THE WRITER'S WORKPLACE
with Readings
Third Edition

THE WRITER'S WORKPLACE
with Readings

Third Edition

Building College Writing Skills

SANDRA SCARRY | *Formerly with the Office of Academic Affairs, City University of New York*

JOHN SCARRY | *Hostos Community College, City University of New York*

Harcourt Brace College Publishers

Fort Worth   Philadelphia   San Diego   New York   Orlando   Austin   San Antonio
Toronto   Montreal   London   Sydney   Tokyo

Publisher	Earl McPeek
Acquisitions Editor	Stephen Dalphin
Marketing Strategist	John Meyers
Developmental Editor	Diane Drexler
Project Editor	Laura Hanna
Art Directors	Brian Salisbury and Burl Sloan
Production Manager	Kathleen Ferguson

Cover illustration: Kurt Gobel

ISBN: 0-15-508174-8

Library of Congress Catalog Card Number: 98-72310

Copyright © 1999, 1997, 1994 by Harcourt Brace & Company

Address for Orders
Harcourt Brace College Publishers, 6277 Sea Harbor Drive, Orlando, FL 32887–6777
1–800–782–4479

Address for Editorial Correspondence
Harcourt Brace College Publishers, 301 Commerce Street, Suite 3700, Fort Worth, TX 76102

Web site Address
http://www.hbcollege.com

Harcourt Brace College Publishers will provide complimentary supplements or supplement packages to those adopters qualified under our adoption policy. Please contact your sales representative to learn how you qualify. If as an adopter or potential user you receive supplements you do not need, please return them to your sales representative or send them to: Attn: Returns Department, Troy Warehouse, 465 South Lincoln Drive, Troy, MO 63379.

Printed in the United States of America

9 0 1 2 3 4 5 6 7   048   9 8 7 6 5 4

Harcourt Brace College Publishers

For Our Students

What shall I do this year? What shall I become? What shall I learn—truly learn and know that I have learned by the time I look at these pages next year?

Lorraine Hansberry
Journal entry of August 23, 1962*

---

*From *To Be Young, Gifted and Black*, adapted by Robert Nemiroff (Englewood Cliffs, NJ: Prentice-Hall, 1969).

PREFACE

Overview

The Writer's Workplace with Readings, third edition, offers a complete writing program for the student who needs additional preparation not only for the present demands of college writing assignments but also for the future demands of the workplace. Each chapter in the book gives the student writer a solid foundation for a thorough understanding of the writing process. The student is invited to explore, step-by-step, each element of good writing, beginning with prewriting techniques and proceeding to grammatically correct sentences, correct word choice, effective paragraphs, and ending with the complete college essay, all the while enjoying a feeling of security and control.

The book is a flexible tool for the teacher and an engaging resource for the student. Instructors may begin their work in virtually any chapter, depending on the needs of the class. Students will find themselves learning sentence, paragraph, or essay skills, as they work from models with compelling content.

An important goal of *The Writer's Workplace with Readings* is to focus on the benefit of collaborative learning. Group activities are designed to encourage critical thinking and appreciation for the ideas of others. Finally, it's attention to the two-fold need of the student writer that leads to the effectiveness of this book. First, the emphasis on process writing nurtures the student's creativity and individuality in the planning and drafting stage. And, at the same time, the book places importance on the mastery of basic writing skills so that the student is able to revise and edit. Teachers of writing and their students should feel assured that *The Writer's Workplace with Readings* is a rich resource they can use with confidence and success.

The organization of *The Writer's Workplace with Readings*

Step I   Looking at the whole

This section introduces the student to the writing process, focusing on short activities that immediately involve the student in journaling, brainstorming, and editing for unity.

Step 2   Creating effective sentences

This section helps students understand a fundamental issue in student writing: the difference between a complete sentence and a fragment or run-on. Instructors will find this sentence building section one of the most comprehensive treatments available, with its multiple practices on each topic so all students have full opportunity to succeed. Furthermore, most of the practices are written in continuous discourse; that is, all the sentences within an exercise explore a single subject. This will interest students in the content as they learn the fundamentals for writing clear and complete sentences.

Step 3   Understanding the power of words

Choosing the correct word can include knowing the difference between *its* and *it's* or understand why the word *kid* is considered slang and usually inappropriate for formal writing. This section is intended as an enjoyable but challenging series of lessons in the use of precise and appropriate language. Working in this section will heighten student awareness of the impact that word choice always has on a piece of writing.

Step 4   Creating effective paragraphs

This section has been described by users as the heart of the book. It is here that students learn to take the mystery out of paragraph construction and to explore the many rhetorical modes for developing these building blocks of the essay. Far from inhibiting students with complicated instructions, this section actively teaches students each element of a particular rhetorical mode. The practice activities in this part of the book are done in the context of outstanding models that inspire students to include specific details in their own writing. As instructors know very well, specific details make all the difference between effective or ineffective student writing.

Step 5   Structuring the college essay

The final goal of most writing programs is to give students an understanding of how to construct an essay that contains a clear thesis statement, fully developed support paragraphs, and a logical conclusion. This section of the book builds on the student's grasp of sentence mechanics and paragraph development, skill taught in the preceding sections, and then adds the more demanding requirements of a longer piece of writing: organizing material, writing the thesis statement and the introduction, making transitions between ideas, building paragraphs, using outside sources, and coming to an appropriate conclusion. This section concludes with the most challenging assignment, composing the persuasive essay, a form that demands careful logic and critical thinking.

Additional readings

Although the book is filled with wonderful examples of professional writing that illustrate the work of different lessons and assignments, the book also includes fourteen additional readings, allowing the instructor a wider range of essays from which to choose. These selections were carefully chosen to serve as additional models of the rhetorical modes taught.

The Working Together feature

The Working Together feature that concludes every chapter offers a variety of activities that encourage students to enter into the collaborative process. Announced by a lively illustration and brief or provocative text, this feature asks students to brainstorm, plan, and write about issues of importance in school and in society. Interesting real-life writing projects such as the resume, the survey, or the newspaper editorial are the focus for group discussion and individual writing responses.

New to *The Writer's Workplace with Readings,* third edition

The authors have listened to the many comments and suggestions from both students and instructors who have used previous editions of the book. The following new features reflect our response to these helpful suggestions.

New to the book's contents

- Many of the Working Together activities are new or revised. These activities focus on engaging students in lively discussion that lead to writing assignments. The topics for these assignments deal with current issues and concerns that students will find useful in other college courses or they are directly connected to the world of work.

- Beginning in the first chapter, there is an increased emphasis on the development of the portfolio, a useful record students can bring with them to their next writing course.

- A new section on Parts of Speech has been added to the second chapter.

- More student essays provide opportunities for critical analysis of writing that is closer to the reality of classroom work than some of the professional models.

- New model essays are included to spark reaction on provocative topics.

- Several new photos and graphics add more visual interest.

- Among the fourteen additional readings are several new selections, chosen for their high interest, cultural diversity, and suitability as models for teaching writing skills and rhetorical modes covered in earlier chapters.

New to the book's design

- Symbols in the margins alert readers whenever one of the following topics is discussed:

  Portfolio Reminders

  Work Related Issues

  Computer References

- Exercises are numbered sequentially within each chapter for easy location.

- The quick-reference chart on combining clauses, located on the inside front cover, has a new, more readable design.

- The material from chapter eight of the second edition has now been divided and expanded into two chapters: the first is devoted to pronouns, the second to parallel structure and modifiers.

- The order of chapters covering description and narration has been reversed so that narration occurs first.

- An additional rhetorical table of contents now includes paragraphs and essays found throughout the text.

Ancillary materials

The Writer's Workplace with Readings is accompanied by one of the most extensive supplementary packages ever. This unique set of materials includes:

Annotated Instructor's Edition with the answers to all the exercises included for the ease of the instructor's classroom use.

The Resource Manual, written by J'laine Robnolt of Westark Community College, contains helpful suggestions for the instructor about developing a syllabus and includes sample syllabi for both sixteen week and ten week semesters.

Instructors will also find additional group exercises, essay prompts, and journal exercises. Also included are essays written by leaders in their fields on important topics such as using tutors in developmental writing, helping students with learning disabilities, taking advantage of the internet, and guidance on the use of the portfolio approach.

The Exercise and Test Book, written by Elisa Affanato of Camden County College, contains one-sided perforated pages of diagnostic tests, grammar exercises, and mastery tests of grammar topics covered in *The Writer's Workplace with Readings*. Answers are provided at the end of the book so that students and tutors may work independently with this material if desired.

The Culture and Grammar Software Series is a series of software programs that teach students basic grammar in a cultural context. Each new program introduces an author and his or her work, along with the culture's music, art, and other literature, while showing students both how to improve their grammar and to become aware of different cultures. Titles in the series include the following:

Title	Grammar Topic
Harlem Renaissance I	Fragments
Harlem Renaissance II	Subject-Verb Agreement
New Mexican Culture	Pronoun-Antecedent Agreement
Miami-Cuban Culture	Run-On Sentences
Vietnamese American Culture	Verb Tenses
Southwest Native American Culture	Writing Style

Other versions in The Writer's Workplace Series

In addition to the most comprehensive version, *The Writer's Workplace with Readings*, six other choices exist to accommodate an instructor's curriculum and classroom needs.

The Writer's Workplace, fifth edition (without readings)

This book contains the same material offered in the textbook with readings, but omits the readings for the convenience of instructors who prefer to use their own collection of readings.

The Three-Book Series (each volume with readings)

The Writer's Workplace: Sentences
The Writer's Workplace: Paragraphs
The Writer's Workplace: Essays

To accommodate a three-course sequence or courses that focus on one skill primarily, this three-book series provides the added option to tailor the material to better suit a specific course offering. The books may be used in sequence, or any one book may be used by itself. The material contained in the exercises and activities in each book are different so that while each of the three books has a sentence-level session, there is no overlap of material. Also, as the series progresses and the writing skills levels increase, the amount of material devoted to sentence-level skills decreases. Each of the three books contains fourteen readings particularly suited to the writing skills being developed in that volume of the series.

The Two-Book Series (with Readings)

The Writer's Workplace: Sentences to Paragraphs

The Writer's Workplace: Paragraphs to Essays

To accommodate a two-course sequence, we also offer a series that divides the material into two separate texts. *The Writer's Workplace: Sentences to Paragraphs* offers the student thorough instruction in sentence construction, word choice, and paragraph writing. *The Writer's Workplace: Paragraphs to Essays* reviews sentence construction and word choice while covering in greater depth the writing of clear, coherent paragraphs leading up to full-length essays. Once again, as in the three-book series, there is no repetition of exercise materials between the two books. Although the books are designed to be used in sequence, each book can also be used by itself in any course whose emphasis matches one of these volumes.

Acknowledgments

We are deeply grateful to those individuals who have contributed to this present edition. First of all, we wish to thank J'laine Robnolt for her willingness to share her talents, her perceptions, and her student's essays with us. We also thank family and friends, among them our daughter Siobhan and our dear friends Janice Paterson Boles, formerly of Miami Dade Community College, and Chantal Burns of the United Nations Headquarters, New York City. Their wonderful insights and ongoing support have sustained us throughout this project.

Our work could not have been successful without the kindness and support of our colleagues at City University, specifically President Isaura Santiago Santiago of Hostos Community College, and Vermell Blanding, of the English Department of Hostos.

We would like to thank the following reviewers for their helpful critiques and recommendations:

Jan Barshis, Harold Washington College; Lisa Berman, Miami Dade Community College; Paul Berman, McLennon Community College; Joann Brown, Miami Dade Community College; Georgia Carmichael, North Harris Community College; Jessica Carroll, Miami Dade Community College; Bill Dodd, Augusta College; Donald Edge, Camdem Community College; Joan Feague, Baker College; Valerie Flournoy, Manatee Community College; Eddye Gallagher, Tarrant County Community College; Stella Gildemeister, Palo Alto Community College; Bonnie Hilton, Broward Community College; Cynthia Krausk, Wilber Wright College; Douglas Kreinke, Sam Houston University; Bill McKeever, Sinclair Community College; Mary Ann Merz, Oklahoma City Community College; Gary L. Myers, Mississippi State University; Troy Nordman, Butler County Community College; Kathleen Olds, Erie Community College; Michael Orlando, Bergen Community College; Abraham Oseroff, Miami Dade Community College; Linda Patterson, State Technical Institute; Beverly Peterson, Penn State Fayette Campus; Sharon Reedy, Pellissippi State Community College; Sandra Rust, Community College of Southern Nevada; Sarah Lee Sanderson, Miami Dade Community College; Sandra Sloan, Heald Business College; Donald Stoddard, Anne Arundel Community College; Linda J. Whisnant, Guilford Technical Community College; David White, Walters State Community College; Melanie Whitebread, Luzerne County Community College.

Finally, we recall with pleasure how each member of the Harcourt Brace team was more than helpful and cooperative at every stage of the editorial and production process, from manuscript to final copy. We are especially grateful to Carol Wada for her vision of the book and her enthusiasm for our work. Her tireless efforts were a constant inspiration to us. Our gratitude also goes to Diane Drexler, who was attentive to every detail and immediately responsive to every need we placed before her. Very special thanks go to Nancy Marcus Land and her staff at the Publication Development Company. Their splendid work on the final editing and design is deeply appreciated.

We know how fortunate we are to have such competent and generous support, and we also realize how lucky we are as writers to find ourselves working together in harmony and agreement. All of these good circumstances have led to this latest edition of *The Writer's Workplace with Readings* along with the fifth edition of *The Writer's Workplace* and all of the ancillary materials. May those who use the book have a similar sense of gratification and success.

BRIEF CONTENTS

CONTENTS

STEP 5 STRUCTURING THE COLLEGE ESSAY 367

RHETORICAL LIST OF PARAGRAPHS AND ESSAYS

The following symbols are used: one paragraph   ¶
                                  two or more paragraphs   ¶'s
                                  complete essay   E

Classification

Argumentation/Persuasion

INDEX   511

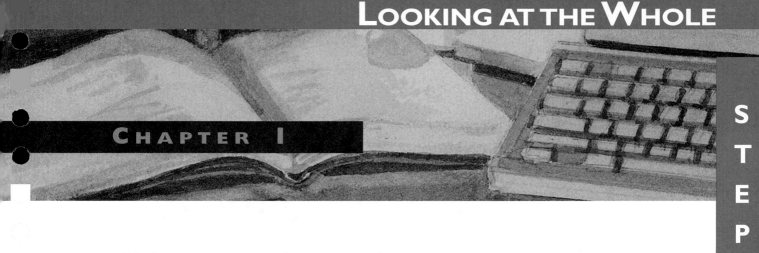

CHAPTER I

Discovering the Writing Process

The written word has undeniable power. Throughout history, words carved on stone buildings have inspired whole populations, while words copied on pieces of paper have changed individual hearts and minds. The words carved on the base of the Statue of Liberty ("Give me your tired, your poor . . .") have given hope to countless numbers of immigrants to the United States; the poet's words ("How do I love thee? Let me count the ways . . .") have helped generations of lovers express their emotions to each other.

Thanks to the written word, the past comes alive and we are able to share in the living hopes and dreams of those who have gone before us. When Frederick Douglass, one of the most articulate African-Americans of the nineteenth century, wrote that he once traded food for reading lessons from his friends, his words invite us to share that very experience from his childhood. "This bread," Douglass later recalled, "I used to bestow upon the hungry little urchins, who, in return, would give me that more valuable bread of knowledge." The writer's words take us back to a neighborhood street nearly two centuries ago, into the mind of a child who was determined to get what he needed.

The words of another writer and speaker take us back into history and into the mind of another great American. In 1863, at the height of the Civil War, Abraham Lincoln gave a three-minute speech at the battlefield in Gettysburg, Pennsylvania. Although the President had worked and reworked every phrase in his speech, few people including Lincoln himself thought that his words would be remembered. He told the assembled crowd that the world might "little note, nor long remember what we say here," but over a century later his Gettysburg Address is still quoted and often memorized. The nobility of his thoughts and the beauty of his words will be cherished as long as great writing is appreciated.

What makes some pieces of writing, like the Gettysburg Address, so powerful that they can change history or inspire generation after generation of readers? What makes some people able to transform the material from their own lives, or from the world around them, into writing that has meaning for so many others? You don't have to be a famous writer or a well-known speaker to write strong words. Each person's life experiences are unique, and everyone must discover the best way to express that uniqueness. The spirit and the intention behind this book is to help you share in the work of professional writers and student writers and to participate in every aspect of the writing process. Your task is to discover the voice that is within you. Writing may not be easy, but it is a skill that can be developed!

Key terms for the writer

Purpose: **The writer's intention.** The possible reasons a writer might have for composing a particular piece range all the way from *entertaining* readers to the more serious purpose of *classifying* information. One journalist might intend to write a totally *factual account* of an event while another journalist might write an *editorial* about that same event. The editorial's purpose might be to persuade readers to change their minds about some aspect of a situation. Without a purpose, a writer will have little sense of direction or little motivation for working so hard.

Audience: **The readers for a particular piece of writing.** Writers need to direct their writing toward a particular audience. To do this effectively, writers need to be aware of the characteristics of those who will read their work. What do these readers already know about the topic? What are their attitudes toward the topic as they begin to read? Knowing something about the audience will help the writer to choose the most effective approach in a piece of writing.

Prewriting: **Activities that writers often use to help them generate ideas for their work.** *Freewriting* and *journal writing* are good techniques to use when exploring topics that relate to real or imaginary events. These explorations can be made at any time and may be reviewed much later when material is needed for writing.

   Brainstorming and *clustering* are techniques for working alone or in groups, to gather information and ideas and discover new ways of organizing those ideas.

   Outlining and *researching* are more formal methods of preparing to write. When you do an outline, you organize material into sections so that the main points are at once distinguishable from the supporting points. When you do research, you are gathering facts and ideas from other writers who are experts on the subjects you are investigating.

Unity: **The relation of all the parts in a piece of writing to the central theme, resulting in a sense of oneness.** Unity is achieved in a piece of writing when the writer makes sure that every sentence in the piece serves the main idea. No detail should be included that is not *directly related* to that main idea. When there is unity, the reader will have no trouble understanding the main point that the writer is making.

Coherence: **The relation of each part (sentence, paragraph, section) to each other part in order to provide clear progression of thought.** A piece of writing needs careful organization of all its parts so that one idea leads logically to the next. To help parts relate to one another, writers use transitional expressions, repetition of key words, and careful pronoun reference.

Elements of good writing

Good writers always have a definite *purpose* when they write; they believe in something very strongly and they want to communicate that belief to others. These writers also want to reach a specific *audience,* so they choose their words to communicate to that audience. As they write, they keep in mind the attitudes and knowledge of their readers. It is essential to recognize good ideas and to have the ability to express those ideas. Closely related to this, good writers possess the ability to give their writing a sense of oneness or wholeness, so their readers will have a feeling of satisfaction when they come to the end of the piece. This is called *unity.* An additional element that may be the hardest to achieve is *coherence*—a clear and logical movement from one part of a piece of writing to the next.

The chart on page 2 contains the important terms and definitions that you will need as you approach the writing process. In Chapter 1, we will examine several of these elements that are at the heart of good writing.

In this chapter, you will study selections by three writers, all of whom come from very different backgrounds. The work of all three writers shows their compelling desire to grow, to understand, and to make progress in their craft. As you examine each selection, you will also focus on a skill that is necessary for you in your own writing development.

Journal writing

Some writers try to understand their lives and explore their own feelings by writing down their thoughts in a relaxed, informal way, often on a daily basis. This is called *journal writing.* Not only writers, but people in all walks of life keep diaries as part of their personal lives, schoolwork, or both.

Reading a journal entry from *Anne Frank's Diary*

One very famous journal writer was Anne Frank, a young Jewish girl who hid from the Nazis in Amsterdam, Holland, in World War II. She and most of her family died in concentration camps just as the war was coming to an end.

> I *know* I can write. A few of my stories are good, my descriptions of the Secret Annex are humorous, much of my diary is vivid and alive, but . . . it remains to be seen whether I really have talent.
>
> "Eva's Dream" is my best fairy tale, and the odd thing is that I don't have the faintest idea where it came from. Parts of "Cady's Life" are also good, but as a whole it's nothing special. I'm my best and harshest critic. I know what's good and what isn't. Unless you write yourself, you can't know how wonderful it is; I always used to bemoan the fact that I couldn't draw, but now I'm overjoyed that at least I can write. And if I don't have the talent to write books or newspaper articles, I can always write for myself. But I want to achieve more than that. I can't imagine having to live like Mother, Mrs. van Daan and all the women who go about their work and are then forgotten. I need to have something besides a husband and children to devote myself to! I don't want to have lived in vain like most people. I want to be useful or bring enjoyment to all people, even those I've never met. I want to go on living even after my death! And that's why I'm so grateful to God for having given me this gift, which I can use to develop myself and to express all that's inside me!

> When I write I can shake off all my cares. My sorrow disappears, my spirits are revived! But, and that's a big question, will I ever be able to write something great, will I ever become a journalist or a writer?
>
> I hope so, oh, I hope so very much, because writing allows me to record everything, all my thoughts, ideals and fantasies.
>
> I haven't worked on "Cady's Life" for ages. In my mind I've worked out exactly what happens next, but the story doesn't seem to be coming along very well. I might never finish it, and it'll wind up in the wastepaper basket or the stove. That's a horrible thought, but then I say to myself, "At the age of fourteen and with so little experience, you can't write about philosophy."
>
> So onward and upward, with renewed spirits. It'll all work out, because I'm determined to write!

When Anne Frank started to keep a journal in 1942, she wrote only for herself, but in 1944 she heard that the Dutch government planned to collect diaries and other accounts of the war. She immediately began to rewrite her diary with the idea that it might eventually be published as a book. She knew that her revised version would reach a larger audience, so Anne started to delete some parts and add new sections to her book. The young diarist was looking toward a wider audience, but she never dreamed that her words would eventually be translated into several languages and be read by millions of people all over the world.

The preceding selection is taken from Anne Frank's diary entry of April 5, 1944, and reveals the young girl's reflections on her literary abilities and her future as a writer.

ACTIVITY I Writing a journal entry of your own

In the selection you have just read, Anne Frank examined her writing talents and made several honest remarks about her abilities. Write a journal entry of your own in which you discuss your strengths or weaknesses in a particular area. You might examine your own skills as a writer, athlete, cook, dancer, musician, or parent. Unless you choose to share your writing with others, you will be writing only for yourself. Writing only for yourself may help you feel more open and relaxed as you work. You also may be able to express more freely the perceptions that lie within you.

_____

_____

_____

_____

_____

_____

_____

_____

_____

_____

_____

_____

_____

_____

_____

_____

_____

_____

_____

_____

_____

_____

_____

_____

_____

_____

_____

_____

_____

When you have finished writing, discuss the assignment with your classmates and your instructor. Did you find the experience enjoyable, or did you feel uncomfortable expressing your thoughts?

Remember that material in a journal may eventually become the basis for a more developed piece of writing. Perhaps your instructor will want you to keep a journal as part of this course.

Your portfolio

Although your instructor may not require you to keep a journal as part of this course, it is a good idea for you to keep a writing portfolio. A portfolio is a special folder that contains a useful record of your work, produced over the course of an entire semester. A portfolio should contain not only finished essays and other samples of writing but also drafts of those pieces. These drafts will show important stages in the writing process and will keep a record of your progress throughout the semester.

A writing portfolio is also helpful for the instructor. When a portfolio is maintained throughout a semester, both instructor and student are able to monitor the progress of different writing tasks. These essays come directly out of classroom instruction, and this confirms the drafting, revising, and editing work of the semester's day-to-day assignments.

In addition to preserving the work of a single course, keeping a portfolio has several other advantages. A portfolio can:

- Provide material for future writing projects.
- Help in determining the final grade for the course.
- Aid instructors in other courses to evaluate the student's writing level.
- Provide a placement evaluation if a student transfers to another college.
- Give evidence to a future employer that the student is ready and able to handle challenging work assignments.
- Show family members and friends a collection of finished pieces that could include a record of childhood experiences, a presentation of family history, or other matters of interest.
- Build a body of work that becomes part of a student's total output, a product in which a student can take pride.

ACTIVITY 2

Purchase some type of expandable folder, preferably one that can be secured with a ribbon or strap so you will not lose your papers. Place a label on the portfolio giving your name, the title of the course you are now taking, the semester and year, and the name of your college. Be sure to leave room for names of future courses and their dates. On a separate piece of paper, create a log or grid:

Date	Title	Purpose
2/15/99	How to Draft on the Computer	Process 1st draft
2/18/99	How to Draft on the Computer	Process 2nd draft

As you place each item in your portfolio, you will be able to make a record of its title, the purpose of the piece, and the date it was submitted. In this way, future readers of your portfolio will be able to trace your progress and see at a glance the number of assignments and range of the work.

Your instructor may have other suggestions to add to these guidelines.

Brainstorming and clustering techniques

It has been said that, because authors reveal themselves whenever they put words on paper, most writing is autobiographical. Richard Wright's *Black Boy* is an autobiographical novel, a work that has become a classic of African-American literature. When Wright published his story in 1945, American society lacked sensitivity to many ethnic issues; indeed, it was a struggle to convince some parts of society that everyone should enjoy equal rights under the law.

Reading from Richard Wright's *Black Boy*

Richard Wright used the writing of *Black Boy* to address not only the issues in his own life, but also the larger issues facing American society. Wright's purposes have been largely fulfilled, and his work continues to reach a larger audience than perhaps he ever envisioned.

In the following selection, Wright remembers a time in his childhood when he was especially eager to learn. Notice how his own determination played an important role in his early education. Also notice the people who helped him fulfill his needs.

In the immediate neighborhood there were many school children who, in the afternoons, would stop and play en route to their homes; they would leave their books upon the sidewalk and I would thumb through the pages and question them about the baffling black print. When I had learned to recognize certain words, I told my mother that I wanted to learn to read and she encouraged me. Soon I was able to pick my way through most of the children's books I ran across. There grew in me a consuming curiosity about what was happening around me and, when my mother came home from a hard day's work, I would question her so relentlessly about what I had heard in the streets that she refused to talk to me.

One cold morning my mother awakened me and told me that, because there was no coal in the house, she was taking my brother to the job with her and that I must remain in bed until the coal she had ordered was delivered. For the payment of the coal, she left a note together with some money under the dresser scarf. I went back to sleep and was awakened by the ringing of the doorbell. I opened the door, let in the coal man, and gave him the money and the note. He brought in a few bushels of coal, then lingered, asking me if I were cold.

"Yes," I said, shivering.

He made a fire, then sat and smoked.

"How much change do I owe you?" he asked me.

"I don't know," I said.

"Shame on you," he said. "Don't you know how to count?"

"No, sir," I said.

"Listen and repeat after me," he said.

He counted to ten and I listened carefully; then he asked me to count alone and I did. He then made me memorize the words twenty, thirty, forty, etc.; then told me to add one, two, three, and so on. In about an hour's time I had learned to count to a hundred and I was overjoyed. Long after the coal man had gone I danced up and down on the bed in my nightclothes, counting again and again to a hundred, afraid that if I did not keep repeating the numbers I would forget them. When my mother returned from her job that night I insisted that she stand still and listen while I counted to one hundred. She was dumfounded. After that she taught me to read, told me stories. On Sundays I would read the newspapers with my mother guiding me and spelling out the words.

Understanding brainstorming and clustering

The writing process starts when we begin to think about our subject, and it comes alive when we start to put words on paper. We have already studied one technique to get started as a writer; this is keeping a journal and using the entries as a way of exploring your potential as a writer. Another technique is to make a listing of your ideas. This can be done in more than one way, including *brainstorming, clustering* (or *mapping,* as it is sometimes called), and *outlining.* Brainstorming and clustering both use free association to help a writer explore a topic and generate ideas.

Brainstorming is the listing of whatever comes to mind when you think about a topic.

When you brainstorm, you do not have to worry about being logical. You allow your mind to come up with a number of words, images, and ideas about the topic. Just relax and allow a variety of thoughts to surface. Trust your mind to generate this list for you.

Suppose, for example, that Richard Wright had used brainstorming as he began to recall his childhood memory. If he had jotted down whatever came to mind, his list might have looked something like this:

> coal man sitting and smoking
>
> cold day
>
> dancing on the bed
>
> mama's surprise
>
> children's school books on the sidewalk
>
> the strange black print
>
> always feeling hungry
>
> Sunday School
>
> asking mama questions
>
> reading Sunday newspapers with mama

Once a writer has a brainstorming list, the next step is to think how the items could be grouped. A writer may now add more items or remove others that do not seem to fit:

> the school children
>
> books on the sidewalk
>
> looking at the black print—so strange
>
> wanted to read
>
> the day the coal man came
>
> he sat and smoked
>
> taught me to count to 100
>
> I was afraid I'd forget
>
> I danced on my bed
>
> stories from mama
>
> reading Sunday newspapers together

Clustering is another method of gathering ideas during the prewriting stage. Clustering is similar to brainstorming, except that when you cluster, you produce a visual map of your ideas rather than a list. You begin by placing a key idea (usually a single word or phrase) in the center of the page. Then you jot down other words and phrases that come to mind as you think about this key idea. As you work, you draw lines or branches to connect the items to each other.

> *Clustering* is the mapping of whatever comes to mind when you think about a topic.

On page 9 is a cluster of words and phrases Richard Wright might have constructed if he had decided to map out his initial ideas.

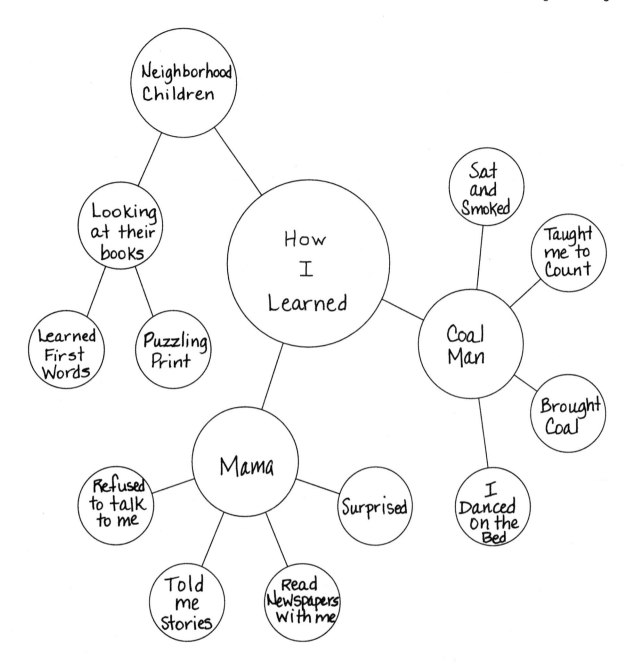

When you use a brainstorming or clustering technique, you will find yourself jotting down some words, images, and ideas that you later might decide not to use. When you come to the point of actually writing, you may include ideas that were not on your brainstorming or clustering list. This points out an important advantage of both of these approaches: You may add details or take away ideas, as you see fit, before you spend much time on the first draft. A second advantage is that by using a prewriting technique, you are giving your mind a chance to retrieve ideas you may not have realized were there. A group of people can use brainstorming and clustering techniques to gather material. This approach works well in the workplace where people are asked to work in teams and pool their ideas. Finally, both brainstorming and clustering can help you place your material in a certain order before you write. No matter what approach you use, the prewriting stage is an important one; the more attention you pay to this stage, the better the chance your best ideas will emerge in your writing.

ACTIVITY 3   **Brainstorming and clustering a topic of your own**

Use both brainstorming and clustering to develop your ideas on one of the following topics:

What I remember when I think about

- my first experiences learning to read
- my early experiences learning math (or another skill)
- my first experience with a computer (or some other machine)

Your chosen topic: _____

Brainstorming list:

_____   _____

_____   _____

_____   _____

_____   _____

_____   _____

_____   _____

Now use the structure below to help you develop your own cluster for the topic you have chosen.

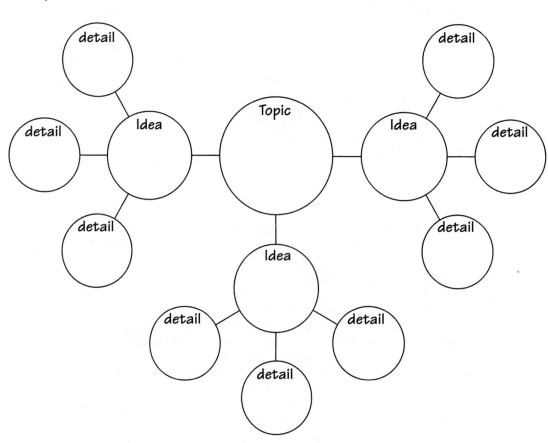

Unity and coherence

When a piece of writing demonstrates both unity and coherence, the quality of that writing greatly increases. ***Unity*** is the result of a writer's ability to make every part of the writing support one central theme or meaning. ***Coherence*** has a closely related purpose: it is the skillful use of more than one technique that leads a reader from one part of the author's work to the next. Writers achieve unity and coherence in a variety of ways, but the result is always a stronger piece of writing.

Studying unity and coherence in the work of William Zinsser

In his book, *Writing with a Word Processor,* the editor and writing teacher William Zinsser provides a frank discussion of his own journey as a writer, from the days of pen and ink to the new technology of computers and word processors. As you read Zinsser's words, think of how many people could be included in his audience—all those people who are anxious about having to learn new technologies for their jobs.

> The hardest thing for me to think about was the idea of getting along without paper. The idea is alien to everything we know in our bones. People have been writing on paper, or papyrus, for four or five thousand years—long enough, anyway, to get into the habit. Paper is where we transact most of the routine business of life: letters, postcards, notes, lists, memos, bills, checks, receipts, notices, reminders to ourselves. Writing something on paper is one of the basic comforts. Even those of us who keep messy desks know that if we just burrow long enough in the piles of stuff we'll find the scrap of paper we're looking for—the one we didn't throw away because we knew that someday we might need it. The nightmare is to lose the crucial nugget of information: the recipe torn from a magazine, the name of the perfect little country inn, the phone number of a plumber who will come on Saturday.
>
> Writers are unusually afraid of loss. The act of writing is so hard that just to get anything on paper is a small victory. A few terrible sentences are better than no sentences at all; they may at least contain a thought worth saving, a phrase that can be reshaped. The important thing is that these fragments exist somewhere in the physical world. The paper that they're written on can be held, stared at, marked up, put aside and reexamined later. Ten or twenty pages can be spread out on the floor and rearranged with scissors and paste. Scissors and paste are honorable writers' tools. So is the floor.
>
> I could hardly imagine throwing all this away—not only the paper itself, but the security blanket. With my new word processor I would type my words and see them materialize on a screen. At that moment the words would, I suppose, exist. But would they *really* exist? Not in any sense that I had ever thought of words before. They would be mere shadows of light. If I pressed the wrong key, couldn't they just vanish into thin air? (No air is thinner than the air into which a writer starting out on a word processor thinks his words will vanish.) Or even if I pressed the right key and stored my words correctly overnight on a disk, would I be able to call them back in the morning? Would I ever see them again? The chances of my never seeing them again struck me as high. I didn't trust what I couldn't hold. Paper was the one reality in writing.
>
> That was my first block. I wondered how I would get past it—and if I would.

The central theme in this selection is the author's fear of writing on the computer instead of with paper and pen. Every sentence in the piece was written with this theme in mind, and because each sentence contributes to this theme, we call this *unified* writing. Good writing always hangs together. It never wanders away from the central theme. For instance, if Zinsser had interrupted his writing to tell us that his daughter just gave birth to a healthy son, or if he stopped to give us the title of a new essay he was working on, the reader would lose track of the focus. The writing would lack unity. Instead, every sentence develops his main idea and by the time we reach the conclusion of the passage, we find Zinsser restating the theme; this time it has even more emphasis than it did at the beginning because of everything the writer has told us in the piece itself. A piece of writing as unified as this one is very satisfying to read. Unity should be one of your major goals as you develop your writing skills.

Understanding *coherence* in a piece of writing is a much more subtle matter. For a piece of writing to be coherent, the reader must be able to move from sentence to sentence with a clear understanding of how one idea leads to the next. For a writer to do this well, a good deal of skill is involved. For Zinsser, much of the coherence he achieves in this piece is through repetition of a key word as he moves to a new sentence. The reader then can follow his thinking as he moves forward.

Study the following breakdown of the sentences in Zinsser's first paragraph:

1st sentence: *idea* of getting along without *paper*

2nd sentence: The *idea* is alien to everything we know in our bones.

3rd sentence: People have been writing on *paper* . . . long enough to get into the habit.

4th sentence: *Paper* is where we transact . . . business.

5th sentence: Writing something on *paper* is one of the basic comforts.

6th sentence: . . . we'll find the scrap of *paper* we're looking for . . .

Now look at the first sentence of the second paragraph. The idea of *loss* is not new. Can you find another form of the word *loss* in the first paragraph? The second paragraph is about a writer's fear of losing an important piece of information. Zinsser uses at least four different words or expressions for these pieces of writing. What are his words? Zinsser achieves coherence by stressing in each sentence of the second paragraph how writers need even small pieces of their writing to exist somewhere so they can be worked on later, if necessary.

Finally, look at the third paragraph and trace the use of the terms *word* or *words* or *them* throughout the paragraph. How many times does Zinsser use *word* or *words*? Coherence can also be achieved by using a pronoun to substitute for a key word. How many times does Zinsser use a pronoun to substitute for *word* or *words*? Zinsser repeated key words and used pronouns to connect his ideas. This will be important for you to think about as you work for coherence in your own writing.

ACTIVITY 4   **Editing for unity**

The following paragraph lacks unity because some sentences do not contribute to the single idea of the paragraph. Study the paragraph closely and cross out all parts that do not contribute to its unity.

Many parents fear the time when their children reach adolescence. When that time does come, some parents are afraid to give their children freedom to make choices. These same parents do not admit that their children have any ideas or feelings that are valid. Many adults like to look back on their childhoods. Pets are often remembered fondly. Conflicts between parents and children are bound to develop. Some conflicts, of course, are a sign of healthy development within the family. Psychologists say that parents should not be fearful when teenagers challenge their authority. Challenging authority is a normal part of the maturing process. Adults without children have none of these concerns. The need for privacy is also a normal emotion during adolescence and should be respected. On the other hand, when the right moment comes along and a teenager wants to talk, parents should not miss the chance. If a teenager prefers to talk to someone other than the parent, that is all right too. Most important of all is the need for parents to be sensitive to the feelings of their teenagers. Remember, adolescence does not last for a lifetime, but hopefully a good relationship between parent and child will last!

Freewriting opportunities

Now that you have studied the work of three different writers, you might want to give some relaxed written responses (freewriting) to ideas suggested by their work.

1. Anne Frank says that she wants to do more than work in the home and then be forgotten: "I need to have something besides a husband and children to devote myself to." What do you want to achieve beyond your day-to-day family chores? Do you agree with Anne Frank, or do you think it is more important to devote yourself to family?

2. In the selection from Richard Wright, the author shows the young boy anxious to learn even before he attends school. He learns from neighborhood children, from the man who delivers coal, and from his mother. What important skill have you learned outside of school? Who has been an important teacher for you outside of the classroom?

3. William Zinsser takes us through a time in his life when he had to make an important but difficult change. Describe a time in your life when you were faced with a challenge. What were your fears and insecurities at the time? How difficult was it for you to meet that challenge?

Looking ahead

For all your future writing assignments, use each of the elements of good writing that you have studied in this chapter. When you write, ask yourself the following questions:

- Have I prepared for my writing by using *prewriting techniques:* journaling, brainstorming, clustering, discussing with others, taking a survey, researching, or outlining?
- Have I thought about my *audience?*
- Did I keep my *purpose* in mind?
- Do I have a *unifying theme* in the piece?
- Does the piece show *coherence*—that is, does each sentence come out of what was written before?

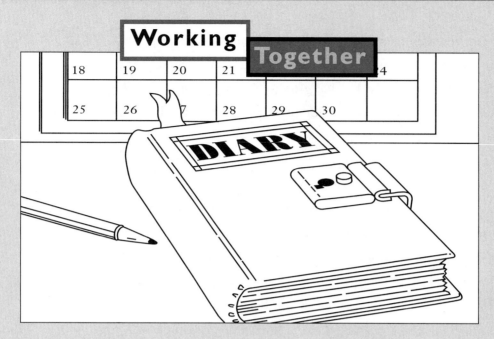

Keeping a Journal

The following excerpts are from *The Diary of Latoya Hunter,* published in 1992. The writer was twelve years old when she kept her journal, a full year of entries showing her experiences in school, her increasing awareness of the world around her, and her desire for independence.

October 6, 1990   Today my friend Isabelle had a fit in her house. It was because of her mother. She's never home and she expects Isabelle to stay by herself. Today she was extra late because she was out with her boyfriend. Isabelle was really mad. She called her father and told him she wanted to live with him because her mother only cared about one person—her boyfriend. She was so upset. She was throwing things all over the place and crying. I never saw her like that before. It was really sad to see. I felt bad when I had to leave her all by herself. I hope she and her mother work it out but all mothers are the same. They think that you're young and shouldn't have an opinion. It's really hard to communicate with my parents. They'll listen to me but that's about it. They hardly take me seriously and it's because of my age. It's like discrimination! If you do speak your mind, you end up getting beaten. The real pain doesn't come from the belt though, it comes from inside. That's the worst pain you could ever feel.

October 8, 1990   Today I saw my old teacher, I was talking about the other day. I thought this should be the day I tell you about him. His name is Robert Pelka. He's a heavy man but that only means there's more of him to love. There's just something about him that makes him impossible not to like. He's warm, caring, loving, and everything else that comes with a great human being. He didn't only teach me academic things like math, English and so on. He taught me how to be openminded to all kinds of people. He did that by making us empathize with other people, in other words, put ourselves in their place and write about it. I went from being a sister of retarded boy named Victor to being a Jewish girl whose family was taken away from me back in the Hitler days.
   Mr. Pelka made things we'd normally learn about from history books sort of come alive, it's like you're there. Those are just some of the things he introduced me to. The things he changed about me are innumerable. The world should know this man. He probably won't go down in any major history books but if this diary counts as a book of history, he just did.

Divide into groups. Each group should choose one of the diary entries to study, with one member of the group reading that entry aloud. If the first entry is selected, you will be discussing parent-child relationships; if the other entry is chosen, you will concentrate on Latoya Hunter's portrait of her teacher.

Each person should then relate a specific past experience, either about a relationship with a parent or a memory of a special teacher. After sharing experiences, members of the group should write down their memories, as if they were writing journal entries.

As you write, keep in mind that all your sentences should relate to the theme you have chosen. Do not stray from the topic. Perhaps your entry could be the start of a journal you will want to keep throughout college and beyond.

Portfolio Suggestion

The entries you studied from *The Diary of Latoya Hunter* contained a story about her friend, Isabelle, and a portrait of her teacher, Robert Pelka. You may want to write short narratives that tell stories of something that happened to you or some of your friends. You might even wish to get into the habit of observing people you encounter in public. You could write brief portraits of these people. The writings can be complete in themselves, or some of them may act as a trigger, helping you to write longer pieces in the future.

Finding Subjects and Verbs in Simple Sentences

Why should we use complete sentences when we write?

We do not always speak in complete sentences. Sometimes we abbreviate a thought into a word or two, knowing that the person to whom we are talking will understand our meaning. We all do this occasionally in our conversations with friends and family.

For example, if a friend walked up to you around lunch time and said, "Lunch?" you would assume that your friend was asking to have lunch with you. While the word "lunch" is not a complete thought, the situation and the way the word was spoken allowed you to guess the probable meaning.

In writing down thoughts, however, a reader (your audience) is not likely to be totally familiar with the thoughts or the circumstances surrounding your words. The reader often cannot interpret or fill in the missing parts. Therefore, *one characteristic of good writing is that all ideas are expressed in complete sentences.*

What is a complete sentence?

> A *complete sentence* must contain a subject and a verb, as well as express a complete thought.
>
> Avon lifts weights.

In this chapter, we will practice finding the subjects and the verbs in some basic sentences. These basic sentences are called *simple sentences* because each of them has only one subject and verb group. (Later we will practice with complex sentences in which two or more ideas are combined giving the sentence more than one subject and verb group.)

How do you find the subject of a sentence?

For most simple sentences, you can find the subject by keeping five points in mind.

1. The subject often answers the question, "Who or what is the sentence about?"
2. The subject often comes early in the sentence.
3. The subject is usually a **noun** or a **pronoun.**
4. Noun or pronoun subjects can be modified by **adjectives.**
5. The subject can be **compound.**

Understanding nouns, pronouns, adjectives, and compound subjects

Nouns

A *noun* is a word that names persons, places, or things.
A *noun* can function as a subject, an object, or a possessive in a sentence.

Subject:	*Avon* lifts weights.
Object:	The coach trained *Avon.*
Possessive:	*Avon's* coach always arrives early.

Nouns can be either *common* nouns or *proper* nouns. Most nouns in our writing are common nouns. They are not capitalized. Proper nouns name particular persons, places, or things. They are always capitalized.

Nouns	
Common	**Proper**
aunt	Aunt Mary
country	Nigeria
watch	Timex

Another way to categorize nouns is into *concrete* or *abstract* nouns. Concrete nouns are all the things we can see or touch, such as desk, car, or friend. Abstract nouns are the things we cannot see or touch, such as justice, honesty, or friendship.

Nouns	
Common	**Abstract**
face	loneliness
people	patriotism
jewelry	beauty

Pronouns

> A *pronoun* is a word used to take the place of a noun. Just like a noun, a pronoun can be used as the subject, the object, or in some cases as a way to show possession.
>
> Subject: *He* lifts weights.
> Object: The coach trained *him*.
> Possessive: *His* coach always arrives early.

Pronouns can also be categorized or divided into groups: *personal, indefinite, relative,* or *demonstrative.* The following chart categorizes pronouns into the four major groups.

Pronouns						
I. Personal Pronouns	**Subjective**		**Objective**		**Possessive**	
	Singular	*Plural*	*Singular*	*Plural*	*Singular*	*Plural*
1st person	I	we	me	us	my (mine)	our (ours)
2nd person	you	you	you	you	your (yours)	your (yours)
3rd person	he	they	him	them	his (his)	their (theirs)
	she		her		her (hers)	
	it		it		its (its)	

2. Relative Pronouns (can introduce noun clauses and adjective clauses)	**3. Demonstrative Pronouns** (can point out the antecedent)	**4. Indefinite Pronouns** (refer to non-specific persons or things)			
who, whom, whose	this	*Singular*			
which	that	everyone	someone	anyone	no one
that	these	everybody	somebody	anybody	nobody
what	those	everything	something	anything	nothing
whoever		each	another	either	neither
whichever		*Singular* or *Plural* (depending on meaning)			
whatever		all	more	none	
		any	most	some	
		Plural			
		both	few	many	several

Adjectives

Noun or pronoun subjects can be modified by **adjectives.**

> An *adjective* is a word that modifies (describes or limits) a noun or a pronoun. Adjectives usually come directly in front of the nouns they modify, but they can also appear later in the sentence and refer back to the noun or pronoun.
>
> *young* Avon
> He is young.

Compound subjects

The subject can be *compound*.

> A **compound subject** is made up of two or more nouns or pronouns joined together by *and, or, either/or,* or *neither/nor*.
>
> *Avon and his coach* lift weights.

PRACTICE   The different kinds of subjects you will encounter in this chapter are illustrated in these seven sentences. Examine each of the sentences and ask yourself who or what each sentence is about. Draw a line under the word you think is the subject in each sentence. Then on the line to the right, indicate what kind of subject (for example, concrete noun or personal pronoun) you have underlined. Be as specific as possible.

1. The young child played.   _____

2. Young Helen Keller played.   _____

3. She played.   _____

4. The park grew chilly.   _____

5. The leaves stirred.   _____

6. A thought suddenly struck her.   _____

7. Her parents and teacher would be
   waiting.   _____

Note: Not every noun or pronoun in a sentence is necessarily the subject of a verb. Nouns and pronouns function as *subjects* and as *objects*. In the following sentence, which noun is the subject and which noun is the object?

Helen drank the water.

For some students, the following exercises will seem easy. However, for many, analyzing the structure of a sentence is unfamiliar. As you practice, get into the habit of referring back to the definitions, charts, and examples. You can, with a little patience, develop an understanding for those words that serve as the subjects of sentences.

EXERCISE 1   **Finding the subject of a sentence**

Underline the subject in each of the following sentences. An example is done for you.

The loudspeaker blared.

1. The train stopped.
2. Steven Laye had arrived!
3. He was afraid.
4. Everything looked so strange.
5. The fearful man held his bag tightly.
6. The tunnel led up to the street.

7. Buses and cars choked the avenues.
8. People rushed everywhere.
9. The noise gave him a headache.
10. Loneliness filled his heart.

Finding the subject of a sentence

Underline the subject in each of the following sentences.

1. The road twisted and turned.
2. A young boy hurried along briskly.
3. He carried an important message.
4. A red-winged blackbird flew overhead.
5. Dark clouds and a sudden wind surprised him.
6. His family would be elated.
7. Someone was raking the leaves.
8. His father called out his name.
9. The old man tore open the envelope.
10. The message was brief.

Finding the subject of a sentence

Underline the subject in each of the following sentences.

1. The Chicago World's Fair opened.
2. Americans had never seen anything like it.
3. Architects had designed a gleaming white city.
4. The buildings and grounds were unique.
5. George Ferris designed an enormous wheel 264 feet high.
6. It could carry sixty passengers per car.
7. The inventor George Westinghouse designed the fair's electric motors and even electric lights.
8. Other fair inventors included Thomas Edison and Alexander Graham Bell.
9. All played an important part.
10. The future seemed bright.

Composing your own sentences

Compose ten sentences to exchange with a classmate. Use each of the following as a subject at least once: (a) proper noun, (b) common noun, (c) abstract noun, (d) compound subject, and (e) pronoun. You may use the words below if you like. Your classmate will read your sentences and with a pencil underline and label each subject with one of the above terms.

Tiger Woods they
golfer skill
trainer and friend P.G.A. Tournament
he

How do you find the subject in sentences with prepositional phrases?

The sentences in Exercises 1 and 2 were short and basic. If we wrote only such sentences, our writing would sound choppy. Complex ideas would be difficult to express. One way to expand the simple sentence is to add prepositional phrases.

Example:

He put his suitcase on the seat.

On is a preposition.

Seat is a noun used as the object of the preposition.

On the seat is the prepositional phrase.

A *prepositional phrase* is a group of words containing a preposition and an object of the preposition with its modifiers. Prepositional phrases contain nouns or pronouns, but these nouns or pronouns are *never* the subject of the sentence.

In sentences with prepositional phrases, the subject may be difficult to spot. What is the subject of the following sentence?

In the young man's apartment, books covered the walls.

In the sentence above, what is the prepositional phrase? Who or what is the sentence about? To avoid making the mistake of thinking that a noun in the prepositional phrase could be the subject, a good practice is to cross out the prepositional phrase.

~~In the young man's apartment~~, books covered the walls.

With the prepositional phrase crossed out, it now becomes clear that the subject of the sentence is the noun *books*.

When you are looking for the subject of a sentence, do not look for it within the prepositional phrase.

You can easily recognize a prepositional phrase because it always begins with a preposition. Study the list on page 23 so that you will be able to recognize quickly all of the common prepositions.

Common prepositions				
about	behind	except	on	toward
above	below	for	onto	under
across	beneath	from	out	underneath
after	beside	in	outside	unlike
against	between	inside	over	until
along	beyond	into	past	up
among	by	like	since	upon
around	despite	near	through	with
at	down	of	throughout	within
before	during	off	to	without

In addition to these common prepositions, English has a number of prepositional combinations that also function as prepositions.

Common prepositional combinations		
ahead of	in addition to	in reference to
at the time of	in between	in regard to
because of	in care of	in search of
by means of	in case of	in spite of
except for	in common with	instead of
for fear of	in contrast to	on account of
for the purpose of	in the course of	similar to
for the sake of	in exchange for	

Creating sentences with prepositional phrases

EXERCISE 5

Use each of the ten prepositions that follow to write a prepositional phrase. Then write a sentence containing that prepositional phrase. An example follows:

Preposition: between

Prepositional Phrase: _between the two barns_

Sentence: _Between the two barns, the old Buick lay rusting._

Notice that when a prepositional phrase begins a sentence, a comma usually follows that prepositional phrase. (Sometimes, if the prepositional phrase is short, the comma is omitted.)

1. Preposition: _in_

   Prepositional Phrase: _In the middle of the lake_

   Sentence: _In the middle of the lake, the boat sank._

2. Preposition: *with*

Prepositional Phrase: _____

Sentence: _____

_____

3. Preposition: *of*

Prepositional Phrase: _____

Sentence: _____

_____

4. Preposition: *from*

Prepositional Phrase: _____

Sentence: _____

_____

5. Preposition: *during*

Prepositional Phrase: _____

Sentence: _____

_____

6. Preposition: *by*

Prepositional Phrase: By the end of the day,

Sentence: By the end of the day, the Student's completed their homework.

7. Preposition: *for*

Prepositional Phrase: For the party

Sentence: For the party, the clown danced.

8. Preposition: *through*

Prepositional Phrase: through rough water

Sentence: The team won the race, through Rough Water.

9. Preposition: *on*

Prepositional Phrase: On the table

Sentence: On the table, books were scattered.

10. Preposition: *beside*

Prepositional Phrase: Beside the door

Sentence: Beside the door, the cat lay to rest.

Finding subjects in sentences with prepositional phrases

Remember that you will never find the subject of a sentence within a prepositional phrase. In each of the following sentences, cross out any prepositional phrases. Then underline the subject of each sentence. An example follows:

On the circus grounds, Lisa wandered among the elephants, horses, and camels.

expresses complete thought

1. Young people in the circus search for travel, adventure, danger, and romance.
2. After a few weeks of pulling cages and sleeping on hay, most of these people get tired of the circus and go back home.
3. The art of clowning, for instance, is very serious work.
4. Today, a circus clown must graduate from Clown College in Venice, Florida.
5. The staff of Clown College looks across the country for applicants.
6. Admission to the college is not easy.
7. Only sixty people out of three thousand applicants are admitted.
8. After ten weeks of training, graduation ceremonies are held.
9. At the ceremony, the clown graduate must perform for three continuous hours.
10. In the past, clowns were not so carefully trained.

Finding subjects in sentences with prepositional phrases

Each of the following sentences contains at least one prepositional phrase. Cross out any prepositional phrases. Then underline the subject in each sentence. An example follows:

In every family, children look for independence.

1. The disappearance of sons and daughters from the lives of their parents can be devastating.
2. In their late teens and early twenties, young people often move away from home.
3. For many of them, a city offers jobs and excitement.
4. With little money and almost no experience, these young people can encounter difficulties of all kinds.
5. The fun of being independent can quickly turn into a nightmare.
6. On the other hand, young adults living with their parents often feel cheated.
7. They have no life of their own.
8. These young adults are frequently treated like children.
9. During this time, parents can be too critical.
10. From the parents' point of view, one decision at this time can determine the direction of their child's life.

What are the other problems in finding subjects?

Sentences with a change in the normal subject position

Some sentences begin with words that indicate that a question is being asked. Such words as *why, where, how,* and *when* give the reader the signal that a question will follow. Such opening words are not the subjects. The subjects will be found later on in these sentences. The following sentences begin with question words:

> Why is *he* going away?
> How did *he* find his sister in the city?

Notice that in each case the subject is not found in the opening part of the sentence. By answering questions or changing the question into a statement, the subject is easier to spot.

> *He* is going away . . .
> *He* found his sister . . .

Using *there* or *here*

Such words as *there* or *here* can never be the subjects of sentences.

> There is a new teacher in the department.
> Here comes the woman now.

Who or what is this first sentence about? This sentence is about a teacher. *Teacher* is the subject of the sentence. Who or what is the second sentence about? This sentence is about a woman. *Woman* is the subject of the second sentence.

Commands

Sometimes a sentence contains a verb that gives an order:

> Go to Chicago.
> Help your sister.

In sentences that give orders, the subject *you* is not written but is understood to be the subject. This is the only case where the subject of a sentence may be left out.

Sentences that contain appositive phrases

> An *appositive phrase* is a group of words in a sentence that gives us extra information about a noun in the sentence.

For example:

> Martin Johnson, the retired salesman, sat at his desk.

In this sentence, the words *the retired salesman* make up the appositive phrase because they give you extra information about Martin Johnson. Notice that commas separate the appositive phrase from the rest of the sentence. If you leave out the appositive phrase when you read this sentence, the thought will still be complete:

> Martin Johnson sat at his desk.

Now the subject is clear: *Martin Johnson.*

> When you are looking for the subject of a sentence, you will not find it within an appositive phrase.

Finding hidden subjects

EXERCISE 8

8.2.00

Each of the following sentences contains an example of a special problem in finding the subject of a sentence. First cross out any prepositional phrases or appositive phrases. Then underline the subject of each sentence. An example follows:

> ~~In every car of the crowded train~~, <u>passengers</u> settled down ~~for the night~~.

1. ~~In the speeding train~~, the <u>child</u> slept.
2. The <u>motion</u> ~~of the railroad cars~~ was relaxing.
3. The child's <u>mother</u>, ~~a tired and discouraged widow~~, put a coat ~~under the child's head for a pillow~~.
4. ~~Outside the window~~, <u>towns</u> and <u>cities</u> sped by ~~in the night~~.
5. Sometimes <u>you</u> could look ~~into people's living rooms~~.
6. There was a <u>silence</u> ~~in the train~~.
7. Why did these <u>people</u> choose ~~to travel at night~~?
8. ~~In most cases~~, <u>children</u> will rest quietly ~~at night~~.
9. The <u>woman</u> ~~with a young child and heavy bags to carry~~ had a difficult time.
10. ~~On the platform~~, an elderly <u>man</u> anxiously waited ~~for the first sight of his grandson~~.

Finding hidden subjects

EXERCISE 9

8.2.00

Each of the following sentences contains an example of a special problem in finding the subject of a sentence. First cross out any prepositional phrases or appositive phrases. Then underline the subject of each sentence. An example follows:

> <u>Disney World</u>, ~~the dream of every child~~, is a favorite destination ~~for family vacations~~.

1. There is a fantasy <u>playland</u> ~~in the state of Florida~~.
2. <u>You</u> Look ~~at a map~~ ~~to find this child's paradise~~.
3. <u>Orlando</u>, the location ~~of Disney World~~, is the place ~~to go~~.
4. Where else can <u>people</u> see toddlers and grownups shaking hands ~~with Mickey Mouse and Minnie Mouse~~?
5. ~~In Disney World~~, <u>everyone</u> is likely ~~to see living cartoon~~ favorites.
6. ~~At breakfast, lunch, and dinner~~, <u>you</u> might shake hands ~~with Pluto Pup, Donald Duck, and Goofy Dog~~.

7. The cleanliness of the place also impresses most families.

8. During the day, there are scores of attractions and activities.

9. Would your parents like to enjoy the cooler and less crowded evening activities?

10. In Disney World, it is hard to tell the children from the adults.

EXERCISE 10   **Finding hidden subjects**

Each of the following sentences contains an example of a special problem in finding the subject of a sentence. First cross out any prepositional phrases or appositive phrases. Then underline the subject of each sentence. An example follows:

What can we learn from the study of an ancient civilization?

You

1. Look at a map of South America.

2. Where is the ancient city of Chan Chan?

3. Here on the coastal desert of northern Peru stand the remains of this city of the kings.

4. Chan Chan, once the fabulously wealthy center of the Chimor, is situated in one of the driest, bleakest regions in the world.

5. This pre-Columbian city in South America is an archaeological treasure.

6. In the ruins of this city, scientists have found fragments to piece together the mystery of the past.

7. How could this civilization have survived this hostile environment and become so advanced?

8. There was an astonishing irrigation system in Chan Chan.

9. Unfortunately for the Chimor, Incas captured the city in the late fifteenth century and carried away much of its wealth.

10. Later, the Spanish armies brought disease and destruction to this desert people.

How do you find the verb of a sentence?

Every sentence must have a verb. Verbs can be divided into three classes.

Action: An *action verb* tells what the subject is doing.

Judith Jamison *danced* in that ballet.

Linking: A *linking verb* indicates a state of being or condition.

The audience *seemed* spellbound.

Helping: A *helping verb* combines with a main verb to form a verb phrase and gives the main verb a special time or meaning.

The audience *may* expect an encore.

Verbs tell time. Use this fact to test for a verb. If you can put the verb into different tenses in the sentence, that word is a verb.

Present: (Today) she *dances.*

Past: (Yesterday) she *danced.*

Future: (Tomorrow) she *will dance.*

Action verbs

Action verbs tell us what the subject is doing and when the action occurs.

The woman *studied* ballet.

What was the woman doing? studying

What is the time of the action? past (-*ed* is the past tense ending)

Action verbs
Most verbs are **action verbs.** Here are a few examples:

arrive	learn	open	watch
leave	forget	write	fly
enjoy	help	speak	catch
despise	make	teach	wait

Finding action verbs

EXERCISE 11

Each of the following sentences contains an action verb. Find the action verb by first underlining the subject of the sentence. Then circle the verb (the word that tells what the subject is doing). Cross out any prepositional phrases. Note also the time of the action: past, present, or future. An example follows:

Many people (begin) hobbies in childhood.

1. Some people collect very strange objects.

2. One man saves the fortunes from fortune cookies.

3. A group in Michigan often trades spark plugs.

4. People in Texas gather many types of barbed wire.

5. One person in New York keeps handouts from the street.

6. Arthur Fiedler hung hundreds of fire hats on pegs around his study.

7. Tom Bloom finds "inspected by" tickets in the pockets of new clothes.

8. Collectors enjoy the search for unusual items.

9. A collection, like odd rocks or unique automobiles, gives a person some individuality.

10. Collections entertain us from childhood to old age.

EXERCISE 12   Finding action verbs

Each of the following sentences contains an action verb. Find the action verb by first underlining the subject of the sentence. Then circle the verb (the word that tells what the subject is doing). Cross out any prepositional phrases. Note also the time of the action: past, present, or future. An example follows:

Attitudes ~~toward medical practices~~ often (change.)

1. Traditional Chinese medicine harnesses ancient healing techniques in the practice of "gigong."
2. Masters of this Chinese practice claim the ability to cure many diseases.

3. The master projects a mysterious force into his students.
4. The student practices for many years.
5. The hands of the Chinese gigong practitioner pound at the air above a patient.

6. Many patients respond to this invisible force.
7. They sway their bodies with the power of the force.
8. Chinese success surprises Western medical authorities.
9. Some doctors conduct research in China in hopes of finding the secrets of this ancient art.
10. Other Western doctors deny the validity of this approach.

Linking verbs

> A *linking verb* is a verb that links the subject of a sentence to one or more words that describe or identify the subject.

For example:

The child (is) a constant dreamer.
She (seems) distracted.
We (feel) sympathetic.

In each of these examples, the verb links the subject to a word that identifies or describes the subject. In the first example, the verb *is* links *child* with *dreamer*. The verb *seems* links the pronoun *she* with *distracted*. Finally, in the third example, the verb *feel* links the pronoun *we* with *sympathetic*.

Common linking verbs	
act	feel
appear	grow
be (am, is, are, was,	look
were, have been)	seem
become	taste

Finding linking verbs

Each of the following sentences contains a linking verb. Find the linking verb by first underlining the subject of the sentence. Then draw an arrow to the word or words that identify or describe the subject. Finally, circle the linking verb. An example follows:

Dreams are very important for many cultures.

1. My dream last night was wonderful.
2. I had become middle-aged.
3. In a sunlit kitchen with a book in hand, I appeared relaxed and happy.
4. The house was empty and quiet.
5. In the morning light, the kitchen felt cozy.
6. The brewing coffee smelled delicious.
7. The bacon never tasted better.
8. I looked peaceful.
9. I seemed to have grown calmer.
10. I felt satisfied with life.

Finding linking verbs

Each of the following sentences contains a linking verb. Find the linking verb by first underlining the subject of the sentence. Then draw an arrow to the word or words that identify or describe the subject. Finally, circle the linking verb. An example follows:

Surprises can be fun.

1. We were anxious to make the evening a success.
2. The apartment looked empty.
3. Everyone remained quiet.
4. Martha turned red at the sound of "Surprise!"
5. She seemed surprised.
6. The music sounded wonderful.
7. The food smelled delicious.
8. All of her presents were lovely.
9. The birthday party was a complete success.
10. Everyone appeared pleased with the evening.

Helping verbs (also called auxiliary verbs)

Some verbs can be used to help the main verb express a special time or meaning.

Auxiliary verbs	Time expressed by auxiliary verbs
He *is sleeping.*	right now
He *might sleep.*	maybe now or in the future
He *should sleep.*	ought to, now or in the future
He *could have been sleeping.*	maybe in the past

Common helping verbs
can, could may, might, must shall, should will, would forms of the irregular verbs *be, do,* and *have.*

Remember that *be, do,* and *have* are also used as the main verbs of sentences. In such cases, *be* is a linking verb while *do* and *have* are action verbs. All the other helping verbs are usually used only as helping verbs.

> *Adverbs* are words that can modify verbs, adjectives, or other adverbs.

Watch out for adverbs that may come in between the helping verb and the main verb.

In the following sentence, the word *often* is an adverb coming between the verb phrase *can frighten.* For a list of common adverbs, see Appendix B: Parts of Speech (p. 467).

Dreams can *often* frighten young children.

EXERCISE 15 Finding helping verbs

Each of the following sentences contains a helping verb in addition to the main verb. In each sentence, first cross out any prepositional phrases and underline the subject. Then circle the entire verb phrase. An example follows:

In some writing classes, students must keep a diary of their work.

1. A diary could be simple or elaborate.

2. In a journal, a person can safely express true feelings without fear of criticism by family or friends.

3. Well-kept diaries have helped to give people insight into the motivations for their actions and have also been a help in dealing with change.

4. Diaries do improve a person's powers of observation to look inwardly at one's own feelings as well as to look outwardly at actual happenings.

5. You will be able to capture your memories.

6. Important, too, would be the development ~~of a writing style~~ and the improvement of language skills.

7. A journal might awaken your imagination.

8. It may unexpectedly bring pleasure and satisfaction.

9. Keener observations will add to the joys of life.

10. You should seriously consider the purchase of one of those lovely fabric-bound notebooks.

Finding helping verbs

Each of the following sentences contains a helping verb. In each sentence, first cross out any prepositional phrases and underline the subject. Then circle the entire verb phrase. An example follows:

~~In this country~~, daycare has become an important issue.

1. How do you start a child care center?

2. First, notices can be put in local churches and supermarkets.

3. Then, you should also use word-of-mouth among your friends.

4. Many parents will need infant care during the day, after-school care, or evening and week-end care.

5. With luck, a nearby doctor may be willing to help with the local health laws and legal requirements.

6. Of course, the licensing laws in your state must be thoroughly researched.

7. Unfortunately, you could have trouble finding a low rent place for your center.

8. Any childcare center will depend on its ever widening good reputation.

9. In good daycare centers, parents are never excluded from meetings or planning sessions.

10. Finally, the center must be more interested in the character of its teachers than in the teachers' degrees.

Parts of speech

In this chapter you have learned how most of the words in the English language function. These categories for words are called *parts of speech*. You have learned to recognize and understand the functioning of *nouns, pronouns, adjectives, verbs, adverbs,* and *prepositions.* (In later chapters you will learn how the *conjunction* functions.) You can review your understanding of these parts of speech as you practice identifying them in the exercises provided here. You may also refer to Appendix B (at the back of the book) for a quick summary whenever you want to refresh your memory.

EXERCISE 17   Identifying parts of speech

In the sentences below, identify the part of speech for each underlined word. Choose from the following list.

a. noun   c. adjective   e. adverb
b. pronoun   d. verb   f. preposition

_____ A _____ 1. Chubby Checker taught the <u>world</u> how to twist.

_____ d _____ 2. Dick Clark, host of American Bandstand, <u>decided</u> he liked "The Twist" and showcased it.

_____ f _____ 3. The song shot up to number one <u>on</u> the pop charts in September of 1960.

_____ C _____ 4. Twisting became the biggest <u>teenage</u> fad.

_____ ~~c~~ B _____ 5. At first, <u>it</u> was considered strictly kid stuff.

C e ✓ 6. Then it became <u>respectable</u> among older groups.

A f ✓ 7. Liz Taylor and Richard Burton were seen twisting in the fashionable night spots of <u>Rome</u>.

_____ f _____ 8. The dance set the pace <u>for</u> a decade.

_____ e _____ 9. The "beautiful people" were seen <u>breathlessly</u> twisting at the Peppermint Lounge in New York.

_____ A _____ 10. The 60s were going to be a reckless and unruly <u>time</u>.

EXERCISE 18   Identifying parts of speech

In the sentences below, identify the part of speech for each underlined word. Choose from the following list.

a. noun   c. adjective   e. adverb
b. pronoun   d. verb   f. preposition

_____ C _____ 1. "The Grand Ole Opry" is a <u>famous</u> radio program.

_____ b _____ 2. <u>It</u> began more than seventy years ago in Nashville, Tennessee.

_____ A _____ 3. By the 1930s, the <u>program</u> was the best source of country music on the radio.

d e ✓ 4. In 1943, the program <u>could</u> be heard in every home in the nation.

_____ C _____ 5. <u>Many</u> people traveled to Nashville.

_____ b _____ 6. <u>They</u> wanted to see the performers for themselves.

_____ e _____ 7. The existing old concert hall, <u>poorly</u> constructed in the nineteenth century, was not an ideal place for modern audiences.

_____ f _____ 8. Television came in during the 1950s, and with it the demand <u>for</u> a new hall.

_____ C _____ 9. Now the Nashville hall is <u>modern</u> and air-conditioned.

_____ d _____ 10. Three million people <u>visit</u> Nashville every year.

Identifying parts of speech

In the sentences below, identify the part of speech for each underlined word. Choose from the following list:

a. noun   c. adjective   e. adverb

b. pronoun   d. verb   f. preposition

_____ 1. The people of the <u>country</u> of Mali, in Africa,

_____ 2. built a mosque out of <u>mud</u> bricks. The Great

_____ 3. Mosque <u>in</u> the town of Djenne was built

_____ 4. by the Mali people sometime <u>between</u> A.D. 1100–

_____ 5. 1300. <u>Most</u> of the leaders of Mali at that time

_____ 6. were <u>Muslims</u>. Djenne became a center of Islamic

_____ 7. learning. When the leader Konboro <u>converted</u> to

_____ 8. Islam he <u>asked</u> a holy man, "How may I please God?"

_____ 9. The holy man said, "<u>Build</u> a mosque. The people

_____ 10. will bless your <u>name</u> for centuries."

Mastery and editing tests

Finding subjects and verbs in simple sentences

In each of the following sentences, cross out any prepositional phrases or appositive phrases. Then underline the subject and circle the complete verb. An example follows:

The main <u>street</u> ~~of Corning, New York,~~ (has been) beautifully (renovated.)

1. Older people today may recall the main street of their home town as a wonderful place forty or fifty years ago.

2. Why can't we have these old main streets back again?

3. In 1970, the National Trust for Historical Preservation began a program to bring new life to the nation's downtown areas.

4. Cities and villages needed new attitudes toward downtown areas.

5. Some local planners began a program to revitalize main streets.

6. One of the most important challenges was to convince businessmen to repair old buildings.

7. Towns quickly saw the value of making changes.

8. Citizens understood the advantages of a comfortable downtown.

9. Now many towns gladly sponsor special events and parades.

10. Will the tradition of personal service return to the American main street?

TEST 2   Finding subjects and verbs in simple sentences

In each of the following sentences, cross out any prepositional phrases or appositive phrases. Then underline the subject and circle the complete verb. An example follows:

~~In the field of writing~~, <u>practice</u> ⟨is⟩ important ~~for growth~~.

1. A certain amount of stress can be a good thing.

2. In many cases, stress motivates us.

3. When does stress become distress?

4. Your own self-awareness is the best place to start.

5. Have there been changes in your sleep or appetite?

6. Are you using alcohol or drugs too much?

7. Anxious people feel trapped by pressure and disappointment.

8. There is usually help from your family and friends.

9. Many can offer you their observations and advice.

10. Clinical depression, a more serious condition, usually responds well to the right combination of psychotherapy and the right medicine.

TEST 3   Finding subjects and verbs in simple sentences

In each of the sentences in the following paragraph, cross out any prepositional or appositive phrases. Then underline the subject and circle the complete verb.

Go West! Western Australia, one of the remaining great boom areas of the world, comprises one-third of the Australian continent. Why did people by the tens of thousands go to western Australia in the late 1800s? In 1894, Leslie Robert Menzies jumped off his camel and landed in a pile of gold nuggets. In less than two hours, this man gathered over a million dollars in gold. He eventually took six tons of gold to the bank by wheelbarrow! Kalgoorlie and Boulder, the two boom towns that grew up there, boast of the richest golden mile in the world. With all the gold seekers, this surface gold did not last very long. Now the only bands of rich ore lie more than 4,000 feet down under the ground. There are many ghost towns with their empty iron houses and run-down chicken coops.

Working Together

Crossword Puzzle: Reviewing the Terms for Sentence Parts

Review the names for sentence parts by doing this crossword puzzle. Feel free to work in pairs. If necessary, look back in the chapter for the answers.

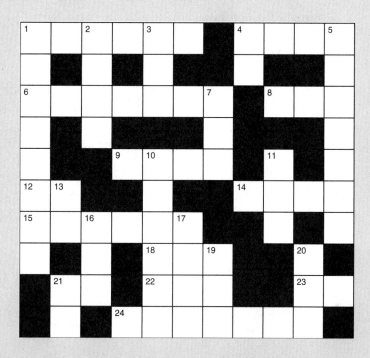

ACROSS

1. Verbs like hop, sing, and play are called _____ verbs.
4. Which of the following is a helping verb?
   hear, when, will, only
6. Every sentence has a _____ and a verb.
8. A helping verb
9. Which of the following is a preposition?
   must, upon, they, open
12. A preposition
14. *Word, witch, wall,* and *willow* are examples of the part of speech called a _____.
15. Most nouns are _____ nouns. They are not capitalized.
18. In the following sentence, which word is an adjective?
   She has pet pigs for sale.
21. Which of the following is a preposition?
   he, be, by, if
22. In the following sentence, which word is an abstract noun?
   The era was not economically successful.
23. A preposition
24. A word that can take the place of a noun.

DOWN

1. *Joy, confidence, peace* are examples of this kind of noun; the opposite of a concrete noun.
2. Which word is the subject in the following sentence:
   Here is the tube of glue for Toby.
3. An indefinite pronoun
4. A plural pronoun
5. *Look, appear, feel,* and *seem* are examples of _____ verbs.
7. Which word is the object of the preposition?
   The car must weigh over a ton.
10. The opposite of a common noun.
11. A personal pronoun
13. A preposition
16. In the following sentence, which word is a helping verb?
   She may pay the fee for her son.
17. Which of the following is a proper noun?
   king, Nero, hero, teen
19. In the following sentence, which word is an adjective?
   Nan quickly ran toward the tan man.
20. Which word is the verb in the following sentence?
   Run down to the car for our bag.
21. A common linking verb.

Making Subjects and Verbs Agree

S T E P 2

Now that we understand that a complete sentence must have a subject for its verb, we will turn our attention to a related problem: making sure the subject and verb agree in the sentence.

What is subject-verb agreement?

> A verb must agree with its subject in number (singular or plural).
> When the subject is a singular noun, the verb takes an *s* in the present tense.
>
> > The baby *sleeps*.
>
> When the subject is a plural noun, the verb does *not* take an *s* in the present tense.
>
> > The babies *sleep*.

Notice that when you add *s* or *es* to an ordinary noun, you form the plural of that noun. However, when you add an *s* to a verb, and you want the verb to be in the present tense, you are writing a singular verb. This rule causes a lot of confusion for student writers, especially those whose first language is not English. It may also be confusing to students who already speak and write English, but whose local manner of speaking does not follow this rule. While there is no one way of speaking that is correct or incorrect, society does recognize a standard form that is agreed upon as acceptable in the worlds of school and business. Since we must all master this standard form, the material contained in this chapter is of the greatest importance to your success in college and beyond.

Pronouns can also present problems for subject-verb agreement

The following chart shows personal pronouns used with the verb *sleep*. After you have studied the chart, what can you tell about the ending of a verb when the subject of that verb is a personal pronoun?

Personal pronouns	
Singular	**Plural**
I sleep	we sleep
you sleep	you sleep
he, she, it sleeps	they sleep

PRACTICE   Underline the correct verb in the following sentences.

1. The dog (bark, barks).
2. It (wake, wakes) up the neighborhood.
3. The neighbors (become, becomes) very angry.
4. These families (deserve, deserves) a quiet Sunday morning.
5. I (throws, throw) an old shoe at the dog.

Pay special attention to the verbs *do* and *be*

Although you may have heard someone say, *It don't matter*, or *We was working*, these expressions are not considered standard English. A singular subject must have a singular verb.

The verb *to do*	
Singular	**Plural**
I do	we
you do	you } do
he	they
she } does	
it	
(never *he don't, she don't, it don't*)	

The verb *to be*			
Present Tense		**Past Tense**	
Singular	*Plural*	*Singular*	*Plural*
I am	we	I was	we
you are	you } are	you were	you } were
he	they	he	they
she } is		she } was	
it		it	
(never *we was, you was,* or *they was*)			

Underline the verb that agrees with the subject.

1. He (doesn't, don't) study in the library anymore.
2. We (was, were) hoping to find him there.
3. The library (doesn't, don't) close until eleven o'clock.
4. (Was, Were) you late tonight?
5. Ann (doesn't, don't) care if you stay until closing time.

Making the subject and verb agree

In the blanks next to each sentence, write the subject of the sentence and the correct form of the verb.

	Subject	Verb
1. My brother (be, is, are) a comedian.	_____	_____
2. We (laughs, laugh) at everything he says.	_____	_____
3. He (expects, expect) us to attend his show tomorrow night.	_____	_____
4. He (doesn't, don't) like us to miss even one performance.	_____	_____
5. Every show (has, have) many comedians on the program.	_____	_____
6. My sister (hopes, hope) to bring her new friend.	_____	_____
7. She (says, say) we will all love him.	_____	_____
8. Yesterday, I (be, was, were) telling my friends to come too.	_____	_____
9. They (was, were) happy to accept.	_____	_____
10. It (promises, promise) to be a great evening.	_____	_____

Making the subject and verb agree

In the blanks next to each sentence, write the subject of the sentence and the correct form of the verb.

	Subject	Verb
1. Many companies today (wants, want) to test their workers for drugs.	_____	_____
2. To many people, it (appears, appear) to be an invasion of privacy.	_____	_____
3. Employers (worries, worry) that bus and train drivers are using drugs on the job.	_____	_____
4. They (doesn't, don't) want to risk the lives of passengers.	_____	_____

5. Even operators of rides in amusement parks (undergoes, undergo) tests. _____ _____

6. Professional athletes on a team (has, have) special problems because of the publicity that surrounds them. _____ _____

7. Some factories (installs, install) hidden video cameras to catch workers using drugs. _____ _____

8. The General Motors Company (worries, worry) enough to hire undercover agents to pretend to be workers, in order to catch drug users. _____ _____

9. In Kansas City, a newspaper wanted to use drug-sniffing dogs, but reporters from the newspaper (was, were) insulted. _____ _____

10. If you (is, are) ever asked to take a drug test, will you be insulted? _____ _____

EXERCISE 3   **Making the subject and verb agree**

In the blanks next to each sentence, write the subject of the sentence and the correct form of the verb.

	Subject	Verb
1. My father and mother (was, were) planning a celebration.	_____	_____
2. They (is, are) celebrating their twenty-fifth wedding anniversary.	_____	_____
3. My sister (doesn't, don't) approve of spending a lot of money.	_____	_____
4. It (doesn't, don't) do any good to argue with her.	_____	_____
5. My mom (spends, spend) several days looking at brochures.	_____	_____
6. They (hasn't, haven't) been on a vacation in over fifteen years.	_____	_____
7. The travel agent (suggests, suggest) a cruise.	_____	_____
8. We (enjoys, enjoy) imagining how much fun they will have.	_____	_____
9. I hope she (doesn't, don't) change her mind at the last minute.	_____	_____
10. A cruise to the Caribbean (sounds, sound) good to me.	_____	_____

Subject-verb agreement with hard to find subjects

As we learned in Chapter 2, a verb does not always immediately follow the subject. Other words or groups of words called phrases (prepositional or appositive phrases, for example) can come between the subject and verb. Furthermore, subjects and verbs can be inverted as they are in questions or sentences beginning with *there* or *here*.

When looking for subject-verb agreement in sentences where the subjects are more difficult to find, keep in mind two points:

- Subjects are not found in prepositional phrases or appositive phrases.
- Subjects can be found after the verb in sentences that are questions and in sentences that begin with *there* or *here*.

Agreement with hidden subjects

EXERCISE 4

Circle the correct verb in each sentence.

1. Here (is, are) a plan about time management.
2. Too much busywork in your day (prevents, prevent) efficiency.
3. A period of time without interruptions (is, are) crucial.
4. People usually (does, do) too many things at once.
5. Why (is, are) frequent breaks important?
6. Constant clutter on people's desks (causes, cause) frustration.
7. Why (does, do) perfectionists have so much difficulty?
8. The habit of procrastination (is, are) another area of time management.
9. There (is, are) also several disastrous activities like television viewing.
10. Children in a family (needs, need) to help with chores.

Agreement with hidden subjects

EXERCISE 5

Circle the correct verb in each sentence.

1. Here (is, are) some basic medical supplies needed for every home.
2. A thermometer in the medicine chest (is, are) crucial.
3. There (is, are) a box of bandages on hand for minor injuries.
4. A vaporizer in the bedroom at night (relieves, relieve) bronchial congestion.
5. Pads of sterile gauze often (tends, tend) to be forgotten.
6. A small bottle of Coca-Cola syrup (proves, prove) helpful for treating stomach upsets.
7. A useful tool, a pair of tweezers, (removes, remove) splinters.
8. In a home ready for emergencies, a list of emergency phone numbers (sits, sit) next to the telephone.
9. Why (has, have) cold compresses been useful in treating sprains?
10. Every person with the desire to be prepared (needs, need) a resource book on first aid at hand.

Special problems with subject-verb agreement

I. Subject-verb agreement with collective (or group) nouns

> **Collective Nouns** name a group of people or things.

Common collective nouns			
audience	committee	group	public
assembly	council	herd	senate
board	crowd	jury	team
class	faculty	orchestra	
club	family	panel	

- Usually, a collective noun takes a singular verb or requires a singular pronoun to refer to that noun. That is because the group acts as a single unit.

  The *class* **is** waiting for **its** turn to use the gym.

- Sometimes a collective noun takes a plural verb or requires a plural pronoun to refer that noun. This applies when the members of a group are acting as individuals, with separate actions as a result.

  The *class* **are** putting on **their** coats.

EXERCISE 6   **Agreement with collective nouns**

Circle the correct verb in each sentence.

1. The Spanish club (is, are) planning refreshments for their next meeting.
2. The trio (performs, perform) mostly on weekends.
3. The group (needs, need) a sponsor for its organization.
4. The faculty (is, are) excited about the proposal.
5. The committee (is, are) undecided who should be invited. (Members are acting as individuals, separate actions)
6. A team (has, have) been selected to compete at the Spanish History Tournament.
7. A crowd usually (attends, attend) the competition.
8. The board of directors (meets, meet) to make the decision.
9. The panel tonight (was, were) discussing the ancient culture of Castille in Spain.
10. The audience (was, were) very appreciative.

Agreement with collective nouns

Circle the correct verb in each sentence.

1. The construction crew (seems, seem) to be guilty of a crime.
2. In this case, the municipal police (accuses, accuse) the crew.
3. A few days later, the same group (files, file) charges.
4. The crew's legal team (defends, defend) them.
5. The public (attends, attend) the trial.
6. The crowd (grows, grow) impatient.
7. The audience (interrupts, interrupt) the proceedings. (Members are acting as individuals, separate actions)
8. The jury (hears, hear) the evidence.
9. The group (has, have) different opinions. (Members are acting as individuals, separate actions)
10. The crowd (waits, wait) to hear the verdict.

2. **Subject-verb agreement with indefinite pronouns**

Care should be taken to learn which indefinite pronouns are singular and which are plural.

Indefinite pronouns			
Indefinite pronouns taking a singular verb:			
everyone	someone	anyone	no one
everybody	somebody	anybody	nobody
everything	something	anything	nothing
each	another	either	neither

Everyone *is* expecting a miracle.

Indefinite pronouns taking a plural verb:

both	few	many	several

The talks between the two countries failed.

Both *were* to blame.

Indefinite pronouns taking a singular or plural verb depending on the meaning in the sentence:

any	all	more	most
none	some		

The books are gone. All *were* very popular.

The sugar is gone. All of it *was* spilled.

EXERCISE 8   **Agreement with indefinite pronouns**

Circle the correct verb in each sentence.

1. Nobody (knows, know) how many drugs are contained in plants that grow in the rainforest.
2. Some (argues, argue) that wonderful drugs could be derived from many plants.
3. Most of the pharmaceutical experts (remains, remain) skeptical.
4. All of the research (is, are) expensive and often (proves, prove) fruitless.
5. Everybody (agrees, agree) the tropical forest is a source of medicine.
6. One of the dangers (is, are) that if we wait, the tropical forest may disappear.
7. One of the two U.S. companies in Costa Rica (is, are) Merck & Company.
8. Each of the companies (is, are) paying the country for the right to search the rainforest.
9. Among scientists, some (recommends, recommend) that governments subsidize drug research.
10. Vincristine and vinblastine are two medicines found in the rainforest; both (is, are) used for cancer treatment.

EXERCISE 9   **Agreement with indefinite pronouns**

Circle the correct verb in the sentences.

1. One of the classic Spanish colonial towns still existing today (**is**, are) St. Augustine, Florida.
2. Almost nobody (**realizes**, realize) the difference between the alligator of the Southern wetlands and the crocodile of southern Florida.
3. Most of the South's coast (**is**, are) lined with barrier islands.
4. Nobody (**reaches**, reach) Florida's Gulf Islands except by boat.
5. One of the special Southern treats (**remains**, remain) a bag of boiled peanuts.
6. Anyone visiting a Southern home (**is**, are) likely to be served iced tea, the "house wine" of the South.
7. (**Doesn't**, Don't) everybody love the music from Mississippi: rock 'n' roll, blues, and country western?
8. Some of the country's most colorful folk art (**is**, **are**) found by driving on the backroads.
9. Not all of the plantation houses in the Old South (looks, **look**) like Tara in *Gone with the Wind*.
10. Southern names can often be distinctive; many of them (uses, **use**) double names like Billie Jean, James Earl, or Peggy Sue.

3. Subject-verb agreement with compound subjects

• If the conjunction used to connect the compound subjects is *and*, the verb is usually plural.

Mary and Steve *are* my good friends.

The exception to this is if the two subjects are thought of as a single unit.

Peanut butter and jelly *is* my favorite sandwich.

- If the conjunction used to connect the compound subjects is *or, nor, either, either/or, neither, neither/nor, not only/but also*, you need to be particularly careful.

The verb is singular if both subjects are singular.

> Mary or Steve *is* going to help me.

The verb is plural if both subjects are plural.

> My friends or my two brothers *are* going to help me.

The verb agrees with the subject closest to the verb if one subject is singular and one subject is plural.

> My friends or my brother *is* going to help me.

Subject-verb agreement with compound subjects

EXERCISE 10

Circle the correct verb in each sentence.

1. Macaroni and cheese (is, are) my son's favorite supper.
2. This meal and others like it (has, have) too much fat.
3. My mother and father, on the other hand, often (enjoys, enjoy) a fruit salad for their main meal.
4. Shopping or cooking habits (needs, need) to be changed.
5. Either a salad or another vegetable with a sprinkling of cheese (is, are) a better choice than macaroni and cheese.
6. Adults and children (does, do) need to watch their diets.
7. Too many pizzas and sodas (is, are) a disaster for people's health.
8. Either the lack of exercise or the eating of fatty foods (causes, cause) more problems than just overweight.
9. Neither potato chips nor buttered popcorn (is, are) a good snack choice.
10. An apple or grapes (makes, make) a better choice.

Subject-verb agreement with compound subjects

EXERCISE 11

Circle the correct verb in each sentence.

1. Students and a teacher (meets, meet) at the University of Indiana to do marriage research.
2. Either Robert Levenson or John Gollman (uses, use) the video to examine how couples interact during arguments.
3. Neither body language nor the spoken words (is, are) unimportant.
4. Criticism, whining, or withdrawal (reveals, reveal) potential trouble.
5. Sweating, blood flow, and heart rate (is, are) also monitored during arguments.
6. Positive moments or good memories (needs, need) to outnumber the negative moments.
7. A man or a woman who (marries, marry) someone with a different fighting style may be doomed to an unhappy marriage.

8. Courtrooms or a baseball field (provides, provide) structured times and places for people to fight.

9. A particular time and a particular place (needs, need) to be set aside for talking about marital problems.

10. A happy husband and wife (gives, give) each other support and friendship.

4. **Subject-verb agreement with unusual nouns**

Don't assume that every noun ending in *s* is plural, or that all nouns that do not end in *s* are singular. There are some exceptions. Here are a few of the most common exceptions.

Some nouns always end in *s*, but are singular.

mathematics	diabetes	United States
economics	measles	Kansas

Some nouns do not end in *s* but are plural.

Nouns with unusual plurals		
	Singular	**Plural**
1. Some foreign words use rules of their languages to make words plural. For example, to the right are four Latin words that show the Latin rule *-um changes to -a to form the plural* are:	bacterium	bacteria
	datum	data
	medium	media
	stratum	strata
2. Some words change internally rather than add -s at the end:	foot	feet
	tooth	teeth
	child	children
	man	men
	woman	women
	mouse	mice
	ox	oxen
	goose	geese
3. Some words remain the same whether singular or plural:	deer	deer
	elk	elk
	fish	fish
	moose	moose

Some nouns have only a plural form.

clothes	scissors	fireworks
headquarters	tweezers	pants

Mastery and editing tests

Making the subject and verb agree

In the blanks next to each sentence, write the subject of the sentence and the correct form of the verb. An example follows:

	Subject	Verb
The eleven proposals for the development of a new building at Columbus Circle (has, have) been submitted to the city.	*proposals*	*have*

1. The price of airline tickets to England (has, have) remained fairly reasonable. _____ _____

2. His decision (requires, require) a lot of thought. _____ _____

3. She (doesn't, don't) know the answers to any of the test questions. _____ _____

4. Either the elevator operator or the security guard (see, sees) every visitor. _____ _____

5. The committee (agree, agrees) to the fund-raising projects for this year. _____ _____

6. Potato chips and soda (makes up, make up) most of her diet. _____ _____

7. One of the people in the audience (is, are) my brother. _____ _____

8. There (was, were) two raccoons sleeping in the barn last night. _____ _____

9. Posted on the bulletin board (was, were) the assignments for the week. _____ _____

10. Everyone (takes, take) the test on Monday. _____ _____

Making the subject and verb agree

In the blanks next to each sentence, write the subject of the sentence and the correct form of the verb.

	Subject	Verb

1. Included in the price of the trip (was, were) five nights in a lovely hotel and all meals. _____ _____

2. Nobody in the family (knows, know) how to swim. _____ _____

3. Jerry and Craig (works, work) well together. _____ _____

4. The student senate (meets, meet) every Tuesday. _____ _____

	Subject	Verb
5. Where (is, are) the wrapping paper for these packages?	_____	_____
6. In the entire building there (is, are) only two windows.	_____	_____
7. Either the fruit pies or that chocolate cake (looks, look) like the best choice for your picnic.	_____	_____
8. Public performances (makes, make) me nervous.	_____	_____
9. One of my most favorite shows (is, are) *Cats*.	_____	_____
10. The book for the report (doesn't, don't) have to be from the reading list.	_____	_____

TEST 3   Making the subject and verb agree

Using your own words and ideas, complete each of the following sentences. Be sure that the verb in each sentence agrees with the subject of that sentence. Use the verbs in the present tense.

1. Our team _____

2. The box of chocolates _____

3. Both of my sisters _____

4. The effects of a pay cut on a family _____
_____

5. Where is _____

6. Not only the teacher but also the students _____
_____

7. The jury _____

8. Each of the contestants _____

9. Do you think there is _____

10. The table of contents in that book _____

Working Together

Conducting an Interview

Choose a partner for this activity. Each of you will take a turn interviewing the other. Allow ten minutes per interview. Use the following questions, as well as any additional questions that may occur to you as you conduct your interview. Take notes on the lines provided.

Suggested Questions for Your Interview

1. What made you decide to go to college?

_____

_____

_____

2. Why did you choose this school?

_____

_____

_____

3. What major field are you going to pursue?

_____

_____

_____

4. What would you like to be doing five years from now?

_____

_____

_____

5. What will be the greatest challenge as you work toward your goal?

_____

_____

_____

6. What do you find is the most enjoyable part of going to college?

_____

_____

_____

7. What has been the least enjoyable aspect of going to college?

_____

_____

_____

After interviewing each other, write a paragraph that could be used to introduce your interviewee to the class. Use the information you have learned from the interview. If time permits, exchange your paragraph for the paragraph written about you. Check the facts for accuracy. For instance, is your name spelled correctly? Does the paragraph have complete sentences and subject-verb agreement?

You and your classmates will enjoy getting to know each other by the sharing of these interviews. (Each person can present another student by reading the paragraph out loud to the class, or by passing the paragraphs around to be read silently.)

Portfolio Suggestion

 Place your interview in your portfolio. In future writing tasks, consider using the interview approach as a technique for gathering material that can be converted quite easily into an essay. Remember that people who write for a living, for example newspaper and magazine writers, depend heavily on interviews for their material. You can, too.

CHAPTER 4

Correcting the Fragment in Simple Sentences

Fragments in everyday conversations

The fragment is a major problem for many student writers. A thought may be clear in a writer's mind, but on paper this same idea may turn out to be incomplete because it does not include a subject, a verb, or express a complete thought. In this section, you will improve your ability to spot incomplete sentences or fragments, and you will learn how to correct them. This practice will help you avoid such fragments in your own writing. Here, for example, is a typical conversation between two people at lunchtime. It is composed entirely of fragments, but the two people who are speaking have no trouble understanding each other.

Ron: Had any lunch?
Jan: A sandwich.
Ron: What kind?
Jan: Ham and Swiss on rye.

If we use complete sentences to rewrite this brief conversation, the result might be the following:

Ron: Did you have any lunch yet?
Jan: Yes, I had a sandwich.
Ron: What kind of sandwich did you have?
Jan: I had a ham and Swiss on rye bread.

In the first conversation, misunderstanding is unlikely since the two speakers stand face to face, see each other's gestures, and hear the intonations of each other's voice in order to help figure out the meaning. These short phrases may be enough for communication since the speakers are using more than just words to convey their thoughts. They understand each other because each one is able to complete the thoughts that are in the other person's mind.

In writing, however, readers cannot be present at the scene to observe the situation for themselves. They cannot be expected to read the author's mind. Only the words grouped into sentences and the sentences grouped into paragraphs provide the clues to the meaning. Since writing often involves thoughts that are abstract and even complex, fragments cause great difficulty and sometimes total confusion for the reader.

EXERCISE 1   Putting a conversation into complete sentences

The following conversation is one that a couple of students might have at the start of their English class. Rewrite the conversation in complete thoughts or standard sentences. Remember the definition of a sentence:

> A *complete sentence* has a subject and a verb and expresses a complete thought.

John: Early again.
Elaine: Want to get a front row seat.
John: Your homework done?
Elaine: Nearly.
John: Think he'll give a quiz today?
Elaine: Hope not.
John: Looks like rain today.
Elaine: Better not; haven't got a bag for these new books.
John: Going to the game Saturday?
Elaine: Probably.

John: *The movie started early again.*
Elaine: *Do you want to get a front row seat?*
John: *Is your homework done?*
Elaine: *I nearly lost my dog.*
John: *Do you think he will give a quiz today?*
Elaine: *I hope not.*
John: *It looks like rain today.*
Elaine: *Better not; I haven't got a bag for these new books.*
John: *Are you going to the game Saturday?*
Elaine: *I probably will not go to the game.*

Remember, when you write in complete sentences, this writing may be somewhat different from the way you would express the same idea in everyday conversation with a friend.

Although you will occasionally spot incomplete sentences in professional writing, you may be sure the writer is using these fragments intentionally. In such cases, the fragment may capture the way a person thinks or speaks, or it may create a special effect. A student developing his or her writing skills should be sure to use only standard sentence form so that thoughts will be communicated effectively. Nearly all the writing you will do in your life—letters to friends, business correspondence, papers in school, or reports in your job—will demand standard sentence form. Fragments will be looked upon as a sign of ignorance rather than creative style!

What is a fragment?

> A *fragment* is a piece of a sentence.

A group of words that looks like a sentence is really a fragment if one of the following is true:

a. The subject is missing:

> Delivered the plans to my office.

b. The verb is missing:

> The architect to my office.

c. Both the subject and verb are missing:

> To my office.

d. The subject and verb are present but the words do not express a complete thought:

> The architect delivered.

Understanding fragments

Each of the ten examples is a fragment. In the blank to the right of each fragment, identify what part of the sentence is missing and needs to be added to make the fragment into a sentence.

a. Add a subject.
b. Add a verb.
c. Add a subject and a verb.
d. The subject and verb are already present, but the sentence needs to express a complete thought.

An example follows:

Fragment	What is missing?
the red fox	b. verb

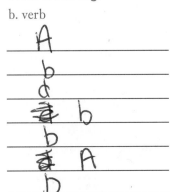

1. returned to the river
2. a bird on the oak branch
3. between the island and the mainland
4. the hawk in a soaring motion
5. the fishing boats on the lake
6. dropped like a stone into the water
7. the silence of the forest

8. carried the fish to the tree

9. the fisherman put

10. into the net

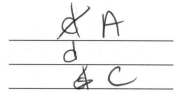

How do you correct a fragment?

1. **Add the missing part or parts.**

Example: Fragment: across the lake
Add: subject and verb
Sentence: I swam across the lake.

Note: The prepositional phrase *across the lake* is a fragment because a prepositional phrase cannot function as the subject or the verb in a sentence. Furthermore, the words *across the lake* do not express a complete thought.

2. **Join the fragment to the sentence that precedes it or to the sentence that follows it, depending on where it belongs.**

If a writer looks at the text where the fragment occurs, often the complete thought is already present. The writer did not recognize that the fragment belonged to the sentence coming before or the sentence following. Study the example below:

Wrong: In the middle of the night, I swam. Across the lake.

The camp counselor was waiting at the other side.

Correct: In the middle of the night, I swam across the lake.

The camp counselor was waiting at the other side.

There can be more than one reason for fragments in a writer's work. A writer may be careless for a moment or may not fully understand all the parts of a sentence. Also, if the writer does not have a clear idea of what he or she is trying to say, fragments and other errors are more likely to occur. Sometimes further thought or another try at expressing the same idea may produce a better result.

In the following two exercises, practice correcting both kinds of fragments.

EXERCISE 3   **Making fragments into sentences**

Change the fragments of Exercise 2 into complete sentences by adding the missing part or parts that you have already identified.

1. returned to the river

_____

2. a bird on the oak branch

_____

3. between the island and the mainland

_____

4. the hawk in a soaring motion

_____

5. the fishing boats on the lake

_____

6. dropped like a stone into the water

_____

7. the silence of the forest

_____

8. carried the fish to the tree

_____

9. the fisherman put

_____

10. into the net

_____

Finding fragments that belong to other sentences

Each of the following passages contains a fragment or two. First, read each passage. Then locate the fragment in each passage. Circle the fragment and draw an arrow to the sentence to which it should be connected. An example follows:

Adelle assisted the dancers. She stood backstage. Between numbers. She helped the ballerinas change costumes.

Fishing is one of the oldest sports in the world. And can be one of the most relaxing. A person with a simple wooden pole and line can have as much fun as a sportsman. With expensive equipment. For busy executives, overworked teachers, and even presidents of nations. Fishing can be a good way to escape from the stress of demanding jobs.

Passage 1

The first electric car was built in 1887. Six years later, it was sold commercially. At the turn of the century, people had great faith in new technology. In fact, three hundred electric taxicabs were operating in New York City by 1900. However, electric cars soon lost their popularity. The new gasoline engine became more widely used. With our concern over pollution. Perhaps electric cars will become desirable once again.

Passage 2

Passage 3   Eskimos obtain most of their food from the sea. They eat seals and walruses. Whales, fish and sea birds in abundance. Eskimos boil some of their food. They eat other foods uncooked because of the scarcity of fuel. Eskimos get important vitamins and minerals. By eating every part of the animal they kill. The heart, the liver, and even the digestive tracts of the animals have great food value for the Eskimos.

What is a phrase?

> A *Phrase* is a group of words that go together, but the group lacks one or more of the elements necessary to be classified as a sentence.

Fragments are usually made up of phrases. These phrases are often mistaken for sentences because they are words that go together as a group. However, they do not fit the definition of a sentence. *Do not confuse a phrase with a sentence.*

How many kinds of phrases are there?

The English language has six phrases (three of which you have already studied in Chapter 2). You should learn to recognize each of these phrases. Remember that a phrase is never a sentence.

1. **Noun phrase:** a noun plus its modifiers

   large square bricks

2. **Prepositional phrase:** a preposition plus its object and modifiers

   around our neighborhood

3. **Verb phrase:** the main verb plus its helping verbs

   is walking

   could have walked

   should have been walking

The three remaining phrases are formed from *verbs.* However, these phrases do not function as verbs in the sentence. Study carefully how to use them.

4. **Participial phrase:**
   How is the participial phrase formed?

   a. the present form of a verb ending in *-ing* and any other words necessary to complete the phrase

      running home

      looking very unhappy

b. the past form of a verb usually ending in -*ed* and any other words necessary to complete the phrase

> greatly disappointed
>
> told tearfully

How does the participial phrase function? Participial phrases function as ***adjectives*** in a sentence. Study how the above phrases could be made into complete sentences. These phrases will function as adjectives for the noun or pronoun that follows.

> *Running home*, the worker lost her wallet.
>
> *Looking very unhappy*, she retraced her steps.
>
> *Greatly disappointed*, she could not find it.
>
> *Told tearfully*, her story saddened her friends.

Students often make the mistake of confusing a participle with a verb. When a participle is used as a verb, there *must* be a helping verb with it.

Incorrect: I running in the marathon

Correct: I *am* running in the marathon.

5. **Gerund phrase:** the present form of a verb ending in -*ing*, and any other words necessary to complete the phrase.

   The gerund phrase functions as a noun.

   a. subject of the sentence:

   > *Running in a marathon* is strenuous exercise.

   b. direct object of the sentence:

   > I like *running in a marathon.*

6. **Infinitive phrase:** *to* plus the verb and any other words necessary to complete the phrase

   > *to run* the race

   Note: The word *to* can also function as a preposition.

   > I ran *to school.*

EXERCISE 5 **Identifying phrases**

Identify each of the underlined phrases in the following sentences.

1. <u>Visiting New York</u> can be a nightmare or a thrill. _____

2. Many people love <u>to see the Broadway shows.</u> _____

3. Museums, restaurants, shopping, and the varied night life offer endless possibilities <u>for the tourist.</u> _____

4. <u>Riding the subways,</u> tourists see another side of New York. _____

5. <u>My brother Don</u> was pickpocketed on a hot and crowded subway last summer. _____

6. <u>Coming from the country,</u> he thought the prices were outrageous and the noise and traffic unbearable. _____

7. Finding a parking spot <u>may have been</u> his most frustrating experience. _____

8. <u>In addition to these problems,</u> the question of physical safety concerns most tourists. _____

9. The city <u>has begun</u> projects to clean up the Times Square area. _____

10. New York's continual fascination is the rich <u>mix of cultures and lifestyles</u> from all over the world. _____

EXERCISE 6 **Identifying phrases**

The following six sentences come from a paragraph by John Steinbeck. Identify each of the underlined phrases.

1. <u>At dawn</u> Cannery Row seems

   <u>to hang suspended</u>

   out of time <u>in a silvery light.</u>

2. The splashing <u>of the waves</u>

   <u>can be heard.</u>

3. <u>Flapping their wings,</u> the seagulls

   come <u>to sit</u> on the roof peaks shoulder to shoulder.

4. Cats drip <u>over the fences</u> and slither like syrup over the ground to look for fishheads.

5. Silent early morning <u>dogs parade</u> majestically.

6. No automobiles <u>are running</u> then.

1. _____

2. _____

3. _____

4. _____

5. _____

6. _____

7. _____

8. _____

9. _____

10. _____

Identifying phrases

Identify each of the underlined phrases.

1. Exploring the farm, I could see the growing
   coffee plants.   _____

2. It is a very difficult job to supervise a farm.   _____

3. Growing any kind of crop is a time-consuming
   procedure.   _____

4. Helped constantly, crops will tend to do well.   _____

5. Appearing very tiny, the coffee plants needed
   more moisture.   _____

6. The plants should have been watered last week.   _____

7. I walked through different parts of the plantation
   to see what other problems I could identify.   _____

8. Around the edge of the farm I could see
   evidence of insect damage to the plants.   _____

9. Their discolored leaves showed signs of
   infestation.   _____

10. Organized properly, this farm could be a source
    of both profit and pride.   _____

Understanding the uses of the present participle

The present participle causes a good deal of confusion for students working with
the fragment. Because the participle can be used sometimes as a verb, sometimes as
an adjective, and sometimes as a noun, you will want to be aware of which of these
uses you intend.

Using the participle in a verb phrase

Below are five present participles. Use each of them as part of a verb phrase in a
sentence. An example follows:

    Present participle: sitting

    Verb phrase: is sitting

    Sentence: The couple is sitting on the balcony.

1. building _____

2. crying _____

3. traveling _____

4. writing _____

5. lacking _____

EXERCISE 9 **Using the participial phrase as an adjective**

Each of the underlined words below is a present participle. Use the word along with the phrase provided to compose sentences in which the phrase functions as an adjective. An example follows:

Present participle: sitting

Participial phrase: sitting on the balcony

Participial phrase used as an adjective phrase in the sentence: Sitting on the balcony, the couple enjoyed the moonlight.

1. Building a house

_____

_____

2. Crying over the broken vase

_____

_____

3. Traveling in Mexico

_____

_____

4. Hastily writing the letter

_____

_____

5. Lacking the courage to tell the truth

_____

_____

EXERCISE 10 **Using the participial phrase as a noun (gerund)**

Each of the underlined words below is a present participle of a phrase. Use each phrase as a noun phrase to create a sentence of your own. An example follows:

Present participle: sitting

Participial phrase: sitting on the balcony

Participial phrase used as a noun phrase in a sentence: Sitting on the balcony is relaxing.

1. Building a house

_____

_____

2. Crying over the broken vase

_____

_____

3. Traveling in Mexico

_____

_____

4. Hastily writing the letter

_____

_____

5. Lacking the courage to tell the truth

_____

_____

How do you make a complete sentence from a fragment that contains a participle?

Fragment: he talking in his sleep

1. Add a helping verb to the participle:

He is talking in his sleep.

2. Change the participle to a different form of the verb:

He talks in his sleep.

3. Use the participle as an adjective, being sure to provide a subject and verb for the sentence:

Talking in his sleep, he muttered something about his boss.

4. Use the participle as a noun:

Talking in his sleep revealed his innermost thoughts.

Correcting the fragment that contains a participle

EXERCISE 11

Make four complete sentences from each of the following fragments. Use the following example as your model.

Fragment: using the back stairway

    a. He is using the back stairway.

    b. He uses the back stairway.

    c. Using the back stairway, he got away without being seen.

    d. Using the back stairway is not a good idea.

1. moving out of the house

    a. _____

    b. _____

    c. _____

    d. _____

2. talking on the telephone

    a. _____

    b. _____

    c. _____

    d. _____

3. driving the car down Highway 60

    a. _____

    b. _____

    c. _____

    d. _____

EXERCISE 12 **Correcting the fragment that contains a participle**

The following passage is made up of fragments containing participles. Rewrite the passage using complete sentences. Use any of the four correction methods discussed above.

I walking through the deserted apartment building. Poking around in piles of junk. The brick walls crumbling. Two children playing in the dismal hallways. Waiting for someone to restore the house to its former glory.

_____

_____

_____

_____

_____

EXERCISE 13 **Correcting the fragment that contains a participle**

The following passage has four fragments containing participles. Circle the fragments. Then rewrite the passage using complete sentences. Use any of the four correction methods discussed previously.

At last taking the driving test. I felt very nervous. My mother was sitting in the back seat. All my papers sitting on the front seat. The inspector got into the car and sat on my insurance form. He looked rather sour and barely spoke to me. Trying not to hit the curb. I parallel parked surprisingly well. I managed to get through all the maneuvers. Now tensely waiting for the results.

_____

_____

_____

_____

_____

Correcting fragments

Rewrite each fragment so that it is a complete sentence.

1. early morning a time of peace in my neighborhood

   _____

   _____

2. the gray mist covering up all but the faint outlines of nearby houses

   _____

   _____

3. the shapes of cars in the streets and driveways

   _____

   _____

4. to sit and look out the window

   _____

   _____

5. holding a steaming cup of coffee

   _____

   _____

6. the only sound the rumbling of a truck

   _____

   _____

7. passing on the highway a quarter-mile away

   _____

   _____

8. children all in their beds

   _____

   _____

9. no barks of dogs

   _____

   _____

10. in this soft, silent dreamworld

   _____

   _____

Correcting fragments

Each of the following groups of words is a phrase. First, name each phrase. Second, make each phrase into a complete sentence.

1. to earn a living

   Name of phrase: _____

   Sentence: _____

   _____

2. from another country

    Name of phrase: _____

    Sentence: _____

    _____

3. hanging dangerously

    Name of phrase: _____

    Sentence: _____

    _____

4. for children of any age

    Name of phrase: _____

    Sentence: _____

    _____

5. making candy

    Name of phrase: _____

    Sentence: _____

    _____

6. to sit outside

    Name of phrase: _____

    Sentence: _____

    _____

7. at the bottom of the hill

    Name of phrase: _____

    Sentence: _____

    _____

8. shaping the dough

    Name of phrase: _____

    Sentence: _____

    _____

9. the heavy oven door

    Name of phrase: _____

    Sentence: _____

    _____

10. walking slowly

    Name of phrase: _____

    Sentence: _____

    _____

Correcting fragments

Each of the following groups of words is a phrase. First, name each phrase. Second, make each phrase into a complete sentence.

1. two champion boxers

   Name of phrase: _____

   Sentence: _____

   _____

2. to watch

   Name of phrase: _____

   Sentence: _____

   _____

3. in the ring

   Name of phrase: _____

   Sentence: _____

   _____

4. hitting each other

   Name of phrase: _____

   Sentence: _____

   _____

5. at each sound of the bell

   Name of phrase: _____

   Sentence: _____

   _____

6. gratefully supported

   Name of phrase: _____

   Sentence: _____

   _____

7. to conduct the fight

   Name of phrase: _____

   Sentence: _____

   _____

8. the screaming fans

   Name of phrase: _____

   Sentence: _____

   _____

   _____

9. by the second round

   Name of phrase: _____

   Sentence: _____

   _____

10. knocked unconscious

    Name of phrase: _____

    Sentence: _____

    _____

Mastery and editing tests

TEST 1   Recognizing and correcting the fragment

The following description of people on a dance floor at the Peppermint Lounge appeared in the *New Yorker*. The description is made up entirely of fragments. Rewrite the description making each fragment into a sentence.

Place always jammed. Huge line outside. Portals closely guarded. Finally made it last night, after hour's wait. Exhilarating experience! Feel ten years younger. Hit Peppermint close to midnight, in blue mood. Inside, found pandemonium. Dance floor packed and popping. Was battered by wild swinging of hips and elbows. . . . Garb of twisters seems to run gamut. Some couples in evening dress, others in T shirts and blue jeans. Young. Old. Businessmen. Crew Cuts. Beatniks.

_____

_____

_____

_____

_____

_____

_____

_____

_____

_____

_____

_____

_____

_____

Recognizing and correcting the fragment

The following paragraph contains fragments. Read the paragraph and underline each fragment. Then rewrite the paragraph being careful to use only complete sentences.

We called it our house. It was only one room. With about as much space as a tent. Painted in a pastel color with a red tiled roof. The front window reaching nearly from the sidewalk to the roof. We could look up and down the street. Sitting indoors on the window seat. Our kitchen was a small narrow area. With the brick stove and two benches to serve as shelves. Three steel bars and a short piece of lead pipe from a scrap heap to make a grate.

HINT:
6 fragments

_____

_____

_____

_____

_____

_____

_____

_____

Recognizing and correcting the fragment

The following paragraph contains fragments. Read the paragraph and underline each fragment. Then rewrite the paragraph being careful to use only complete sentences.

That afternoon the street was full of children. Taking a shower in the rain. Soaping themselves and rushing out into the storm. To wash off the suds. In a few minutes, it was all over. Including the rubdown. The younger children took their showers naked. Teetering on the tips of their toes and squealing to one another. The stately coconut palm in one corner of the patio. Thrashed its branches high over the dripping children bouncing on the cobblestones.

HINT:
7 fragments

_____

_____

_____

_____

_____

_____

_____

Examining an Advertisement for Fragments

1. Read the Bankers Trust advertisement illustrated here. Notice that the advertisement is composed in a short, snappy way that is appealing but grammatically incorrect. Why do you think an advertiser would write in this way? When we write for school or for work, our compositions must contain only complete sentences. Rewrite all of the fragments you find in the advertisement, making a complete and separate sentence out of each fragment.

Advertising companies devote a great deal of their time and attention to market research. This research helps the industry target its message to the most likely audience for their product or service. Who is the advertiser in this newspaper ad? Who is the intended audience? What is product or service being advertised?

Suggestion

now to clip magazine or newspaper advertisements that you find appealing or tive. Save them in your portfolio until you have gathered enough material to ssay on how advertisers direct their messages to specific audiences.

CHAPTER 5

Combining Sentences Using the Three Methods of Coordination

So far you have worked with the simple sentence. If you review some of these sentences (such as the practice sentences on page 40), you will see that writing only simple sentences results in a choppy style and also makes it difficult to express more complicated ideas. You will need to understand the possible ways of combining simple sentences. In this chapter, you will practice the skill of combining sentences using *coordination*.

1st Method: Use a comma plus a coordinating conjunction.
2nd Method: Use a semicolon, an adverbial conjunction, and a comma.
3rd Method: Use only a semicolon.

What is coordination?

Coordination is the combining of two simple sentences (which we will now refer to as independent clauses) that are related and contain ideas of equal importance. The result is a compound sentence.

Note: Don't be confused by the term *independent clause*. A *clause* is a group of words having a subject and a verb. An *independent clause* (IC) is a clause that could stand alone as a simple sentence. You may think of these terms in the following way:

simple sentence   = one independent clause
compound sentence = two independent clauses joined by coordination

First method: Use a comma plus a coordinating conjunction

> The most common way to form a compound sentence is to combine independent clauses using a comma plus a coordinating conjunction.

IC	, coordinating conjunction	IC
He spoke forcefully	, and	I felt compelled to listen.

Because there are only seven common coordinating conjunctions and three pairs of coordinating conjunctions, a little time invested in memorizing the list would be time well spent. By doing this now, you will avoid confusion later on when you must use a different set of conjunctions to combine clauses.

Connectors: Coordinating conjunctions	
and	*Used in Pairs*
but	either . . . or
or, nor	neither . . . nor
for (meaning *because*)	not only . . . but also
yet	
so	

PRACTICE   In each of the following compound sentences, draw a single line under the subject and draw two lines under the verb for each independent clause. Then circle both the coordinating conjunction and the comma. An example follows:

The speaker rose to his feet, and the room became quiet.

1. The audience was packed, for this was a man with an international reputation.

2. He could have told about all his successes, but instead he spoke about his disappointments.

3. His words were electric, so the crowd was attentive.

4. I should have brought a tape recorder, or at least I should have taken notes.

Did you find a subject and verb for both independent clauses in each sentence?

Now that you understand the structure of a compound sentence, you need to think about the meanings of the different coordinating conjunctions and how they can be used to show the relationship between two ideas, each idea being given equal importance.

Meanings of coordinating conjunctions	
to add an idea:	and
to add an idea when the first clause is in the negative:	nor
to contrast two opposing ideas:	but, yet
to introduce a reason:	for
to show a choice:	or
to introduce a result:	so

Combining sentences using coordinating conjunctions

EXERCISE I

Each of the following examples contains two simple sentences that could be related by combining them with a coordinating conjunction. Decide what relationship the second sentence has to the first, and then select the conjunction that will make sense. Then write the new compound sentence.

Two simple sentences:

She broke her arm.

She couldn't play in the finals.

Relationship of second sentence to first: *result*
Conjunction that introduces this meaning: *so*
New compound sentence:

She broke her arm, so she couldn't play in the finals.

1. Mr. Watson is kind and patient.
   His brother is sharp and nagging.

   Relationship of 2nd sentence to 1st: ___Contrast___

   Conjunction that introduces this meaning: ___but___

   _____

   _____

2. The two adults are having great difficulty.
   They are trying to raise a teenager.

   Relationship of 2nd sentence to 1st: ___to introduce a reason___

   Conjunction that introduces this meaning: ___for___

   _____

   _____

3. Young Michael has no family of his own.
   He feels angry and alone.

   Relationship of 2nd sentence to 1st: ___introduce a result___

   Conjunction that introduces this meaning: ___so___

   _____

   _____

4. Michael hasn't been doing well in school.

   He isn't involved in any activities outside school.

   Relationship of 2nd sentence to 1st: *to Add An idea When 1st Clause is neg.*

   Conjunction that introduces this meaning: *nor*

   _____

   _____

5. Mr. Watson encouraged Michael to do volunteer work at the hospital.

   This might give Michael the satisfaction of helping other people.

   Relationship of 2nd sentence to 1st: *to introduce A result*

   Conjunction that introduces this meaning: *So*

   _____

   _____

6. Mr. Watson's brother wanted Michael to spend more time on his homework.

   He also wanted him to get a job that would bring in some money to help with expenses.

   Relationship of 2nd sentence to 1st: *to Add An idea*

   Conjunction that introduces this meaning: *And*

   _____

   _____

7. Michael liked going to the hospital.

   He was doing something important.

   Relationship of 2nd sentence to 1st: *To introduce A Reason*

   Conjunction that introduces this meaning: *for*

   _____

   _____

8. He didn't earn any money.

   He liked helping people.

   Relationship of 2nd sentence to 1st: *To Add An Idea when 1st is Neg.*

   Conjunction that introduces this meaning: *nor*

   _____

   _____

9. Michael now wants to have a career working in a hospital.

   He will have a reason to work harder in school.

   Relationship of 2nd sentence to 1st: *To intro A Result*

   Conjunction that introduces this meaning: *So*

   _____

   _____

10. Mr. Watson thinks the hospital work was a good idea.

His brother has to agree.

Relationship of 2nd sentence to 1st: _____Contrast_____

Conjunction that introduces this meaning: _____but_____

_____

_____

Combining sentences using coordinating conjunctions

For each example, add a second independent clause using the given coordinating conjunction. Be certain that your new sentence makes sense.

1. Richard Gere is my favorite actor, and _____

_____

2. I loved the movie *Red Corner*, but _____

_____

3. Either I go to a movie on Friday night, or _____

_____

4. I would like to have dinner in a fine restaurant, but _____

_____

5. The weather this Friday night is supposed to be cold and wet, so _____

_____

6. My friend Craig cannot go with me, for _____

_____

7. I can't borrow my friend's car, nor _____

_____

8. Not only are the beverages there too expensive, _____

_____

9. It would be nice to own a video machine, for _____

_____

10. Watching videos at home is cheap, yet _____

_____

Combining sentences using coordinating conjunctions

For each example, add a second independent clause using the given coordinating conjunction. Be certain that your new sentence makes sense.

1. (but) The two detectives carefully checked the scene for fingerprints *but they forgot to check the attic.*

2. (and) The safe was open *, and the jewels were taken.*

3. (so) There was no sign of forced entry *, so the officer could not make an arrest ~~be~~ anyone.*

4. (nor) The restaurant owner could not be found *, nor the employees were working.*

5. (for) Suddenly they became interested in one of the tables *for they purchased ~~the tables~~ the table*

6. (so) The missing tablecloth could be significant *the tablecloth was missing*

7. (and) One detective looked in the closets _____

8. (or) They might find another clue _____

9. (yet) There were no witnesses _____

10. (or) Either they get a break in the case _____

Composing compound sentences

Compose ten of your own compound sentences using the coordinating conjunctions indicated.

1. and _____

2. but _____

3. or _____

4. for (meaning *because*) _____

5. yet _____

6. so _____

_____

7. nor _____

_____

8. neither/nor _____

_____

9. not only/but also _____

_____

10. either/or _____

_____

Second method: Use a semicolon, an adverbial conjunction, and a comma

> A second way to form a compound sentence is to combine independent clauses by using a semicolon, an adverbial conjunction, and a comma.

IC	; adverbial conjunction,	IC
I had worked hard	; therefore,	I expected results.

The conjunctions used for this method are called **adverbial conjunctions** (or conjunctive adverbs). These conjunctions have meanings similar to the common coordinating conjunctions, but they sound slightly more formal than the shorter conjunctions such as *and* or *but*. These connecting words give a compound sentence more emphasis.

He was late, and he had the wrong documents.

He was late; furthermore, he had the wrong documents.

Connectors: Frequently used adverbial conjunctions		
Addition (and)	**Alternative (or)**	**Result (so)**
In addition	instead	accordingly
also	on the other hand	consequently
besides	otherwise	hence
furthermore		therefore
moreover	**Contrast (but)**	thus
	however	
	nevertheless	
	nonetheless	
Likeness	**Emphasis**	**To Show Time**
likewise	indeed	meanwhile
similarly	in fact	

PRACTICE   In each of the following compound sentences, draw a single line under the subject and draw two lines under the verb for both independent clauses. Then circle the semicolon, adverbial conjunction, and comma. For example:

The jet was the fastest way to get there; moreover, it was the most comfortable.

1. The restaurant is always too crowded on Saturdays; nevertheless, it serves the best food in town.

2. The land was not for sale; however, the house could be rented.

3. The lawsuit cost the company several million dollars; consequently, the company went out of business a short time later.

4. The doctor told him to lose weight; furthermore, she instructed him to stop smoking.

EXERCISE 5   ## Combining sentences using adverbial conjunctions

Combine each pair of sentences below to make a compound sentence. Use a semicolon, an adverbial conjunction, and a comma. Be sure the conjunction you choose makes sense in the sentence. For example:

Two simple sentences: Our family would like to purchase a computer.

We must wait until prices come down further.

Compound sentence: Our family would like to purchase a computer; however, we must wait until prices come down further.

1. Most people have preferred to write with a pen or pencil.
   The computer is quickly becoming another favorite writing tool.
   most people have preferred to write with a pen or pencil, And

2. Computers provide a powerful way to create and store pieces of writing.
   They will become even more important in the future. (Show result.)
   ; hence,

3. Some people do not like the idea of using electronics to create words.
   The modern typewriter is also an electronic tool. (Show contrast.)
   ; however,

4. Computers have already revolutionized today's offices.
   No modern business can afford to be without them. (Show emphasis.)
   in fact

5. Many schools are using computers in the classroom.
   These same schools are helping students prepare for their working careers.
   (Add an idea.)
   furthermore
   _____

   _____

6. The prices of many computers are coming down these days.
   Owning a computer is a real possibility. (Show result.)
   therefore
   _____

   _____

7. Some children know more about computers than many adults.
   Some children are teaching the adults. (Show emphasis.)
   in fact
   _____

   _____

8. Professional writers have become enthusiastic about the use of computers.
   Some writers still use paper and pencil. (Show contrast.)
   nevertheless
   _____

   _____

9. The electronic revolution has just begun.
   The nation faces a great challenge to keep up with such a fast-growing revolution. (Show result.)
   consequently
   _____

   _____

10. We have many technological aids to writing.
    The source for all our ideas is still the human brain. (Show contrast.)
    however
    _____

    _____

Combining sentences using adverbial conjunctions

EXERCISE 6

Combine each pair of sentences below to make a compound sentence. Use a semi-colon, an adverbial conjunction, and a comma. Be sure the conjunction you choose makes sense in the sentence.

1. She doesn't like her job anymore.
   She cannot find another job that pays as well.

   _____

   _____

2. The office is clean and spacious.
   Her coworkers are very kind.

   _____

   _____

3. The work is very repetitious and boring.
   She finds herself looking at her watch twenty times a day.

   _____

   _____

4. Her best qualities are carefulness and industriousness.
   Her problem is a need for excitement and challenge.

   _____

   _____

5. She long ago learned everything about the job.
   She now has no sense of growth or personal satisfaction.

   _____

   _____

6. Even some doctors sometimes grow tired of their jobs.
   They have invested too much time and energy to change careers.

   _____

   _____

7. One solution could be the establishment of regular retraining programs.
   A person with years of experience in one field might leave it all behind for something new.

   _____

   _____

8. Society would lose the benefit of their expertise.
   Individuals would lose the chance to be at the top of their fields.

   _____

   _____

9. Some large companies move employees around every few years.
   Workers seem energized by new surroundings and people.

   _____

   _____

10. Perhaps every ten years we should all switch jobs.
    We had better make the best of our situations.

    _____

    _____

Combining sentences using adverbial conjunctions

For each example, add the suggested adverbial conjunction and another independent clause that will make sense. Remember to punctuate correctly.

1. (however) We were told not to leave the building; *however,* *everyone decided to leave.*

2. (therefore) I hadn't done the homework very carefully; *therefore* *my grade was affected.*

3. (otherwise) He accepted the job he was offered; *otherwise* *he will remain unemployed.*

4. (instead) Matthew doesn't like office work, *instead, he* *would be playing golf.*

5. (in fact) The running shoes are expensive, *in fact,* *the dress shoes are more expensive*

6. (furthermore) The doctor advised my father to stop smoking _____

_____

7. (consequently) The hurricane struck last night _____

_____

8. (meanwhile) I worked feverishly for days on the report _____

_____

9. (nevertheless) The young singer was nervous _____

_____

10. (moreover) The car is the fastest way to get to work _____

_____

Third method: Use a semicolon

The third and less commonly used way to form a compound sentence is to combine two independent clauses by using only a semicolon.

IC	;	IC
He arrived at ten	;	He left at midnight.

This third method of combining sentences is used less often. No connecting word is used. The semicolon takes the place of the conjunction.

Two independent clauses:	Last year I read F. Scott Fitzgerald's *The Great Gatsby.*
	Tonight I saw the movie version of his *Tender Is the Night.*
Compound sentence:	Last year I read F. Scott Fitzgerald's *The Great Gatsby*; tonight I saw the movie version of his *Tender Is the Night.*

The semicolon was used in this example to show that the contents of both sentences are closely related and therefore could be combined in one sentence.

When sentences are combined by using a semicolon, the grammatical structure of each sentence is often similar:

The women pitched the tents; the men cooked the dinner.

EXERCISE 8   **Combining sentences using the semicolon**

For each of the independent clauses below, add your own independent clause that has a similar grammatical structure or is a closely related idea. Join the two clauses with a semicolon. An example follows:

Independent clause: He wrote the speech.

Compound sentence: He wrote the speech; she gave it.

1. The apartment was light and airy.

_____

_____

2. Shoppers were pushing grocery carts down the aisles.

_____

_____

3. I plan to learn two foreign languages.

_____

_____

4. I tried to explain.

_____

_____

5. Many teenagers spend hours listening to rock music.

_____

_____

Combining sentences using the semicolon

For each of the independent clauses that follow, add your own independent clause that has a similar grammatical structure or is a closely related idea. An example follows:

> **Independent clause:** The guests are putting on their coats.
>
> **Compound sentence:** The guests are putting on their coats; the cab is at the door.

1. The pickup truck was filled with old furniture.

   _____

   _____

2. Children played in the streets.

   _____

   _____

3. We expected them to understand.

   _____

   _____

4. The older men wore ties.

   _____

   _____

5. She hoped her friend would soon call.

   _____

   _____

Mastery and editing tests

Combining sentences using coordination

Combine each pair of sentences below to make a compound sentence. Choose from the three methods you have studied in this chapter. Be sure that the conjunctions you choose clearly show the relationships between the ideas.

1. The large rain forests of Africa and South America are in danger.
   They can never be replaced.

   _____

   _____

2. The varieties of insects and animals in the rain forest are enormous.
   Their destruction means the loss of the world's greatest biological laboratory.

   _____

   _____

3. Many countries are cutting down their rain forests every year.
   The world's natural resources are steadily decreasing.

   _____

   _____

4. Scientists are concerned about the loss of animal and plant species in the rain forest.
   They are trying to slow down this destruction.

   _____

   _____

5. The governments of the world should be concerned about the loss of the rain forests.
   They are not doing enough to stop the developers.

   _____

   _____

6. The rain forests could be a valuable source of medical knowledge.
   The forests are also an invaluable source of timber and other products.

   _____

   _____

7. Most people in our country have never seen a rain forest.
   They find it difficult to imagine how beautiful it is.

   _____

   _____

8. Rain forests appear to be fertile.
   They actually have very poor soil for growing crops.

   _____

   _____

9. Many animals of the rain forest have not yet been studied by scientists.
   Many plants may still hold the secret to medical cures.

   _____

   _____

10. Some developers pride themselves in the cutting down of the rainforests.
    Most scientists are deeply disturbed by this monumental destruction of nature.

    _____

    _____

Combining sentences using coordination

Using each of the five following simple sentences as an independent clause, construct a compound sentence. Use each of the three possible methods at least once.

1. The beach was crowded. (Add an idea.)

   _____

   _____

2. The first apartment had no bedroom. (Show a contrast.)

   _____

   _____

3. January had been bitterly cold. (Show a result.)

   _____

   _____

4. The young model wore dark glasses. (Introduce a reason.)

   _____

   _____

5. The community waited for news. (Show time.)

   _____

   _____

Combining sentences using coordination

Construct a compound sentence by adding another independent clause to each of the five simple sentences (or independent clauses) that follow. Use any one of the three methods of coordination.

1. Babysitters should stay awake.

   _____

   _____

2. A good babysitter will play with the children.

   _____

   _____

3. A parent should not expect a babysitter to do cleaning.

   _____

   _____

4. A list of emergency numbers should be left by the telephone.

   _____

   _____

5. A young babysitter should be escorted home.

   _____

   _____

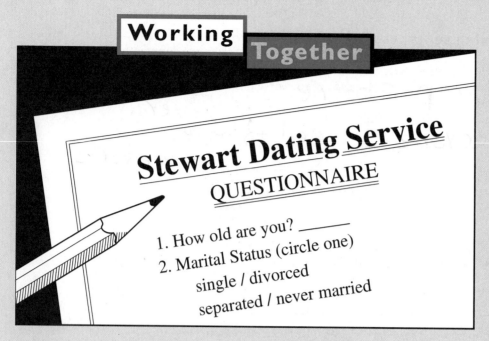

Stewart Dating Service

QUESTIONNAIRE

1. How old are you? _____
2. Marital Status (circle one)
   single / divorced
   separated / never married

Brainstorming with Others for Ideas

An important part of the writing process is being able to brainstorm before you actually write. If you are lucky enough to be able to do this with a group of people, you are likely to be inspired with new or different ideas. Also, brainstorming usually stimulates each group member to stretch his or her own thinking on a given topic. Approach the following question by brainstorming for ideas:

How can a single person create opportunities to meet someone for a possible special relationship?

Many single people want to develop friendships that may lead to lasting relationships or even marriage. However, these people may not believe that going to singles bars, for example, is the best way to meet people. What are some ideas for a single person who wants to meet people and develop lasting relationships?

Divide into groups to discuss the issue. Although everyone should take notes, choose one person to record the important points made during the discussion. This formal list is important for two reasons. First, others may need to hear some of the points repeated later, and second, your instructor will want to see your list in order to evaluate your group effort.

After discussing the issue for approximately twenty minutes, review the points that have been made. Each person should then put the items into a certain order, numbering them according to the importance placed on each idea that came out of the group discussion. This order may differ from person to person, depending on individual experiences and private opinions. These ordered lists will now become the plans students may use to write about this issue.

Use the last minutes of class to come together and share the brainstorming experience. Did each group get down to work and develop possible solutions to the situation? Did each person finish with an ordered list?

Portfolio Suggestion

Save the ordered list in your portfolio. Even if you do not use the list now, this material could be the basis for a paragraph or essay on the topic at some future time.

CHAPTER 6

Combining Sentences Using Subordination

S
T
E
P

2

In Chapter 5, when you used *coordination*, each clause of the resulting *compound sentence* carried ideas of equal weight. However, writers often want to combine ideas that are not equally important. This is done by using two different sets of connecting words, creating a **complex sentence.** This method of combining ideas is called **subordination** because one idea will be dependent on (or subordinate to) the other. In this chapter, you will learn how to write complex sentences by using subordination. Exercises will help you to do the following:

- Recognize the difference between **independent** and **dependent clauses.**
- Use two types of dependent clauses for writing complex sentences:
    1. A dependent clause beginning with a **subordinating conjunction.**
    2. A dependent clause beginning with a **relative pronoun.**

What is subordination?

Subordination is the combining of two clauses containing ideas that are not equally important. The more important idea is called the *independent clause* and the less important idea is called the *dependent clause.* The result is a *complex sentence.*

In *coordination*, you used certain connecting words called *coordinating conjunctions* or *adverbial conjunctions* to combine ideas. In *subordination*, you use two different sets of connecting words: *subordinating conjunctions* or *relative pronouns.*

What is the difference between an independent and dependent clause?

An independent clause stands alone as a complete thought; it could be a simple sentence.

Independent clause: I drank the water.

A dependent clause begins with a connecting word, and although the thought has a subject and a verb, it does not stand alone as a complete thought. The idea needs to be completed.

Dependent clause: When I drank the water, . . .

Before you write your own complex sentences, practice the following exercises to be sure you understand the difference between an independent clause and a dependent clause.

EXERCISE 1 ## Recognizing dependent and independent clauses

In the blank to the side of each group of words, write the letters IC if the group is an independent clause (a complete thought) or DC if the group of words is a dependent clause (not a complete thought, even though it contains a subject and a verb).

DC 1. while the photographer was getting ready

DC 2. before the show began

IC 3. I seldom go to the movies by myself

DC 4. even if it rains

IC 5. the Monopoly game lasted five hours

DC 6. whenever I see you

DC 7. since I did not take the medicine

IC 8. I spent the day in bed

DC 9. when I was sitting on the crosstown bus

DC 10. until the day he died

EXERCISE 2 ## Recognizing dependent and independent clauses

In the blank to the side of each group of words, write the letters IC if the group is an independent clause (a complete thought) or DC if the group of words is a dependent clause (not a complete thought, even though it contains a subject and a verb).

DC 1. when his back was turned

IC 2. he stared at his watch angrily

DC 3. even though I offered to walk with him

IC 4. this was a new development

IC 5. I was so astonished

DC 6. unless I acted at once

DC 7. after my brother arrived

IC 8. I had to be very quiet

DC 9. sometimes I pinched him

DC 10. as he lay sleeping

Recognizing dependent and independent clauses

In the blank to the side of each group of words, write the letters IC if the group is an independent clause (a complete thought) or DC if the group of words is a dependent clause (not a complete thought, even though it contains a subject and a verb).

_____ 1. William Faulkner was a regional writer

_____ 2. he was born near Oxford, Mississippi

_____ 3. where he lived and died

_____ 4. even if he used the dialect of the area

_____ 5. some of his books share the same characters and themes

_____ 6. because Faulkner devoted many pages to greed, violence, and meanness

_____ 7. until the year he died

_____ 8. he won the Nobel Prize in 1950

_____ 9. when he became one of America's greatest writers

_____ 10. although Faulkner departed from the traditional style of prose

Using subordinating conjunctions

Study the list of subordinating conjunctions in the chart that follows. The use of one of these connecting words signals the beginning of a dependent clause. It is a good idea to memorize them just as you did the coordinating conjunctions. The different groups of connecting words have different principles for punctuation, so you really need to memorize them in these groups.

Connectors: Common subordinating conjunctions		
after	if, even if	unless
although	in order that	until
as, as if	provided that	when, whenever
as long as, as though	rather than	where, wherever
because	since	whether
before	so that	while
even though	though	

The next chart contains the subordinating conjunctions grouped according to their meanings. When you use one of these conjunctions, you must be sure that the connection made between the independent clause and the dependent clause is the meaning you intend.

Function of subordinating conjunctions	
To introduce a *condition:*	if, even if, as long as, provided that, unless (after a negative independent clause)
I will go as long as you go with me.	
I won't go unless you go with me.	
To introduce a *contrast:*	although, even though, though
I will go even though you won't go with me.	
To introduce a *cause:*	because, since
I will go because the meeting is very important.	
To show *time:*	after, before, when, whenever, while, until (independent clause is negative).
I will go whenever you say.	
I won't go until you say it is time.	
To show *place:*	where, wherever
I will go wherever you send me.	
To show *purpose:*	in order that, so that
I will go so that I can hear the candidate for myself.	

You have two choices of how to write a complex sentence. You can begin with the independent clause, or you can begin with the dependent clause.

First way:	**IC**	**IC**
Example:	We can finish our homework	if Barbara leaves.

Second way:	**DC**	**,**	**IC**
Example:	If Barbara leaves	,	we can finish our homework.

Notice that only the second version uses a comma; this is because the second version begins with the dependent clause. When a sentence begins with the independent clause, no comma is used. Your ear may help you with this punctuation. Read a sentence that begins with a dependent clause. Do you notice that there is a tendency to pause at the end of that dependent clause? This is a natural place to put a comma.

PRACTICE

Use a subordinating conjunction to combine each of the following pairs of sentences. Remember, the independent clause will contain the more important idea in the sentence.

1. Use the subordinating conjunction *after:*

>   Joseph went out to celebrate.
>
>   He won the wrestling match.

   a. Begin with the independent clause:

   _____

   b. Begin with the dependent clause:

   _____

2. Use the subordinating conjunction *when:*

>   Carla returned from Venezuela this spring.
>
>   The family was excited.

   a. Begin with the independent clause:

   _____

   b. Begin with the dependent clause:

   _____

Combining sentences using subordination

EXERCISE 4

Use each of the following subordinating conjunctions to compose a complex sentence. An example has been done for you.

Subordinating conjunction: *after*

Complex sentence: *After* the game was over, we all went out for pizza.

Remember that a complex sentence has one independent clause and at least one dependent clause. Every clause must have a subject and a verb. Check your sentences by underlining the subject and verb in each clause.

Can you explain why the following sentence is not a complex sentence?

>   After the game, we all went out for pizza.

After the game is a prepositional phrase. *After*, in this case, is a preposition. It is not used as a subordinating conjunction to combine clauses.

1. as if

   _____

   _____

2. before

   _____

   _____

3. until

_____

_____

4. although

_____

_____

5. because (Begin with the independent clause. Traditional English grammar
   frowns on beginning a sentence with _because_. Ask your instructor for his or her
   opinion.)

_____

_____

EXERCISE 5   **Combining sentences using subordination**

Combine each pair of sentences using subordination. Look back at the list of subordinating conjunctions if you need to.

1. He was eating breakfast.
   The results of the election came over the radio.

   _____

   _____

2. The town council voted against the plan.
   They believed the project was too expensive.

   _____

   _____

3. I will see Maya Angelou tonight.
   She is speaking at the university.

   _____

   _____

4. The worker hoped for a promotion.
   Not one person in the department had received a promotion last year.

   _____

   _____

5. The worker hoped for a promotion.
   He made sure all his work was done accurately and on time.

   _____

   _____

Combining sentences using subordination

On a separate piece of paper, rewrite the following paragraph using subordination to combine some of the sentences wherever you feel it would be effective. Discuss your choices with your classmates. You might want to discuss places where coordination might be a good choice.

At the present time, the United States recycles 10 percent of its trash. It burns another 10 percent. The remaining 80 percent is used as landfill. Over the next few years, many of our landfills will close. They are full. Some of them are leaking toxic wastes. Some parts of the Northeast already truck much of their trash to landfills in Pennsylvania, Ohio, Kentucky, and West Virginia. The garbage continues to pile up. The newspapers print stories about it every week. Trash is not a very glamorous subject. People in every town talk about the problem. One magazine, called *Garbage*, is printed on recycled paper. No town ever before gathered together information about garbage. The town of Lyndhurst, New Jersey, began what is the world's only garbage museum. One landfill now has a restaurant on its premises. Another landfill displays some of its unusual garbage. It displays these objects like trophies. We really want to solve the garbage problem. We must change our "buy more and throw everything old away" mentality.

Using a relative pronoun to create a complex sentence

Often sentences can be combined with a relative pronoun.

Common relative pronouns		
who		
whose	}	refers to people
whom		
which		refers to things
that		refers to people and/or things

Combining sentences with a relative pronoun:

Two simple sentences:

The researcher had a breakthrough.

He was studying diabetes.

These sentences could sound short and choppy. To avoid this choppiness, a writer might want to join these two related ideas with a relative pronoun.

Correctly combined:

The researcher *who* was studying diabetes had a breakthrough.

Incorrectly combined:

The researcher had a breakthrough *who* was studying diabetes.

Note: The relative pronoun *who* and its clause *who was studying diabetes* refers to *researcher*. The *who* clause must be placed immediately after the word *researcher*.

> The relative pronoun and its clause must immediately follow the word it relates to.

Now we could join a third idea:

Third idea:

He reported the breakthrough to the press.

Combining sentences using two relative pronouns:

The researcher *who* was studying diabetes had a

breakthrough, *which* he reported to the press.

PRACTICE **Combining sentences using relative pronouns**

Combine each of the three pairs of sentences into one complex sentence by using a relative pronoun. Do not use commas. An example follows:

First sentence:	That woman created the flower arrangement.
Second sentence:	She visited us last weekend.
Combined sentence:	That woman who visited us last weekend created the flower arrangement.

1. The chemistry lab is two hours long.
   I attend that chemistry lab.

   Combined: _____

   _____

   _____

2. The student assistant is very knowledgeable.
   The student assistant is standing by the door.

   Combined: _____

   _____

   _____

3. The equipment was purchased last year.
   The equipment will make possible some important new research.

   Combined: _____

   _____

   _____

How do you punctuate a clause with a relative pronoun?

Punctuating relative clauses can be tricky because there are two types of relative clauses:

1. **Some relative clauses are essential to the meaning of the sentence.** They *do not* require commas.

> Never eat fruit *that isn't washed first.*

The basic meaning of the sentence is not "never eat fruit." The relative clause is necessary to restrict the meaning. This clause is called a **restrictive clause** and does not use commas to set off the clause. *Note:* The pronoun *that* is usual in such a case.

2. **Some relative clauses are *not* essential to the meaning of the sentence.** They *do* require commas.

> Mother's fruit salad, *which consisted of grapes, apples, and walnuts,* was delicious.

In this sentence, the relative clause is not essential to the main idea. In fact, if the clause were omitted, the main idea would not be changed. This clause is called a **nonrestrictive clause.** Commas are required to indicate the information is nonessential. *Note:* The pronoun *which* is usual in such a case.

Punctuating a clause with relative pronouns

PRACTICE

Choose whether or not to insert commas in the following sentences. Use the following examples as your models.

> The man *who is wearing the Hawaiian shirt* is the bridegroom.

In the sentence above, the bridegroom can only be identified by his Hawaiian shirt. Therefore, the relative clause *who is wearing the Hawaiian shirt* is essential to the meaning. No commas are necessary.

> Al, *who was wearing a flannel shirt,* arrived late to the wedding.

In the sentence above, the main idea is that Al was late. What he was wearing is not essential to that main idea. Therefore, commas are needed to set off this nonessential information.

1. The poem that my classmate read in class was very powerful.
2. The teacher who guided our class today is my favorite college professor.
3. The biology course which met four times a week for two hours each session was extremely demanding.
4. You seldom learn much in courses that are not demanding.
5. My own poetry which has improved over the semester has brought me much satisfaction.

Now you are ready to practice joining your own sentences with relative pronouns, being sure to punctuate carefully. The following exercises ask you to insert a variety of relative clauses into simple sentences.

EXERCISE 7   **Combining sentences using relative pronouns**

Add a relative clause to each of the following ten sentences. Use each of the possibilities at least once: *who, whose, whom, which, that.* Be sure to punctuate correctly. An example has been done for you.

Simple sentence: The leader was barely five feet tall.

Complex sentence: The leader, who was always self-conscious about his height, was barely five feet tall.

1. The president _____
   asked his advisors for help.

2. His advisors _____
   met with him in his office.

3. The situation _____
   was at a critical point.

4. Even his vice president _____
   appeared visibly alarmed.

5. Stacked on the table, the plans _____
   _____ looked impressive.

6. The meeting _____
   began at 2 o'clock.

7. Every idea _____
   was examined in great detail.

8. Several maps _____
   showed the area in question.

9. One advisor _____
   was vehemently opposed to the plan.

10. Finally the group agreed on a plan of action _____

EXERCISE 8   **Combining sentences using relative pronouns**

Combine the following pairs of sentences using a relative pronoun.

1. Stress can do a great deal of harm.
   We experience stress every day.

   _____

   _____

2. People often use food to help them cope.
   Some people work long hours at demanding jobs.

   _____

   _____

3. The practice of eating to cope with stress is often automatic.
   The practice of eating to cope often goes back to childhood.

   _____

   _____

4. Foods can actually increase tension.
   People turn to foods in times of stress.

   _____

   _____

5. Sweet foods are actually not energy boosters.
   Sweet foods are popular with people who need a lift.

   _____

   _____

6. Another substance is caffeine.
   People use other substances to get an energy boost.

   _____

   _____

7. One of the biggest mistakes people make is to use alcohol as an aid to achieving calm.
   Alcohol is really a depressant.

   _____

   _____

8. People should eat three light meals a day and two small snacks.
   People want to feel a sense of calm.

   _____

   _____

9. Getting enough protein is also important in keeping an adequate energy level.
   An adequate energy level will get you through the day.

   _____

   _____

10. Most important is to eat regularly so you will avoid binges.
    Binges put on pounds and drain you of energy.

    _____

    _____

<u>EXERCISE 9</u>   **Combining sentences using relative pronouns**

Combine the following pairs of sentences using a relative pronoun.

1. Murray, Kentucky, is a Norman Rockwell painting come to life.
   It is in the middle of America's heartland.

   _____

   _____

2. You will soon notice the blue, clean lakes.
   They are bustling with activity.

   _____

   _____

3. The town is surrounded by water.
   This water is perfect for sailing, water-skiing, fishing, and relaxing.

   _____

   _____

4. Scouting enthusiasts enjoy the National Scouting Museum.
   The museum has exhibits for hands-on experience.

   _____

   _____

5. The same museum has a large collection of paintings by Norman Rockwell.
   His work reflects the surrounding landscape.

   _____

   _____

6. Murray State University is an important part of local life.
   The University often has inexpensive concerts and other activities.

   _____

   _____

7. The Homestead is a working farm.
   It shows the way families lived a century ago.

   _____

   _____

8. The Homestead also puts on old-fashioned weddings.
   The wedding parties are made up of actors and actresses in beautiful antique attire.

   _____

   _____

9. People can see herds of buffalo.
   People like to see rare sights.

   _____

   _____

10. At the end of the day, you can enjoy the local cooking.
    Murray is famous for its local cooking.

    _____

    _____

Mastery and editing tests

Combining sentences with a subordinating conjunction or a relative pronoun   TEST 1

Combine each of the following pairs of sentences using either a subordinating conjunction or a relative pronoun.

1. I live alone with two dogs.
   They sleep on the braided rug in my bedroom.

   _____

   _____

2. The police stood by the door.
   They blocked our entrance.

   _____

   _____

3. She wore high heels.
   They made marks in the wooden floor.

   _____

   _____

4. My aunt is a tyrant.
   Her name is Isabel.

   _____

   _____

5. Her outfit was classy.
   Her hair was dirty and unattractive.

   _____

   _____

6. The interviewer did not smile.
   He discovered we had a friend in common.

   _____

   _____

7. I had a test the next day.
   I stayed up to watch a Bette Davis movie.

   _____

   _____

8. The skater fell and broke his arm.
   He was trying to skate backward.

   _____

   _____

9. For a moment her face glowed with pleasure.
   Her face was usually serious.

   _____

   _____

10. I was thinking.
    The toast burned.

    _____

    _____

TEST 2 Combining sentences using coordination and subordination

Now you are ready to have some fun! James Thurber, a famous American humorist, wrote a magazine article that gave a portrait of a man named Doc Marlowe. Below are some simple sentences made from one of his paragraphs. Look over the sentences, and then rewrite the paragraph combining sentences wherever you think it would improve the meaning and style. Don't be afraid to change the wording slightly to accommodate the changes you want to make. Although your instructor can provide Thurber's original version, there is more than one way to revise the paragraph.

   I met Doc Marlowe at old Mrs. Willoughby's rooming house. She had been a nurse in our family. I used to go and visit her over weekends sometimes. I was very fond of her. I was about eleven years old then. Doc Marlowe wore scarred leather leggings and a bright-colored bead vest. He said he got the vest from the Indians. He wore a ten-gallon hat with kitchen matches stuck in the band, all the way around. He was about six feet four inches tall, with big shoulders, and a long, drooping mustache. He let his hair grow long, like General Custer's. He had a wonderful collection of Indian relics and six-shooters. He used to tell me stories of his adventures in the Far West. His favorite expressions were "Hay, boy!" and "Hay, boy-gie!" He used these the way some people now use "Hot dog!" or "Doggone!" I thought he was the greatest man I had ever seen. He died. His son came in from New Jersey for the funeral. I found

out something. He had never been in the Far West in his life. He had been
born in Brooklyn.

Thurber's version

_____

_____

_____

_____

_____

_____

_____

_____

_____

_____

Working Together

Writing a News Report

1. A good news report should answer the questions of who, what, when, where, why, and how:

   Who was involved in the event?

   What exactly happened?

   When did the event take place?

   Where did the event take place?

   Why did the event take place?

   How did the event take place?

   The newspaper account at the right reports on one school district's decision on the celebration of a traditional holiday. Use a highlighter pen to mark those specific sentences in the newspaper account that answer each of the above questions. Then use this information to fill in each blank space that follows. Be sure to answer with complete sentences. Your sentences will provide a good summary of this news event.

When: ~~Friday~~ August 28, 2000

Where: Football Practice

Who: Chris Dalman San Francisco 49er offensive line man

What: neck injury

How: ~~football practice~~

Why: repeated injuries to the neck

What additional information would you like to have known? _____

_____

_____

_____

_____

_____

Portfolio Suggestion

You may want to clip newspaper and magazine articles that are of interest to you. Perhaps you will want to save all the articles you can find on particular subjects, such as those that are related to your field of study or those that involve community issues that you care about. These news articles can provide interesting facts and examples that you will be able to use in future essays for this and other courses.

District's Ban On Halloween Riles Parents

SAN FRANCISCO, Oct. 12 (AP)—The Los Altos School Board has added Halloween—and all its trappings—to its list of holidays that may not be celebrated in district schools because of their underlying religious themes. The board's action has angered some parents in the upscale Bay Area community, and many plan to protest it at a board meeting on Monday.

One parent, Patrick Ferrell, said his 7-year-old daughter said that her teacher had told the class that "the Halloween parade would feed the devil."

"We sanitize our schools and then wonder why our kids come out politically corrected," Mr. Ferrell said today.

The board president, Phil Faillace, sees it differently.

Mr. Faillace said that since January the board had examined the curriculum to eliminate practices that appeared to favor any one belief, and that Christmas, Hanukkah and Easter celebrations had long been banned.

"The board has to acknowledge Halloween's roots in Druid ceremonies and in a Celtic festival for Samhain, the Celts' god of the dead," Mr. Faillace wrote in a school bulletin that announced the Halloween celebration ban.

The policy means no Halloween parties on school time, no Halloween parade, a tradition in some schools, and no witches pasted on class windows, "unless they serve some curricular objective," Mr. Faillace said.

—*New York Times*, October 13, 1995

CHAPTER 7

Correcting the Run-On

In conversation, as we relate an event that involves a series of connected actions, we may string together our thoughts as if they were just one long thought. Here is what one person who was involved in a car accident recently reported to the police officer who arrived on the scene:

> I was driving along on Route 80 and my daughter asked my wife to change the radio station and my wife told my daughter to do it herself so she unhooked her seatbelt and reached over from the back seat to change the station but then her brother tickled her and she lost her balance and fell on the gear shift and that moved the gear into neutral so the car instantly lost power and that's when we were hit by the van behind us.

The man relating the accident ran each part of this entire event together without any separation. As a result, the account appears as a ***run-on sentence.*** Whoever must write the report of this accident needs to use a more acceptable form. You cannot combine independent clauses without some kind of punctuation.

What is a run-on?

> ***Run-on-sentences*** are independent clauses that have been combined incorrectly.

How many kinds of run-ons are there?

Run-on sentences occur when the writer is either unable to recognize where one complete idea has ended and another idea begins or is not sure of the standard ways of connecting the ideas. Certain marks of punctuation show where two clauses join. Other punctuation signifies the end of the thought. One of three mistakes is commonly made:

1. *The fused run-on:* Two or more independent clauses are run together without any punctuation.

incorrect: I met Charlyce we soon became friends.

2. *The comma splice:* Two or more independent clauses are run together with only a comma.

incorrect: I met Charlyce, we soon became friends.

3. *The "and" run-on:* Two or more independent clauses are connected with a coordinating conjunction but there is no punctuation.

incorrect: I met Charlyce and we soon became friends.

How do you make a complete sentence from a run-on?

Guide for correcting run-ons

1. Make two sentences with end punctuation.
   correct: I met Charlyce. We soon became friends.

2. Make a compound sentence using one of the three methods of coordination.
   correct: I met Charlyce, and we soon became friends.

   I met Charlyce; furthermore, we soon became friends.

   I met Charlyce; we soon became friends.

3. Make a complex sentence using subordination.
   correct: Soon after I met Charlyce, we became friends.

   Charlyce and I became friends soon after we met.

Note: See inside cover for quick review of coordination and subordination.

EXERCISE 1 **Recognizing and correcting run-ons**

Here is the same run-on sentence that you read at the beginning of this chapter. Rewrite the report correctly. Put a period at the end of each complete thought. You may have to omit some of the words that loosely connect the ideas, or you may want to use coordination and subordination. Remember to make each new sentence begin with a capital letter.

I was driving along on Route 80 and my daughter asked my wife to change the radio station and my wife told my daughter to do it herself so she unhooked her seatbelt and reached over from the back seat to change the station but then her brother tickled her and she lost her balance and fell on the gear shift and that moved the gear into neutral so the car instantly lost power and that's when we were hit by the van behind us.

_____

_____

_____

_____

_____

Recognizing and correcting run-ons

EXERCISE 2

The following story is written as one sentence. Rewrite the story correctly. Put a period at the end of each complete thought. You may have to omit some of the words that loosely connect the ideas, or you may want to use coordination and subordination. Remember to make each new sentence begin with a capital letter.

My best friend is accident-prone if you knew her you'd know that she's always limping, having to write with her left hand or wearing a bandage on her head or ankle, like last week for example she was walking down the street minding her own business when a shingle from someone's roof hit her on the head and she had to go to the emergency room for stitches, then this week one of her fingers is purple because someone slammed the car door on her hand sometimes I think it might be better if I didn't spend too much time with her you know her bad luck might be catching!

_____

_____

_____

_____

_____

_____

Recognizing and correcting run-ons

EXERCISE 3

The following story is written as one sentence. Rewrite the story correctly. Put a period at the end of each complete thought. You may have to omit some of the words that loosely connect the ideas, or you may want to use coordination and subordination. Remember to make each new sentence begin with a capital letter.

One morning, not too early, I will rise and slip downstairs to brew the coffee and no baby will wake me up and no alarm clock will rattle my nerves and the weather will be so warm that I will not have to put on my coat and hat to go out for the paper there will be no rush I will go to the refrigerator and take out eggs and sausage the bathroom will be free so I will be able to take a shower with no one knocking on the door and I will not have to run up and down the stairs first looking for someone's shoes and then for someone's car keys I will leisurely fix my hair and pick out a lovely suit to wear the phone might ring and it will be a friend who would like to have lunch and share the afternoon with me money will be no problem maybe we'll see a movie or drive to the nearby city to visit a museum and the countryside will be beautiful and unspoiled my life will seem fresh and promising.

_____

_____

_____

_____

_____

_____

_____

_____

_____

_____

EXERCISE 4 **Revising run-ons**

Each of the following examples is a run-on. Supply four possible ways to revise each run-on. Use the guide on page 104 if you need help.

1. Intelligence tests for children are not always useful they are a basic tool for measurement in most schools.

   Two simple sentences:

   _____

   _____

   Two kinds of compound sentence:

   a. _____

   _____

   b. _____

   _____

   Complex sentence:

   _____

   _____

2. Many people are opposed to gambling in all its forms they will not even buy a lottery ticket.

   Two simple sentences:

   a. _____

   b. _____

   Two kinds of compound sentence:

   a. _____

   _____

   b. _____

   _____

Complex sentence:

_____

_____

3. Travel is a great luxury one needs time and money.

Two simple sentences:

_____

_____

Two kinds of compound sentence:

a. _____

b. _____

Complex sentence:

_____

_____

Revising run-ons

EXERCISE 5

Each of the following examples is a run-on. Supply four possible ways to revise each run-on. Use the guide on page 104 if you need help.

1. The airline has begun its new route to the islands everyone is looking forward to flying there.

Two simple sentences:

_____

_____

Two kinds of compound sentence:

a. _____

_____

b. _____

_____

Complex sentence:

_____

_____

2. The movie begins at nine o'clock let's have dinner before the show.

Two simple sentences:

_____

_____

Two kinds of compound sentence:

a. _____

_____

b. _____

_____

Complex sentence:

_____

_____

3. The studio audience screamed at the contestant they wanted her to try for the big prize.

Two simple sentences:

_____

_____

Two kinds of compound sentence:

a. _____

_____

b. _____

_____

Complex sentence:

_____

_____

EXERCISE 6 **Revising run-ons**

Each of the following examples is a run-on. Supply four possible ways to revise each run-on. Use the guide on page 104 if you need help.

1. We didn't start our trip until noon it was pouring.

Two simple sentences:

_____

_____

Two kinds of compound sentence:

a. _____

b. _____

Complex sentence:

_____

_____

2. After many years, women finally won the right to vote the struggle for equal rights is now found in other areas besides politics.

Two simple sentences:

_____

_____

Two kinds of compound sentence:

a. _____

_____

b. _____

_____

Complex sentence:

_____

_____

3. Mrs. Brighton takes in student lodgers every year she likes to have people in the house.

Two simple sentences:

a. _____

b. _____

Two kinds of compound sentence:

a. _____

_____

b. _____

_____

Complex sentence:

_____

_____

Mastery and editing tests

TEST 1 Editing for run-ons

Edit the following paragraph, correcting all seven run-on sentences.

In 1990, John Ehrlichman drove 600 miles in Russia talking to ordinary citizens, Soviet workers were quick to talk about their everyday troubles. The dismal state of the economy was evident everywhere. Cars waited for hours in line to get gasoline people were lined up at stores to buy anything the stores might be happening to sell that day. It's a way of life to the people in the Soviet Union. Russians are deeply distressed for the privileged hierarchy still enjoys fine housing and imported delicacies while the masses cope with grinding shortages. Doctors work in old facilities and they have little medicine or basic equipment like antibiotics or disposable syringes. Meat is very scarce even if a farmer is very productive. Twenty-five percent of his food spoils en route. The United States feeds all its people with 2 million farmers, Russia can't feed its people with 24 million farmers and 4 million bureaucrats to tell the farmers what to do. At one factory where Ehrlichman visited, he was told to be careful where he walked because the ground was saturated with sulfuric acid and it would eat up his shoes. In other places, he could see pipes discharging untreated waste chemicals into the marshlands and rivers. The city of Novgorod hopes its sister city, Rochester, New York, will help Novgorod obtain instruments to test the purity of the air, they cannot enforce pollution laws without such equipment.

TEST 2 Editing for run-ons

Edit the following paragraph, correcting all six run-on sentences.

In laboratory experiments, scientists have discovered a diet which extends the life of their animals up to 50 percent or more. This diet prevents heart disease, diabetes, and kidney failure and it greatly retards all types of cancer. It even slows down the aging process of cataracts, gray hair, and feebleness. Staying on this diet keeps the mind flexible and the body active to an almost biblical old age! These rats, fish, and worms stay very slim, they are fed a diet of necessary vitamins and nutrients, but only 65 percent of the calories of the animal's normal diet. Every creature fed this restricted diet has had a greatly extended life span. Richard Weindruch, a gerontologist at the National Institute on Aging in Bethesda, Maryland, says the results of caloric restriction are spectacular. Gerontologists have tried many things to extend life but this is the only experiment that works every time in the lab. Animals who received enough protein, vitamins, and minerals to prevent malnutrition survived to a grand old age and it does not seem to matter whether they eat a diet composed largely of fats or carbohydrates. Researchers warn against people undertaking this diet too hastily, it is easy to become malnourished. Dr. Roy

Walford is a pioneer in the field from the University of California he believes humans could live to an extraordinarily advanced age if they were to limit their caloric intake.

Editing run-ons

Edit these ten run-on sentences.

1. Many parents worry that their children are not reading others worry about what they are reading.
2. Most children are not reading anything at all, the home is filled with the sounds from stereos and television sets.
3. Children should have library cards and parents should accompany them regularly to the library to pick out books.
4. Children need to see their parents reading magazines, books, and newspapers reflect the tastes and interests of the adults in a home.
5. Books can be bonds between children and their parents so parents should read aloud to their children as often as possible.
6. What do you think of parents who are not involved in the school they are usually quick to go and make a complaint about a teacher.
7. Maps are wonderful geography lessons and they remind us that we are not at the center of the world.
8. Some parents think their child is gifted, it is a mistake to let a child think this.
9. Memorizing poetry should be encouraged we learn the rhythms of our language and strengthen our speech and writing.
10. A child who doesn't read will be at the mercy of radical groups reading encourages children to think through many issues which they might not normally experience themselves.

Conducting a Survey

A writer can obtain information for an essay in a number of different ways. One very good way is to gather material by conducting a survey, using a group of people who have something in common. For this exercise, you will participate in a survey of the students in your class. This survey will question students to discover their attitudes and experiences with writing. The members of your class may add their own questions, or they may change the questions suggested here.

Use the following procedure below:

1. Remove the survey page from your textbook.

2. Put your name or an assigned number in the top right-hand corner of the survey for purposes of identification.

3. Answer the survey questions as completely and honestly as possible.

4. Select two persons who will collect all the surveys and lead the class in tallying the information. One person can read off the responses; the other person can put the information on a blackboard where everyone can view the information and take their own notes.

Portfolio Suggestion

 With the information gathered from the survey, compose an essay that describes the attitudes and experiences of your classmates when it comes to writing. Keep this essay, as well as the survey results, in your portfolio. You may want to use these survey results for other writing in the future.

Student Questionnaire

1. Where do you do your best writing—in the library, at home, or someplace else? What makes some places better than others?

   _____

   _____

   _____

   _____

   _____

   _____

2. Is a certain time of day better for you than other times? When do you concentrate the best?

   _____

3. How long can you write with concentration before you have to take a break?

   _____

4. What fears do you have when you write?

   _____

5. What do you believe is your major weakness as a writer?

   _____

6. Are you comfortable using a computer to compose?

   _____

7. In high school, how many of your classes included writing opportunities? How often did you write?

   _____

8. Keeping in mind that most people today use a telephone to keep in touch, how often do you find yourself writing a letter?

   _____

9. Which of the following best describes your feeling about writing at this point in your school career?

   _____ I enjoy writing most of the time.

   _____ I occasionally like to write.

   _____ I usually do not like to write.

   _____ I don't have any opinion about writing at all.

How could the responses in this survey be used as the basis for an essay? What could be the purpose of such an essay?

CHAPTER 8

Making Sentence Parts Work Together: Pronouns

Sentence parts work together to make meaning clear. In Chapter 3, you practiced making subjects and verbs agree (showing singular or plural). In this chapter, you will focus on the two major issues for using pronouns correctly:

- Pronouns and case
- Pronoun-antecedent agreement

Pronouns and case

Many personal pronouns change in form depending on how they are used in the sentence; that is, they can be used as subjects, objects, possessives, or reflexives.

> I gave *him their* instructions *myself.*
>
> He gave *me their* instructions *himself.*

The chart on page 116 may be useful as a reference.

In general, most of us use pronouns in the correct case without thinking. Three constructions, however, require some special attention:

Comparisons

Compound constructions

Use of *who/whom*

Pronouns and case				
	Pronouns used as subjects	Pronouns used as objects	Pronouns used as possessives	Pronouns used as reflexives
Singular	I	me	my, mine	myself
	you	you	you, yours	yourself
	he	him	his	himself
	she	her	hers	herself
	it	it	its	itself
Plural	we	us	our, ours	ourselves
	you	you	your, yours	yourselves
	they	them	their, theirs	themselves
Singular or Plural	who	whom	whose	

Note: There are no such forms as *hisself* or *theirselves*.

Note: Do not confuse *whose* with *who's* or *its* with *it's*. (*Who's* means *who is* and *it's* means *it is*.)

I. Comparisons

In a comparison, picking the correct pronoun is easier if you complete the comparison.

> That swimmer is much stronger than (he, him, his).
>
> That swimmer is much stronger than (he, him, his) is.

The second sentence shows that *he* is the correct form because the pronoun is used as the subject for the clause *he is*.

PRACTICE Circle the correct pronoun in each of the sentences below.

1. My brother did not enjoy the vacation as much as (I, me, mine).

   Hint: Try completing the comparison:

   > My brother did not enjoy the vacation as much as (I), me, mine) did.

2. The altitude in Quito affected my brother more than (I, me).

   Hint: Try completing the comparison:

   > The altitude in Quito affected my brother more than it affected (I, me).

EXERCISE I ## Choosing the correct pronoun in comparisons

Circle the correct pronoun in each of the sentences below.

1. I am as deeply involved in this report as (they, them).
2. Karen's research has been more extensive than (we, us, our, ours).

3. She studied the final report less than (I, me).
4. Unfortunately, the competing report was just as attractive as (we, us, our, ours).
5. Their company had acquired fewer clients than (we, us).
6. Our policies are much better than (them, theirs).
7. The contract was awarded to us rather than to (they, them).
8. The results will matter more to the client than to (she, her).
9. I will celebrate much longer tonight than (she, her).
10. An immediate vacation is more important for me than for (he, him).

2. Compound constructions

When you have a compound subject or a compound object, choosing the correct pronoun is easier if you read the sentence without one of the pronouns.

> Today, you and (I, me) should buy the tickets.
>
> Today, (I, me) should buy the tickets.

PRACTICE

1. Developers and (he, him) hope to renovate that building.

   Hint: Try the sentence without *Developers*.

   (He, Him) hopes to renovate that building.

2. They spoke to the construction company and (I, me).

   Hint: Try the sentence without *construction company*.

   They spoke to (I, me).

Choosing the correct pronoun in compound constructions   EXERCISE 2

Circle the correct pronoun in each of the sentences.

1. Sara called from Washington to speak with Leslie and (I, me).
2. Both Damon and (I, me) keep a daily journal.
3. Today we received the letters from you and (she, her).
4. Among Sasha, Jerry, and (I, me), Sasha is the best writer.
5. Karen and (she, her) are hoping for good grades this term.
6. Because Martin and (she, her) decided to go, the group could no longer fit into one car.
7. (He, Him) and (I, me) handed our journals in to the professor.
8. When we were sick, my aunt ran lots of errands for Kathleen and (I, me).
9. The dinner gave Mike and (he, him) the chance to be together.
10. The two men, (he, him) and Mike, were brothers.

3. Who/whom constructions

The use of these two pronouns is at times confusing to most of us. When in doubt, you need to consider if the pronoun is used in a subject position or in an object position.

Subject position: *Who* is going with you to the performance?

Object position: *Whom* did the director choose for the solo?

To whom did the director give the solo?

If there is more than one clause in the sentence, you will find it helpful to cross out everything except the clause with the *who/whom*. Then you can focus on how *who/whom* functions in its own clause.

PRACTICE   1. She is the friend (who, whom) I treasured.

look at: (who, whom) I treasured

2. She is the friend (who, whom) I knew could be trusted.

look at: (who, whom) could be trusted

3. I don't know (who, whom) should do the work

4. That is the girl (who, whom) I hope will win.

EXERCISE 3   ## Choosing the correct pronoun using who/whom

Circle the correct pronoun in each of the sentences.

1. (Who, Whom) is singing at the choral concert tonight?
2. (Whoever, Whomever) sold us the tickets gave us the best seats in the house.
3. From (who, whom) can we obtain a program?
4. (Who, Whom) of these singers can you tell needs more practice?
5. The director gave the solo parts to (whoever, whomever) was qualified.
6. Our eyes were glued on (whoever, whomever) was singing the lead.
7. (Who's, Whose) solo did you think was performed with the most musicality?
8. (Whoever, Whomever) played the piano accompaniment did a wonderful job.
9. Just between the two of us, (who, whom) do you believe is the more musically inclined?
10. (Who's, Whose) music was left on the piano?

In order to avoid confusion, remember you can always cross out other clauses in the sentence so you can concentrate on the clause in question.

~~I don't know~~ (who, whom) ~~I think~~ should do the work.

~~That is the girl~~ (who, whom) ~~I believe~~ was dancing.

Use the following exercises to practice all three constructions that you have studied.

Choosing correct pronoun forms

Circle the correct pronoun in each of the sentences below.

1. Matthew and (she, her) presented the project today.
2. Between you and (I, me), I think it was outstanding.
3. Their visual materials will help (whoever, whomever) will study the project later.
4. He is usually a better speaker than (she, her).
5. (Whoever, Whomever) heard them agreed that it was an impressive presentation.
6. (Who, Whom) do you think made the best points?
7. I am not as deeply involved in my project as (they, them).
8. Their research was much more detailed than (us, our, ours).
9. The professor gave both Carolyn and (he, him) A's.
10. My partner and (I, me) will have to work harder to reach this standard.

Choosing correct pronoun forms

Circle each correct pronoun in the following paragraph.

When my mother and (I, me) decided to care for my very ill father at home, some of our friends objected. My sister and (they, them) said we would be exhausted and unable to handle the stress. To (who, whom) could we go for help in the middle of the night? My father, (who, whom) we believed would be happier at home, had been our first consideration. Of course, we would have benefited if my mother or (I, me) had been a nurse. However, we did have a visiting nurse available at times. We were more confident than (they, them) that we could handle the situation.

Pronoun-antecedent agreement

When we use a pronoun in our writing, that pronoun must refer to a word used previously in the text. This word is called the *antecedent*.

> An *antecedent* is a word (or words) that a pronoun replaces.
>
> The pool was crowded. It was a popular place on a hot summer day.

In this example, the pronoun *It* replaces the word *pool*. *Pool*, in this case, is referred to as the *antecedent* to the pronoun *it*.

Study the next three pronoun-related issues, each one a source of trouble for writers.

I. A pronoun must agree in number (singular or plural) with any other word to which it refers. The following sentence contains a pronoun-antecedent disagreement in **number:**

Lacks agreement: *Everyone* worked on *their* final draft.

The problem in this sentence is that *everyone* is a singular word, but *their* is a plural pronoun. You may have often heard people use the plural pronoun *their* to refer to a singular subject. In fact, the above sentence may sound correct, but it is still a mistake in formal writing. Here are two other approaches that writers often use:

Sexist: Everyone worked on *his* final draft.

Although you may often encounter this approach in current writing, it is unpopular because it is widely considered a sexist construction.

Awkward: Everyone worked on *his or her* final draft.

This form is technically correct, but if it is used several times it sounds awkward and repetitious.

The best solution may be to revise such a construction so that the antecedent is plural:

Pronouns agree: *All* the students worked on *their* final drafts.

Another problem with pronoun-antecedent agreement in number occurs when a demonstrative pronoun *(this, that, these, those)* is used with a noun. That pronoun must agree with the noun it modifies:

Singular: this kind, that type

Incorrect: *These kind* of shoes hurt my feet.

Correct: *This kind* of shoe hurts my feet.

Plural: these kinds, those types

Incorrect: *Those type* of cars always need oil.

Correct: *Those types* of cars always need oil.

PRACTICE   Rewrite each of the following sentences so that the pronoun agrees with its antecedent in *number.*

1. Everyone should bring their suggestions to the meeting.

   _____

   _____

2. This sorts of clothes are popular now.

   _____

   _____

3. No one knew what they were doing.

   _____

   _____

4. If the bird watchers hope to see anything, one must get up early.

   _____

   _____

5. These type of book appeals to me.

_____

_____

2. **Pronouns must also agree with their antecedents in *person*.** The following sentence contains a pronoun-antecedent disagreement in **person:**

> *Lacks agreement:* When mountain climbing, *one* must maintain *your*
> concentration at all times.

When you construct a piece of writing, you choose a "person" as the voice in
that piece of writing. Some teachers ask students not to choose the first person *I*
because they believe such writing sounds too personal. Other teachers warn students not to use *you* because it is too casual. Whatever guidelines your teacher
gives you, the important point is to be consistent in person.

Below are some examples in which the pronouns agree:

> When mountain climbing, *you* must maintain *your* concentration at all
> times.

> When mountain climbing, *I* must maintain *my* concentration at all times.

> When mountain climbing, *we* must maintain *our* concentration at all times.

PRACTICE

Correct each of the following sentences so that the pronoun agrees with its *antecedent in person.*

1. I enjoy math exams because you can show what you know.
2. When I took geometry, we discovered that frequent review of past assignments
   helped make the course seem easy.
3. People always need to practice your skills in order not to forget them.
4. Math games can be fun for one if you have a spirit of curiosity.
5. When studying math, you must remember that we have to "use it or lose it."

**3. The antecedent of a pronoun should not be *missing, ambiguous,* or
*repetitious.***

a. **Missing antecedent:**

> In Florida, *they* have many beautifully developed retirement areas.

Possible revision:

> Florida has many beautifully developed retirement areas.

Explanation: In the first sentence, who is *they?* If the context has not told us
that *they* refers to the government or to the developers, then the antecedent
is missing. The sentence should be rewritten in order to avoid *they.*

b. **Ambiguous antecedent:**

> Margaret told Lin that *she* needed to earn one thousand dollars during
> the summer.

Possible revision:

> Margaret said that Lin needed to earn one thousand dollars during
> the summer.

Explanation: In the first example, *she* could refer to either Margaret or Lin.
The sentence should be revised in a way that will avoid this confusion.

c. **Repetitious pronoun and antecedent:**

> The newspaper article, *it* said that Earth Day, 1990, reestablished man's commitment to the earth.

Possible revision:

> The newspaper article said that Earth Day, 1990, reestablished man's commitment to the earth.

Explanation: The subject should be either *article*, or if there is already an antecedent, *it*. Using both the noun and the pronoun results in needless repetition.

PRACTICE Rewrite the following sentences so that the antecedents are not *missing*, *ambiguous*, or *repetitious*.

1. The biologist asked the director to bring back his microscope.

   _____

   _____

2. In the report, it says that the number of science and engineering students seeking doctoral degrees has fallen fifty percent since the mid-sixties.

   _____

   _____

3. At the laboratory, they said the research had run into serious difficulties.

   _____

   _____

4. The testing equipment was accidentally dropped onto the aquarium, and it was badly damaged.

   _____

   _____

5. I don't watch the 10 o'clock news anymore because they have become too slick.

   _____

   _____

EXERCISE 6 **Making pronouns and antecedents agree**

The following sentences contain errors with pronouns. Revise each sentence so that pronouns agree with their antecedents, and so that there are no missing, ambiguous, or repetitious antecedents.

1. His father mailed him his high school yearbook.

   _____

   _____

2. No one wants their income reduced.

   _____

   _____

3. When a company fails to update its equipment, they often pay a price in the long run.

_____

_____

4. The woman today has many more options open to them than ever before.

_____

_____

5. Everybody knows their own strengths best.

_____

_____

6. Each of the workers anticipates their summer vacation.

_____

_____

7. If the campers want to eat quickly, each one should help themselves.

_____

_____

8. These sort of bathing suits look ridiculous on me.

_____

_____

9. On the application, it says you must pay a registration fee of thirty-five dollars.

_____

_____

10. The doctor said that those type of diseases are rare here.

_____

_____

Making pronouns and antecedents agree

EXERCISE 7

Each of the following sentences may contain an error with pronouns. Revise each sentence so that pronouns agree with their antecedents, and so that there are no missing, ambiguous or repetitious antecedents. If a sentence is correct, mark a C on the line provided.

1. The teacher suggested to the parent that he might have been too busy to have noticed the child's unhappiness.

_____

_____

2. The county submitted their proposal for the bridge repairs.

_____

_____

3. We all rushed to our cars because you had to wait for the thunderstorm to stop.

_____

_____

4. A young person does not receive enough advice on how they should choose their career.

_____

_____

5. These type of watches are very popular.

_____

_____

6. People were taken forcibly from our homes.

_____

_____

7. No one brought their books today.

_____

_____

8. The college it is holding homecoming weekend on October 5.

_____

_____

9. They call it the "Hoosier" state.

_____

_____

10. Anyone who fails the final will be unlikely to get his or her diploma.

_____

_____

EXERCISE 8   **Making pronouns and antecedents agree**

Each of the following sentences contains an error in pronoun-antecedent agreement. Revise each sentence so that pronouns agree with their antecedents, and so that there are no missing, ambiguous, or repetitious antecedents.

1. Let me tell you a story that one shivers to tell.

2. In April, Sheila went with her friend Melissa to the motor vehicle bureau where she passed her driver's test.

3. Later that month, Sheila asked her mother if she could run an errand.

4. Sheila drove to an unfamiliar town where they had never been before.

5. The radio it reported the driving was dangerous due to both rain and fog.

6. On a dark and rainswept road, Sheila drove through a stop sign at an intersection, and another driver did not see it in time to stop.

7. I believe Sheila was a good driver, but the police didn't agree with it.

8. The doctor told Sheila's parents that they did everything possible to save her.

9. Everyone feels the shock of their loss.

10. The police say those type of accidents are unfortunately very common with inexperienced drivers.

Mastery and editing tests

Using pronouns correctly

TEST 1

Each of the following sentences contains pronouns. Revise each sentence to correct any errors in pronoun case, any pronouns that do not agree with their antecedents, or any missing, ambiguous, or repetitive antecedents. If the sentence does not contain an error, mark it with a "C."

1. One should plant flowers if you like improving your front yard.

   _____

   _____

2. His friend sent him his favorite coffee.

   _____

   _____

3. In the book, it said that fish oil is good to take for arthritis.

   _____

   _____

4. My mom and me have a great day planned on Saturday.

   _____

   _____

5. Whom do you think is coming to our art show?

   _____

   _____

6. They ought to fix these potholes outside our school.

   _____

   _____

7. The customer and she agreed on a price.

   _____

   _____

8. That athlete is much faster than me.

   _____

   _____

9. These sorts of chairs tend to be uncomfortable.

   _____

   _____

10. He did all the work on the house hisself.

_____

_____

TEST 2   **Using pronouns correctly**

Each of the following sentences contains pronouns. In each case, revise the sentence if there is an error in pronoun case, if pronouns do not agree with their antecedents, or if there are missing, ambiguous, or repetitious antecedents. If the sentence does not contain an error, mark it with a "C."

1. Michael told John that he had won the raffle.

_____

_____

2. The report said they would do their best to get the workers a raise.

_____

_____

3. Those type of desserts are too rich for me.

_____

_____

4. Tomorrow you and me are going out to lunch.

_____

_____

5. We wondered who had made the delicious cake.

_____

_____

6. One should never doubt your ability to learn a new skill.

_____

_____

7. Mr. Baker is a better math teacher than her.

_____

_____

8. They tried to program the computer theirselves.

_____

_____

9. The poem it was beautiful to hear read out loud.

_____

_____

10. Everyone remembered to bring his books to class.

_____

_____

Using pronouns correctly

Each of the following sentences contains pronouns. In each case, revise the sentence if there is an error in pronoun case, if pronouns do not agree with their antecedents, or if there are missing, ambiguous, or repetitious antecedents. If the sentence does not contain an error, mark it with a "C."

1. In the ad it said you should send a resume.

   _____

   _____

2. To who do you think we should send these bulletins?

   _____

   _____

3. A pharmacist must triple check every order he fills.

   _____

   _____

4. Just between you and I, the firm is in financial trouble.

   _____

   _____

5. Those lessons helped Karen more than him.

   _____

   _____

6. We always buy these type of coats.

   _____

   _____

7. The bank warns people that you should always keep a careful balance of your checkbooks.

   _____

   _____

8. Janelle's sister brought her plan to the council.

   _____

   _____

9. The assignments they are going to require library research.

   _____

   _____

10. Everyone did his or her part.

   _____

   _____

Preserving Family History

The photograph shows a family portrait from the turn of the century. What is the earliest photograph you have of members of your own family? What documents (such as birth certificates) do you have that give you some information about these relatives? What stories have you been told about them? What do you believe you can tell about them from looking at their photographs? If you have no photos, what information have you gathered from family stories you may have heard? Use the next twenty minutes to write freely on this subject. When you have finished your work, exchange your paper with another student. Look for sentences that contain the kinds of errors you have studied so far: subject-verb agreement, pronoun-antecedent agreement, parallel structure, and misplaced and dangling modifiers. Mark sentences that need revision by using the correction symbols listed inside the back cover of this book.

Portfolio Suggestion

Save the freewriting you have done on your family's history. This is a topic that you may want to return to again and again. Children will appreciate all the stories and memories you can gather about your relatives. This may be one of the greatest gifts you can give your family.

Making Sentence Parts Work Together: Parallel Structure and Modifiers

In addition to the work of Chapter 3 (Making verbs agree with their subjects) and the work of Chapter 8 (Making pronouns agree with their antecedents), two other topics concerned with sentence parts working together remain to be studied:

- Parallel structure
- Misplaced or dangling modifiers

Parallel structure: Making a series of words, phrases, or clauses balanced within the sentence

Which one of the following sentences achieves a better balanced structure?

> His favorite hobbies are playing the trumpet, listening to jazz, and to go to concerts.

> His favorite hobbies are playing the trumpet, listening to jazz, and going to concerts.

If you selected the second sentence, you made the better choice. The second sentence uses parallel structure to balance the three phases in the series (playing, listening, and going). By matching each of the items in the series with the same *-ing* structure, the sentence becomes easier to understand and more pleasant to read. You can make words, phrases, and even sentences in a series parallel:

1. Words in a series should be the same parts of speech.

Not parallel: The town was small, quiet, and the atmosphere was peaceful.
(The series is composed of two adjectives and one clause.)

Parallel: The town was small, quiet, and peaceful.
(*Small, quiet,* and *peaceful* are adjectives.)

2. Phrases in a series should be the same kinds of phrases (*infinitive phrases, prepositional phrases, verb phrases, noun phrases, participial phrases*).

Not parallel: Her lost assignment is in her closet, on the floor, and a pile of clothes is hiding it.
(two prepositional phrases and one clause)

Parallel: Her lost assignment is in her closet, on the floor, and under a pile of clothes.
(three prepositional phrases beginning with *in*, *on*, and *under*)

3. Clauses in a series should not be mixed with phrases.

Not parallel: The street was narrow, the shops were charming, and crowds in the cafe.
(The series is composed of two clauses and one phrase.)

Parallel: The street was narrow, the shops were charming, and the cafe was crowded.
(The series is composed of three clauses.)

PRACTICE   Each of the following sentences has an underlined word, phrase, or clause that is not parallel. Make the underlined section parallel.

1. My favorite armchair is lumpy, worn out, and <u>has dirt spots everywhere</u>.

_____

_____

2. She enjoys reading novels, studying the flute, and <u>sews her own clothes</u>.

_____

_____

3. He admires teachers who make the classroom an exciting place and <u>willingly explaining material more than once</u>.

_____

_____

Revising sentences for parallel structure

Each of the following sentences needs parallel structure. Underline the word, phrase, or clause that is not parallel and revise it so that its structure will balance with the other items in the pair or series. An example has been done for you.

Not parallel: The best leather comes from Italy, from Spain, and is imported from Brazil.

Parallel: The best leather comes from Italy, Spain, and Brazil.

1. Winter in Chicago is very windy and has many bitterly cold days.

_____

_____

2. I would prefer to fix an old car to watching television.

_____

_____

3. George is a helpful neighbor, a loyal friend, and dedicated to his children.

_____

_____

4. The apartment is crowded and without light.

_____

_____

5. The dancer is slender and moves gracefully.

_____

_____

6. The nursery was cheerful and had a lot of sun.

_____

_____

7. My friend loves to play chess, to read science fiction, and working out at the gym.

_____

_____

8. For homework today I must read a chapter in history, do five exercises for Spanish class, and working on my term paper for political science.

_____

_____

9. The painting reveals the artist's talent and it is imaginative.

_____

10. The cars race down the track, turn the corner at great speed, and then they are heading for the homestretch.

_____

_____

EXERCISE 2 Each of the following sentences needs parallel structure. Underline the word, phrase, or clause that is not parallel and revise it so that its structure will balance with the other items in the pair or series.

1. The dog had to choose between jumping over the fence or he could have dug a hole underneath it.

   _____

   _____

2. She disliked going to the beach, hiking in the woods, and she didn't care for picnics, either.

   _____

   _____

3. As I looked down the city street, I could see the soft lights from restaurant windows, I could hear the mellow sounds of a nightclub band, and carefree moods of people walking by.

   _____

   _____

4. The singers have been on several road tours, have recorded for two record companies, and they would also like to make a movie someday.

   _____

   _____

5. They would rather order a pizza than eating their sister's cooking.

   _____

   _____

6. I explained to the teacher that my car had broken down, my books had been stolen, and I left my assignment pad home.

   _____

   _____

7. That night the prisoner was sick, discouraged, and she was filled with loneliness.

   _____

   _____

8. As the truck rumbled through the street, it suddenly lurched out of control, smashed into a parked car, and then the truck hit the storefront of my uncle's hardware store.

   _____

   _____

9. The teacher is patient, intelligent, and demands a lot.

   _____

   _____

10. He was determined to pass the math course, not only to get his three credits but also for a sense of achievement.

   _____

   _____

Revising sentences for parallel structure

Each of the following sentences needs parallel structure. Underline the word, phrase, or clause that is not parallel and revise it so that its structure will balance with the other items in the pair or series.

1. The first-grade teacher told us that our child was unruly, mischievous, and talked too much.

   _____

   _____

2. The dog's size, its coloring, and whenever it barked reminded me of a wolf.

   _____

   _____

3. Carol is not only very talented, but she is also acting kindly to everyone.

   _____

   _____

4. He dried the dishes; putting them away was the job of his wife.

   _____

   _____

5. Jordan would rather travel and see the world than staying home and reading about other places.

   _____

   _____

6. For weeks he tried to decide if he should major in chemistry, continue with accounting, or to take a year off.

   _____

   _____

7. Her depression was a result of the loss of her job, the breakdown of her marriage, and a teenage daughter who was a problem.

   _____

   _____

8. She must either cut back on her expenses or selling her car.

   _____

   _____

9. His office is without windows, on the fourth floor, and you have to go down a dark hallway to get there.

   _____

   _____

10. He went through four years of college, one year of graduate school, and he has spent one year teaching seventh-grade science.

   _____

   _____

Misplaced and dangling modifiers

Notice how the meaning changes in each of the following sentences, depending on where the modifier *only* is placed:

Only Charlene telephoned my brother yesterday.

Charlene *only* telephoned my brother yesterday.

Charlene telephoned *only* my brother yesterday.

Charlene telephoned my *only* brother yesterday.

Charlene telephoned my brother *only* yesterday.

Modifiers are words or groups of words that function as adjectives or adverbs.

my *only* brother

the marine *who is my brother*

only yesterday

A modifier must be placed close to the word, phrase, or clause that it modifies in order to be understood by the reader.

Misplaced modifiers

Be especially careful in your own writing when you use the words in the following list. They are often misplaced.

Modifiers often misplaced				
almost	exactly	just	nearly	scarcely
even	hardly	merely	only	simply

A *misplaced modifier* is a modifier that has been placed in a wrong, awkward, or ambiguous position.

Below are examples of some special problems that can happen when modifiers are not used correctly. Study how the sentences have been revised, so you will be able to correct any misplaced or dangling modifiers in your own writing.

1. The modifier is in the wrong place.

   Wrong: The salesperson sold the used car to the customer *that needed extensive body work.*

   Who or what needed body work—the customer or the car?

   Revised: The salesperson sold the customer the used car *that needed extensive body work.*

2. The modifier is positioned awkwardly, interrupting the flow of the sentence, as in the following split infinitive.

> *Awkward:*   Alex planned to exactly arrive on time.
>
> The infinitive "to arrive" should not be split.
>
> *Revised:*   Alex planned to arrive exactly on time.

3. The modifier is in an ambiguous position; that is, it could describe the word or words on either side of it (sometimes called a *squinting modifier*).

> *Squinting:*   Ms. Douglass having arranged other parties secretly planned the surprise party for her friend.
>
> Did she secretly arrange parties or secretly plan the surprise party?
> From the wording, you cannot tell which is the correct interpretation.
>
> *Revised:*   Having arranged other parties, Ms. Douglass secretly planned the surprise party for her friend.

Dangling modifiers

A *dangling modifier* is a modifier without a word, phrase, or clause that the modifier can describe.

> *Dangling:*   Working on the car's engine, the dog barked all afternoon.
>
> Who is working on the engine? Was it the dog?
>
> *Revised:*   Working on the car's engine, I heard the dog barking all afternoon.
>
> or
>
> The dog barked all afternoon while I was working on the car's engine.

Revising misplaced or dangling modifiers

EXERCISE 4

Revise each sentence so there is no dangling modifier.

1. Victor fed the dog wearing his tuxedo.

   _____

   _____

2. Visiting Yellowstone National Park, Old Faithful entertained us by performing on schedule.

   _____

   _____

3. Hoping to see the news, the television set was turned on by seven o'clock.

   _____

   _____

4. A woodpecker was found in Cuba that had been considered extinct.

_____

_____

5. After running over the hill, the farm was visible in the valley below.

_____

_____

6. The truck caused a traffic jam, which was broken down on the highway, for miles.

_____

_____

7. Hanging from the ceiling in her bedroom, she saw three spiders.

_____

_____

8. After wiping my glasses, the redbird flew away.

_____

_____

9. Howling without a stop, I listened to the neighbor's dog all evening.

_____

_____

10. After painting my room all afternoon, my cat demanded her dinner.

_____

_____

EXERCISE 5 Revising misplaced or dangling modifiers

Revise each sentence so there is no dangling modifier.

1. Leaping upstream, we fished most of the day for salmon.

_____

_____

2. At the age of ten, my family took a trip to Washington, D.C.

_____

_____

3. Skimming every chapter, my biology textbook made more sense.

_____

_____

4. Running up the stairs, the train had already left for Philadelphia.

_____

_____

5. Working extra hours last week, my salary increased dramatically.

_____

_____

6. We watched a movie in the theater which we had paid five dollars to see.

_____

_____

7. Dressed in a Dracula costume, I thought my son looked perfect for Halloween.

_____

_____

8. Last week while shopping, my friend's purse was stolen.

_____

_____

9. While eating lunch outdoors, our picnic table collapsed.

_____

_____

10. Our car is in the parking lot with two bags of groceries unlocked.

_____

_____

Mastery and editing tests

Revising sentences for parallel structure and correct use of modifiers   TEST 1

Each sentence has an error in parallel structure or in the use of a modifier. Revise each sentence so that it is correct.

1. He devoured the bone, tore up his new bed, and jumping up on the new sofa.

_____

_____

2. The student almost received enough money from his aunt to pay for his semester's tuition.

_____

_____

3. She returned from vacation rested, with a great deal of energy, and happy.

_____

_____

4. Josef managed to find time to coach the team with two other day jobs.

_____

_____

5. When acting on the stage, a good memory helps.

_____

_____

6. Discovered by accident, the football fan brought the diamond ring to the lost and found.

_____

_____

7. Books were piled on the reading tables, magazines were tossed, and scraps of paper everywhere.

_____

_____

8. Being nearly deaf, the whistle of the train did not warn him of the danger.

_____

_____

9. I would rather read a good mystery than to watch television.

_____

_____

10. The bus driving through the fog slowly came into view.

_____

_____

TEST 2   Revising sentences for parallel structure and correct use of modifiers

Each sentence has an error in parallel structure or in the use of a modifier. Revise each sentence so that it is correct.

1. The job demands computer skills, math ability, and with accounting background.

_____

_____

2. My sister is not only a talented musician, but she is also teaching with great success.

_____

_____

3. Raking the leaves this morning, over one hundred geese flew overhead.

_____

_____

4. Follow the directions for writing the essay carefully.

_____

_____

5. The astronomer completed the calculation at the observatory that he had been working on for nearly a decade.

_____

_____

6. We should bring a picnic lunch rather than to pay for an expensive restaurant lunch somewhere.

_____

_____

7. My older brother is guilty of lecturing me instead of a good example.

_____

_____

8. The new highway follows the river, bypasses the small towns, and you can save a lot of time.

_____

_____

9. He only ordered an appetizer.

_____

_____

10. She mowed the lawn, repaired the broken window, and a huge pile of newspapers to be recycled.

_____

_____

Revising sentences for parallel structure and correct use of modifiers TEST 3

Each sentence has an error in parallel structure or in the use of a modifier. Revise each sentence so that it is correct.

1. After the move, he slumped into a chair, grabbed a bottle of soda, and with a wish for a good book.

_____

_____

2. My friend is generous, hard-working, and a talker.

_____

_____

3. The members of Congress would rather stonewall the proposal than to pass the new law.

_____

_____

4. When covered with thin ice, you should not skate on the lake.

_____

_____

5. Last year, the citizen just paid half of his taxes.

_____

_____

6. From the airport, I will either take the bus or the shuttle to the hotel.

_____

_____

7. For the holidays, we plan to do some cooking, see a few good movies, and listening to jazz.

_____

_____

8. Working late into the night, the page numbering on my report kept printing out wrong.

_____

_____

9. The crime not only involved the chief officer but also several of his assistants.

_____

_____

10. The witness told the whole story from the beginning of the incident to when the suspects were arrested.

_____

_____

Developing a Resume

The following is a draft of a resume written by a college student who is looking for a summer job. Study the resume and then answer the questions that follow it.

Gary Sommers
645 Franklin AVe.
Norman, Oklahoma
Home Telephone: 662-1919

<u>Present Job Objective</u>	A summer position as an assistant in ~~teh~~ *the* mayor's office
<u>Education</u>	High School Diploma, Kennedy High School, Norman, Oklahoma
	B.A., Business Administration, University of Oklahoma Expected date of graduation: june 2000
	Courses in Business and Computers: Principles of Accounting, Microeconomic Theory, Problem solving and Structured Programming, Computer Systems and Assembly

<u>WORK EXPERIENCE</u>

9/96 to present	Tutor, Math Lab, University of Oklahoma
1993–1995	Summer Volunteer at Camp Sunshine, a day camp for disabled children

<u>Special skills:</u>   fluent in spanish

<u>Computer Skills:</u> familiar with Microsoft Word, EXCEL,

<u>Interests:</u> soccer, guitar

<u>REFERENCES:</u> Available on request

Questions for Resume Editing

1. Can you find any typos, misspelled words, or errors in capitalization or punctuation?
2. Can you find anything inconsistent in the design or layout? (Look for places where parallel structures are needed.)
3. What do you think about Mr. Sommers correcting an error using pen rather than reprinting a corrected version? What conclusion might the potential employer have?
4. Is there any information that is missing?
5. Why has the person not included such facts as date of birth or marital status?
6. How does a person go about obtaining references? How many references does one need?
7. How could this person highlight his interest in the particular job for which he is applying?

Portfolio Suggestion: Write Your Own Resume

Using the same general headings as contained in this sample resume, write your own resume. Copy it onto a disk of your own that you will keep. Remember to update the resume regularly. You may have more than one version depending on what experiences or skills you want to emphasize.

Practicing More with Verbs

So far in this book, you have already learned a great deal about verbs. In Chapter 2, you learned how to recognize the verb in a sentence. In Chapter 3, you learned that verbs must agree with their subjects. Chapter 4 discussed how to form participles, gerunds, and infinitives from the verb. This chapter will continue your study of verbs focusing on:

- Principal parts of irregular verbs
- How to use the present perfect and past perfect tenses
- Sequence of tenses
- How to avoid unnecessary shifts in verb tense
- The difference between active or passive voice
- The subjunctive mode
- Confusions with *should* and *would*

What are the principal parts of the irregular verbs?

The English language has more than one hundred verbs that do not form the past tense or past participle with the usual *-ed* ending. Their forms are irregular. When you listen to children aged four or five, you often hear them utter expressions such as "Yesterday I *cutted* myself." Later on, they will hear that the verb "cut" is unusual, and they will change to the irregular form, "Yesterday I *cut* myself." The best way to learn these verbs is to listen to how they sound. You will find an extensive list of these verbs in the appendix of this book. Pronounce them out loud over and over until you have learned them. If you find that you don't know a particular verb's meaning, or you cannot pronounce a verb and its forms, ask your instructor for help. Most irregular verbs are very common words that you will be using often in your writing and speaking. You will want to know them well.

Practicing 50 irregular verbs

The three principal parts of irregular verbs		
Base Form	**Past Tense**	**Past Participle**
(also called Dictionary Form, Infinitive Form, or Simple Form)		*(used with perfect tenses after "has," "have," "had," "will have" or with passive voice after the verb "to be.")*
ride	rode	ridden

Eight verbs that do not change their forms (notice they all end in -t or -d)		
Base Form	**Past Tense**	**Past Participle**
bet	bet	bet
cost	cost	cost
cut	cut	cut
fit	fit	fit
hit	hit	hit
hurt	hurt	hurt
quit	quit	quit
spread	spread	spread

Two verbs that have the same simple present form and the part participle		
Base Form	**Past Tense**	**Past Participle**
come	came	come
become	became	become

PRACTICE   Fill in the correct form of the verb in each of the following sentences.

(cost)   1. Last year the tuition for my education _____ seven percent more than the year before.

(quit)   2. I have _____ trying to guess my expenses for next year.

(spread)   3. The message has _____ that college costs continue to spiral.

(hit)   4. Most parents have been _____ with large tax increases.

(become)   5. Financing a child's higher education has _____ a difficult task.

Twenty verbs that have the same simple past form and past participle		
Base Form	**Past Tense**	**Past Participle**
bend	bent	bent
lend	lent	lent
send	sent	sent
spend	spent	spent
creep	crept	crept
keep	kept	kept
sleep	slept	slept
sweep	swept	swept
weep	wept	wept
teach	taught	taught
catch	caught	caught
bleed	bled	bled
feed	fed	fed
lead	led	led
speed	sped	sped
bring	brought	brought
buy	bought	bought
fight	fought	fought
think	thought	thought
seek	sought	sought

Fill in the correct form of the verb in each of the following sentences.

PRACTICE

(buy)   1. Last year the school district _____ new chemistry texts.

(spend)   2. Some parents felt they had _____ too much money on these new books.

(bleed)   3. They claimed the taxpayers were being _____dry.

(keep)   4. These parents argued that the school should have _____ the old books.

(think)   5. The teachers _____ the old books were worn out.

9.13.00 Wednesday

Twenty verbs that have all different forms		
Base Form	**Past Tense**	**Past Participle**
blow	blew	blown
fly	flew	flown
grow	grew	grown
know	knew	known
throw	threw	thrown
begin	began	begun
drink	drank	drunk
ring	rang	rung
shrink	shrank	shrunk
sink	sank	sunk
sing	sang	sung
spring	sprang	sprung
swim	swam	swum
bite	bit	bitten (or bit)
hide	hid	hidden (or hid)
drive	drove	driven
ride	rode	ridden
stride	strode	stridden
rise	rose	risen
write	wrote	written

PRACTICE   Fill in the correct form of the verb in each of the following sentences.

(sing)   1. Last night, the tenor _sang_ "The Flower Song" from *Carmen*.

(grow)   2. Over the past few performances, his audiences have _grown_

(begin)   3. I first _began_ to enjoy his singing when I heard his voice on the radio last spring.

(hide)   4. I have never _hidden_ my admiration for the tenor voice.

(know)   5. Famous tenors like Enrico Caruso, John McCormack, and Luciano Pavarotti are _known_ all over the world.

EXERCISE 1   ## Knowing the irregular verb forms

Supply the past form or the past participle for each verb in parentheses.

Ever since people _began_ to write, they have _written_ about the great the great mysteries in nature. For instance, why did the dinosaurs disappear? In
(begin)   (write)

the past, no one _knew_ why. Scientists now have _bet_ on one strong possibility.
(know)   (bet)

That possibility is that sixty-five million years ago, a six-mile-wide chunk of rock _hit_ the earth and _threw_ up a thick cloud of dust. The dust _kept_ the
(hit)   (throw)   (keep)

sunlight from the earth; therefore, certain life forms disappeared. Some scientists have _thought_ (think) that this could also have _shrunk_ (shrink) the earth's animal population by as much as seventy percent. Other scientists are not so sure that this is the answer. They believe time has _hid_ (hide) the real reason for the disappearance of the dinosaurs.

Knowing the irregular verb forms

EXERCISE 2

Supply the past form or the past participle for each verb in parentheses.

Medical researchers have _sought_ (seek) a cure for the common cold, but so far they have _fought_ (fight) without success. The cold virus has _spread_ (spread) throughout the world and the number of cold victims has _risen_ (rise) every year. Past experience has _taught_ (teach) us that people who have _drank_ (drink) plenty of liquids and taken aspirin get over colds more quickly than those who have not, but this is is not a good enough remedy. People once believed that if you _feed_ (feed) a fever, you starved a cold, but recent research has _lead_ (lead) to a disclaimer of this belief. It has _cost_ (cost) a lot of time and effort in the search for a vaccine, but so far the new knowledge has not _brought_ (bring) a cure.

Knowing the irregular verb forms

EXERCISE 3

Rewrite the following paragraph in the past tense.

The jockey drives his pickup truck to the race track. He strides into the stalls where the horses are kept. His head swims with thoughts of the coming race. He springs into the saddle and rides to the starting gate. The bell rings and the horses fly out of the gate. They speed around the first turn. The crowd grows tense, and excitement spreads as the horses near the finish line.

_____

_____

_____

_____

_____

Appendix A at the back of this book gives an alphabetical listing of nearly every irregular verb. Use that list to supply the correct form for each verb in the following exercises.

EXERCISE 4   Additional irregular verbs

Supply the past form of the past participle for each verb in parentheses.

1. We _caught_ four trout in the stream.
    (to catch)
2. The burglar _crept_ up the fire escape.
    (to creep)
3. The audience _fled_ when the singer attempted the high notes.
    (to flee)
4. The pipe _busted_ yesterday; we are waiting for a plumber.
    (to burst)
5. He has _ridden_ aimlessly around the city for several hours.
    (to ride)
6. The firefighters _slid_ down the ladder.
    (to slide)
7. The elevator _rose_ quickly to the tenth floor.
    (to rise)
8. She had _quit_ her job before the baby was born.
    (to quit)
9. The pond was _frozen_ enough for ice skating.
    (to freeze)
10. He had washed and _wrang_ out all his clothes in the bathtub.
    (to wring)

EXERCISE 5   Additional irregular verbs

Read the following paragraph and find the ten irregular verbs that are written incorrectly. In the spaces provided, write the correct forms of the ten irregular verbs.

Mr. Weeks, an alumnus of our university, had gave a large sum of money to the school just before he died. A committee was choosen to study how the money should be used. Each member thunk about the possibilities for several weeks before the meeting. Finally, the meeting begun in late November. Each member brung his ideas. One gentleman fealt the school should improve the graduate program by hiring two new teachers. Another committee member layed down a proposal for remodeling the oldest dormitory on campus. Janice Spaulding had a writen plan for increasing the scholarships for deserving students. A citizen unexpectedly swang open the door and strode into the room. She pleaded with the school to provide more programs for the community. After everyone had spoke, the committee was asked to make a more thorough study of each project.

1. _Given_
2. _Chosen_
3. _thought_
4. _began_
5. _brought_
6. _Written_
7. _Swung_
8. _Felt_
9. _laid_
10. _Spoken_

Additional irregular verbs

Supply the past form or the past participle for each verb in parentheses.

1. We _____ in the lake last summer.
   (to swim)
2. The director _____ a solution to the problems.
   (to seek)
3. The family _____ bitterly over the death of the child.
   (to weep)
4. The clerk _____ the clock before going home.
   (to wind)
5. The door seemed to be _____.
   (to stick)
6. The dog _____ itself as it came out of the water.
   (to shake)
7. The youth _____ he was telling the truth.
   (to swear)
8. Yesterday, the food had ____ on the table all day without being touched.
   (to lie)
9. My friend _____ her first child in a taxicab on the way to the hospital.
   (to bear)
10. The hosts _____ their guests to drink in their home.
    (to forbid)

How many verb tenses are there in English?

Since the next sections of this chapter concern common problems with tense, a chart of the English Verb Tenses is given in case you want to refer to this list from time to time. Not all languages express time by using exactly the same verb tenses. Students for whom English is a second language know that one of their major tasks in learning English is to understand how to use each of these tenses. Along with the name of each verb tense, the chart gives a sentence using that particular tense.

English verb tenses	
present	I walk
present continuous	I am walking
present perfect	I have walked
present perfect continuous	I have been walking
past	I walked
past continuous	I was walking
past perfect	I had walked
past perfect continuous	I had been walking
future	I will walk
future continuous	I will be walking
future perfect	I will have walked
future perfect continuous	I will have been walking

Note: The perfect tenses need special attention since they are generally not well understood or used consistently in the accepted way.

How do you use the present perfect and the past perfect tenses?

Forming the perfect tenses

Present perfect tense: *has* or *have* + past participle of the main verb

has worked

have worked

Past perfect tense: *had* + past participle of the main verb

had worked

What do these tenses mean?

> The ***present perfect tense*** describes an action that started in the past and continues to the present time.

Jennifer *has worked* at the hospital for ten years.

This sentence indicates that Jennifer began to work at the hospital ten years ago and is still working there now.

Examine the following time line. What does it tell you about the present perfect tense?

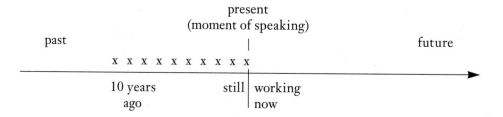

Other example sentences of the present perfect tense:

She *has studied* violin since 1980.

I *have* always *appreciated* his generosity.

> The ***present perfect tense*** can also describe an action that has just taken place, or an action where the exact time in the past is indefinite.

Has Jennifer *found* a job yet?

Jennifer *has* (just) *found* a new job in Kansas City.

Have you ever *been* to San Diego?

Yes, I *have been* there three times.

If the time were definite, you would use the simple past:

Jennifer *found* a new job yesterday.

Yes, I *was* there last week.

> The *past perfect tense* describes an action that occurred in the past before another activity or another point of time in the past.

Jennifer *had worked* at the hospital for ten years *before* she *moved* away.

In this sentence, there are two past actions: Jennifer *worked*, and Jennifer *moved*. The action that took place first is in the past perfect *(had worked)*. The action that took place later, and was also completed in the past, is in the simple past *(moved)*.

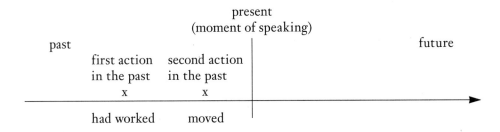

Other example sentences using the past perfect tense:

I *had* just *finished* when the bell *rang*.

He *said* that Randall *had told* the class about the experiment.

We *had provided* the information *long before* last week's meeting.

PRACTICE

Complete each of the following sentences by filling in each blank with either the present perfect tense or past perfect tense of the verb given.

1. Yolanda told us that she _____ in Fort Worth before she moved to
   (live)
   Mexico City.

2. Mexico City _____ visitors for many years.
   (fascinate)

3. This city _____ the third largest city in the world, and people
   (become)
   _____ it grow larger every year.
   (watch)

4. The suburbs of the city_____ old villages that_____ peacefully
   (replace)   (exist)
   since the days of the Aztecs.

5. Today, Mexico City _____ a computer-controlled subway system to deal
   (build)
   with its huge transportation problem.

What is the sequence of tenses?

> The term *sequence of tenses* refers to the proper use of verb tenses in complex sentences (sentences that have an independent clause and a dependent clause).

The following guide shows the relationship between the verb in the independent clause (IC) and the verb in the dependent clause (DC).

Sequence of tenses		
Independent Clause	**Dependent Clause**	**Time of the DC in Relation to the IC**
If the tense of the independent clause is in the present (He *knows*), here are the possibilities for the dependent clause.		
	that she *is* right.	same time
He knows	that she *was* right.	earlier
	that she *will be* right.	later
If the tense of the independent clause is in the past (He *knew*), here are the possibilities for the dependent clause.		
	that she *was* right.	same time
He knew	that she *had been* right.	earlier
	that she *would be* right.	later
If the independent clause is in the future (He *will tell*), here are the possibilities for the dependent clause.		
	if she *goes*.	same time
He will tell us	if she *has gone*.	earlier
	if she *will go*.	later

PRACTICE In each of the following sentences, the verb in the independent clause has been underlined. Choose the correct verb tense for the verb in the dependent clause. Use the guide above if you need help.

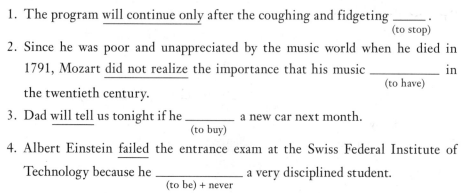

1. The program <u>will continue</u> only after the coughing and fidgeting _____ .
   (to stop)

2. Since he was poor and unappreciated by the music world when he died in 1791, Mozart <u>did not realize</u> the importance that his music _____ in the twentieth century.
   (to have)

3. Dad <u>will tell</u> us tonight if he _____ a new car next month.
   (to buy)

4. Albert Einstein <u>failed</u> the entrance exam at the Swiss Federal Institute of Technology because he _____ a very disciplined student.
   (to be) + never

5. Einstein only <u>studied</u> subjects that he _____ .
   (to like)

6. Cancer researchers <u>think</u> it's likely that a cure for most cancers _____
   _____(to be) + soon_____
   found.

7. We <u>know</u> that science ___ now close to finding a cure for leukemia.
   _____(to be)_____

8. The interviewer <u>felt</u> that the young woman _____ more than she was telling
   _____(to know)_____
   him.

9. The doctor went into the operating room. She <u>hoped</u> that the operation
   _____ out all right.
   _____(to turn)_____

10. The doctor came out of the operating room. She <u>said</u> that the operation
    _____ well.
    _____(to go)_____

Avoid unnecessary shift in verb tense

Unless there is some reason to change tenses, inconsistent shifting from one tense
to another should be avoided. Study the following examples:

Shifted tenses: The customer *asked* (past tense) to see the manager. He *was* (past
tense) angry because every jacket he *tries* on (Why present tense?)
has (Why present tense?) something wrong with it. A button was
(past tense) missing on the first, the lining *did* not *fit* (past tense)
right on the second, and the collar *had* (past tense) a stain on the
third.

Revised: The customer *asked* (past tense) to see the manager. He *was* (past
tense) angry because every jacket he *tried* on (past tense) *had* (past
tense) something wrong with it. A button *was* (past tense) missing
on the first, the lining *did* not *fit* (past tense) right on the second,
and the collar *had* (past tense) a stain on the third.

Note: When the subject is a created work, such as a book, play, poem, or piece of music,
be especially careful about the verb tense. Although the work was created in the past, it
is still enjoyed in the present. In this case, the present tense is used.

Shakespeare's *Hamlet* <u>is</u> a great play. It <u>was written</u> four centuries ago.

Correcting unnecessary shift in verb tense

EXERCISE 7

Each sentence has an unnecessary shift in verb tense. Revise each sentence so that
the tenses remain consistent.

1. After I complete that writing course, I took the required history course.

   _____

   _____

2. In the beginning of the movie, the action was slow; by the end, I am sitting on
   the edge of my seat.

   _____

   _____

3. The textbook gives the rules for writing a bibliography, but it didn't explain how to do footnotes.

_____

_____

4. While working on her report in the library, my best friend lost her note cards and comes to me for help.

_____

_____

5. The encyclopedia gave several pages of information about astronomy, but it doesn't give any information about "black holes."

_____

_____

6. The invitation requested that Juan be at the ceremony and that he will attend the banquet as well.

_____

_____

7. This is an exciting book, but it had too many characters.

_____

_____

8. The senator was doing just fine until along comes a younger and more energetic politician with firm support from the middle class.

_____

_____

9. At the end of *Gulliver's Travels*, the main character rejects the company of people; he preferred the company of horses.

_____

_____

10. My sister arrives, late as usual, and complained that her dinner was cold.

_____

_____

EXERCISE 8   **Correcting unnecessary shift in verb tense**

The following paragraph contains unnecessary shifts in verb tense. Change each incorrect verb to its proper form.

The writer Willa Cather (1873–1947) grew up in Red Cloud, Nebraska, at a time when many parts of the United States were still undeveloped. In 1890 she went to college in Lincoln, Nebraska, when it was still a small town; the university is made up of only a few buildings. After graduating, she tried teaching and writing in Pittsburgh, but in New York she becomes a real success, doing magazine work and writing fiction. Later, she traveled to other parts of the country to find inspiration for her novels and short stories. She visits the Southwest to get inspiration for her novel *The Song of the Lark*, and she went to New Mexico to find material for one of her most popular books, *Death Comes for the Archbishop*. Her most famous book is *My Antonia*, a novel that told about life in the American West. In that book we see both a portrait of America and a picture of Willa Cather's own mind.

Correcting unnecessary shift in verb tense

EXERCISE 9

The following paragraph contains unnecessary shifts in verb tense. Change each incorrect verb to its proper form.

Charles Dickens was a nineteenth-century author whose work is well known today. One of the reasons Dickens remained so popular is that so many of his stories are available not only as books but also as movies, plays, and television productions. We all knew from our childhood the famous story of Uncle Scrooge and Tiny Tim. Often we saw a television version of *A Christmas Carol* at holiday time. If we have never read the story of Oliver Twist in book form, we might see the musical *Oliver!* Also, there was a movie version of *Great Expectations*. Many students still studied *A Tale of Two Cities* in high school. No matter how many adaptations of Dickens's books we see, people seem to agree that there was no substitute for the books themselves. At first, the vocabulary seemed hard to understand, but if we concentrate on the story and read a chapter or two every day, we will find ourselves not only comprehending these wonderful stories but loving the richness of Dickens's use of language.

What is the difference between the passive voice and the active voice?

Passive and active voice

In the *active voice,* the subject does the acting:

The committee made the decision.

Choose the active voice generally in order to achieve direct, economical and forceful writing. Most writing, therefore, should be in the active voice.

In the *passive voice,* the subject is acted upon:

The decision was made by the committee.

or

The decision was made.

Notice in these passive sentences, the actor is not only deemphasized by moving out of the subject place but may be omitted entirely from the sentence.

Choose the passive voice to deemphasize the actor or to avoid naming the actor altogether.

Study the three sentences that follow. All three state the fact of President Kennedy's assassination. Discuss with your classmates and instructor what would cause a writer to choose each of the following sentences to express the same basic fact.

1. Lee Harvey Oswald shot President John F. Kennedy in 1963.

2. President John F. Kennedy was shot by Lee Harvey Oswald in 1963.

3. President John F. Kennedy was shot in 1963.

How do you form the passive voice?

Forming the passive voice			
Subject Acted Upon	**+ Verb "To Be"**	**+ Past Participle**	**+ "by" Phrase (Optional)**
The race	was	won	(by the runner)
The fish	was	cooked	(by the chef)
The books	are	illustrated	(by the artists)

EXERCISE 10   Fill in the following chart by showing how the sentences in the active voice could be put into passive voice and how the sentences in the passive voice could be put into the active voice. Then discuss with your classmates and instructor the circumstances under which you would choose active or passive voice to express these ideas.

Active voice

1. *The child dialed the wrong number.*

2. *My grandmother crocheted the sweater very carefully.*

3. The tornado struck Cherry Creek last spring.

4. The wind blew the leaves across the yard.

5. *In the 60's, fashionable young men and women wore platform shoes.*

Passive voice

1. The wrong number was dialed by the child.

2. The sweater was crocheted very carefully by my grandmother.

3. *Cherry Creek was struck by a tornado last spring.*

4. *The leaves were blown across the yard by the wind.*

5. In the 60s, platform shoes were worn by many fashionable young men and women.

EXERCISE 11   ## Active and passive voice

Fill in the following chart by showing how the sentences in the active voice could be put into passive voice and how the sentences in the passive voice could be put into the active voice. Then discuss with your classmates and instructor the circumstances under which you would choose active or passive voice to express these ideas.

Active voice

1. The jury announced the verdict after five hours of deliberation.

2. *Elvis Presley Created modernpop music.*

3. The sleet turned the old municipal building into an ice castle.

4. *Someone smuggled the priceless vase.*

5. *Television viewers paid more Attention And concern over the Super Bowl than over the outbreak of Conflict involving the U.S.*

Passive voice

1. *After five hours of deliberation the verdict WAS Announced by the Jury.*

2. Modern pop music was created by Elvis Presley.

3. *The old municiple building was turned into An ice castle by the sleet.*

4. The priceless vase was smuggled by someone out of the country.

5. More attention and concern were shown by television viewers over the Super Bowl than over the outbreak of a conflict involving the United States.

What is the subjunctive?

> The *subjunctive* is an as yet unrealized situation.

Recognize the three instances that call for the subjunctive:

1. Unreal conditions using *if* or *wish*

If he were my teacher, I would be pleased.

I *wish* he were my teacher.

2. Clauses starting with *that* after verbs such as *ask, request, demand, suggest, order, insist,* or *command*

I *demand* that she work harder.

Sullivan *insisted* that Jones report on Tuesday.

3. Clauses starting with *that* after adjectives expressing urgency, as in *it is necessary, it is imperative, it is urgent, it is important,* and *it is essential*

It is necessary that she wear a net covering her hair.

It is essential that Robert understand the concept.

In each of these three instances, notice that the verb following the italicized word or phrase does not agree with its subject. (The third person plural form of the verb without the *s* is used in these cases.)

PRACTICE   In the following sentences, circle the subjunctives (the subjects and verbs that do not agree). Underline the word or phrase that determines the subjunctive. An example has been done for you.

Truman <u>suggested</u> that the ⟨country adopt⟩ the Marshall plan in 1947.

1. When President Roosevelt died in 1945, the law required that Vice President Truman take over immediately.
2. It was essential that President Truman act quickly and decisively.
3. Truman must have wished that he were able to avoid using the atomic bomb to bring an end to World War II.
4. He felt it was necessary that the United States help Europe recover from the destruction of World War II.
5. President Truman always insisted that other countries be economically strong.

Confusions with *should* and *would*

Do not use more than one modal auxiliary (*can, may, might, must, should, ought*) with the main verb.

Incorrect: Matt *shouldn't ought* to sell his car.

Correct: Matt *ought not* sell his car.

  or

  Matt *shouldn't* sell his car.

Do not use *should of, would of,* or *could of* to mean *should have, would have,* or *could have.*

Incorrect: Elana *would of* helped you if she *could of.*

Correct: Elana *would have* helped you if she *could have.*

Mastery and editing tests

TEST 1   Solving problems with verbs

Revise each of the following sentences to avoid problems with verbs.

1. He hadn't ought to drive so fast.

2. The officer said that the motorist drove through a red light.

3. I wish I was a senior.

4. She sung for a huge crowd Saturday night.

5. I was shook up by the accident.

6. The map was studied by the motorist. (use active voice)

_____

7. My father ask me last night to help him build a deck.

_____

8. I should of kept the promise I made.

_____

9. I insist she keeps her clothes on her side of the room.

_____

10. The ship sunk off the coast of Florida.

_____

Solving problems with verbs

TEST 2

Some of the verbs in the following paragraph are incorrect. Find the errors and correct them.

When the day arrived, my mother was jubilant. We drive to the synagogue. My aunt Sophie and her daughters comes with us. Once in the temple, the women were not allowed to sit with the men. They had to go upstairs to their assigned places. I was ask to keep my hat on and was given a shawl to wear which I seen before. I was suppose to watch for the rabbi to call me. My turn finally come. I was brung to a table in the front. There I read from the Bible in Hebrew. I knew I could of read louder, but I was nervous. My mother had said that if I was good, she would be especially proud of me, so I done my best. Afterward, I was took by my mother and other relatives to a fine kosher restaurant where we celebrated. I receive a fine gold watch.

Solving problems with verbs

TEST 3

Some of the verbs in the following paragraph are incorrect. Find the errors and correct them.

I knowed I was in big trouble in chemistry when I took a look at the midterm exam. My semester should of been a lot better. The first week I had my new textbook, I lend it to a friend who lost it. Then I catched a cold and miss two classes. When I finally start off for class, I missed the bus and walked into the classroom half an hour late. The teacher scowls at me and ask to speak to me after class. I always use to sit in the front row so I could see the board and hear the lectures, but since I am late, I will have to take a seat in the last row. I wish I was able to start this class over again the right way. No one had ought to have such an unlucky start in any class.

Working Together

Summarizing a Class Discussion

Topic: What wage should a person be able to earn?

We often hear people being outraged over the amounts of money people in some professions can earn. For instance, some sports figures and entertainers can earn millions every year, while a daycare worker who cares for a community's children, or a postal worker who has responsibility for the mail, will not earn that much in an entire lifetime.

Select a person from the class to be the recorder—the person who will write on the board the major points made during the discussion. Each person will be responsible to keep his or her own notes. Be sure that everyone is given an opportunity to voice an opinion. Consider the following questions in discussing this complicated topic:

1. In the United States today, how are wages determined? Give specific examples. Explain why this may be different in other countries.

2. Do you think there should be a minimum wage law? Do you think there should be a maximum wage law?

3. What is the present minimum wage? Do you believe this is a living wage?

4. Do you think some people's work is more valuable than the work of others and therefore should be paid with more money, or should everyone receive the same amount, whether or not the work is considered valuable to society?

Portfolio Suggestion

Reserve the last half hour of class for each student to write a summary of the class discussion. At many meetings in the workplace, employees are expected to take notes on the discussions and remember the main ideas brought up, especially when those ideas involve decisions made and actions that must be implemented. You may be asked to record the minutes, which is to make a formal document that summarizes everything that is discussed. Remember, a summary does not contain the opinions of just the writer. It must include all the important ideas that were generated in the discussion. The writer should express which ideas the class seemed in agreement about and which ideas the class disagreed about.

CHAPTER 11

Using Correct Capitalization and Punctuation

S
T
E
P

2

Ten basic rules for capitalization

Many people are often confused or careless about the use of capital letters. Sometimes writers capitalize words without thinking, or they capitalize "important" words without really understanding what makes them important enough to deserve a capital letter. The question of when to capitalize words becomes easier to answer when you study the following rules and carefully apply them to your own writing.

1. Capitalize the first word of every sentence.

2. Capitalize the names of specific things and places.

Specific buildings:

> I went to the Jamestown Post Office.
>
> > but
>
> I went to the post office.

Specific streets, cities, states, countries:

> She lives on Elam Avenue.
>
> > but
>
> She lives on the same street as my mom and dad.

Specific organizations:

> He collected money for the March of Dimes.
>
> but
>
> Janice joined more than one club at the school.

Specific institutions:

> The loan is from the First National Bank.
>
> but
>
> The loan is from one of the banks in town.

Specific bodies of water:

> My uncle fishes every summer on Lake Chautauqua.
>
> but
>
> My uncle spends every summer at the lake.

3. Capitalize days of the week, months of the year, and holidays. Do not capitalize the names of seasons.

> The last Thursday in November is Thanksgiving Day.
>
> but
>
> I cannot wait until spring.

4. Capitalize the names of all languages, nationalities, races, religions, deities, and sacred terms.

> My friend who is Ethiopian speaks very little English.
>
> The Koran is the sacred book of Islam.

5. Capitalize the first word and every important word in a title. Do not capitalize articles, prepositions, or short connecting words in the title.

> *For Whom the Bell Tolls* is a famous novel by Ernest Hemingway.
>
> Her favorite short story is "A Rose for Emily."

6. Capitalize the first word of a direct quotation.

> The teacher said, "You have been chosen for the part."
>
> but
>
> "You have been chosen," she said, "for the part."

Note: *for* is not capitalized because it is not the beginning of the sentence in quotation marks.

7. Capitalize historical events, periods, and documents.

> The American Revolution
>
> The Colonial Period
>
> The Bill of Rights

8. **Capitalize the words north, south, east, and west when they are used as places rather than as directions.**

> He comes from the Midwest.
>
> but
>
> The farm is about twenty miles west of Omaha.

9. **Capitalize people's names.**

Proper names:

> George Hendrickson

Professional titles when they are used with the person's proper name:

> Judge Samuelson   but   the judge
>
> Professor Shapiro   but   the professor

Term for a relative (like mother, sister, nephew, uncle) when it is used in the place of the proper name:

> I told Grandfather I would meet him later.

Note: terms for relatives are not capitalized if a pronoun, article, or adjective is used with the name.

> I told my grandfather I would meet him later.

10. **Capitalize brand names.**

> Lipton's Noodle Soup   but   noodle soup
>
> Velveeta Cheese   but   cheese

Capitalization (on Test)

EXERCISE 1

Capitalize wherever necessary.

1. The italian student got a job in the school cafeteria.

2. Our train ride through the canadian rockies was fabulous.

3. The author often made references in his writing to names from the bible.

4. A student at the university of delaware was chosen for the national award.

5. My uncle's children always have a party on halloween.

6. I met the president of american telephone and telegraph company last friday at a convention in portland, oregon.

7. In 1863 president Lincoln wrote his famous emancipation proclamation.

8. My niece said, "why don't you consider moving farther south if you hate the winter so much?"

9. The united auto workers voted not to go on strike over the new contract.

10. A very popular radio program in the east is called a prairie home companion.

Capitalization

Capitalize wherever necessary.

1. Every tuesday the general visits the hospital.

2. On one level, the book *the lord of the rings* can be read as a fairy tale; on another level, the book can be read as a christian allegory.

3. The golden gate bridge in san francisco may be the most beautiful bridge in the world.

4. She is the sister of my french teacher.

5. I've always wanted to take a trip to the far east in spring.

6. The kremlin, located in moscow, once housed the soviet government.

7. I needed to see dr. Madison, but the nurse told me the doctor would not be in until next week.

8. He shouted angrily, "why don't you ever arrive at your history class on time?"

9. The scholastic aptitude test will be given on january 18.

10. While yet a teenager growing up in harlem, james Baldwin became a baptist preacher.

Capitalization

Capitalize wherever necessary.

1. The lawyer's office is located on south pleasant street.

2. My uncle lives farther south than grandmother.

3. I'd like to move to the south if I could find a job there.

4. The well-known anthropologist Margaret Mead was for many years director of the museum of natural history in new york city.

5. The constitution of the united states was signed in constitution hall on september 17, 1787.

6. Sculptor John Wilson was commissioned to create a bust of rev. Martin Luther King, jr.

7. The money will be funded partly from the national endowment for the arts.

8. I read the magazine article in *newsweek* while I was waiting in the dentist's office yesterday.

9. The tour took the retired teachers above the arctic circle.

10. Many gerber baby foods no longer have sugar and salt.

Eight basic uses of the comma

You may feel uncertain about when to use the comma. The starting point is to concentrate on a few basic rules. These rules will cover most of your needs.

The tendency now in English is to use fewer commas than in the past. There is no one complete set of rules on which everyone agrees. However, if you learn these basic eight, your common sense will help you figure out what to do in other cases. Remember that a comma usually signifies a pause in a sentence. As you read a sentence out loud, listen to where you pause within the sentence. Where you pause is often your clue that a comma is needed. Notice that in each of the examples for the following eight uses, you can pause where the comma is placed.

1. Use a comma to separate items in a series (more than two items).

> I was angry, fretful, and impatient.
>
> I was dreaming of running in the race, finishing among the top ten, and collapsing happily on the ground.

- Some writers omit the comma before the *and* that introduces the last item.

  > I was angry, fretful and impatient.

- When an address or date occurs in a sentence, each part is treated like an item in a series. A comma is put after each item, including the last:

  > I lived at 428 North Monroe Street, Madison, Wisconsin, for many years.
  >
  > I was born on August 18, 1965, in the middle of a hurricane.

- A group of adjectives may not be regarded as a series if some of the words "go together." You can test this by putting *and* between each item. If you can put *and* between two adjectives, use a comma.

  > I carried my *old, dark green* coat.

In each of the following sentences, insert commas wherever they are needed.

PRACTICE

1. Problems with the water supply of the United States Europe Canada and other parts of the world are growing.
2. Water is colorless tasteless odorless and free of calories.
3. You will use on an average day twenty-four gallons of water for flushing thirty-two gallons for bathing and washing clothes and twenty-five gallons for other uses.
4. It took 120 gallons of water to create the eggs you ate for breakfast 3,500 gallons for the steak you might eat for dinner and over 60,000 gallons to produce the steel used to make your car.
5. On November 14 1977 officials discovered a major body of polluted water in Oswego New York.

2. **Use a comma along with a coordinating conjunction to combine two simple sentences (also called independent clauses) into a single compound sentence. (See Chapter 5 on coordination.)**

> The house was on fire, but I was determined not to leave my place of safety.

Be careful that you use the comma with the conjunction only when you are combining sentences. If you are combining only words or phrases, no comma is used.

> I was safe but not happy.
>
> My mother and father were searching for me.
>
> She was neither in class nor at work.

PRACTICE In each of the following sentences, insert commas wherever they are needed.

1. The most overused bodies of water are our rivers but they continue to serve us daily.
2. American cities often developed next to rivers and industries followed soon after in the same locations.
3. The people of the industrial age can try to clean the water they use or they can watch pollution take over.
4. The Great Lakes are showing signs of renewal yet the struggle against pollution there must continue.
5. Many people have not yet been educated about the dangers to our water supply nor are all our legislators fully aware of the problem.

3. **Use a comma to follow introductory words, expressions, phrases, or clauses.**

A. Introductory words (such as *yes, no, oh, well*)

> Oh, I never thought he would do it.

B. Introductory expressions (transitions such as *as a matter of fact, finally, secondly, furthermore, consequently*)

> Therefore, I will give you a second chance.

C. Introductory phrases

Long prepositional phrase: In the beginning of the course, I thought I would never be able to do the work.

Participial phrase: Walking on tiptoe, the young mother quietly peeked into the nursery.

Infinitive phrase: To be quite honest, I don't believe he's feeling well.

D. Introductory dependent clauses beginning with a subordinating conjunction (See Chapter 6.)

> When the food arrived, we all grabbed for it.

In each of the following sentences, insert commas wherever they are needed.

1. To many people from the East the plans to supply more water to the western states seem unnecessary.
2. However people in the West know that they have no future without a good water supply.
3. When they entered Salt Lake Valley in 1847 the Mormons found dry soil that needed water before crops could be grown.
4. Confidently the new settlers dug ditches that brought the needed water.
5. Learning from the past modern farmers are trying to cooperate with nature.

4. **Use commas surrounding a word, phrase, or clause when the word or group of words interrupts the main idea.**

A. Interrupting word

We will, however, take an X-ray.

B. Interrupting phrase

Prepositional phrase: I wanted, of course, to stay.

Appositive phrase: Ann, the girl with the braids, has a wicked sense of humor.

C. Interrupting clause

He won't, I think, try that again.

Ann, who wears braids, has a wicked sense of humor.

• Sometimes the same word, phrase, or clause can be used in more than one way. Often this changes the rule for punctuation.

The word *however*

Use commas if the word interrupts in the middle of a clause.

We will, however, take an X-ray.

Use a semicolon and a comma if the word connects two independent clauses.

We will take an X-ray; however, the doctor cannot read it today.

The relative clause *who wears braids*

Use commas if the clause interrupts and is not essential to the main idea.

My sister, who wears braids, has a wicked sense of humor.

Do not use commas if the clause is part of the identity, necessary to the main idea.

The girl who wears braids is my sister.

The clause *who wears braids* is necessary for identifying which girl is the sister.

PRACTICE In each of the following sentences, insert commas wherever they are needed.

1. Some parts of our country I believe do not have ample supplies of water.
2. The rocky soil of Virginia for example cannot absorb much rainwater.
3. Johnstown, Pennsylvania an industrial city of 48,000 is situated in one of the most flood-prone valleys of America.
4. It is not therefore a very safe place to live.
5. The Colorado which is one of our longest rivers gives up most of its water to farmers and cities before it can reach the sea.

5. **Use a comma around nouns in direct address. (A noun in direct address is the name or title used in speaking to someone.)**

I thought, Maria, that I saw your picture in the paper.

PRACTICE In each of the following sentences, insert commas wherever they are needed.

1. Dear your tea is ready now.
2. I wonder Jason if the game has been canceled.
3. Dad could I borrow five dollars?
4. I insist sir on speaking with the manager.
5. Margaret is that you?

6. **Use a comma in numbers of one thousand or larger.**

1,999

1,999,999,999

PRACTICE In each of the following numbers, insert commas wherever they are needed.

1. 4876454
2. 87602
3. 156439600
4. 187000
5. 10000000000000

7. **Use a comma to set off exact words spoken in dialogue.**

"Let them," she said, "eat cake."

Note: The comma as well as the period is always placed inside the quotation marks.

PRACTICE In each of the following sentences, insert commas wherever they are necessary.

1. "I won't" he insisted "be a part of your scheme."
2. He mumbled "I plead the Fifth Amendment."
3. "I was told" the defendant explained "to answer every question."
4. "This court case" the judge announced "will be televised."
5. "The jury" said Al Tarvin of the press "was hand-picked."

8. Use a comma where it is necessary to prevent a misunderstanding.

Before eating, the cat prowled through the barn.

In each of the following sentences, insert commas wherever they are needed.

1. Kicking the child was carried off to bed.
2. To John Russell Baker is the best columnist.
3. When you can come and visit us.
4. Whoever that is is going to be surprised.
5. Skin cancer seldom kills doctors say.

Using the comma correctly

In each of the following sentences, insert commas wherever they are needed.

1. The penguins that live in an area of South Africa near the coast are an endangered species.
2. One breeding ground for these penguins tiny Dassen Island is northwest of Cape Town.
3. Today fewer than sixty thousand penguins can be found breeding on this island.
4. At one time seabirds that stole the penguins' eggs were the only threat to the funny-looking birds.
5. These days human egg collectors not to mention animals that simply take the eggs are constantly reducing the penguin population.
6. However the worst threat to the penguins is oil pollution.
7. If a passing tanker spills oil many penguins can die.
8. In 1971 an oil tanker the *Wafra* spilled thousands of gallons of oil off the coast of southern Africa.
9. Whenever there is an oil spill near this area the number of healthy penguins declines.
10. The ideal situation of course is to make the oil tankers take a completely different route.

Using the comma correctly

In each of the following sentences, insert commas wherever they are needed.

1. Abraham Lincoln was born on February 12 1809 in Kentucky.
2. In December 1816 after selling most of their possessions the Lincoln family moved to Indiana.
3. During their first weeks in Indiana the family hunted for food drank melted snow and huddled together for warmth.
4. After a little formal education Lincoln worked on a ferryboat on the Ohio River.
5. The first large city that Lincoln visited was New Orleans an important center of trade in 1828.

6. Among the 40000 people Lincoln found himself with on that first visit there were people from all the states and several foreign countries.

7. New Orleans also showed Lincoln such city luxuries as fancy clothes gleaming silverware expensive furniture and imported china and glassware.

8. As a result of this visit Lincoln must have compared the log cabin of his childhood with the wealthy houses of this big city.

9. A few years later Lincoln became a merchant but his failure in business left him in debt for over ten years.

10. We should be grateful that Lincoln who started off in a business career turned his attention to politics.

EXERCISE 6   Using the comma correctly

In each of the following examples, insert commas wherever they are needed.

1. The Hope Diamond is one of the most famous if not *the* most famous gems in the world.

2. Mined in India the diamond reached Europe in 1668 along with the story that there was a curse on the stone.

3. The curse or so the legend goes is that bad fortune followed the diamond because it had been stolen from a temple in India.

4. The curse may be true since nearly all of its owners including Marie Antoinette of France a French actress who was shot to death and an American woman whose children were killed in accidents have met with tragedy.

5. Well if we cannot share in the history of the Hope Diamond we can see it in the Smithsonian Institution in our nation's capital.

6. Other gems not as famous have served people throughout history as payments for ransom as bribes and as lavish wedding presents.

7. One of the most famous mines in South America is in Colombia where an emerald mine started in 1537 is still being worked today.

8. Some gems are difficult to find but as the earth's crust changes rough stones may find their way into streams rivers and other bodies of water where they may be found.

9. In several parts of the world notably Africa and South America the greatest number of diamonds emeralds amethyst topaz and other precious and semi-precious stones are to be found.

10. We could travel to these places if we had the time the money and the interest.

Three uses for the apostrophe

1. To form the possessive:

A. Add *'s* to singular nouns:

the pen of the teacher = the teacher*'s* pen

the strategy of the boss = the boss*'s* strategy

the work of the week   = the week*'s* work

Watch out that you choose the right noun to make possessive. Always ask yourself *who* or *what* possesses something. In the sentences above, the teacher possesses the pen, the boss possesses the strategy, and the week possesses the work.

Note these unusual possessives:

Hyphenated words:	mother-in-law*'s* advice
Joint possession:	Lucy and Desi*'s* children
Individual possession:	John's and Steve*'s* ideas

B. Add *'s* to irregular plural nouns that do not end in *-s*.

the hats of the children = the children*'s* hats

the harness for the oxen = the oxen*'s* harness

C. Add *'s* to indefinite pronouns:

everyone's responsibility

somebody's wallet

Indefinite pronouns			
anyone	everyone	no one	someone
anybody	everybody	nobody	somebody
anything	everything	nothing	something

Possessive pronouns in English *(his, hers, its, ours, yours, theirs, whose)* do *not* use an apostrophe.

Whose key is this?

The key is *his.*

The car is *theirs.*

D. Add an apostrophe only to regular plural nouns ending in *-s*.

the coats of the ladies = the ladies' coats

the store of the brothers = the brothers' store

• A few singular nouns ending in the *s* or *z* sound are awkward-sounding if another *s* sound is added. You may drop the final *s*. Let your ear help you make the decision.

Jesus' robe *not* Jesus's robe

Moses' law *not* Moses's law

2. To form certain plurals in order to prevent confusion, use 's.

A. Numbers: 100's

B. Letters: *a*'s and *b*'s

C. Years: 1800's or 1800s

D. Abbreviations: Ph.D.'s

E. Words referred to in a text: He uses too many *and*'s in his writing.

Note: Be sure not to use the apostrophe to form a plural in any case other than these.

3. To show where letters have been omitted in contractions, use an apostrophe.

cannot   = can't

should not = shouldn't

will not   = won't (the only contraction that changes its spelling)

I am   = I'm

she will   = she'll

EXERCISE 7   Using the apostrophe

Fill in each of the blanks below using the rules you have just studied for uses of the apostrophe.

1. rays of the sun   the _Sun's_ rays
2. sleeve of the dress   the ~~dress's~~ sleeve _dress's_
3. length of the room   the _room's_ length
4. the house of Antony and Maria   _Antony and Maria's_ house
   (joint possession)
5. the idea of nobody   _nobodies_ idea
6. The book belongs to him.   The book is _his_
7. in the century of 1700   in the _1700's_
8. That is her opinion.   _That's_ her opinion.
9. shirts for boys   _boys'_ shirts
10. the cover of the book   the _book's_ cover

EXERCISE 8   Using the apostrophe

Fill in each of the blanks below using the rules you have just studied for uses of the apostrophe.

1. clarity of the ice   the _ice's_ clarity
2. the flight of the geese   the _Geese's_ flight
3. the work of Ann and Chris   _Ann's, Chris's_ work
   (individual possession)

4. the plan of someone   ___Someone's___ plan

5. The drums belong to her.   The drums are ___her's___

6. the terrible year of two   the terrible ___years' two's___

7. We cannot leave yet.   We ___can't___ leave yet.

8. the leaves of the tree   the ___tree's___ leaves

9. the cheese of the farmers   the ___farmer's___ cheese

10. the life-style of my brother-in-law   my ___brother-in-law's___ life-style

Using the apostrophe

Fill in each of the blanks below using the rules you have just studied for uses of the apostrophe.

1. the engine of the train   the ___train's___ engine

2. the spirit of the class   the ___class's___ spirit

3. the center for women   the ___women's___ center

4. the wish of everybody   ___everybody's___ wish

5. The toys belong to them.   The toys are ___theirs___ theirs

6. The child mixes up *b* and *d*.   The child mixes up ___b's, d's___

7. I will not leave this house.   I ___won't___ leave this house.

8. the grain of the wood   the ___wood's___ grain

9. the verdict of the jurors   the ___jurors'___ verdict

10. the policies of Ridge School and
    Orchard School (individual possession)   ___Ridge school's___ policies ___Orchard school's___

Other marks of punctuation

Four uses for quotation marks

1. **For a direct quotation:**

"Please," I begged, "don't go away."

Not for an indirect quotation:

I begged her not to go away.

2. **For material copied word for word from a source:**

According to *Science* magazine, "In an academic achievement test given to 600 sixth-graders in eight countries, U.S. kids scored last in mathematics, sixth in science, and fourth in geography."

[Handwritten notes in margin: 9.18.00 monday / correct form of the verb / Active/Passive / Possesives / Capitization of Proper nouns / Writing sample usining 4 Supporting detail]

3. For titles of shorter works such as short stories, one-act plays, poems, articles in magazines and newspapers, songs, essays, and chapters of books:

> "A Modest Proposal," an essay by Jonathan Swift, is a masterpiece of satire.

> "The Lottery," a short story by Shirley Jackson, created a sensation when it first appeared in the *New Yorker*.

4. For words used in a special way:

> "Duckie" is a term of affection used by the British, the way we would use the word "honey."

Underlining

> Underlining is used in handwriting or typing to indicate a title of a long work such as a book, full-length play, magazine, or newspaper. (In print, such titles are put in italics.)

In print: Many famous short stories have first appeared in the *New Yorker*.

In type or handwriting: Many famous short stories have first appeared in the <u>New Yorker</u>.

PRACTICE   In each of the following sentences, insert quotation marks wherever they are needed.

1. The Gift of the Magi is one of the short stories contained in O. Henry's book *The Four Million*.
2. Franklin Delano Roosevelt said, We have nothing to fear but fear itself.
3. The president told his cabinet that they would have to settle the problem in the next few days.
4. Punk is a particular form of rock music.
5. She read the article Trouble in Silicon Valley in last February's *Newsweek*.

If these five sentences were handwritten or typed, which words would have to be underlined?

Three uses for the semicolon

1. To join two independent clauses whose ideas and sentence structure are related:

> He decided to consult the map; she decided to ask the next pedestrian she saw.

2. To combine two sentences using an adverbial conjunction:

> He decided to consult the map; however, she decided to ask the next pedestrian she saw.

3. **To separate items in a series when the items themselves contain commas:**

> I had lunch with Linda, my best friend; Mrs. Zhangi, my English teacher; and Jan, my sister-in-law.

If the writer had used only commas to separate items in the last example, the reader might think six people had gone to lunch.

PRACTICE

In each of the following sentences, insert a semicolon wherever needed.

1. One of the best ways to remember a vacation is to take numerous photos one of the best ways to recall the contents of a book is to take notes.
2. The problem of street crime must be solved otherwise, the number of vigilantes will increase.
3. The committee was made up of Kevin Corey, a writer Anita Lightburn, a professor and T. P. O'Connor, a politician.
4. The bank president was very cordial however, he would not approve the loan.
5. Robots are being used in the factories of Japan eventually they will be common in this country as well.

Four uses for the colon

1. **After a complete sentence when the material that follows is a list, an illustration, or an explanation:**

A. A list:

> Please order the following items: five dozen pencils, twenty rulers, and five rolls of tape.

> Notice that in the sentence below, no colon is used because there is not a complete sentence before the list.

> The courses I am taking this semester are Freshman Composition, Introduction to Psychology, Art Appreciation, and Survey of American Literature.

B. An explanation or illustration:

> She was an exceptional child: at seven she was performing on the concert stage.

2. **For the salutation of a business letter:**

> To whom it may concern:

> Dear Madam President:

3. **In telling time:**

> We will eat at 5:15.

4. Between the title and subtitle of a book:

Plain English Please: A Rhetoric

PRACTICE   In each of the following sentences, insert colons where they are needed.

1. Three pianists played in New York on the same weekend Andre Watts, Claudio Arrau, and Jorge Bolet.
2. The official has one major flaw in his personality greed.
3. The restaurant has lovely homemade desserts such as German chocolate layer cake and baked Alaska.
4. The college offers four courses in English literature Romantic Poetry, Shakespeare's Plays, The British Short Story, and The Modern Novel.
5. Arriving at 615 in the morning, Marlene brought me a sausage and cheese pizza, soda, and a gallon of ice cream.

The dash and parentheses

The comma, dash, and parentheses can all be used to show an interruption of the main idea. The particular form you choose depends on the degree of interruption.

> Use the dash for a less formal and more emphatic interruption of the main idea.

He came—I thought—by car.

She arrived—and I know this for a fact—in a pink Cadillac.

> Use the parentheses to insert extra information that some of your readers might want to know but that is not at all essential for the main idea. Such information is not emphasized.

Johann Sebastian Bach (1685–1750) composed the "Preludes and Fugues."

Plea bargaining (see 3.4) was developed to speed court verdicts.

PRACTICE   Insert dashes or parentheses wherever needed.

1. Herbert Simon is and I don't think this is an exaggeration a genius.
2. George Eliot her real name was Mary Ann Evans wrote *Silas Marner.*
3. You should in fact I insist see a doctor.
4. Unemployment brings with it a number of other problems see the study by Brody, 1982.
5. Mass media television, radio, movies, magazines, and newspapers are able to transmit information over a wide range and to a large number of people.

Other marks of punctuation

In each of the following sentences, insert marks of punctuation wherever they are needed.

1. To measure crime, sociologists have used three different techniques official statistics, victimization surveys, and self-report studies.
2. The Bells is one of the best-loved poems of Edgar Allan Poe.
3. The lake this summer has one major disadvantage for swimmers seaweed.
4. E. B. White wrote numerous essays for adults however, he also wrote some very popular books for children.
5. Tuberculosis also known as consumption has once again become a serious health issue.
6. The Victorian Period 1837–1901 saw a rapid expansion in industry.
7. He promised me I know he promised that he would come to my graduation.
8. Do you know what the French expression déjà vu means?
9. She wanted to go to the movies he decided to stay home and see an old film on his new videocassette recorder.
10. She has the qualifications needed for the job a teaching degree, a pleasant personality, two years' experience, and a love of children.

Other marks of punctuation

In each of the following sentences, insert marks of punctuation wherever they are needed.

1. Many young people have two feelings about science and technology awe and fear.
2. The three people who helped work out the real estate transaction were Mr. Doyle, the realtor Mrs. White, the bank officer and Scott Castle, the lawyer.
3. The book was entitled English Literature The Victorian Age.
4. I decided to walk to school, she said, because the bus fare has been raised again.
5. She brought the following items to the beach a bathing suit, towel, sunglasses, and several books.
6. The conference I believe it is scheduled for sometime in January will focus on the development of a new curriculum.
7. The song Memories comes from the Broadway show Cats.
8. The complex lab experiment has these two major problems too many difficult calculations and too many variables.
9. The mutt that is to say my dog is smarter than he looks.
10. Violent crime cannot be reduced unless the society supports efforts such as strengthening the family structure, educating the young, and recruiting top-notch police.

EXERCISE 12   Other marks of punctuation

In each of the following sentences, supply marks of punctuation wherever they are needed.

1. Star Wars is the popular term for the development of atomic weapons for use in space.
2. Remember, the doctor told the patient, the next time I see you I want to see an improvement in your condition.
3. The student's short story Ten Steps to Nowhere appeared in a collection entitled The Best of Student Writing.
4. The report stated specifically that the company must if it wanted to grow sell off at least ten percent of its property.
5. The foreign countries she visited were Mexico, Israel, and Morocco.
6. My father enjoyed spending money my mother was frugal.
7. These students made the high honor roll David Hyatt, Julie Carlson, and Erica Lane.
8. The scientist showed the class a glass of H_2O water and asked them to identify the liquid.
9. He said that he would give us an extension on our term papers.
10. The work was tedious nevertheless, the goal of finding the solution kept him motivated.

Mastery and editing tests

TEST 1   Editing for correct capitalization and punctuation

Read the following paragraph and insert the correct capitalization and marks of punctuation wherever they are needed.

will rogers 1879–1935 is often remembered as the cowboy philosopher. He was born on november 4 1879 on a ranch near oologah oklahoma. After two years in a military academy he left school and became a cowboy in the texas panhandle. Then he drifted off to argentina later he turned up in south africa as a member of texas jacks wild west circus. He was one of the best ropers of all times but his real talent was his ability as a writer. He became famous for his homespun humor and his shrewd timely comments on current events. his comments on the news appeared in 350 daily newspapers. He always began a performance by saying all I know is what I read in the papers. This saying became a byword in the 1920s. Rogers married betty blake an arkansas school teacher in 1908 and together they had four children. Although he started his motion picture career in 1918 it was not until 1934 that he made his first appearance in a stage play ah wilderness! by Eugene O'Neill. Unfortunately Rogers was killed the next year in a plane crash near Point Barrow Alaska on his way to the orient.

Editing for correct capitalization and punctuation

Read the following paragraph and insert the correct capitalization and marks of punctuation wherever they are needed.

Albert schweitzer was a brilliant german philosopher physician musician clergyman missionary and writer on theology. Early in his career he based his philosophy on what he called reverence for life. He felt a deep sense of obligation to serve mankind. His accomplishments as a humanitarian were great consequently he was awarded the nobel peace prize in 1952. Before Schweitzer was 30 he had won an international reputation as a writer on theology as an organist and authority on organ building as an interpreter of the works of Johann Sebastian Bach and as an authority on bachs life. When he became inspired to become a medical missionary he studied medicine at the university in strasbourg Germany. He began his work in french equatorial africa now called gabon in 1913 where his first consulting room was a chicken coop. Over the years he built a large hospital where thousands of Africans were treated yearly. He used his $33000 Nobel prize money to expand the hospital and set up a leper colony in fact he even designed all the buildings. One of Schweitzers many famous books which you might like to find in the library is entitled out of my life and thought. His accomplishments were so many music medicine scholarship theology and service to his fellow man.

Editing for correct capitalization and punctuation

Read the following paragraph and insert the correct capitalization and marks of punctuation wherever they are needed.

valentines day is celebrated on february 14 as a festival of romance and affection. People send their sweethearts greeting cards that ask won't you be my valentine? Children like to make their own valentines from paper doilies red construction paper bright foils and wallpaper samples. These customs probably came from an ancient roman festival called lupercalia which took place every february 15. The festival honored juno the roman goddess of women and marriage and pan the god of nature. Young men and women chose partners for the festival by drawing names by chance from a box. After exchanging gifts they often continued to enjoy each others company long after the festival and many were eventually married. After the spread of christianity churches tried to give christian meaning to the pagan festival. In the year 496 the pope changed the lupercalia festival of february 15 to saint valentines day on February 14 but the sentimental meaning of the old festival has remained to the present time. saint valentine is believed to be a priest who was jailed for aiding the persecuted christians. People believe he cured the jailkeepers daughter of blindness. According to the book popular antiquities which was written in 1877 people were observing this holiday in england as early as 1446. One account tells of young men wearing the names of their ladies on their sleeves for several days. The expression he wears his heart on his sleeve probably came from this custom. In the united states valentines day became popular in the 1800s at the time of the civil war. Many of the valentines of that period were hand painted and today their beautiful decorative qualities make them collectors items.

Working Together

Writing a Restaurant Review

What is your idea of the perfect job? Some people might think that eating out all the time and then writing reviews of the restaurants visited would be the perfect occupation.

Read this typical newspaper review of a neighborhood restaurant. The review contains certain important information that a reader would want to know, such as location, days and hours of operation, menu, atmosphere, price, and unique features.

Divide into groups. Together compose a restaurant review. (It would be nice if your group could actually go to the eatery you choose to write about.) First, decide what factors should be considered for the review. Each person should have fifteen minutes to compose his or her part of the review. Allow half an hour at the end to put the parts together and to decide on an introduction and a conclusion to the review.

Portfolio Suggestion

Keep this review in your portfolio. Keep in mind that whenever you eat out, attend a concert, or visit a museum, these are places that reviewers go and write their critiques. You can, too!

DINING OUT

If you appreciate authentic Chinese food, you should go for lunch or dinner to the Golden Fortune Restaurant, located at 99 Elm Avenue in Ellington. It is just above the South Side Plaza, walking distance from the center of town. The Golden Fortune Restaurant is the kind of restaurant you will want to visit more than once. The food is expertly prepared, the prices are very moderate, and the service is always friendly. We particularly liked the warm and relaxed atmosphere, partly the result of soft classical music playing in the background.

Many of the lunch and dinner selections at the Golden Fortune are traditional, with a few surprises. All of the vegetables used are fresh, and there is a choice of white or brown rice. The appetizers are large enough to serve two people. On our first visit, we were delighted with the combination platter. It is the most popular appetizer on the menu because it allows diners to sample a half dozen of the house specialties.

One unique touch at this restaurant is the choice of 24 different teas. Instead of the ordinary pot of green tea that is placed in front of you in most Chinese restaurants, at the Golden Fortune you have a wide variety to choose from. These include green tea with passion fruit, peach tea, or even milk tea with oatmeal. Customers enjoy trying new combinations each time they visit. Our favorite is the black tea with plum. If you like, you may bring your own wine or beer, and the waiters will be happy to serve it.

Some of the most popular main courses are beef with garlic sauce, crispy honey chicken on a bed of rice and vegetables, and a variety of delicious stir-fry dishes. If you choose a stir-fry at the Golden Fortune, you may select a favorite sauce and type of noodle along with a meat or fish, and the kitchen will make up the dish you want.

The Golden Fortune is open for lunch from noon to 4 P.M. and for dinner from 5 P.M. until 11 P.M. every day of the week. No reservations are needed. For take out orders, call 548-4407 after 11 A.M.

Review: Using All You Have Learned

Revising more fragments and run-ons

By now, you have learned to recognize the basic fragment or run-on error in your writing. You have worked with revising fairly uncomplicated sentences so that they are correct.

This chapter presents sentences that are more complicated. Even though a sentence may have more than one dependent clause and several phrases, you must always remember that the sentence must have an independent clause with a subject and verb. For example:

> When my family finally went on a vacation which was to take us across Canada by train, we never guessed that my two younger brothers would come down with the chicken pox on the second day.

Cross out all dependent clauses and phrases. Can you find the independent clause? What is the subject? What is the verb? *We never guessed* is the independent clause. All other parts of the sentence are dependent clauses that include many prepositional phrases.

The following exercises require mastery of all the skills you have learned in this unit on the sentence. See if you can now revise these more complicated sentences to rid them of fragments and run-ons.

EXERCISE 1 **Correcting more fragments and run-ons**

Read each example. If you think the example is a complete sentence, place a C beside the number of the sentence. If you think the example is not correct, revise it so that the sentence is complete. Use the methods you have studied for coordination and subordination.

1. Dinner in India is an experience that Western people find very strange things we take for granted are not always available there.

   _____

   _____

2. Whenever you eat an Indian meal you are not given anything to drink it is not considered appropriate to drink a beverage with a meal.

   _____

   _____

3. Indian food is eaten with the right hand, you pick up a piece of bread or some rice and scoop up some food.

   _____

   _____

4. However, when water for rinsing the fingers is given to you at the end of the meal.

   _____

   _____

5. Because Indian food is so spicy and there are so many different pickles and relishes that are served with nearly every meal.

   _____

   _____

6. Indians serve plain yogurt with their meals in order to comfort the mouth after spicy foods have been eaten.

   _____

   _____

7. The habit of chewing betel leaves and betel nuts aiding digestion and sweeten the breath.

   _____

   _____

8. Breakfast in India, unlike breakfast in the United States.

   _____

   _____

9. For breakfast, people in India eat dishes of rice and lentils in addition a special lentil soup is part of their first meal of the day.

   _____

   _____

10. Often trying different kinds of food but sometimes thinking the best meal of all is a good juicy steak.

_____

_____

Correcting more complicated fragments and run-ons

Read each example. If you think the example is a complete sentence, place a C beside the number of the sentence. If you think the example is not correct, revise it so that the sentence is complete. Use the methods you have studied for coordination and subordination.

1. Because the Golden Gate Bridge has been freshly painted with a color that blends beautifully with the color of the sunset.

_____

_____

2. The roses which are in full bloom in Golden Gate Park.

_____

_____

3. On Fisherman's Wharf, a few men are sitting together talking about the days when the fish were plentiful they caught so many that they thought the supply would never run out.

_____

_____

_____

4. Some people, thinking that the famous cable cars of San Francisco are noisier now that they have been repaired.

_____

_____

5. If you visit San Francisco and you are planning some trips into the surrounding countryside.

_____

_____

6. The city itself has cable cars as well as buses and trolleys, they make up one of the easiest-to-use public transportation systems in the country.

_____

_____

7. San Francisco is an easy place to see two or three days will permit you to enjoy most of the city's highlights.

_____

_____

8. On a weekend everyone trying to see Fisherman's Wharf, Nob Hill, the Union Square shopping district, and North Beach.

_____

_____

9. You should take a tour of the famous Alcatraz prison where convicts once spent many years behind bars now tourists walk at leisure.

_____

_____

10. For a taste of the local history, you could visit Fort Point, a fortress built during the Civil War to guard the entrance to the bay.

_____

_____

Editing sentences for errors

In the following exercises, you will find all types of sentence problems that you have studied in Step 2. If you think an example is correct, mark it with a *C*. If you think there is an error, correct the error so that the sentence is correct.

Major sentence errors

Fragments

Run-ons

Incorrect punctuation

Sentence parts that do not work together

EXERCISE 3   **Editing sentences for errors**

The following examples contain sentence errors studied in Step 2. If you think an example is a complete and correct sentence, mark it with a *C*. If the example has errors, correct them. An example has been done for you.

Incorrect: A group of Gypsies who now live in Ireland.

Correct: A group of Gypsies now live in Ireland.

or

A group of Gypsies, who now live in Ireland, make their living by repairing pots and pans.

1. Gypsies now living in many countries of the world.

_____

_____

2. The international community of scientists agree that these Gypsies originally came from India thousands of years ago. (Hint: Look at subject and verb.)

_____

_____

3. After the original Gypsies left India they went to Persia there they divided into groups.

_____

_____

4. One branch of Gypsies went west to Europe the other group decided to go east.

_____

_____

5. In the middle ages 476–1453 some gypsies lived in a fertile area of greece called little egypt.

_____

_____

6. Gypsies often found it hard to gain acceptance in many countries. Because of their wandering lifestyle.

_____

_____

7. Although the Gypsies needed the protection from the pope in Rome.

_____

_____

8. In the year 1418 when large bands of Gypsies passed through Hungary and Germany where the emperor offered them his protection.

_____

_____

9. Between the fifteenth and eighteenth centuries, every country of Europe had Gypsies however not every one of those countries enjoyed having them as guests.

_____

_____

10. Today Gypsy families may be found from Canada to Chile living much as his ancestors did thousands of years ago.

_____

_____

Editing sentences for errors

The following examples contain sentence errors studied in Step 2. If you think the example is a complete and correct sentence, mark it with a C. If the example has errors, correct them. An example has been done for you.

Incorrect: Most of us buy our food in stores, people in more than one part of the world still hunt for their food.

Correct: While most of us buy our food in stores, people in more than one part of the world still hunt for their food.

1. For the eskimos of alaska, hunting for whales are important for the economy of the people.

   _____

   _____

2. One of the most respected members of the Eskimo community.

   _____

   _____

3. In the spring, the Eskimos who know that the whaling season is about to begin set up camps to prepare for the hunt.

   _____

   _____

4. The arrival of some Eskimos from faraway places just to be present at the hunt.

   _____

   _____

5. Children are excused from school for as long as six weeks they help with the work of the camp.

   _____

   _____

6. While the men go out in their boats, the women and children stay in camp cooking meals and to take care of the dog teams.

   _____

   _____

7. Sometimes a period of several days go by with no success for the boat crews.

   _____

   _____

8. Eventually, the people in the camps hear the shouts of the boat crews a whale has been caught.

   _____

   _____

9. Eskimos use every part of the captured whales the blubber is used for fuel, the meat is eaten, and the internal organs are fed to the dogs.

   _____

   _____

10. Because the Eskimos are careful hunters and only kill what they use.

    _____

    _____

Editing sentences for errors

The following examples contain sentence errors studied in Step 2. If you think an example is a complete and correct sentence, mark it with a C. If the example has errors, correct them. An example has been done for you.

Incorrect: Although there are many tricks that we would like to teach our pets.

Correct: Although there are many tricks that we would like to teach our pets, few of us have the time and patience required for a training program.

1. Porpoises also known as dolphins are amazing animals.

_____

_____

2. Porpoises are known for the following tricks they can play baseball and basketball jump through hoops ring bells and raise flags.

_____

_____

3. Porpoises are able to use a kind of radar to find objects it cannot see.

_____

_____

4. The wonderful ability of porpoises to imitate human speech.

_____

_____

5. A movie and a television series with a real porpoise named flipper.

_____

_____

6. Trained porpoises now do tricks for thousands of people, who are in zoos and marinelands from Florida to Hawaii.

_____

_____

7. Because they like to ride in the waves made by the boat.

_____

_____

8. The first step in training a porpoise is to observe their natural behavior.

_____

_____

9. Porpoises have always been helpful and friendly toward humans indeed stories of their good relationships with people go back thousands of years.

_____

_____

10. If you throw a ball to a porpoise he will probably throw it back to you.

_____

_____

Editing a student essay

Read the essay through once for meaning. Then return to the beginning and read each sentence carefully to analyze its parts. Look for sentence level errors and word level errors. The margins show editing and correction symbols to help you locate problems. See the inside back cover for the explanation of these symbols.

Batman Will Always Get the Bad Man

1st 3 sentences
are choppy.

wc, p

sp,

~, t

Television shows can be teaching guides for parents. Television shows can help portray ideas. Good versus evil has been a topic for many generations. Shows such as Batman and Superman demonstrate this idea. The idea that you can be anything you want to be is represented on the show "Dr. Quin, Medicine Woman". "Bonanza" is a show that also demonstrated certain ideals.

Combine these
two sentences.

Batman and Superman are characters that have been on television for many years. The significance of their success is not that they have super powers. Their success is that they have taught us good can prevail. Batman and Super-man have seen the big screen (movies) and the small screen (television). Series after series have used them. These characters have been revised many times.

Frag

Their costumes made to fit the new styles. The character has not been altered. They both have been heroes and role models for children.

Sp

Sp, p, t, p, t

awk, t

t

apos, t

t

t, p

p

"Dr. Quin, Medicine Woman" is a fairly new show to television. It portrays a women who beat the odds, and became a doctor. The era, in which she lived, said she was supposed to be a homemaker. Her desire was to be a doctor, and she achieved it. After she became a doctor, the townsmen were against her practice because it did not conform to societies standards. She proved that if you put your mind to it, you can succeed. As a parent, this should be an idea you want portrayed to your children. This show has also portrayed the injustices of society. One episode was on prejudice, and how wrong it is. This show has dealt with many aspects of life, and is a good learning tool for children.

"Bonanza" is a program that has taught many lessons. This show is   *t*

about a man and his three sons. The man, Ben Cartwright, is a widower. His

three sons Adam, the oldest; Hoss, the middle child; and Little Joe, his   *Frag*

youngest son. They are living in the gunslinger days. On one episode, Ben was

shot. His three sons all were out to get the man they suspected for it. Each   *~, wf,*

child had a different suspect. The kids were out looking for their man. Each boy   *wc, t*

found their man. When they found their man, they were faced with the idea of   *choppy, agr*

killing him. They wrestled with the idea of hurting someone who hurt their   *agr, wc*

father. They each believed their father was dead. Should they kill another   *agr, wdy*

because of what he did or did not do? They faced this argument. Adam and Hoss   *log, wc*

quickly decided they could not kill another. Little Joe, a hot-headed boy pointed,

a riffle at the man. With his finger poised on the trigger and the gun cocked,   *sp*

he could not pull the trigger. He to could not justify killing the man. This   *sp*

show displayed the ability to control ones self. Every child young and old can   *wc, sp*

relate and learn from this idea.

Many shows on television have had an impact on our children. They can

teach us values and morals. In many ways, shows have told stories the ancients

have been handing down for years. The only thing to be aware of is the shows   *wc*

that degrade the values and morals. I believe TV can be a useful tool in edu-   *no abbr*

cating and entertaining children. If one monitors TV shows that their children   *agr, abbr*

watch, the TV can be a great tool. TV shows with good moral and values will   *abbr, wf*

live for ever because they are worth watching. So, Mr. Ed will always make good   *sp*

horse sense. Batman and Superman will always save the day.

by Patricia Britt

Working Together

Composing a Test as a Joint Effort

The class should divide into two or more groups. Each group will create an exam that reviews the most important lessons learned so far in your course. Your group must first decide on a plan. Take the following points into consideration:

1. You might decide to give each person in the group a certain chapter or topic to cover. This person would be responsible for developing a specified number of questions on that chapter or topic.

2. Tests can use a variety of types of test questions such as multiple choice, fill in the blank, true/false, short answer, editing, or essay questions. What types of questions does your group think will be best for this test?

3. How many questions will there be and how will you distribute the points? (For example, 25 questions of four points each would add up to 100%.)

4. How much time will each person have to write his or her test questions?

5. When you come together afterwards, everyone will need to read over all the test items for final approval from members of the group. You will undoubtedly have some questions that need more work. Are there any directions needed?

6. Will one group member be willing to set up the test on the computer and print out enough copies for the entire class?

When the tests are copied, the groups should exchange tests. Students can take the test either in class or as a homework assignment.

Portfolio Suggestion

Keep a copy of the tests developed by the class. Write a reaction to the experiences of both developing a test and taking a test. Consider the following issues:

1. Were the questions in the tests too easy or too hard?

2. Was the distribution of points fair?

3. Was there a variety of activities in the test or were the questions all of the same type? Why should it matter if there are a variety of types of test questions or not?

4. Were the directions clear?

5. What is the value of making a test as a way of reviewing material?

6. What are the problems in making a fair test?

CHAPTER 13

Choosing Words That Work

S
T
E
P

3

Using words rich in meaning

Writing is a constant search to find the right word to express thoughts and feelings as accurately as possible. When a writer wants to be precise or wants to give a flavor to a piece of writing, the creative possibilities are almost endless for word choice and sentence construction. The creative writer looks for words that have rich and appropriate meanings and associations.

For instance, if you were describing a young person under five years of age, you might choose one of these words:

imp	brat	preschooler
toddler	tot	youngster
child		

Some words have no associations beyond their strict dictionary meaning. These words are said to be neutral. Which word in the list is the most neutral, with the least negative or positive emotional associations?* The person who is writing a brochure for a nursery school would probably choose the word *preschooler* because it identifies the age of the child. A person talking about a child who has just learned to walk would possibly use the word *toddler* because it carries the association of a small child who is toddling along a bit unsteadily. What informal and unkind word might an angry older sibling shout when a younger brother or sister has just colored all over a favorite book?†

---

* Your answer should be *child.*
† Your answer to the second question should be *brat.*

EXERCISE 1 **Using words rich in meaning**

The five words in Column A all have the basic meaning of *thin*. For each word, however, an additional meaning makes the word richer and more specific. Match each word in Column A with the letter of the definition from Column B that best fits the meaning of the word.

Column A

_____ 1. slender

_____ 2. emaciated

_____ 3. lean

_____ 4. skinny

_____ 5. gaunt

Column B

a. unattractively thin

b. thin and bony with a haggard appearance

c. gracefully long and slim

d. containing little fat, in shape, fit

e. extremely thin, undernourished, and sickly

Most languages are rich with words that describe eating. Column A contains a few English words about eating. Match each word in Column A with the letter of the definition from Column B that best fits the meaning of the word.

Column A

_____ 1. taste

_____ 2. devour

_____ 3. nibble

_____ 4. gorge

_____ 5. gnaw

_____ 6. snack

Column B

a. to eat with small quick bites

b. to bite or chew on something persistently

c. to eat between meals

d. to test the flavor of a food

e. to stuff oneself with food

f. to eat up greedily

EXERCISE 2 **Using words rich in meaning**

The words *eat*, *drink*, *hit*, or *walk* are common neutral words. Underneath each neutral term are four words, each one having its own more precise meaning. In each case, give a definition for each word.

Example: crunch—to eat with a noisy crackling sound

to eat

1. gobble _____

2. savor _____

3. munch _____

4. chomp _____

to drink

1. sip _____

2. gulp _____

3. slurp _____

4. lap _____

to hit

1. swat _____

2. slap _____

3. paddle _____

4. flog _____

to walk

1. lumber _____

2. amble _____

3. stride _____

4. roam _____

Understanding loaded words: Denotation/connotation

The careful writer must consider more than the dictionary meaning of a word. Some words have different meanings for different people.

> The *denotation* of a word is its strict dictionary meaning.
>
> The *connotation* of a word is the meaning (apart from the dictionary meaning) that a person attaches to a word because of the person's personal experience with the word.
>
> **word:** liberal
>
> **denotation:** to favor nonrevolutionary progress or reform
>
> **possible connotations:** socially active, free thinking, too generous, far left, favoring many costly government programs

Politicians are usually experts in understanding the connotations of a word. They know, for instance, that if they want to get votes in a conservative area, they should not refer to their views as liberal. The strict dictionary meaning of *liberal* is "to favor nonrevolutionary progress or reform," certainly an idea that most people would support. However, when most people hear the words *liberal* or *conservative,* they bring to the words many political biases and experiences from their past: their parents' attitudes, the political and social history of the area in which they live, and many other factors that may correctly or incorrectly color their understanding of a word.

Choosing words that are not neutral but that have more exact or appropriate meanings is a powerful skill for your writing, one that will help your reader better understand the ideas you want to communicate. As your vocabulary grows, your writing will become richer and deeper. Your work will reflect your understanding of all the shades of meanings that words can have.

EXERCISE 3   **Denotation/connotation**

In this exercise you have the opportunity to think of words that are richer in associations than the neutral words that are underlined in the sentences below. Write your own word choice in the space to the right of each sentence. Discuss with others in your class the associations you make with the words you have chosen.

1. I live in a house at the edge of town.   _____

2. I walk home from work every night.   _____

3. Usually the same person is always walking
   behind me.   _____

4. She is always carrying a lot of stuff.   _____

5. She looks as if she is very old.   _____

6. She has marks all over her face.   _____

7. Sometimes I try to talk to her.   _____

8. She has such an unusual look in her eyes.   _____

9. Sometimes I can hear her talking to herself.   _____

10. At night when I am sitting in my favorite
    armchair, I often think of her and wish she could
    tell me the story of her life.   _____

EXERCISE 4   **Denotation/connotation**

The following sentences contain words that may have positive or negative associations for you. Read the sentences and study the underlined words. Below each sentence, write the emotional meaning the underlined words have for you. Discuss your answers with your classmates.

1. The dog stood at the door; his size was quite astounding.

   _____

   _____

2. The foreigner approached the ranch slowly.

   _____

   _____

3. His pick-up truck was parked in front.

   _____

   _____

4. A woman and child were peering out from behind the stained glass window.

   _____

   _____

5. The stranger carried a long object of some kind.

   _____

   _____

Your instructor may ask you to rewrite these sentences. If you do, change each sentence so that there is no chance to make a negative association or feel a sense of threat. In order to give a different emotional tone to the sentences, you may change the actual word or add adjectives or phrases to modify the word. Words have the power to arouse people when there may be no intent to inflame such sentiments.

Wordiness: In writing, less can be more!

In his book *The Elements of Style*, the famous writer E.B. White quotes his old teacher William Strunk, Jr. who said that a sentence "should contain no unnecessary words" and a paragraph "no unnecessary sentences." Strunk's philosophy of writing also includes the commandment he gave many times in his class at Cornell University, "Omit needless words!" It was a lesson that E.B. White took to heart, with wonderful results that we see in his own writing.

Below is a summary of some important ways you can cut the actual number of your words in order to strengthen the power of your ideas. As you read each example of wordiness, notice how the revision has cut out unnecessary words.

Wordy Expressions	Revision
1. Avoid redundancy.	
circle around	circle
blue in color	blue
past history	history
connect together	connect
true fact	fact
2. Avoid wordy phrases.	
in the event that	if
due to the fact that	because
for the stated reason that	because
in this day and age	today
at this point in time	now
in the neighborhood of	about
3. Avoid overuse of the verb *to be*.	
The man is in need of help.	The man needs help.
4. Avoid repeating the same word too many times.	
The book is on the table. The book is my favorite. I have read the book five times.	The book on the table is my favorite. I have read it five times.
5. Avoid beginning a sentence with *there is* or *it is* whenever possible.	
There are two major disadvantages to the new proposal.	The new proposal has two major disadvantages.

Wordy Expressions	Revision

6. Avoid flowery or pretentious language.

It is delightful to contemplate the culinary experience we will enjoy after the termination of this cinematic event.	I can't wait until we have pizza after the movie.

7. Avoid apologetic, tentative expressions.

In my opinion, the grading policy for this course should be changed.	The grading policy for this course should be changed.
Right now, it seems to me that finding a job in my field is very difficult.	Right now, finding a job in my field is very difficult
In this paper, I will try to explain my views on censorship of the campus newspaper.	Censoring the campus newspaper is a mistake.

EXERCISE 5   Revising wordy sentences

For each of the following sentences, underline the part that is unnecessarily wordy, and on the line below revise the sentence.

1. The date for the final completion of your project is May 18.

    _____

    _____

2. The thought of the exam is causing her to be in a constant state of tension.

    _____

    _____

3. There is no better place to study than in our library.

    _____

    _____

4. Some people have the belief that astrology is a science.

    _____

    _____

5. We are all in a need of better organizational skills.

    _____

    _____

6. As far as mechanical ability is concerned, Mike is very handy.

    _____

    _____

7. She is in the process of cooking dinner.

    _____

    _____

8. Due to the fact of the rain, the game will be cancelled.

   _____

   _____

9. In my opinion, it would seem to me that the reasons for unemployment are complex.

   _____

   _____

10. The box had an oblong shape.

    _____

    _____

Revising wordy sentences

EXERCISE 6

For each of the following sentences, underline the part that is unnecessarily wordy, and on the line below revise the sentence.

1. The gentleman is of a kindly nature.

   _____

   _____

2. I was told he is a male actor.

   _____

   _____

3. The price was in the neighborhood of fifty dollars.

   _____

   _____

4. In regard to the letter, it was sent to the wrong address.

   _____

   _____

5. It is everyone's duty to be in attendance at the meeting today.

   _____

   _____

6. My best friend is above me in height.

   _____

   _____

7. I tiptoed down the stairs on my toes in order to surprise everyone.

   _____

   _____

8. They made the discovery that I was not upstairs.

   _____

   _____

9. A member of the teaching staff at this institution of higher learning failed to submit in a timely fashion the fruits of my endeavors for the course during this entire period from September to December.

_____

_____

10. Even though I am not an expert, I think that more neighborhood health clinics are needed.

_____

_____

Recognizing appropriate language for formal writing

In speaking or writing to our family and friends, an informal style is always appropriate because it is relaxed and conversational. On the other hand, writing and speaking in school or at work requires a more formal style, one that is less personal and more detached in tone. In formal writing situations, slang is not appropriate and any use of language that is seen as sexist or disrespectful to any individual or groups of individuals is not at all acceptable.

> *Slang* is a term that refers to a special word or expression that a particular group of people use, often with the intention of keeping the meaning to themselves. A characteristic of a slang word or expression is that it is often used only for a limited period of time and then is forgotten. For example:
>
> The party was *grand*. (1940s)
>
> The party was *awesome*. (1990s)

Slang or informal words	Acceptable
bucks	dollars
kids	children
cops	police
a bummer	a bad experience
off the wall	crazy
yummy	delicious
chow	food

> **Clipped language** is the use of shortened words to make communication more relaxed and informal. Clipped language is not appropriate usage in more formal writing, which requires standard English.

Clipped language	Acceptable
doc	doctor
fridge	refrigerator
pro	professional
t.v.	television

Sexist language is the use of single gender nouns or pronouns to refer to both men and women. This was standard usage in the past, but writers and publishers today avoid such language.

Sexist: Everyone must bring *his* project on Tuesday.

Three options for revising a sentence with sexist language:

1. Revise the sentence using plural pronouns and plural antecedents.

   All students must bring *their* projects on Tuesday.

2. Change the pronoun to an article.

   Everyone must bring *the* project on Tuesday.

3. Change the sentence into the passive.

   All projects must be brought to class on Tuesday.

Sexist language	Acceptable
fireman	firefighter
mailman	mail carrier
stewardess	flight attendant
common man	average person
actress	actor
mankind	humanity
The teacher is an important man. He can influence the lives of many children in the community.	Teachers are important people. They can influence the lives of many children in a community.

Trite expressions (or clichés) are those expressions which may have been fresh at one time but now have become stale from overuse.

Trite expressions	Acceptable
cool as a cucumber	calm
mad as a hornet	angry
a golden opportunity	an exceptional opportunity
blind as a bat	blind
busy as a bee	busy
dead as a doornail	dead
slowly but surely	gradually
without rhyme or reason	senseless

EXERCISE 7   **Recognizing inappropriate language for formal writing**

The following sentences contain words that are informal, slang, or sexist. Circle the word in each sentence that is inappropriate for formal writing, and on the line to the right of each sentence, provide a more formal word or expression to replace the informal word.

1. Melanie brought her box along to the party for some music. _____

2. She told her friends to chill out. _____

3. The entire evening turned out to be a bummer. _____

4. The businessmen in the community support the science project. _____

5. The time has come to level with the director. _____

6. The first experiment turned out to be a downer. _____

7. The scientist has guts to continue the research. _____

8. The entire lab is a dump. _____

9. The guys often spend the night there. _____

10. They work until two or three in the morning and then crash. _____

EXERCISE 8   **Recognizing inappropriate language for formal writing**

The following sentences contain words that are informal, slang, or sexist. Circle the word in each sentence that is inappropriate for formal writing, and on the line to the right of each sentence, provide a more formal word or expression to replace the informal word.

1. Don't bug me about studying. _____

2. I aced the last French test. _____

3. Bring me some grub tonight. _____

4. He's my buddy. _____

5. What's the lousy weather like outside? _____

6. That idea doesn't grab me just right. _____

7. I still have a crush on that intern. _____

8. The medical doctor is a well-respected person in most communities; he is considered a role model for our children. _____

9. I think it's gonna be nice tomorrow. _____

10. I ain't seen the new neighbors yet. _____

Studying a student essay for word choices

Making better word choices

When Sandra Russell wrote an essay on the experience of living through a tornado, she composed more than one draft. Below are six sentences that the student could have written when she worked on the first draft of her essay.

Rewrite each of the sentences. Your revisions could include different word choices or added words, phrases, and clauses that make the sentences more descriptive and interesting.

1. All afternoon clouds were getting dark.

   _____

   _____

2. I could see lightning and hear thunder.

   _____

   _____

3. She took my hand and took me to the storm cellar.

   _____

   _____

4. We sat in the cellar.

   _____

   _____

5. Stuff lay around our yard.

   _____

   _____

6. The storm came through my neighborhood destroying lots of property.

   _____

   _____

Sharing sentence revisions

Now, share your revised sentences with other members of your class. For each of the six sentences, write three revised examples on the board for the class to review.

Working with a student essay

Next, read the complete student essay out loud. Following the reading, search through the essay to discover how Sandra Russell expressed these six ideas that you have revised. Underline each of the six sentences as you find them. Discuss with class members how these ideas were successfully expressed by the student writer.

Bad Weather

I was born in Booneville, Arkansas, and grew up on a small farm about five miles south of Paris. Naturally, I grew up in an area where tornados are feared each spring. I didn't really understand this until one humid, still night in April of 1985.

All afternoon, dark threatening clouds had been building up in the west, blocking out the sun. I could see the lightning dance about the sky, as the thunder responded by shaking the ground beneath my feet. The wind softly stirred the tree tops but then quickly died as it got darker and darker.

I walked outside and listened to the silence ringing in my ears. In the distance I could hear a rumble, soft at first but slowly and steadily intensifying. My mom came outside and stood at my side and listened to the rumbling noise. Everything was still, nothing dared to move. Even my dog Moose lay quietly, as if punished, in his doghouse. It was almost as if he knew what was about to happen.

"Mama, what's that noise?" I asked her, but she didn't answer. She grabbed my hand and dragged me to the storm cellar. I didn't have time to argue with her before I heard the rumble nearly upon us. We huddled in the musty smelling cellar. The roar was so loud it hurt my ears. I could hear the whistling of the wind above us. I cried and screamed for the awful noise of the whistle to stop, but no one could hear me above the ferocious noise. The rumble barreled on us and it seemed as if it would never end. The air was still in the dark cellar, but I could hear it as it moved violently above our heads. I didn't think the thundering noise would ever end.

I hadn't realized that I had quit breathing until it finally stopped. I drew a quick breath and thanked God it was over and my mother and I were safe. We crawled out of the cellar and took the first real look at our home. Trees were uprooted. Glass and boards and even a stop sign lay scattered around our yard. The roof on our house was damaged and a few windows were broken out, but that was all. Even most of our animals we had survived that day, including Moose.

That night I'll never forget. A moderately sized tornado (about an F3 on the Fujita scale) ripped through my neighborhood, destroying ten houses and damaging fifty others. No tornado warnings were issued for that area until ten minutes after it was already over, but still no one was seriously injured. The local television station didn't even bother to comment on their mistake. Until that night I never realized that something could happen that could change the way you feel about something for the rest of your life. I look at the television and see the tornado, hurricane, and even flood victims with new eyes. They are real, just like me.

by Sandra Russell

Mastery and editing tests

Editing for wordiness

Below is an introductory paragraph of five sentences, taken from a student essay. Find the example of wordiness in each sentence of the paragraph and correct it as you rewrite the paragraph.

In this paragraph, I am going to try to name some of the earliest Spanish settlements in the New World. In 1513, for example, an event of considerable magnitude took place in Florida when Ponce de Leon landed there. In a similar exploratory fashion, Hernando de Soto landed in the same area in 1539. Florida has become noteworthy for another reason: it is the site, at St. Augustine, of the oldest permanent settlement in the United States. All explorers in those days had to be of a courageous nature, but Spanish explorers were especially brave because they were among the first to set foot in the New World.

_____

_____

_____

_____

_____

_____

_____

_____

Editing for inappropriate language

Each sentence in the following paragraph contains an example of inappropriate language. Rewrite the paragraph revising all language to be acceptable as formal writing.

When my sis was hired by a major electronics company last summer, we were a little worried about her. She had flunked math in school, so we wondered if she had chosen the right kind of company. The person who had the job before her was let go because he had an attitude. Imagine our surprise when she soon announced that she had been selected chairman of an important committee at work. She said that she really didn't want to be in a leadership position, but we all knew she was nuts about it.

_____

_____

_____

_____

_____

_____

_____

Working Together

Being Tactful in the Workplace

Words are charged with meanings that can be encouraging and supportive or hurtful and wounding. Although workers in government buildings and other public places are there to help the public, they often are so overwhelmed or overworked that they do not always respond in a positive way. Below are seven comments that might be heard in an office where a person has gone to get help. In each case, revise the language so that the comment is more encouraging.

a. I don't have any idea what you're talking about.

_____

_____

b. Why don't you learn to write so people can read it?

_____

_____

c. We don't accept sloppy applications.

_____

_____

d. How old are you anyway?

_____

_____

e. Can't you read directions?

_____

_____

f. What's the matter with you? Why can't you understand this simple procedure?

_____

_____

g. I don't have time today for people like you!

_____

_____

Share some of these revisions with each other. Then, as a class, discuss some of your individual experiences involving incidents where the use of language made you or someone you know feel hurt or upset. You may remember incidents from a campus office, a local bank, or a local shop. How could a change of language have made the situation better?

Portfolio Suggestion

Using the Working Together activity and using class discussion, write on one of the following:

- The importance of using polite language in the workplace. (You can use the examples given during classroom discussion.)

- Advice to employers on training their employees how to speak to people on the job.

- The difficulty workers have because many customers or clients are rude. (If you have had a job, you may have examples of some of these experiences. How did you deal with the situation?)

Paying Attention to Look-Alikes and Sound-Alikes

Many words are confusing because they either sound alike or look alike, but they are spelled differently and have different meanings. Master the words in each group before proceeding to the next group. The first column lists the word, the second column gives the definition, and the third column gives a sentence using the word correctly.

Group I: Words that sound alike

1. **aural/oral**

aural	related to hearing	The child has *aural* nerve damage.
oral	related to the mouth	The student wrote an *oral* report.

2. **buy/by**

buy (verb)	to purchase	He hopes to *buy* a car.
by (prep.)	near; past; not later than	Let's meet *by* the clock. They drive *by* my house every morning. Please arrive *by* six o'clock.

3. **capital/capitol**

capital (adj.)	major; fatal	He made a *capital* improvement on his home. The governor opposes *capital* punishment.

capital (noun)	leading city; money	The *capital* (city) of Wyoming is Cheyenne. The retailer has *capital* to invest.
capitol	a legislative building	The dome of the state *capitol* (building) is gold.

4. close/clothes

close	to shut	*Close* the door.
clothes	garments	The *clothes* were from the GAP.

Note: Cloth is a piece of fabric, not to be confused with clothes, which is always plural.

5. coarse/course

coarse (adj.)	rough; common or of inferior quality	He told a *coarse* joke. The coat was made from a *coarse* fabric.
course (noun)	direction; part of a meal; a unit of study	What is the *course* of the spaceship? The main *course* of the meal was served. This is a required *course*.

6. complement/compliment

complement (noun)	something that completes	The library has a full *complement* of books.
(verb)	to complete	Her shoes *complement* the outfit.
compliment (noun)	an expression of praise	The chef received a *compliment*.
(verb)	to praise	He *complimented* the chef.

7. forward/foreword

forward	to send on to another address; moving toward the front or the future; bold	Please *forward* my mail. He took one step *forward*. She is very *forward* when she speaks.
foreword	introduction to a book	Read the *foreword* first.

8. passed/past

passed (verb)	moved ahead	She *passed* the test.
past (noun)	time before the present	Don't live in the *past*.
past (prep.)	beyond	He walked *past* the house.
past (adj.)	no longer current	This *past* year has been cold.

9. plain/plane

plain (adj.)	ordinary; clear	His *plain* clothing was of good quality. We appreciated the *plain* directions.
plain (noun)	flat land without trees	They crossed the *plain* by covered wagon.

| plane | an aircraft; a flat, level surface; a carpenter's tool for leveling wood; a level of development | 159 passengers were on the *plane*. The *planes* of the crystal shone. A carpenter's *plane* and saw are needed. They think on a different *plane*. |

10. presence/presents

| presence | the state of being present; a person's manner | His *presence* is needed. She has a wonderful *presence*. |
| presents | gifts | The child's birthday *presents* were many. |

Group 1 words

EXERCISE 1

Fill in the blanks in each of the following sentences by choosing the correct word to complete that sentence.

1. When I telephoned the doctor, he warned me that the _____ medicine
   (aural, oral)
   was to be used only in my child's ear; this medicine was not an _____
   (aural, oral)
   medicine.

2. _____ the time I arrived at the store, the sale was over and I could not
   (Buy, By)
   _____ what I needed.
   (buy, by)

3. The senators met in Athens, the _____ of Greece, to discuss the ques-
   (capital, capitol)
   tion of _____ punishment.
   (capital, capitol)

4. I hurried to bring several yards of wool _____ to the tailor, who
   (clothes, close, cloth)
   will make some new winter _____ for my family; I knew he would
   (clothes, close, cloth)
   _____ at five o'clock.
   (close, clothes, cloth)

5. I would have enjoyed the _____, but some of the students told
   (coarse, course)
   _____ jokes during every class.
   (coarse, course)

6. She always wears clothes that _____ each other, but she never
   (complement, compliment)
   expects a _____ .
   (complement, compliment)

7. I looked _____ to reading the new book so much that I read the
   (forward, foreword)
   _____ the very first day.
   (forward, foreword)

8. I have spent the _____ few days wondering if I _____ the exam.
   (passed, past)   (passed, past)

9. The storm had been raging over the _____ for hours when the
   (plain, plane)
   _____ suddenly went down.
   (plain, plane)

10. Each year the mayor always _____ an award as well as several lovely
    (presence, presents)
    _____ to outstanding members of the community.
    (presence, presents)

Group I words

Edit the following paragraph for word confusions. Circle the errors and write the correct words on the lines below the paragraph.

Wolfgang Mozart was a child star of the eighteenth century. At three years old, he could pick out chords and tunes on the piano. Buy age four, he was composing at the piano. As a musical genius, Mozart had an extremely well-developed oral sense. When Mozart was only six, he and his sister played before the emperor in Vienna, the capitol of Austria. The emperor paid Mozart a complement by having his portrait painted. Another one of the empress's presence was an embroidered suit of cloths. Throughout the coarse of his lifetime, Mozart wrote a good deal of church music, sonatas, operas, chamber music, and much more. Like many great artists of the passed, he was ahead of his time and thought on such a different plain that he was not fully appreciated in his own time. Today, Mozart is recognized as one of the greatest composers in all of history. You might be interested in reading a book of Mozart's letters which has been published in English. Be sure to read the forward.

_____   _____

_____   _____

_____   _____

_____   _____

Group II: Words that sound alike

1. principal/principle

principal (adj.)	most important; main	The *principal* dancer was superb. What is the *principal* reason for your decision?
principal (noun)	the head of a school; a sum of money	The *principal* of the school arrived late. The *principal* and interest on the loan were due.
principle (noun)	a rule or standard	He is a man of *principle*.

2. rain/reign/rein

rain	water falling to earth in drops	I'm singing in the *rain*.
reign	a period of rule for a king or queen	When was the *reign* of Henry the Eighth?
rein	a strap attached to a bridle, used to control a horse	I grabbed the pony's frayed *rein*.

3. **sight/site/cite**

sight	the ability to see; a view	His *sight* was limited. The Grand Canyon is an awesome *sight*.
site	the plot of land where something is located; the place for an event	Here is the *site* for the new courthouse.
cite	to quote as an authority or example	Please *cite* the correct law.

4. **stationary/stationery**

stationary (adj.)	standing still	He hit a *stationary* object.
stationery (noun)	writing paper and envelopes	She wrote the letter on her *stationery*.

5. **to/too/two**

to (prep.)	in a direction toward	We walked *to* the movies.
too (adv.)	also; very	We walked home *too*. The tickets were *too* expensive.
two	number	She has *two* children.

6. **vain/vane/vein**

vain	conceited; unsuccessful	He was attractive but *vain*. We made a *vain* attempt.
vane	an ornament which turns in the wind (often in the shape of a rooster and seen on tops of barns)	The weather *vane* pointed southwest.
vein	a blood vessel; the branching framework of a leaf; an area in the earth where a mineral like gold or silver is found; a passing attitude	The *veins* carry blood to the heart. The miner found a *vein* of silver. She spoke in a humorous *vein*.

7. **waist/waste**

waist	The middle portion of a body or garment	His *waist* was 36 inches around.
waste (verb)	to use carelessly	He *wasted* too much time watching television.
waste (noun)	discarded objects	The *waste* was put in the garbage.

8. **weather/whether**

weather (noun)	atmospheric conditions	The *weather* in Hawaii is gorgeous.
whether (conj.)	if it is the case that	I'll go *whether* or not I'm finished.

9. **whole/hole**

whole	complete	He ate the *whole* apple.
hole	an opening	I found a *hole* in the sock.

10. write/right/rite

write	to form letters and words; to compose	I will *write* a poem for your birthday.
right	correct	What is the *right* answer?
	to conform to justice, law, or morality	Trial by jury is a *right* under the law.
	toward a conservative point of view	The senator's position is to the *right*.
rite	a traditional, often religious ceremony	A birthday is a *rite* of passage.

EXERCISE 3   Group II words

Fill in the blanks in each of the following sentences by choosing the correct word to complete that sentence.

1. The _____ was respected because he would not compromise his one
   (principal, principle)
   fundamental _____ .
   (principal, principle)

2. The museum had on display a horse's _____ that dated from the
   (rain, reign, rein)
   _____ of Henry the Eighth.
   (rain, reign, rein)

3. You do not have to _____ statistics to convince me of the importance of
   (sight, site, cite)
   caring for my _____ .
   (sight, site, cite)

4. He bought the _____ from a clerk who said nothing and remained
   (stationary, stationery)
   _____ all the time behind the counter.
   (stationary, stationery)

5. I want _____ go _____ the movies, and I hope you do _____ .
   (to, too, two)   (to, too, two)   (to, too, two)

6. I could tell the actress was _____ when she kept hiding a long blue
   (vain, vane, vein)
   _____ on her leg.
   (vain, vane, vein)

7. It is a _____ of time to try and get him to admit the size of his _____ .
   (waist, waste)   (waist, waste)

8. We always listen to the _____ report _____ it's right
   (weather, whether)   (weather, whether)
   or wrong.

9. I am telling you the _____ story about the _____ in our new carpet.
   (whole, hole)   (whole, hole)

10. Every American has the _____ to participate in the religious
    (right, write, rite)
    _____ of his or her own choosing.
    (right, write, rite)

Group II words

Edit the following paragraph for word confusions. Circle the errors and write the correct words on the lines below the paragraph.

The dance performance I attended last weekend at our local community college was a spectacular site. The hole piece told the story of a queen who was so vein that she brought about her own downfall with her selfishness. The principle dancer who played the queen danced the part with remarkable sensitivity and grace. At first the queen was such an unlikable character: not only was she manipulative and greedy, but she felt it was her rite to put her own needs above all others. Yet by the end, one didn't know weather to hate her or pity her. Her subjects denounce the queen and storm the castle, to. The queen looks out at the chaos and realizes her rain is coming to an end. As she stands stationery in her room looking out of her window, she hears the many cries of her subjects who are determined to destroy her, and she realizes for the first time that it was her own vanity and selfishness that led to these sad events. The last moments of the piece show the queen dancing alone in her room. She wraps a black scarf around her waste as the curtain comes down.

_____   _____

_____   _____

_____   _____

_____   _____

_____   _____

Group III: Words that sound alike

1. it's/its

   | it's | contraction of *it is* | *It's* early. |
   | its | possessive pronoun | *Its* tail is short. |

2. they're/their/there

they're	contraction of *they are*	*They're* happy.
their	possessive pronoun	*Their* children are beautiful.
there	at that place	Look over *there*.

3. we're/were/where

we're	contraction of *we are*	*We're* happy.
were	past tense of *are*	They *were* happy.
where	at or in what place	*Where* are we?

4. who's/whose

   | who's | contraction of *who is* | *Who's* the author of this book? |
   | whose | possessive pronoun | *Whose* clothes are these? |

5. you're/your

you're   contraction of *you are*   *You're* the boss.

your   possessive pronoun   *Your* team has won.

Group III words

Fill in the blanks in each of the following sentences by choosing the correct word to complete that sentence.

1. _____ obvious that the car has lost _____ muffler.
   (It's, Its)   (it's, its)

2. The dog has no license, so _____ possible _____ owner doesn't care
   (it's, its)   (it's, its)
   about the dog very much.

3. When _____ in school, _____ parents work in the
   (they're, their, there)   (they're, their, there)
   restaurant_____ on the corner.
   (they're, their, there)

4. Now that _____ living in the country, _____ expenses
   (they're, their, there)   (they're, their, there)
   are not so great, so they might stay_____.
   (they're, their, there)

5. _____ hoping our friends _____ not hurt at the place
   (We're, Were, Where)   (we're, were, where)
   _____ the accident occurred.
   (we're, were, where)

6. _____ did the coupons go that _____ saving?
   (We're, Were, Where)   (we're, were, where)

7. _____ car is double-parked outside, and_____ going to move it?
   (Who's, Whose)   (who's, whose)

8. _____ the pitcher at the game today, and _____ glove will
   (Who's, Whose)   (who's, whose)
   he use?

9. When _____ a father,_____ free time is never guaranteed.
   (you're, your)   (you're, your)

10. Please give me _____ paper when _____ finished writing.
    (you're, your)   (you're, your)

Group III words

Edit the following paragraph for word confusions. Circle the errors and write the correct words on the lines below the paragraph.

    Psychologists tell us that laughter is found only among human beings. Of all the animals, were the only ones who laugh. Psychologists are interested in what makes people laugh, but so far there best explanations are only theories. From a physical point of view, your healthier if you laugh often. Its good for you're lungs. Its an outlet for extra energy. Among it's other effects are the release of anxieties and anger. The comedian, who's job depends on figuring out what makes people laugh, often pokes fun at the behavior of other people. However, a joke about New Jersey might not be funny in front of an audience of people who like living their. We're all familiar with jokes that are in bad taste. Its the purpose of jokes to make people conform to acceptable standards.

_____   _____
_____   _____
_____   _____
_____   _____
_____   _____

Group IV: Words that sound or look almost alike

1. **accept/except**

accept (verb)	to receive; to admit; to regard as true or right	I *accept* with pleasure. I *accept* responsibility. I *accept* your apology.
except (prep.)	other than, but	Everyone *except* me was ready.

2. **advice/advise**

advice (noun)	opinion as to what should be done about a problem	I need good *advice*.
advise (verb)	to suggest; to counsel	He *advised* me to take a different course.

3. **affect/effect**

affect (verb)	to influence; to change	Smoking will *affect* your health.
effect (noun)	result	The *effect* of the hurricane was evident.
(verb)	to bring about a result	The hurricane *effected* a devastating change in the community.

4. **breath/breathe**

breath (noun)	air that is inhaled or exhaled	You seem out of *breath*.
breathe (verb)	to inhale or exhale	Don't *breathe* in these fumes.

5. **choose/chose**

choose (present tense)	select	Today I *choose* the purple shirt.
chose (past tense)	selected	Yesterday I *chose* the red one.

6. **conscience/conscious/conscientious**

conscience	recognition of right and wrong	His *conscience* bothered him.
conscious	awake; aware of one's own existence	The patient was *conscious*.
conscientious	careful; thorough	The student was *conscientious* about doing her homework.

7. costume/custom

costume	a special style of dress for a particular occasion	The child wore a clown *costume* for Halloween.
custom	a common tradition	One *custom* at Thanksgiving is to serve turkey.

8. council/counsel/consul

council (noun)	a group that governs	The student *council* meets every Tuesday.
counsel (verb)	to give advice	Please *counsel* the arguing couple.
counsel (noun)	advice; a lawyer	The couple needs *counsel*. The prisoner has requested *counsel*.
consul	a government official in the foreign service	He was appointed a *consul* by the president.

9. desert/dessert

desert (verb)	to abandon	Don't *desert* me now.
desert (noun)	barren land	The cactus flowers on the *desert* are beautiful.
dessert	last part of a meal, often sweet	We had apple pie for *dessert*.

10. diner/dinner

diner	a person eating dinner; a restaurant with a long counter and booths	The *diner* waited for her check. I prefer a booth at the *diner*.
dinner	main meal of the day	What is for *dinner*?

EXERCISE 7   Group IV words

Fill in the blanks in each of the following sentences by choosing the correct word to complete that sentence.

1. The judge refused to_____ most of the evidence _____ for the
   (accept, except)   (accept, except)
   testimony from one witness.

2. I need some good_____; is there anyone here who could _____ me?
   (advice, advise)   (advice, advise)

3. How does the allergy medicine_____you? Some medicine may have an
   (affect, effect)
   adverse side _____.
   (affect, effect)

4. The patient was told to _____ deeply and exhale slowly; the doctor
   (breath, breathe)
   could see her _____in the chilly winter air.
   (breath, breathe)

5. Today we _____ fruit for a snack; in the past we usually_____
   (choose, chose)   (choose, chose)
   junk food.

6. The thief, when he became _____, gave himself
   (conscience, conscientious, conscious)
   up to police because his _____ was bothering him.
   (conscience, conscientious, conscious)

7. Before you visit a foreign country, you should read about its _____
   (costumes, customs)
   so that you will not unknowingly offend someone.

8. The town _____ met to discuss a new ordinance.
   (council, counsel, consul)

9. We made a chocolate layer cake for _____ ; don't _____ me
   (desert, dessert)   (desert, dessert)
   until we eat it all.

10. All I want for _____ is a salad; do you think I can get a good one at
    (diner, dinner)
    this _____ ?
    (diner, dinner)

Group IV words

EXERCISE 8

Edit the following paragraph for word confusions. Circle the errors and write the correct words on the lines below the paragraph.

    For thousands of years, it has been a costume to enjoy wine. Today, some people chose to drink wine with diner, while others wait until desert. There are wine clubs where people look for advise as to what they should drink; these people are very conscience that they should do the correct thing. Others look for council in magazines which tell them how to chose the correct wine for the right food. They except the words of the experts, but the prices of some wines would take your breathe away.

_____ _____

_____ _____

_____ _____

_____ _____

_____ _____

Group V: Words that sound or look almost alike

1. emigrate/immigrate; emigrant/immigrant

emigrate:	to leave a country	They *emigrated* from Europe.
immigrate:	to come into a country	Many people have *immigrated* to the United States.
emigrant:	a person who leaves one country to settle in another	Each *emigrant* brought hopes and dreams.
immigrant:	a person who comes into a country to settle there	Nearly every *immigrant* landed first at Ellis Island.

2. farther/further

farther	greater distance (physically)	They had to walk *farther* down the road.
further	greater distance (mentally); to help advance a person or a cause	The speaker made a *further* point. The tutor will *further* my chances on the exam.

3. loose/lose

loose	not tightly fitted	The dog's collar is *loose*.
lose	unable to keep or find; to fail to win	Don't *lose* your keys. Don't *lose* the game.

4. personal/personnel

personal	relating to an individual; private	He asked for his *personal* mail.
personnel	people employed by an organization	All *personnel* in the company were interviewed.

5. quiet/quit/quite

quiet	free from noise; calm	They loved the *quiet* village.
quit	to give up; to stop	He *quit* smoking.
quite	completely	She is *quite* well again.

6. receipt/recipe

receipt	a bill marked paid	No exchanges can be made without a *receipt*.
recipe	a formula to prepare a mixture, especially in cooking	I found my *recipe* for caramel flan.

7. special/especially

special (adj.)	not ordinary	We're planning a *special* weekend.
especially (adv.)	particularly	She is *especially* talented in art.

8. than/then

than	used to make a comparison	This cake is sweeter *than* that one.
then	at that time; in that case	First he was late; *then* he blamed me.

9. thorough/though/thought/through/threw

thorough (adj.)	accurate and complete	She always does a *thorough* job.
though (adv. conj.)	however, despite the fact	I worked even *though* I was exhausted.
thought (verb)	past tense of to think	I *thought* about my goals.
through (prep.)	to enter one side and exit from the other side	We drove *through* the tunnel.

Note: *Thru* is not considered standard spelling.

threw (verb)	past tense of to throw	He *threw* the ball to me.

10. use/used to

use	to bring or put into service, to make use of	Present: I usually *use* a bike to get to school.
		Past: Yesterday, I *us*ed my father's car.
used to	an expression that indicates an activity that is no longer done in the present	I *used to* take the bus to school, but now I ride my bike.
	accustomed to or familiar with	I am not *used to* walking to school.

Group V words

EXERCISE 9

Fill in the blank in each of the following sentences by choosing the correct word to complete that sentence.

1. My parents _____ from Greece.
   (emigrated, immigrated)

2. Let's not travel any _____ tonight.
   (farther, further)

3. Your belt is too _____.
   (loose, lose)

4. Most of the _____ at this company are well trained.
   (personal, personnel)

5. Please be _____ while she is performing.
   (quiet, quit, quite)

6. Keep this _____ for tax purposes.
   (receipt, recipe)

7. He made a _____ trip to visit his daughter.
   (special, especial, especially)

8. I would rather read a good book _____ listen to television.
   (than, then)

9. When she walked _____ the door, he didn't recognize
   (thorough, though, through, threw)
   her even _____ he had known her all his life.
   (thorough, though, through, threw)

10. I am not _____ to staying up so late.
    (use, used)

Group V words

EXERCISE 10

Edit the following paragraph for word confusions. Circle the errors and write the correct words on the lines below the paragraph.

Advertising is very old: some advertisements on paper go back farther than three thousand years. In ancient Greece, it was quiet common to see signs advertising different kinds of services, but it was not until printing was invented that modern advertising was born. In Europe, in the seventeenth century, they use to place ads in newspapers; some of these ads were personnel messages, but most were for business. When many emigrants came to the United States, they used advertisements to get jobs; we can imagine them going thorough each newspaper very carefully. Today, advertising is all around us, special on television. If we are not careful, we can loose our focus when we watch some programs. For example, when a commercial interrupts a chef who is giving us a receipt for a complicated new dish, we are likely to remember the flashy commercial better then the chef's directions.

_____	_____
_____	_____
_____	_____
_____	_____
_____	_____

Group VI: lie/lay; rise/raise; sit/set

These six verbs are perhaps the most troublesome verbs in the English language. Not only must you learn their principal parts, which are irregular and easily confused with each other, but in addition, one set is reflexive and cannot take an object while the other set must always take a direct object.

First, learn the principal parts of the three reflexive verbs whose action is accomplished by the subject only.

Reflexive verbs: Lie—rise—sit

When these reflexive verbs are used, the subject is doing the action without any help. No other person or object is needed to accomplish the action. _Reflexive verbs never take an object._

I _lie_ down.
I _rise_ up.
I _sit_ down.

Principal parts of reflective verbs lie—rise—sit				
Verb Meaning	**Present**	**Present Participle**	**Past**	**Past Participle**
to lie = to recline	lie	lying	lay	has or have lain
to rise = to stand up or move upward	rise	rising	rose	has or have risen
to sit = to take a sitting position	sit	sitting	sat	has or have sat

Here are some additional examples of reflexive verbs:

The cat is lying on the rug.
The sun rose in the East.
The woman sat on the sofa.

Fill in each blank below with the correct form of one of the reflexive verbs.

1. The sun is _____ at about 6 A.M. this week.
2. He _____ at 7 o'clock every morning.
3. He is _____ at the breakfast table by 7:30.
4. He will not _____ down again until after midnight.
5. His cat is always _____ on the rug.
6. Yesterday he _____ there for seven hours without moving.

Verbs requiring a direct object: Lay—raise—set

These three verbs *always* require a direct object.

I lay the book down.
I raise the flag.
I set the table.

Principal parts of the verbs lay—raise—set				
Verb Meaning	**Present**	**Present Participle**	**Past**	**Past Participle**
to lay = to put something	lay	laying	laid	has or have laid
to raise = to move something up	raise	raising	raised	has or have raised
to set = to place something	set	setting	set	has or have set

Here are some additional examples of these verbs:

The cat *laid her ball* on the rug.

The sunshine *raised our spirits*.

The woman *set her hat* on the sofa.

Fill in each blank with the correct form of the verb and its direct object.

1. The postal worker _____ the _____ on the back porch.
2. The father _____ his _____ to be a sensitive individual.
3. We _____ the _____ on the counter.

EXERCISE 11   **Group VI words**

Fill in the blanks with the correct form of the verbs.

1. I have _____ the suitcases in your room.

2. I am _____ in my favorite rocking chair.

3. She likes me to _____ by her bed and read to her in the evening.

4. Last spring the manufacturers _____ the prices.

5. Yesterday the price of the magazine _____ by a dime.

6. When I entered the room, the woman _____ to greet me.

7. The woman _____ her head when I entered the room.

8. I usually _____ down in the afternoon.

9. The auto mechanic is _____ under the car.

10. I can't remember where I _____ my keys.

EXERCISE 12   **Group VI words**

Fill in the blanks with the correct form of the verbs.

1. The cat has _____ in the sun all day.
   (lie, lay)

2. If you feel sick, _____ down on that bed.
   (lie, lay)

3. The elevator always _____ quickly to the tenth floor.
   (rise, raise)

4. The boss _____ her salary twice this year.
   (rise, raise)

5. The parents _____ down the law when their son came home late.
   (lie, lay)

6. The carpenters _____ the roof when they remodeled the house.
   (rise, raise)

7. The dog _____ up every night and begs for food.
   (sit, set)

8. Last week I _____ in front of my television set nearly every night.
   (sit, set)

9. I always watch the waiter _____ on a stool after his shift is done.
   (sit, set)

10. We have _____ a plate of cookies and milk out for Santa Claus every
    (sit, set)
    year since the children were born.

Mastery and editing tests

Choosing correct words

Fill in the blanks with the correct form of the verbs.

One of the _____ ways to identify people is the use of fingerprints.
(principal, principle)
Each set of fingers has _____ unique pattern of ridges and designs. In the
(it's, its)
_____, this knowledge was not recognized as useful, but one hundred years
(passed, past)
ago, during the _____ of Queen Victoria, an Englishman named Sir
(rain, reign, rein)
Edward Henry devised a _____ system of identifying _____ prints
(hole, whole)   (who's, whose)
belong to whom. During the _____ of his investigation, he discovered
(coarse, course)
that we really have two layers of skin, and where _____ joined, the
(they're, their, there)
upper layer of skin forms a number of ridges. These ridges are divided by type,
into loops, double loops, arches, whorls, and accidentals. _____ studying these
(Buy, By)
different patterns, we are able to match people with _____ prints.
(they're, their, there)

Choosing correct words

Fill in the blanks with the correct form of the verbs.

Coffee has a long history and an interesting one. Long before it was brewed,
coffee was enjoyed _____ or mixed with vegetables and eaten as food.
(plain, plane)
The _____ of the first cultivated coffee was most likely Kaffa, a part of
(sight, site, cite)
Ethiopia not far from the _____ of that country. That is_____
(capital, capitol)   (we're, were, where)
coffee most likely got _____ name. _____, in the fourteenth century,
(it's, its)   (Than, Then)
merchants came across the _____ from Arabia to Kaffa, obtained coffee
(desert, dessert)
seeds, and began to grow coffee in their own countries. The people of Arabia
were _____ happy to enjoy coffee,_____ because it took the
(quite, quit, quiet)   (special, especially)
place of alcohol, which they were not allowed to drink. The first _____
(lose, loose)
coffee beans came to Europe in 1615, and the drink has remained popular ever
since.

TEST 3   Choosing correct words

Fill in the blanks with the correct form of the verbs.

People have pierced their ears _____
(thorough, though, thought, through, threw)
every period of recorded history. Ancient Egyptians, Persians, Hebrews,
and others would _____ pieces of gold and silver with jewels, pearls, and
(sit, set)
other precious stones. Some earrings would hang from the ear, while
others would _____ against the earlobe itself. They even _____
(lie, lay)   (use, used)
to hang earrings from the statues of their gods and goddesses. When the
Egyptians put mummies in their tombs, they place would place earrings in
the coffin as a decoration for the person to wear in the afterlife. Centuries
ago, both men and women wore earrings, and one Roman emperor
thought his people were becoming _____ _____. He spoke
(to, too, two)   (vain, vane, vein)
out against the use of earrings and _____ stated that men could
(farther, further)
not wear them. We do not know how people reacted to that announcement,
but there would be an uproar today because everyone sees wearing their
jewelry as a _____. Can you imagine police officers trying to enforce
(right, write, rite)
a law that forbids such a popular _____? Hardly anyone would
(costume, custom)
_____ such a regulation today.
(accept, except)

Using Editing Symbols

Freewriting topic:

> It is Saturday morning. A friend calls you and wants to know if you would like to spend the day together. You realize you are free that day. How would you like to spend that time with your friend?

Each person should write freely on this topic for at least fifteen minutes. Even though you are freewriting without a chance to draft and revise, try to make your work readable by writing on every other line. Be sure to use very legible handwriting. If you have a computer at your table, this will be no problem! Write your name on the back of the paper.

At the end of fifteen minutes, exchange your paper with another student in the class. Do not worry if you did not put down all that you wanted to say.

Now, taking the paper that you have been given, turn it over and under the name of the student who wrote it, write "corrected by" and put your own name. Next, take your textbook and turn to the inside back cover where you will find the symbols that writers use to make corrections on student papers.

As you carefully read the paper you have been given, examine each word to see if you can find three or four *word level errors*, and each sentence to see if you can find one or two *sentence level errors*. When you find what you believe is an error, underline it or circle it, and then mark it with the appropriate symbol. If you are uncertain about an error, consult with someone else in the class. For those who think they have a paper without any errors, ask yourself if that paper has too many simple sentences and not enough variety of sentence types. You might count how many of the sentences are simple sentences. What about word choices? Should the student find more interesting words in the revision? If so, indicate places where this should be done. Were the details specific enough to be interesting?

Your instructor may now want to collect these papers to make additional corrections or to see how well the members of the class worked as editors. Do not be discouraged if you were unable to spot all the errors in the paper you were marking. It is difficult to look at writing in an analytical way, especially if you are not in the habit of doing this.

Portfolio Suggestion

You may want to make a copy of the editing and correction symbols to keep in your portfolio. When papers you write for future courses are returned to you, these symbols may be helpful in understanding the teacher's marks. You will then be able to refresh your memory by referring to the editing symbols (inside the back cover).

CHAPTER 15

Working with Paragraphs: Topic Sentences and Controlling Ideas

What is a paragraph?

> A *paragraph* is a group of sentences that develops one main idea. A paragraph may stand by itself as a complete piece of writing, or it may be a section of a longer piece of writing, such as an essay.

No single rule will tell you how long a paragraph should be, but if a paragraph is too short, the reader will feel that basic information is missing. If the paragraph is too long, the reader will be bored or confused. An effective paragraph is always long enough to develop the main idea that is being presented. A healthy paragraph usually consists of at least six sentences and no more than ten or twelve sentences. You have undoubtedly read paragraphs in newspapers that are only one sentence long, but in fully developed writing one sentence is usually not an acceptable paragraph.

What does a paragraph look like?

Some students come to college unaccustomed to using margins, indentation, and complete sentences, which are essential parts of paragraph form. Study the following paragraph to observe the standard form.

S
T
E
P

4

First word indented.
Consistent margin of
at least one inch on
each side.
Blank space after the
final word.

I got the job. I worked in a bank's city collection department. For weeks I was like a mouse in a maze: my feet scurried. Every seventh day I received thirteen dollar bills. It wasn't much. But, standing beside the pneumatic tube, unloading the bundles of mail that pelted down and distributing them according to their texture, size, and color to my superiors at their desks, I felt humble and useful.

EXERCISE 1   **Standard paragraph form**

Write the following six sentences in standard paragraph form. As you write, use margins, indentation, and complete sentences. Each sentence must begin with a capital letter and end with a period, question mark, or exclamation point.

1. In the large basement of the school, thirty families huddled in little groups of four or five.
2. Volunteer workers were busy carrying in boxes of clothing and blankets.
3. Two Red Cross women stood at a long table sorting through boxes to find sweaters and blankets for the shivering flood victims.
4. One heavyset man in a red woolen hunting jacket stirred a huge pot of soup.
5. Men and women with tired faces sipped their steaming coffee and wondered if they would ever see their homes again.
6. Outside the downpour continued.

> In the large basement of the school, thirty families huddled in little groups of four or five. Volunteer workers were busy carrying in boxes of clothing and blankets. Two Red Cross women stood at a long table sorting through boxes to find sweaters and blankets for the shivering flood victims. One heavyset man in a red woolen hunting jacket stirred a huge pot of soup.

EXERCISE 2   **Standard paragraph form**

Write the following seven sentences in standard paragraph form. As you write, use margins, indentation, and complete sentences. Each sentence must begin with a capital letter and end with a period, question mark, or exclamation point.

1. Friday afternoon I was desperate to get my English homework finished before I left the campus.
2. The assignment was due on Monday, but I really wanted my weekend free.
3. As I sat at the table in the library, I could see dictionaries and other reference books on the nearby shelves.

4. I felt in a good mood because I knew that if I had to find information for my assignment, it would be available to me.

5. The only worry I had was whether or not I would be interrupted by my friends who might stop by, wanting to chat.

6. Luckily, I worked along with no interruptions and was able to finish my work by five o'clock.

7. My weekend was saved!

_____

_____

_____

_____

_____

_____

_____

_____

_____

_____

_____

_____

What is a topic sentence?

> A *topic sentence* states the main idea of a paragraph. It is the most general sentence of the paragraph. All the other sentences serve to explain, describe, extend, or support this main-idea sentence.

Most paragraphs you read will begin with the topic sentence. However, some topic sentences come in the middle of the paragraph; others come at the end. Some paragraphs have no stated topic sentence at all; in those cases, the main idea is implied. Students are usually advised to use topic sentences in all their work in order to be certain that the writing has a focus and develops a single idea at a time. Whether you are taking an essay exam in a history course, doing a research paper for a sociology course, or writing an essay in a composition course, thoughtful use of the topic sentence will always bring better results. Good topic sentences help both the writer and the reader to think clearly about the main points.

Below are two paragraphs. Each paragraph makes a separate point, which is stated in its topic sentence. In both of these paragraphs, the topic sentence happens to be first. Read the paragraphs and notice how the topic sentence is the most general sentence; it is the main idea of each paragraph. The other sentences explain, describe, extend, or support the topic sentence.

> ### Model paragraph 1
>
> *I went through a difficult period after my father died.* I was moody and sullen at home. I spent most of the time in my bedroom listening to music on the radio, which made me feel even worse. I stopped playing soccer after school with my friends. My grades in school went down. I lost my appetite and seemed to get into arguments with everybody. My mom began to look worried, but I couldn't bring myself to participate in an activity with any spirit. It seemed life had lost its joy for me.

> ### Model paragraph 2
>
> *Fortunately, something happened that spring that brought me out of my depression.* My uncle, who had been crippled in the Vietnam War, came to live with us. I learned many years later that my mother had asked him to come and live with us in the hope that he could bring me out of myself. I, on the other hand, was told that it was my responsibility to help my uncle feel at home. My mother's plan worked. My uncle and I were both lonely people. A friendship began that was to change both our lives for the better.

EXERCISE 3   Finding the topic sentence of a paragraph

Each of the following five paragraphs contains a topic sentence that states the main idea of the paragraph. Find which sentence best states the main idea and underline it. The topic sentence will not always be the first sentence of the paragraph.

1. Mountains of disposable diapers are thrown into garbage cans every day. Tons of yogurt containers, soda cans, and other plastic items are discarded without so much as a stomp to flatten them out. If the old Chevy is not worth fixing, tow it off to sit with thousands of others on acres of fenced-in junkyards. Radios, televisions, and toasters get the same treatment because it is easier and often less expensive to buy a new product than to fix the old one. Who wants a comfortable old sweater if a new one can be bought on sale? No thought is given that the new one will soon look like the old one after two or three washings. We are the great "Let's junk it" society!

2. Anyone who has been in the hospital with a serious illness can tell you that the sight of a good nurse is the most beautiful sight in the world. Today, the hospital nurse has one of the hardest jobs of all. Although a doctor may direct the care and treatment of a patient, it is the nurse who must see to it that this care and treatment is carried out. A nurse must pay attention to everything, from the condition of the hospital bed to the scheduling of medication throughout the day and night. In addition to following a doctor's orders for the day, the nurse must respond to whatever the patient might need at any given moment. A sudden emergency requires the nurse to make an immediate judgment: can the situation be handled with or without the doctor being called in? More recently, nurses have become increasingly burdened by paperwork and other administrative duties. Many people worry that the increasing demands on nurses will take them away from what they do best, namely, taking care of people on a one-to-one basis.

3. Anything can happen at a county agricultural fair. It is the perfect human occasion, the harvest of the fields and of the emotions. To the fair come the man and his cow, the boy and his girl, the wife and her green tomato pickle, each anticipating victory and the excitement of being separated from his money by familiar devices. It is at a fair that man can be drunk forever on liquor, love, or fights; at a fair that your front pocket can be picked by a trotting horse looking for sugar, and your hind pocket by a thief looking for his fortune.

4. This was one of the worst situations I had ever been in. There was a tube in my nose that went all the way to the pit of my stomach. I was being fed intravenously, and there was a drain in my side. Everybody came to visit me, mainly out of curiosity. The girls were all anxious to know where I had gotten shot. They had heard all kinds of tales about where the bullet struck. The bolder ones wouldn't even bother to ask: they just snatched the cover off me and looked for themselves. In a few days, the word got around that I was in one piece.

5. On hot summer days, the only room of the house that was cool was the sunporch. My mother brought out all her books and papers and stacked them up on the card table. There she would sit for hours at a stretch with one hand on her forehead trying to concentrate. Baby Kathleen would often sit in her playpen, throwing all her toys out of the pen or screeching with such a piercing high pitch that someone would have to come and rescue mom by giving the baby a cracker. Father would frequently bring in cups of tea for everyone and make mother laugh with his Irish sense of humor. It was there I would love to curl up on the wicker sofa (which was too short for my long legs even at twelve) and read one of the forty or fifty books I had bought for ten cents each at a local book fair. The sounds of neighborhood activities—muted voices, a back door slamming, a dog barking—all these were a background that was friendly yet distant. During those summer days, the sunporch was the center of our lives.

Finding the topic sentence of a paragraph

EXERCISE 4

Each of the following five paragraphs contains a topic sentence that states the main idea of the paragraph. Find which sentence best states the main idea and underline it. The topic sentence will not always be the first sentence of the paragraph.

1. Last evening at a party, a complete stranger asked me, "Are you a Libra?" Astrology is enjoying increasing popularity all across the United States. My wife hurries every morning to read her horoscope in the paper. At the local stores, cards, books, T-shirts, and other useless astrological products bring fat profits to those who have manufactured them. Even some public officials, like the British royal family, are known to consider the "science" of astrology before scheduling an important event.

2. Travelers to the United States have usually heard about the wonders of Niagara Falls and the Grand Canyon. These same tourists are not always so aware that an impressive variety of other sights awaits them in this country. The spectacular beauty of the Rocky Mountains and the wide majesty of the Mississippi River are sure to please the tourist. The green hills and valleys of the East are a contrast to the purple plains and dramatic skies of the West. The sandy beaches of the southern states are becoming increasingly popular. Even the area of the Great Lakes becomes a center of activity for boating, fishing, and swimming throughout the summer months.

3. When you remember something, your brain uses more than one method to store the information. You have short-term memory, which helps you recall recent events; you have long-term memory, which brings back items that are further in the past; and you have deep retrieval, which gives you access to long-buried information that is sometimes difficult to recall. Whether these processes are chemical or electrical, we do not yet know, and much research remains to be done before we can say with any certainty. The brain is one of the most remarkable organs, a part of the body that we have only begun to investigate. It will be years before we even begin to understand all its complex processes.

4. Some of the homes were small with whitewashed walls and thatched roofs. We were eager to see how they were furnished. The living rooms were simple, often with only a plain wooden table and some chairs. The tiny bedrooms usually had room for only a single bed and a small table. Occasionally, a bedroom would be large enough to have a stove made of richly decorated tiles. Visiting these houses was an experience that would always stay in our memory. All of the windows held boxes for flowers so that even in the dark of winter there was the promise of a blaze of colors in the spring.

5. Advertisements that claim you can lose five pounds overnight are not to be trusted. Nor are claims that your luck will change if you send money to a certain post office box in a distant state. You should also avoid chain letters you receive in the mail that promise you large amounts of money if you will cooperate and keep the chain going. Many people are suspicious of the well-publicized million-dollar giveaway promotions that seem to offer enormous cash prizes, even if you do not try the company's product. We should always be suspicious of offers that promise us something for little or no effort or money.

EXERCISE 5   **Finding the topic sentence of a paragraph**

The topic sentence is missing in each of the following four paragraphs. Read each paragraph carefully and circle the letter of the best topic sentence for that paragraph.

Ninety-five percent of the population in China had been illiterate. He knew that American public schools would take care of our English, but he had to be the watchdog to nurture our Chinese knowledge. Only the Cantonese tongue was ever spoken by him or my mother. When the two oldest girls arrived from China, the schools of Chinatown received only boys. My father tutored his daughters each morning before breakfast. In the midst of a foreign environment, he clung to a combination of the familiar old standards and what was permissible in the newly learned Christian ideals.

a. Education was always a priority in our family.
b. My father made sure that his sons received a proper education.
c. Learning Cantonese was an essential part of my education.
d. My father believed that the girls deserved educational opportunities just as much as the boys in the family.

How to hold a pair of chopsticks (palm up, not down); how to hold a bowl of rice (one thumb on top, not resting in an open palm); how to pass something to elders (with both hands, never one); how to pour tea into the tiny, handleless porcelain cups (seven-eighths full so that the top edge would be cool enough to hold); how to eat from a center serving dish (only the piece in front of your place; never pick around); not to talk at table; not to show up outside of one's room without being fully dressed; not to be late, ever; not to be too playful—in a hundred and one ways, we were molded to be trouble-free, unobtrusive, quiescent, cooperative.

a. From a very young age, I was taught proper table manners.

b. Very early in my life, the manners of a Chinese lady were taught to me.

c. Many Chinese customs differ from the customs in America.

d. Learning manners in a Chinese-American household.

I was never hungry. Though we had no milk, there was all the rice we wanted. We had hot and cold running water—a rarity in Chinatown, as well as our own bathtub. Others in the community used the YWCA or YMCA facilities, where for twenty-five cents, a family could draw six baths. Our sheets were pieced from dishtowels, but we had sheets. I was never neglected, for my mother and father were always at home. During school vacation periods, I was taught to operate many types of machines—tacking (for pockets), overlocking (for the raw edges of seams), buttonhole, double seaming; and I learned all the stages in producing a pair of jeans to its final inspection, folding, and tying in bundles of a dozen pairs by size, ready for pickup. Denim jeans are heavy—my shoulders ached often. My father set up a modest nickel-and-dime piecework reward for me, which he recorded in my own notebook, and he paid me regularly.

a. Learning the family trade.

b. Life in Chinatown for most people was very hard.

c. Learning how to sew was an important part of my upbringing.

d. Life was often hard, but there was little reason for unhappiness.

Mother would clean our living quarters very thoroughly, decorate the sitting room with flowering branches, fresh oranges, and arrange candied fruits or salty melon seeds for callers. All of us would be dressed in bright new clothes, and relatives or close friends, who came to call, would give each of us a red paper packet containing a good luck coin—usually a quarter. I remember how my classmates would gleefully talk of *their* receipts. But my mother made us give our money to her, for she said that she needed it to reciprocate to others.

a. I always enjoyed dressing up for Chinese holidays.

b. Each holiday was unique and had its own special blend of traditions and festivities.

c. The Chinese New Year, which would fall sometime in late January or early February, was the most special time of the year.

d. There was much work to be done during times of celebration.

How can you tell a topic sentence from a title?

The topic sentence works like a title by announcing to the reader what the paragraph is about. However, keep in mind that the title of an essay or book is usually a single word or short phrase, whereas the topic sentence of a paragraph must *always* be a complete sentence.

Title: Backpacking in the mountains

Topic sentence: Backpacking in the mountains last year was an exciting experience.

Title: The stress of college registration

Topic sentence: College registration can be stressful.

EXERCISE 6   **Distinguishing a topic sentence from a title**

Each of the following ten examples is either a title (T) or a topic sentence (TS). In each of the spaces provided, identify the example by writing T or TS.

_____ 1. The benefits of a college education

_____ 2. The outstanding achievements of aviator Charles Lindbergh

_____ 3. The president's cabinet faced two major problems

_____ 4. The basis of the Arab-Israeli Conflict

_____ 5. The Japanese diet is perhaps the healthiest diet in the world

_____ 6. The astounding beauty of the Rocky Mountains at dusk

_____ 7. The finest sports car on the market

_____ 8. Fast-food restaurants are popular with families having small children

_____ 9. The expense of maintaining a car

_____ 10. Maintaining a car is expensive

EXERCISE 7   **Distinguishing a topic sentence from a title**

Each of the following ten examples is either a title (T) or a topic sentence (TS). In each of the spaces provided, identify the example by writing T or TS.

_____ 1. Dreams can be frightening

_____ 2. The advantages of getting a job after high school

_____ 3. *Grumpy Old Men* was an unusual movie because it portrayed the unpopular subject of growing old

_____ 4. The home of my dreams

_____ 5. Walking on the beach at sunset calms me down after a stressful day at work

_____ 6. Making your own clothes requires great patience as well as skill

_____ 7. Selecting the right camera for an amateur

_____ 8. Finding the right place to study was my most difficult problem at college

_____ 9. The worst bargain of my life

_____ 10. The old car I bought from my friend's father turned out to be a real bargain

EXERCISE 8   **Distinguishing a topic sentence from a title**

Each of the following ten examples is either a title (T) or a topic sentence (TS). In each of the spaces provided, identify the example by writing T or TS.

_____ 1. How to make friends at college and still have time to study

_____ 2. With the widespread use of computers, word processing skills are needed for many jobs

_____ 3. The disadvantages of living alone

_____ 4. The fight to keep our neighborhood park

_____ 5. The peacefulness of a solitary weekend at the beach

_____ 6. Our investigation into the mysterious death of Walter D.

_____ 7. The flea market looked promising

_____ 8. The two main reasons why divorce is common

_____ 9. The single life did not turn out to be as glamorous as I had hoped

_____ 10. The increasing popularity of board games

How do you find the topic in a topic sentence?

To find the topic in a topic sentence, ask yourself what subject the writer is going to discuss. In the first sentence that follows, the topic is underlined for you. Underline the topic in the second example.

Backpacking in the mountains last year was an exciting experience.

College registration can be stressful.

Finding the topic in the topic sentence

EXERCISE 9

Find the topic in each of the following topic sentences. For each example, ask yourself this question: What topic is the writer going to discuss? Then underline the topic.

1. Remodeling an old house can be frustrating.
2. College work demands more independence than high school work.
3. A well-made suit has three easily identified characteristics.
4. Growing up near a museum had a profound influence on my life.
5. My favorite room in the house would seem ugly to most people.
6. A student who goes to school full time and also works part time has to make careful use of every hour.
7. One of the disadvantages of skiing is the expense.
8. Spanking is the least successful way to discipline a child.
9. An attractive wardrobe does not have to be expensive.
10. Of all the years in college, the freshman year is usually the most demanding.

Finding the topic in the topic sentence

EXERCISE 10

Find the topic in each of the following topic sentences. For each example, ask yourself this question: What topic is the writer going to discuss? Then underline the topic.

1. Taking care of a house can easily be a full-time job.
2. Many television news programs are more interested in providing entertainment than newsworthy information.
3. One of the undisputed goals in teaching is to be able to offer individualized instruction.
4. Whether it's a car, a house, or a college, bigger isn't always better.

5. Violence on television is disturbing to most child psychologists.
6. In today's economy, carrying at least one credit card is probably advisable.
7. Much highway advertising is not only ugly but also distracting for the driver.
8. Figuring out a semester course schedule can be a complicated process.
9. In recent years, we have seen a dramatic revival of interest in quilting.
10. The grading system of the state university is quite different from that of the small liberal arts college in my hometown.

EXERCISE 11 Finding the topic in the topic sentence

Find the topic in each of the following topic sentences. For each example, ask yourself this question: What topic is the writer going to discuss? Then underline the topic.

1. To my surprise, the basement had now been converted into a small studio apartment.
2. Of all the presidents, Abraham Lincoln probably enjoys the greatest popularity.
3. Scientists cannot yet explain how an identical twin often has an uncanny knowledge of what the other twin is doing or feeling.
4. If you don't have a car in the United States, you have undoubtedly discovered that public transportation is in a state of decay.
5. When we met for dinner that night, I was shocked at the change that had come over my friend.
6. According to the report, current tax laws greatly benefit those who own real estate.
7. Marian Anderson, the famous singer, began her career in a church choir.
8. As we rode into town, the streets seemed unusually empty.
9. The United Parcel Service offers its employees many long-term benefits.
10. Many people claim that clipping coupons can save them as much as 30 percent of their food bill.

What is a controlling idea?

A topic sentence should contain not only the topic but also a controlling idea.

> The *controlling idea* of a topic sentence is the attitude or point of view that the writer takes toward the topic.
> Backpacking trips are *exciting*.

A particular topic, therefore, could have any number of possible controlling ideas, all depending on the writer's attitude. Three writers on the same topic of backpacking might have different points of view:

A family backpacking trip can be much more *satisfying* than a trip to an amusement park.

or

Our recent backpacking trip was a *disaster*.

or

A backpacking trip *should be a part of every teenager's experience*.

How do you find the controlling idea of a topic sentence?

When you look for the controlling idea of a topic sentence, ask yourself this question: What is the writer's attitude toward the topic?

In each of the following examples, underline the topic and circle the controlling idea.

Sealfon's Department Store is my favorite store in town.

Sealfon's Department Store is too expensive for my budget.

Finding the controlling idea

EXERCISE 12

Below are ten topic sentences. For each sentence, underline the topic and circle the controlling idea.

1. Vigorous exercise is a good way to reduce the effects of stress on the body.
2. Buffalo and Toronto differ in four major ways.
3. Television violence causes aggressive behavior in children.
4. Athletic scholarships available to women are increasing.
5. Caffeine has several adverse effects on the body.
6. Graham Kerr, the galloping gourmet, is an amusing personality.
7. Training a parakeet to talk takes great patience.
8. Babysitting for a family with four preschool children was the most difficult job I've ever had.
9. The hours between five and seven in the morning are my most productive.
10. The foggy night was spooky.

Finding the controlling idea

EXERCISE 13

Below are ten topic sentences. For each sentence, underline the topic and circle the controlling idea.

1. Piano lessons turned out to be a disaster.
2. The training of Japanese policemen is quite different from American police training.
3. An Olympic champion has five distinctive characteristics.
4. The candidate's unethical financial dealings will have a negative impact on this campaign.
5. A bicycle ride along the coast is a breathtaking trip.
6. The grocery store is another place where people waste a significant amount of money every week.

7. Being an only child is not as bad as people think.
8. Rewarding children with candy or desserts is an unfortunate habit of many parents.
9. A childhood hobby often develops into a promising career.
10. The writing of a dictionary is an incredibly detailed process.

EXERCISE 14 **Finding the controlling idea**

Below are ten topic sentences. For each sentence, underline the topic and circle the controlling idea.

1. Learning to type takes more practice than talent.
2. Shakespeare's plays are difficult for today's students because English has undergone many changes since the sixteenth century.
3. Atlanta, Georgia, is one of the cities in the Sunbelt that is experiencing significant population growth.
4. Half a dozen new health magazines are enjoying popularity.
5. The importance of good preschool programs for children has been sadly underestimated.
6. The disposal of toxic wastes has caused problems for many manufacturers.
7. Censorship of school textbooks is a controversial issue in most towns.
8. Finding an inexpensive method to make salt water drinkable has been a difficult problem for decades.
9. Developing color film is more complicated than developing black and white.
10. The cloudberry is one of the rare berries of the world.

Choosing your own controlling idea

Teachers often assign one general topic on which all students must write. Likewise, when writing contests are announced, the topic is generally the same for all contestants. Since very few people have exactly the same view or attitude toward a topic, it is likely that no two papers would have the same controlling idea. There could be as many controlling ideas as there are people to write them. The secret of writing a good topic sentence is to find the controlling idea that is right for you.

EXERCISE 15 **Choosing controlling ideas to write topic sentences**

Below are two topics. For each topic, think of three different possible controlling ideas, and then write a different topic sentence for each of these controlling ideas. An example is done for you.

Topic: My mother

Three possible controlling ideas:

1. Unusual childhood
2. Silent woman
3. Definite ideas about alcohol

Three different topic sentences:

1. My mother had a most unusual childhood.
2. My mother is a very silent woman.
3. My mother has definite ideas about alcohol.

1. **Topic:** My grandmother

First controlling idea: _____

First topic sentence: _____

_____

Second controlling idea: _____

Second topic sentence: _____

_____

Third controlling idea: _____

Third topic sentence: _____

_____

2. **Topic:** California

First controlling idea: _____

First topic sentence: _____

_____

Second controlling idea: _____

Second topic sentence: _____

_____

Third controlling idea: _____

Third topic sentence: _____

_____

Choosing controlling ideas to write topic sentences

EXERCISE 16

Below are two topics. For each topic, think of three different possible controlling ideas, and then write a different topic sentence for each of these controlling ideas. An example is done for you.

Topic: The movie *Apollo 13*

Three possible controlling ideas:

1. Filled with suspense
2. Reveals the bravery of the astronauts
3. Explores the importance of teamwork

Three different topic sentences:

1. *Apollo 13* is a movie filled with suspense.
2. *Apollo 13* is a movie that reveals the bravery of the astronauts when faced with life and death situations.
3. *Apollo 13* is a movie that explores the importance of teamwork.

1. **Topic:** Thanksgiving

First controlling idea: _____

First topic sentence: _____

_____

Second controlling idea: _____

Second topic sentence: _____

_____

Third controlling idea: _____

Third topic sentence: _____

_____

2. **Topic:** Working in a nursing home

First controlling idea: _____

First topic sentence: _____

_____

Second controlling idea: _____

Second topic sentence: _____

_____

Third controlling idea: _____

Third topic sentence: _____

_____

EXERCISE 17   Choosing controlling ideas to write topic sentences

Below are two topics. For each topic, think of three different possible controlling ideas, and then write a different topic sentence for each of these controlling ideas. An example is done for you.

Topic: Fitness and health

Three possible controlling ideas:

1. The growth of new lines of products
2. Increased popularity of health clubs
3. Use of exercise videos and equipment at home

Three different topic sentences:

1. Recent years have seen the creation of entire lines of products devoted to fitness and health.
2. The high level of interest in physical fitness and health has resulted in a widespread growth of health clubs across the country.
3. A person can improve his or her health by exercising at home with a professional video or working out on one of the many pieces of equipment available for private use.

1. **Topic:** Rap music

First controlling idea: _____

First topic sentence: _____

_____

Second controlling idea: _____

Second topic sentence: _____

_____

Third controlling idea: _____

Third topic sentence: _____

_____

2. **Topic:** Junk food

First controlling idea: _____

First topic sentence: _____

_____

Second controlling idea: _____

Second topic sentence: _____

_____

Third controlling idea: _____

Third topic sentence: _____

_____

Mastery and editing tests

Further practice writing the topic sentence

TEST 1

Develop each of the following topics into a topic sentence. In each case, the controlling idea is missing. First, decide on an attitude you might take toward the topic. Then use that attitude to write your topic sentence. When you are finished, underline your topic and circle your controlling idea. Be sure your topic sentence is a complete sentence and not a fragment. An example has been done for you.

Topic: My brother's car accident

Controlling idea: Tragic results

Topic sentence: My brother's car accident had (tragic results) for the entire family.

1. **Topic:** Teaching a child good manners

Controlling idea: _____

Topic sentence: _____

_____

2. **Topic:** Two years in the military

Controlling idea: _____

Topic sentence: _____

_____

3. **Topic:** Living with your in-laws

   Controlling idea: _____

   Topic sentence: _____

   _____

4. **Topic:** Moving to a new location

   Controlling idea: _____

   Topic sentence: _____

   _____

5. **Topic:** Going on a diet

   Controlling idea: _____

   Topic sentence: _____

   _____

TEST 2 Further practice writing the topic sentence

Develop each of the following topics into a topic sentence. In each case, the controlling idea is missing. First, decide on an attitude you might take toward the topic. Then use that attitude to write your topic sentence. When you are finished, underline your topic and circle your controlling idea. Be sure your topic sentence is a complete sentence and not a fragment.

1. **Topic:** Camping

   Controlling idea: _____

   Topic sentence: _____

   _____

2. **Topic:** Vegetarians

   Controlling idea: _____

   Topic sentence: _____

   _____

3. **Topic:** Noisy neighbors

   Controlling idea: _____

   Topic sentence: _____

   _____

4. **Topic:** Driving lessons

   Controlling idea: _____

   Topic sentence: _____

   _____

5. **Topic:** Subways

   Controlling idea: _____

   Topic sentence: _____

   _____

Further practice writing the topic sentence

Develop each of the following topics into a topic sentence. In each case, the controlling idea is missing. First, decide on an attitude you might take toward the topic. Then use that attitude to write your topic sentence. When you are finished, underline your topic and circle your controlling idea. Be sure your topic sentence is a complete sentence and not a fragment.

1. **Topic:** Computer programming

   Controlling idea: _____

   Topic sentence: _____

   _____

2. **Topic:** Body piercing

   Controlling idea: _____

   Topic sentence: _____

   _____

3. **Topic:** Allergies

   Controlling idea: _____

   Topic sentence: _____

   _____

4. **Topic:** Motorcycles

   Controlling idea: _____

   Topic sentence: _____

   _____

5. **Topic:** Eating out

   Controlling idea: _____

   Topic sentence: _____

   _____

Working Together

Exploring Controlling Ideas

Topic: Marriage

To develop an essay on any given topic, a writer has an almost endless number of possible controlling ideas from which to choose. Student writers often express amazement when they discover how another writer has approached a given topic. "I never thought of doing that," they say. Let's explore some of these possible approaches to a topic as we brainstorm for different controlling ideas on the topic of *marriage*.

What follows is an example of just one controlling idea on marriage that uses comparison or contrast as a method of development.

> My parents' marriage was *a completely different arrangement from my own.*

Begin by dividing into groups. Each person in each group should provide at least two controlling ideas for possible use in a piece of writing on marriage. One person in the group should bring all the controlling ideas together and make up a single list that will be shared with the entire class. Finally, all the groups should come together and share their lists. How many different controlling ideas have come out of the work of all the groups? Do these controlling ideas cover all the different methods for developing ideas discussed in this textbook?

Portfolio Suggestion

Each student in the class should copy the list of controlling ideas developed by the class. Organize the ideas into groups according to each group's most obvious method of development: description, example, narration, process, classification, cause and effect, definition, comparison and contrast, or argument. Save this list in your portfolio as a reminder of the ways you could develop your personal thinking on a given topic.

Choose the controlling idea that is most interesting to you and then write a piece on this aspect of marriage.

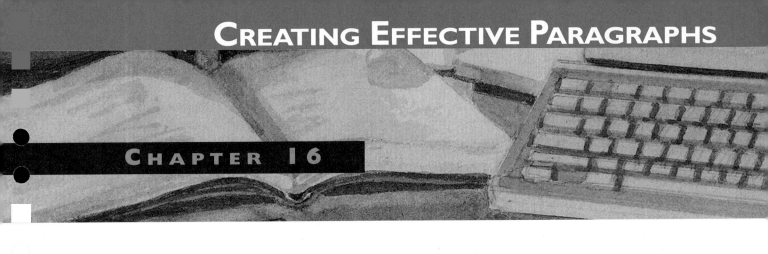

CHAPTER 16

Working with Paragraphs: Supporting Details

What is a supporting detail?

Once you have constructed a topic sentence including the topic and its controlling idea, you are ready to support your statement with details. The quality and number of these details will largely determine the effectiveness of your writing. You can hold your readers spellbound with your choice of details or you can lose your readers' interest because your details are not effective.

> A *supporting detail* is a piece of evidence used by the writer to make the controlling idea of the topic sentence convincing and interesting to the reader. A piece of evidence might include a descriptive image, an example taken from history or personal experience, a reason, a fact (such as a statistic), a quotation from an expert, or an anecdote to illustrate a point.
>
> *Poor supporting detail:*   Many people died of the flu in the 1960s.
>
> *Effective supporting detail:* In 1968, 70,000 people died of the Hong Kong flu in the United States.

As we work through the chapters that follow, you will have opportunities to become familiar with using all of these kinds of supporting details.

As you choose your supporting details, keep in mind that the readers do not necessarily have to agree with your point of view. However, your supporting details must be good enough so that your readers will at least respect your attitude. Your goal should be to educate your readers. Try to give them understanding about your

STEP 4

subject. Don't assume they know about or are interested in your topic. If you provide enough interesting and specific details, your readers will feel they have learned something new about the subject, and this alone is a satisfying experience for most people.

Supporting details will encourage the readers to keep reading, will make your points more memorable, and will give pleasure to the readers who are learning new material or picturing the images you have created.

The following selection is an example of a paragraph that provides effective details in order to support the point of the topic sentence.

> Everyone has heard of sure-fire formulas to prevent getting a cold. Popular home methods include a cold shower, regular exercise, and a hot rum toddy. Some people swear by cod-liver oil, tea with honey, citrus fruit juices, or keeping one's feet dry. Americans spent billions last year for cold and cough remedies. Advertisers have claimed preventive and curative virtues for vitamins, alkalizers, lemon drinks, antihistamines, decongestants, timed-release capsules, antibiotics, antiseptic gargles, bioflavonoids, nose drops and sprays, and a variety of other products. There are at least 3 over-the-counter products, most of which are a combination of ingredients sold for the treatment of symptoms of the common cold. Many of these drugs neither benefit nor harm the cold victim, but there is no doubt that they benefit the drug manufacturers! Now—just as fifty years ago—Americans on average will suffer two to three colds a year, with the infectious stages lasting about a week, regardless of any physical measure, diet, or drug used. U.S. Public Health Service studies show that, during the winter quarter of the year, 50 percent of the population experiences a common cold; during the summer quarter, the figure drops to 20 percent. The increased incidence of colds in winter reflects the fact that people spend more time indoors, thereby allowing the viruses to travel from person to person. In fact, one is less likely to catch a cold after exposure to the elements than after mixing with a convivial group of snifflers and sneezers at a fireside gathering.

PRACTICE Using the lines provided, copy the topic sentence from the previous paragraph. Answer the questions about the supporting details for the topic sentence.

Topic sentence: _____

_____

What are some examples of home remedies?

_____

_____

What are some examples of over-the-counter remedies?

_____

_____

What fact is given?

_____

_____

What expert is named? What is the statistic given by that source?

_____

_____

Finding the topic sentence and supporting details

In each paragraph below, find the topic sentence and the sentences of supporting details.

1. Saturday afternoon was a blessed time on the farm. First of all, there would now be no mail in till Monday afternoon, so that no distressing business letters could reach us till then, and this fact in itself seemed to close the whole place in, as within an *enceinte* [a circular enclosure]. Secondly, everybody was looking forward to the day of Sunday, when they would rest or play all the day, and the Squatters could work on their own land. The thought of the oxen on Saturday pleased me more than all other things. I used to walk down to their paddock at six o'clock, when they were coming in after the day's work and a few hours' grazing. Tomorrow, I thought, they would do nothing but graze all day.

FROM ISAK DINESEN,
Out of Africa

Topic sentence: _____

First reason: _____

_____

_____

Second reason: _____

_____

Third reason: _____

2. More people watched the Superbowl than watched Neil Armstrong's walk on the moon. Fifteen percent of all television programs produced are sports programs. Professional football games have a yearly attendance of over ten million spectators and both baseball leagues together draw over three million spectators every year. In one year, North American spectators spent over $3 million for tickets to sports events. There probably is not a person in the United States who does not recognize a picture of Muhammad Ali, and who cannot identify a picture of the soccer star Pele? The popularity of sports is enormous.

ADAPTED FROM RONALD W. SMITH AND ANDREA FONTANA,
Social Problems

Topic sentence: _____

First statistical fact: _____

_____

Second statistical fact: _____

_____

_____

Examples of recognizable sports stars: _____

_____

EXERCISE 2 **Finding the topic sentence and supporting details**

In each paragraph below, find the topic sentence and the sentences of supporting details.

1. Hilda takes an enormous amount of space, though so little time, in my adolescence. Even today, her memory stirs me; I long to see her again. She was three years older than I, and for a short while all I wanted was to look like, sound like, and dress like her. She was the only girl I knew who told me I wrote excellent letters. She made a plaster cast of my face. She had opinions on everything. She took a picture of me, at sixteen, which I have still. She and I were nearly killed, falling off a hillside road in her small car. Hilda was so full of life, I cannot believe her dead.

FROM HAN SUYIN,
A Mortal Flower

Topic sentence: _____

_____

First example: _____

_____

Second example: _____

Third example: _____

Fourth example: _____

Fifth example: _____

Sixth example: _____

2. A steadily accumulating body of evidence supports the view that cancers are caused by things that we eat, drink, breathe, or are otherwise exposed to. That evidence is of three kinds. First, the incidence of many types of cancers differs greatly from one geographic region of the world to another. Second, when groups of people permanently move from one country to another, the incidence of some types of cancer changes in their offspring. For example, when Japanese move to this country, the relatively high rate of occurrence of stomach cancer they experience in Japan falls so that their children experience such cancer only a fifth as frequently, the same incidence as other Americans. Orientals have low incidence of breast cancer, but when they come to the United States, it increases sixfold. Third, we are becoming aware of an increasing number of chemical pollutants in air and water and food that have proven to be cancer-producing.

FROM MAHLON B. HOAGLAND,
The Roots of Life

Topic sentence: _____

_____

First piece of evidence: _____

_____

Second piece of evidence (and example): _____

_____

_____

Third piece of evidence: _____

_____

Finding the topic sentence and supporting details

In each paragraph below, find the topic sentence and the sentences of supporting details.

1. New York is a center for odd bits of information. New Yorkers blink twenty-eight times a minute, but forty when tense. . . . A Park Avenue doorman has parts of three bullets in his head—there since World War I. Several young gypsy daughters, influenced by television and literacy, are running away from home because they don't want to grow up and become fortune-tellers. Each month a hundred pounds of hair is delivered to Louis Feder on 545 Fifth Avenue, where blonde hairpieces are made from German women's hair; brunette hairpieces from Italian women's hair; but no hairpieces from American women's hair which, says Mr. Feder, is weak from too-frequent rinses and permanents.

FROM GAY TALESE,
"Nocturne, New York"

Topic sentence: _____

First example: _____

Second example: _____

_____

Third example: _____

_____

Fourth example: _____

_____

_____

_____

2. Fairness is the ability to see more than one side in a situation, and sometimes it even means having the ability to decide against your own interests. For example, in San Antonio, Texas, a woman was locked in a bitter custody dispute that involved her thirteen-year-old son. The mother loved her son and wanted custody of him, even though she had a major health problem. She listened patiently while her ex-husband argued for full custody of the child. The woman felt that she had presented a good case before the judge, but when the boy was asked for his feelings in the matter, the mother found herself faced with a difficult situation: her son wanted to live with his father. Fairness to the child led the mother to give up her fight. Fairness, she discovered, is often painful because it means recognizing what is right instead of insisting on your own personal bias.

Topic sentence: _____

_____

Anecdote: _____

_____

_____

_____

_____

_____

Avoid restating the topic sentence

You should be able to recognize the difference between a genuine supporting detail and a simple restatement of the topic sentence. The following is a poor paragraph because all its sentences merely restate the topic sentence.

> The wedding day was the highest point in a girl's life—a day to which she looked forward all her unmarried days and to which she looked back for the rest of her life. All the events of the day were unlike any other day in her life before or after. Everyone would remember this day. Each event was unforgettable. The memories would last a lifetime. A wedding was the beginning of living "happily ever after."

By contrast, this paragraph, "From Popping the Question to Popping the Pill" by Margaret Mead, has good supporting details:

> The wedding day was the highest point in a girl's life—a day to which she looked forward all her unmarried days and to which she looked back for the rest of her life. The splendor of her wedding, the elegance of dress and veil, the cutting of the cake, the departure amid a shower of rice and confetti, gave her an accolade of which no subsequent event could completely rob her. Today people over fifty years of age still treat their daughter's wedding this way, prominently displaying the photographs of the occasion. Until very recently, all brides' books prescribed exactly the same ritual they had prescribed fifty years before. The etiquette governing wedding presents—gifts that were or were not appropriate, the bride's maiden initials on her linen—was also specified. For the bridegroom the wedding represented the end of his free, bachelor days, and the bachelor dinner the night before the wedding symbolized this loss of freedom. A woman who did not marry—even if she had the alibi of a fiance who had been killed in war or had abilities and charm and money of her own—was always at a social disadvantage while an eligible bachelor was sought after by hostess after hostess.

EXERCISE 4 **Distinguishing a supporting detail from a restatement of the main idea**

Each of the following topic sentences is followed by four additional sentences. Three of these additional sentences contain acceptable supporting details, but one of the sentences is simply a restatement of the topic sentence. In the space provided, identify each sentence as SD for supporting detail or R for restatement.

1. I am surprised when I think how neat I used to be before school started.

   _____ a. In my closet, I had my clothes arranged in matching outfits with shoes, hats, and even jewelry to go with them.

   _____ b. I always used to take great pride in having all my things in order.

   _____ c. If I opened my desk drawer, compartments of paper clips, erasers, staples, pens, pencils, stamps, and rulers greeted me without one lost penny or safety pin out of place.

   _____ d. On top of my chest of drawers sat a comb and brush, two oval frames with pictures of my best friends, and that was all.

2. Iceland has a very barren landscape.

_____ a. One-tenth of the island is covered by ice.

_____ b. There is not a single forest on the entire island.

_____ c. Nearly everywhere you look in Iceland, you see vast desolate areas.

_____ d. Three-fourths of the island is uninhabitable.

3. Until recently, books have been the most important method of preserving knowledge.

_____ a. Without books, much of the knowledge of past centuries would have been lost.

_____ b. Leonardo da Vinci kept notebooks of his amazing inventions and discoveries.

_____ c. During the Middle Ages, monks spent their entire lives copying books by hand.

_____ d. The Library of Congress in Washington, D.C., is given a copy of every book published in the United States.

4. Most people no longer wonder whether cigarette smoking is bad for their health.

_____ a. Following the evidence from over 30,000 studies, a federal law requires that cigarette manufacturers place a health warning to all smokers on their packages.

_____ b. Studies have shown that smoking presently causes nearly 80 percent of lung cancer deaths in this country.

_____ c. Few authorities today have any doubts about the connection between cigarette smoking and poor health.

_____ d. We know that 30 percent of the deaths from coronary heart disease can be attributed to smoking.

5. When the Mexican earthquake struck in 1985, scientists and city planners learned a great deal about the kinds of buildings that can survive an earthquake.

_____ a. Buildings that had foundations resting on giant rollers suffered very little damage.

_____ b. Buildings that were made only of adobe material simply fell apart when the earthquake struck.

_____ c. Many of the modern buildings were designed to vibrate when earthquakes occur, so these received the least amount of shock.

_____ d. After the earthquake was over, officials realized why some buildings were destroyed while others suffered hardly any damage at all.

Recognizing a supporting detail from a restatement of the main idea

EXERCISE 5

Each of the following topic sentences is followed by four additional sentences. Three of these additional sentences contain acceptable supporting details, but one of the sentences is simply a restatement of the topic sentence. In the space provided, identify each sentence as SD for supporting detail or R for restatement.

1. In the last thirty years, the number of people living alone in the United States has increased by 400 percent.

   _____ a. People are living alone because the number of divorces has dramatically increased.

   _____ b. Many young people are putting off marriage until they are financially more secure or emotionally ready.

   _____ c. More and more Americans are finding themselves living alone.

   _____ d. An increasing percentage of our population is the age group over sixty-five, among whom are many widows and widowers.

2. Today, people are realizing the disadvantages of using credit cards too often.

   _____ a. People should think twice before using their cards.

   _____ b. Interest rates on credit cards can reach alarming rates.

   _____ c. Credit cards encourage buying on impulse, rather than planning a budget carefully.

   _____ d. Many credit card companies charge an annual fee for the privilege of using cards.

3. The evidence of health problems among people living near Love Canal in upstate New York has been dramatic.

   _____ a. In a professional analysis done by Buffalo scientist Beverly Paigen, out of 245 homes, she found 34 miscarriages, 18 birth defects, 19 nervous breakdowns, 10 cases of epilepsy, and high rates of hyperactivity and suicide.

   _____ b. On October 4, 1978, a little boy suffering with nosebleeds, headaches, and dry heaves died of kidney failure; he often played in the polluted creek behind his house.

   _____ c. Ann Hillis's first baby was born so badly deformed that doctors could not determine the sex of the child.

   _____ d. The story of Love Canal is filled with human tragedy.

4. Since World War II, the status of women in Japan has changed.

   _____ a. In 1947, women won the right to vote.

   _____ b. The women's position in Japanese society has altered over the past forty-five years.

   _____ c. Many Japanese women now go on to get a higher education.

   _____ d. Women can now own property in their own name and seek divorce.

5. Certain factors which cannot be changed have been shown to contribute to heart attacks and stroke.

   _____ a. Three out of four heart attacks and six out of seven strokes occur after the age of sixty-five, so age is definitely a factor.

   _____ b. Heart attacks and strokes have many causes, some of which we can do nothing about.

   _____ c. African Americans have nearly a 45 percent greater risk of having high blood pressure, a major cause of heart attacks and strokes.

   _____ d. Men are at greater risk than women in their chance of suffering from cardiovascular disease.

How do you make supporting details specific?

Students often write paragraphs that are made up only of general statements. When you read such paragraphs, you doubt the author's knowledge and you suspect that the point being made may have no basis in fact. Here is one such paragraph that never gets off the ground.

> Doctors are terrible. They cause more problems than they solve. I don't believe most of their treatments are necessary. History is full of the mistakes doctors have made. We don't need all those operations. We should never ingest all those drugs doctors prescribe. We shouldn't allow them to give us all those unnecessary tests. I've heard plenty of stories that prove my point. Doctors' ideas can kill you.

Here is another paragraph on the same topic. This topic is much more interesting and convincing because the writer has made use of supporting details rather than general statements.

> Evidence shows that "medical progress" has been the cause of tragic consequences and even death for thousands of people. X-ray therapy was thought to help patients with tonsillitis. Now many of these people are found to have developed cancer from these X-rays. Not so long ago, women were kept in bed for several weeks following childbirth. Unfortunately, this cost many women their lives since they developed fatal blood clots from being kept in bed day after day. One recent poll estimates that 30,000 people each year die from the side effects of drugs that were prescribed by doctors. Recently, the Center for Disease Control reported that 25 percent of the tests done by clinical laboratories were done poorly. All this is not to belittle the good done by the medical profession, but to impress on readers that it would be foolish to rely totally on the medical profession to solve all our health problems.

This paragraph is much more likely to be of real interest. Even if you would like to disprove the author's point, it would be very hard to dismiss these supports, which are based on facts and information that can be researched. Because the author sounds reasonable, you can respect him even if you have a different position on the topic.

In writing effectively, the ability to go beyond the general statement and get to the accurate pieces of information is what counts. A writer tries to make his or her reader an expert on the subject. Readers should go away excited to share with the next person they meet the surprising information they have just learned. A writer who has a statistic, a quotation, an anecdote, a historical example, or a descriptive detail has the advantage over all other writers, no matter how impressive these writers' styles may be.

Good writing, therefore, is filled with supporting details that are specific, correct, and appropriate for the subject. Poor writing is filled with generalizations, stereotypes, vagueness, untruths, and even sarcasm and insults.

<u>EXERCISE 6</u>   **Creating supporting details**

Below are five topic sentences. Supply three supporting details for each one. Be sure each detail is specific and not general or vague.

1. The first semester in college can be overwhelming.

    a. _____

    b. _____

    c. _____

2. Designer clothing is a bad investment.

    a. _____

    b. _____

    c. _____

3. Dr. Kline is an easy teacher.

    a. _____

    b. _____

    c. _____

4. It is difficult to stop snacking between meals.

    a. _____

    b. _____

    c. _____

5. My sister is the sloppiest person I know.

    a. _____

    b. _____

    c. _____

<u>EXERCISE 7</u>   **Creating supporting details**

Below are five topic sentences. Supply three supporting details for each one. Be sure each detail is specific and not general or vague.

1. December has become a frantic time at our house.

    a. _____

    b. _____

    c. _____

2. My best friend can often be very immature.

    a. _____

    b. _____

    c. _____

3. Each sport has its own peculiar injuries associated with it.

    a. _____

    b. _____

    c. _____

4. My car is on its "last wheel."

    a. _____

    b. _____

    c. _____

5. Watching too much television has serious effects on family life.

    a. _____

    b. _____

    c. _____

Creating supporting details

EXERCISE 8

Below are five topic sentences. Supply three supporting details for each one. Be sure each detail is specific and not general or vague.

1. Maintaining a car is a continual drain on one's budget.

    a. _____

    b. _____

    c. _____

2. Climate can affect a person's mood.

    a. _____

    b. _____

    c. _____

3. Last year I redecorated my bedroom.

    a. _____

    b. _____

    c. _____

4. Washington, D.C., is the best city for a family vacation.

    a. _____

    b. _____

    c. _____

5. The amateur photographer needs to consider several points when selecting a camera.

    a. _____

    b. _____

    c. _____

Recording Family Traditions

Celebrations are important milestones in the living traditions of individuals, groups, and even entire nations. Traditional celebrations give affirmation to people's lives and help them feel connected to each other. Celebrations also support a country's need to preserve a sense of its own history. The photograph shows children at the Martin Luther King, Jr. School in Phoenix, Arizona, as they celebrate the birthday of their school's namesake.

Divide into groups. Make a list of celebrations (such as birthdays or Thanksgiving) celebrated by the members of each group. Next, consider what makes each celebration special. If you were to write about each holiday, what supporting details would you use? In the case of Thanksgiving, for example, the details would probably center around the meal that would be served. For how many other celebrations named by your group would this be true?

Each person should then write a paragraph describing a chosen celebration. Be sure to have a topic sentence and at least eight more sentences that support the topic sentence. Be sure that these eight sentences provide details that will help the reader construct a picture of the event.

Exchange papers. After you have read the paper you have been given, mark it in the following ways:

1. Underline the topic sentence.

2. Make a + sign in front of the sentence you believe contains the most effective supporting detail.

3. Make an "X" in front of the sentence you believe has the weakest supporting detail.

4. Using the editing symbols from the inside back cover of your book, mark any errors that you find.

5. In the upper right-hand corner rate the paper:

    1 = Uses specific details throughout

    2 = Uses specific details most of the time

    3 = Uses specific details sometimes

    4 = Almost never uses specific details

Continued

Use the following as a guide:

Too General (rating = #4):

We had turkey with stuffing every year.

Better:

Mamma cooked a fresh turkey with the same chestnut stuffing every year.

Much more specific (rating = #1):

Mamma always bought a fresh turkey from Ike at the meat market down the street. She was up by 5 A.M. Thanksgiving morning to start making the chestnut stuffing. Every year, she said, "Let's try a different stuffing this time," but we all shouted, "No, no, we want the chestnut stuffing."

6. Select a sentence you believe is too general. Rewrite it with more specific details that you think would make the sentence more interesting. Write your new version at the bottom of the student's paper.

Portfolio Suggestion

 When your paragraph has been returned to you, mark it as your first draft. Write a second version in which you make your details more specific. Label this your second draft. Be sure to show both versions to someone who can comment on your changes. Are you happier with the second version? Save both versions in your portfolio.

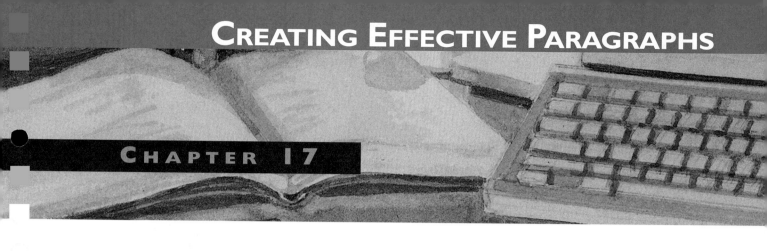

CHAPTER 17

Developing Paragraphs: Narration

What is narration?

> *Narration* is the oldest and best-known form of verbal communication. It is, quite simply, the telling of a story.

Every culture in the world, past and present, has used narration to provide entertainment as well as information for the people of that culture. Since everyone likes a good story, the many forms of narration, such as novels, short stories, soap operas, and full-length movies, are always popular.

The following narrative paragraph, taken from Helen Keller's autobiography, tells the story of this young girl's realization that every object has a name. The paragraph shows the enormous difficulties faced by a seven-year-old girl who was unable to see, hear, or speak.

The morning after my teacher came she led me into her room and gave me a doll. The little blind children at the Perkins Institution had sent it and Laura Bridgman had dressed it; but I did not know this until afterward. When I had played with it a little while, Miss Sullivan slowly spelled into my hand the word "d-o-l-l." I was at once interested in this finger play and tried to imitate it. When I finally succeeded in making the letters correctly, I was flushed with childish pleasure and pride. Running downstairs to my mother I held up my hand and made the letters for doll. I did not know that I was spelling a word or even that words existed; I was simply making my fingers go in monkey-like imitation. In the days that followed I learned to spell in this uncomprehending way a great many words, among them *pin*, *hat*, *cup* and a few verbs like *sit*, *stand*, and *walk*. But my teacher had been with me several weeks before I understood that everything has a name.

Working with narration: Using narration to make a point

At one time or another you have met a person who loves to talk on and on without making any real point. This person is likely to tell you everything that happened in one day, including every cough and sideways glance. Your reaction to the unnecessary and seemingly endless supply of details is probably one of fatigue and hope for a quick getaway. This is not narration at its best! A good story is almost always told to make a point: it can make us laugh, it can make us understand, or it can change our attitudes.

When Helen Keller tells the story of her early experiences with her teacher, she is careful to use only those details that are relevant to her story. For example, the doll her teacher gave her is an important part of the story. Not only does this doll reveal something about Helen Keller's teacher and her other friends, but it also reveals the astounding fact that Helen began to understand that objects have names. We see the beginning of Helen's long struggle to communicate with other people.

EXERCISE 1   Using narration to make a point

Each of the following examples is the beginning of a topic sentence for a narrative paragraph. Complete each sentence by providing a controlling idea that could be the point for the story.

1. Since my family is so large (or small), I have had to learn to _____

   _____

2. When I couldn't get a job, I realized *I could not* _____
   shop.

3. After going to the movies every Saturday for many years, I discovered _____

   _____

4. When I arrived at the room where my business class was to meet, I found _____

   _____

5. When my best friend got married, I began to see that _____

   _____

EXERCISE 2   Using narration to make a point

Each of the following examples is the beginning of a topic sentence for a narrative paragraph. Complete each sentence by providing a controlling idea that could be the point for the story.

1. When I looked more closely at the man, I realized that _____

   _____

2. When the president finished his speech, I concluded that _____

   _____

3. By the end of the movie, I decided that _____

_____

4. After I changed the course as well as the teacher, I felt _____

_____

5. When I could not get past the office secretary, I realized that _____

_____

Using narration to make a point

EXERCISE 3

Each of the following examples is the beginning of a topic sentence for a narrative paragraph. Complete each sentence by providing a controlling idea that could be the point for the story.

1. When the art teacher tore up my sketches in front of the class, I decided

_____

_____

2. When there were no responses to my ad, I concluded _____

_____

3. After two days of trying to sell magazine subscriptions, I knew _____

_____

4. After I had actually performed my first experiment in the lab, I understood

_____

_____

5. The first time I tried to cook a dinner for a group of people, I found out

_____

_____

Coherence in narration: Placing details in order of time sequence

Ordering details in a paragraph of narration usually follows a time sequence. That is, you tell what happened first, then next, and next, until finally you get to the end of the story. An event could take place in a matter of minutes or over a period of many years.

In the following paragraph, the story takes place in a single day. The six events that made the day a disaster are given in the order in which they happened. Although some stories flash back to the past or forward to the future, most use the natural chronological order of the events.

My day was a disaster. First, it had snowed during the night, which meant I had to shovel before I could leave for work. I was mad that I hadn't gotten up earlier. Then I had trouble starting my car, and to make matters worse, my daughter wasn't feeling well and said she didn't think she should go to school. When I eventually did arrive at school, I was twenty minutes late. Soon I found out the secretary had forgotten to type the exam I was supposed to give my class that day. I quickly had to make another plan. By three o'clock, I was looking forward to getting my paycheck. Foolish woman! When I went to pick it up, the girl in the office told me that something had gone wrong with the computers. I would not be able to get my check until Tuesday. Disappointed, I walked down the hill to the parking lot. There I met my final defeat. In my hurry to park the car in the morning, I had left my parking lights on. Now my battery was dead. Even an optimist like me had the right to be discouraged!

EXERCISE 4   Working for coherence: Using details in order of time sequence

Each of the topics below is followed by supporting details. These supporting details are not given in any order. Put the events in order according to time sequence by placing the appropriate number in the space provided.

1. A fight in my apartment building

   _____ Some of the neighbors became so frightened that they called the police.

   _____ The man and the woman began to fight around six o'clock.

   _____ When the police came, they found the couple struggling in the kitchen.

   _____ The neighbors heard the man's voice shouting angrily.

   _____ There were no arrests, but the police warned both individuals not to disturb the peace again.

2. An important invitation

   _____ On the day of the party Louise asked her boss if she could leave an hour or two early in order to have time to get ready.

   _____ When Louise was invited to the party, she was very excited.

   _____ Four days before the party, she finally got up enough nerve to call Bob and ask him to go with her.

   _____ One week before the party she bought a new dress even though she could not afford one.

   _____ Still holding the invitation, she searched through her closet, but all her dresses looked so dull and unfashionable.

EXERCISE 5   Working for coherence: Using details in order of time sequence

Each of the topics below is followed by supporting details. These supporting details are not given in any order. Put the events in order according to time sequence by placing the appropriate number in the space provided.

1. From the life of Amelia Earhart, pioneer aviator and writer

   _____ Amelia Earhart was born in Atchison, Kansas, in 1897.

   _____ Before 1920, she worked as a nurse's aide.

   _____ When she was sixteen, her family moved to St. Paul, Minnesota.

   _____ Four years after her history-making flight across the Atlantic, she made her solo flight across that same ocean.

   _____ After learning to fly in the early 1920s, she became, in 1928, the first woman to cross the Atlantic, although on that trip she was a passenger and not a pilot.

_____ Three years after her solo Atlantic flight, she became the first person to fly from Hawaii to California.

_____ On her last flight, in 1937, she was lost at sea; no trace of her was ever found.

2. From the life of Sojourner Truth, crusader, preacher, and the first African-American woman to speak out against slavery

_____ Sojourner Truth began life as a slave when she was born in 1797, but she was set free in 1827.

_____ She was forty-six when she took the name of Sojourner Truth.

_____ She was received by Abraham Lincoln in the White House the year before that president was assassinated at the end of the Civil War.

_____ She spent her final years giving lectures throughout the North.

_____ In 1850 she traveled to the West, where her speeches against slavery and for women's rights drew large crowds.

_____ At the beginning of the Civil War she was active in gathering supplies for the black regiments that were fighting in the war.

_____ Not long after her first trip west, she settled in Battle Creek, Michigan.

Working for coherence: Using details in order of time sequence

EXERCISE 6

Each of the topics below is followed by supporting details. These supporting details are not given in any order. Put the events in order according to time sequence by placing the appropriate number in the space provided.

1. The novel *Gone With the Wind* by Margaret Mitchell

_____ A widow for the second time, Scarlett marries Rhett Butler, but the marriage is not a happy one.

_____ Scarlett O'Hara, the daughter of Gerald O'Hara, the owner of Tara Plantation, is in love with Ashley Wilkes as the Civil War begins.

_____ When Ashley Wilkes marries Melanie Hamilton, Scarlett marries Melanie's brother Charles, who is soon killed in the war. At the same time, Scarlett is interested in the blockade runner Rhett Butler.

_____ By the time Scarlett discovers that she truly loves Rhett Butler after all, Rhett announces that it is too late and that he is leaving her forever.

_____ Scarlett marries a store owner, Frank Kennedy, who pays the back taxes on Tara. Kennedy is killed by Union Troops.

2. The novel *Great Expectations* by Charles Dickens

_____ Pip realizes Miss Havisham has had nothing to do with his inheritance.

_____ Pip, an orphan, is born and raised in a small English village by a blacksmith, Joe Gargery, and his sister.

_____ After his adventure with the convict, Pip works in a mansion near his home for a Miss Havisham, a crazed old woman who still wears the wedding dress she wore on the day her bridegroom failed to show up for the wedding.

_____ One day, Pip sees a stranger in the marshes near his home. The man asks Pip to bring him food and a filing iron—he is an escaped convict.

_____ Pip is contacted by a lawyer, who tells him that he must leave Miss Havisham and go to London, all expenses paid, to begin life as a gentleman.

_____ On his twenty-first birthday, Pip receives a visitor; it is the convict, Abel Magwitch, whom he had helped years before—it is he who has given Pip the money.

Transitions and time order

> Words and phrases that help a reader move smoothly from one idea to another and make the proper connection between those ideas are called *transitions.*

Although transitions must not be over-used, they are important tools for every writer. Here is the Helen Keller paragraph you studied earlier, but this time printed with each of the transitional words and phrases in boldface.

The morning after my teacher came she led me into her room and gave me a doll. The little blind children at the Perkins Institution had sent it and Laura Bridgman had dressed it; but I did not know this **until afterward.** When I had played with it **a little while,** Miss Sullivan slowly spelled into my hand the word "d-o-l-l." I was **at once** interested in this finger play and tried to imitate it. When I **finally** succeeded in making the letters correctly, I was flushed with childish pleasure and pride. Running downstairs to my mother I held up my hand and made the letters for doll. I did not know that I was spelling a word or even that words existed; I was simply making my fingers go in monkey-like imitation. **In the days that followed** I learned to spell in this uncomprehending way a great many words, among them *pin, hat, cup* and a few verbs like *sit, stand,* and *walk.* But my teacher had been with me **several weeks** before I understood that everything has a name.

Notice how the time transitions used in this paragraph make the order of events clear. "*The morning after* my teacher came" gives the reader the sense that the action of the story is being told day by day. In the second sentence Helen Keller gives information she learned later—*afterward.* The writer then tells us that when she played with the doll *a little while,* she suddenly—*at once*—became interested in the connection between an object and the word for that object. This realization was one of the central lessons in young Helen Keller's education, and it became the starting point for all of her later learning. She uses two more transitional phrases to tell us about the beginning of this education: *In the days that followed,* we learn, she mastered a great many words, although it took her *several weeks* before she learned the even more important concept that everything had a name. Much of the meaning of this paragraph would not have been clear without the careful use of these time transitions.

Working with transitions

Using the transitions given in the list below or using ones you think of yourself, fill in each of the blanks in the following student paragraph.

at once	later, later on	after a little while
immediately	now, by now	first, first of all
soon afterward	finally	then
suddenly	in the next moment	next

    I arrived at Aunt Lorinda's in the middle of a heat wave. It was 105 in the shade and very humid. Aunt Lorinda as usual greeted me with the list of activities she had scheduled for the day. _____ we went to the attic to gather old clothes for the Salvation Army. I nearly passed out up in the attic. Sweat poured down my face. Aunt Lorinda, in her crisp cotton sundress, looked cool and was obviously enjoying herself. "If you see something you want, take it," she said graciously. "It's so nice of you to give me a hand today. You're young and strong and have so much more energy than I." _____ her plans included the yard work. I took off my shirt and mowed the lawn while my eighty-year-old aunt trimmed hedges and weeded the flower beds. _____ it was time to drive into the dusty town and do errands. Luckily, Auntie stayed behind to fix lunch and I was able to duck into an air-conditioned coffee shop for ten minutes' rest before I dropped off the old clothes at the Salvation Army. I wasn't anxious to find out what help I could be to my aunt in the afternoon. I hoped it wouldn't be something like last year when I had to put a new roof on the old shed in the backyard. I could feel the beginning of a painful sunburn.

Working with transitions

Below is a narrative paragraph. Make a list in the spaces provided of all the transitions of time that give order to the paragraph.

    In the meantime, Jason skated along feeling in the best of moods. He was aware every moment that he was wearing his new pair of roller blades, and several times he even visibly smiled from so much inner pleasure. He hardly noticed when suddenly he found himself skating down his own street. Immediately, neighborhood children spotted him and ran up to him calling to him by name, "Jason, Jason, where did you get those skates?" In a short time, Jason found himself surrounded by nine or ten children who were running alongside of him. Finally, with a flair, he turned, stopped dead and blurted out happily, "It's my birthday today!"

_____   _____

_____   _____

_____   _____

_____   _____

Working with transitions

Below is a narrative paragraph from a story by the Russian writer Ivan Turgenev. Make a list of all the transitions of time that give order to the paragraph.

I went to the right through the bushes. Meantime the night had crept close and grown up like a storm cloud; it seemed as though, with the mists of evening, darkness was rising up on all sides and flowing down from overhead. I had come upon some sort of little, untrodden, overgrown path; I walked along it, gazing intently before me. Soon all was blackness and silence around—only the quail's cry was heard from time to time. Some small nightbird, flitting noiselessly near the ground on its soft wings, almost flapped against me and scurried away in alarm. I came out on the further side of the bushes, and made my way along a field by the hedge. By now I could hardly make out distant objects; the field showed dimly white around; beyond it rose up a sullen darkness, which seemed moving up closer in huge masses every instant. My steps gave a muffled sound in the air that grew colder and colder. The pale sky began again to grow blue—but it was the blue of night. The tiny stars glimmered and twinkled in it.

_____   _____

_____   _____

_____   _____

Writing the narrative paragraph step by step

To learn a skill that has so many different demands, the best approach is to work step by step so that one aspect can be worked on at a time. This will ensure that you are not missing a crucial point or misunderstanding a part of the whole. There certainly are other ways to go about writing an effective paragraph, but here is one logical method you can use to achieve results.

Steps for writing the narrative paragraph

1. Study the given topic and then plan your topic sentence with its controlling idea.
2. List all the events that come to your mind when you think about the story you have chosen.
3. Then choose the five or six most important events from your list.
4. Put your list in order.
5. Write one complete sentence for each of the events you have chosen from your list.
6. Write a concluding statement that gives some point to the events of the story.
7. Finally, copy your sentences into standard paragraph form.

Writing the narrative paragraph step by step

This exercise will guide you through the construction of a complete narrative paragraph. Start with the suggested topic. Use the seven steps above to help you work through each stage of the writing process.

Topic: Every family has a favorite story they like to tell about one of their members, often something humorous that happened to one of them. There are also crises and tragic moments in the life of every family. Choose a story, funny or tragic, from the life of a family you know.

1. Topic sentence: _____

_____

2. Make a list of events.

    a. _____

    b. _____

    c. _____

    d. _____

    e. _____

    f. _____

    g. _____

    h. _____

    i. _____

    j. _____

3. Circle the five or six events you believe are the most important for the point of the story.

4. Put your final choices in order by numbering each of them.

5. Using your final list, write at least one sentence for each event you have chosen.

    a. _____

    _____

    b. _____

    _____

    c. _____

    _____

    d. _____

    _____

    e. _____

    _____

    f. _____

    _____

g. _____

_____

6. Write a concluding statement. _____

_____

_____

7. On a separate piece of paper, copy your sentences into standard paragraph form.

EXERCISE 11   **Writing the narrative paragraph step by step**

This exercise will guide you through the construction of a complete narrative paragraph. Start with the suggested topic. Use the seven steps on page 268 to help you work through each stage of the writing process.

Topic: Tell the story of an incident you witnessed, one that revealed an unfortunate lack of sensitivity (or even cruelty) on someone's part. What did you observe the person doing? How did other people react? What did you do or wish that you had done in response to this incident?

1. Topic sentence: _____

_____

2. Make a list of events.

a. _____

b. _____

c. _____

d. _____

e. _____

f. _____

g. _____

h. _____

i. _____

j. _____

3. Circle the five or six events you believe are the most important for the point of the story.

4. Put your final choices in order by numbering each of them.

5. Using your final list, write at least one sentence for each event you have chosen.

a. _____

_____

b. _____

_____

c. _____

_____

d. _____

_____

e. _____

_____

f. _____

_____

g. _____

_____

6. Write a concluding statement. _____

_____

_____

7. On a separate piece of paper, copy your sentences into standard paragraph form.

On your own: Writing narrative paragraphs from model paragraphs

The story of how you faced a new challenge

Write a paragraph telling the story of a day or part of a day in which you faced an important challenge of some kind. It could have been a challenge you faced in school, at home, or on the job. The following paragraph by the journalist Betty Rollin is an example of such an experience.

Assignment 1

> **Model paragraph**
>
> When I awoke that morning I hit the floor running. I washed my face, brushed my teeth, got a pot of coffee going, tightened the sash on my bathrobe, snapped my typewriter out of its case, placed it on the kitchen table, retrieved my notes from the floor where they were stacked in Manila folders, unwrapped a pack of bond paper, put the top sheet in the typewriter, looked at it, put my head on the keys, wrapped my arms around its base and cried.

Ten suggested topics

1. The day I started a new job
2. My first day in history class
3. The day I began my first term paper
4. The day I tried to wallpaper my bedroom
5. The morning of my big job interview
6. Facing a large debt
7. Trying to reestablish a friendship gone sour
8. The day I started driving lessons
9. Coping with a death in the family
10. The day I faced a deadline

The story of an unpleasant fight or argument

Assignment 2   Write a paragraph in which you tell the story of a fight or confrontation you either witnessed or became involved in. Choose an experience that left a deep impression on you. What are the important details of the incident that remain most clearly in your mind? The following paragraph is from Albert Halper's short story "Prelude."

Model paragraph

But the people just stood there afraid to do a thing. Then while a few guys held me, Gooley and about four others went for the stand, turning it over and mussing and stamping on all the newspapers they could find. Syl started to scratch them, so they hit her. Then I broke away to help her, and then they started socking me too. My father tried to reach me, but three guys kept him away. Four guys got me down and started kicking me and all the time my father was begging them to let me up and Syl was screaming at the people to help. And while I was down, my face was squeezed against some papers on the sidewalk telling about Austria and I guess I went nuts while they kept hitting me, and I kept seeing the headlines against my nose.

Ten suggested topics   A confrontation between

1. A police officer and a guilty motorist
2. A teacher and a student
3. An angry customer and a store clerk
4. A frustrated parent and a child
5. A manager and an unhappy employee
6. A judge and an unwilling witness
7. A museum guard and a careless tourist
8. A politician and an angry citizen
9. A mugger and a frightened victim
10. An engaged couple about to break up

The beginning of a special relationship

Assignment 3   Write a paragraph that tells the story of how you became close to another person. Select one particular moment when the relationship changed from casual friendliness to something deeper and more lasting. Perhaps you shared an experience that brought you together. The following paragraph is taken from Morley Callaghan's short story "One Spring Night."

Model paragraph

Bob had taken her out a few times when he had felt like having some girl to talk to who knew him and liked him. And tonight he was leaning back good-humoredly, telling her one thing and then another with the wise self-assurance he usually had when with her; but gradually, as he watched her, he found himself talking more slowly, his voice grew serious and much softer, and then finally he leaned across the table toward her as though he had just discovered that her neck was full and soft with her spring coat thrown open, and that her face under her little black straw hat tilted back on her head had a new, eager beauty. Her warm, smiling softness was so close to him that he smiled a bit shyly.

Ten suggested topics

1. My relationship with a teacher
2. My relationship with a fellow student
3. A moment when I understood my clergyman in a new way
4. When I learned something new about a neighborhood merchant
5. When I shared an experience with a fellow worker
6. When I made friends with someone older or younger than myself
7. When my relationship with my brother or sister changed
8. The moment when my attitude about a grandparent changed
9. When a stranger became a friend
10. When a relationship deepened

You won't believe what happened to me today!

Tell the story of a day you found yourself in a difficult or frustrating situation. The following example is from Berton Roueche's short story "Phone Call." *Assignment 4*

> ### Model paragraph
>
> I got out of the truck and got down on my knees and twisted my neck and looked underneath. Everything looked O.K. There wasn't anything hanging down or anything. I got up and opened the hood and looked at the engine. I don't know too much about engines—only what I picked up working around Lindy's Service Station the summer before last. But the engine looked O.K., too. I slammed down the hood and lighted a cigarette. It really had me beat. A school bus from that convent over in Sag Harbor came piling around the bend, and all the girls leaned out the windows and yelled. I just waved. They didn't mean anything by it—just a bunch of kids going home. The bus went on up the road and into the woods and out of sight. I got back in the truck and started it up again. It sounded fine. I put it in gear and let out the clutch and gave it the gas, and nothing happened. The bastard just sat there. So it was probably the transmission. I shut it off and got out. There was nothing to do but call the store. I still had three or four deliveries that had to be made and it was getting kind of late. I knew what Mr. Lester would say, but this was one time when he couldn't blame me. It wasn't my fault. It was him himself that told me to take this truck.

Ten suggested topics

1. When I ran out of money
2. When I ran out of gas
3. When I was accused of something I didn't do
4. When I was stopped by the police (or by some other authority)
5. When I was guilty of . . .
6. When something terrible happened just before a big date
7. When the weather didn't cooperate
8. When I locked myself out of the house
9. When I couldn't reach my family by phone
10. When my typewriter broke down the night before a paper was due

A memorable experience from childhood

Assignment 5   Write a paragraph in which you remember a special moment from your childhood. The following example is from George Orwell's novel *Coming Up for Air*.

> ### Model paragraph
>
> It was an enormous fish. I don't exaggerate when I say it was enormous. It was almost the length of my arm. It glided across the pool, deep under water, and then became a shadow and disappeared into the darker water on the other side. I felt as if a sword had gone through me. It was by far the biggest fish I'd ever seen, dead or alive. I stood there without breathing, and in a moment another huge thick shape glided through the water, and then another and then two more close together. The pool was full of them. They were carp, I suppose. Just possibly they were bream or tench, but more probably carp. Bream or tench wouldn't grow so huge. I knew what had happened. At some time this pool had been connected with the other, and then the stream had dried up and the woods had closed round the small pool and it had just been forgotten. It's a thing that happens occasionally. A pool gets forgotten somehow, nobody fishes in it for years and decades and the fish grow to monstrous sizes. The brutes that I was watching might be a hundred years old. And not a soul in the world knew about them except me. Very likely it was twenty years since anyone had so much as looked at the pool, and probably even old Hodges and Mr. Farrel's *bailiff* had forgotten its existence.

bailiff:
in England, a person who looks after a large estate

Ten suggested topics

1. The first time I went swimming
2. My first time on a roller coaster (or on another ride)
3. A frightening experience when I was home alone
4. My most memorable Halloween (or other holiday)
5. The best birthday party I ever had
6. My first bicycle (or car)
7. The greatest present I ever received
8. A memorable visit to a favorite relative
9. My first time traveling alone
10. The first time I went camping

Telling Stories That Make a Point

Aesop is believed to have been a Greek slave who lived about 2,500 years ago. He created over 200 fables, many of which have become part of our international literary heritage. The following example of his work is a classic fable, one that has a timeless moral.

> A farmer realized he was dying. He did not want to leave this world without being sure that all of his sons knew how to be good farmers. He called them to his bedside and said, "My sons, I am about to depart from this world. Before I go, however, I want you to search for what I have hidden in the vineyard. When you find it, you will possess all that I am able to leave you."
>
> The young men were convinced their father had buried some great treasure on the property. After he died, they all took their shovels and dug up every part of the vineyard. They found no treasure at all, but their digging helped the grapevines so much that the next year's harvest saw the best crop of grapes in many years.
>
> *Moral: Our greatest treasure is what comes from our own hard work.*

Group Discussion

Wouldn't all of us like to get something for nothing? Share with your classmates a current story of someone you know or have heard about, who, like the sons of the farmer in the fable above, wanted to get something for nothing. (Do you know people who gamble? Do you know people who expect their relatives to keep supporting them? Do you know anyone who has inherited money?)

Then, share with your classmates a story about someone you know or have heard about who achieved something by working very hard. Do you think Aesop's moral is true, namely, that what we achieve by our own hard work is the greatest treasure?

Portfolio Suggestion

Write a true story or a fictional tale of one of the following:

1. What happened to someone who wanted to get something for nothing?

2. What happened to someone who, by his or her own hard work, achieved something significant?

Give your story the same one-sentence moral that Aesop gave to his fable, or using the same one-sentence model, make up your own moral.

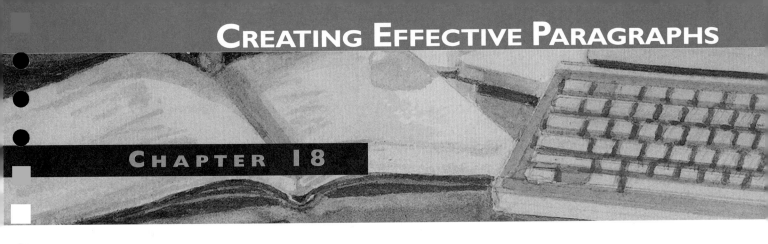

Developing Paragraphs: Description

What is description?

Writers frequently use description as a method of supporting the topic sentence of a paragraph. For example, the openings of many novels begin with paragraphs of description. Authors want their readers to be able to imagine the setting for their stories. In this chapter, we will examine the kinds of specific details that writers use in order to build effective descriptive paragraphs. We will also study the need to create an overall impression in our writing. Too many images, or images not carefully chosen, will greatly weaken the writing. Finally, as with all writing, we must consider what is the logical method for putting the details in order.

When you write descriptively, it is the use of **sensory images** that will largely determine whether or not your reader will be able to imagine what you are describing.

> *Sensory images* are those details that relate to our senses: sight, smell, touch, taste, or hearing.
>
> *Not descriptive:* It was morning in Harrington.
>
> *Descriptive:* As thick fog rolled down the rocky hills and into the sleepy village of Harrington, the early morning chirping of birds and the calls of one lone wolf fell strangely silent.

When you use details that relate to at least some of the five senses, you help your reader more clearly imagine the physical places, people, and objects in your writing.

S
T
E
P

4

Effective descriptive writing also gives the reader a definite sense that the details have been chosen to produce an overall impression.

> The ***dominant impression*** is the overall impression created by a descriptive piece of writing. This impression is often summed up by one word or phrase in the topic sentence.
>
> *Topic sentence without a dominant impression:*   It was morning in Harrington.
>
> *Topic sentence with a dominant impression:*   Early morning in Harrington was *eerie*.

A third important consideration in descriptive writing is the question of how to put the supporting details for that topic sentence into a logical order.

> ***Order*** in descriptive writing is often a *spatial order*. Details can be given as one's eyes might move, for example, from top to bottom, left to right, outside to inside, or around in a circle.

The following example of descriptive writing shows all of the elements of an effective description. As you read this description of a typical neighborhood delicatessen, note the specific details and the sensory images the writer uses. After you have read the whole description, ask yourself what dominant impression the writer wants us to have of the place.

The delicatessen was a wide store with high ceilings which were a dark brown color from many years of not being painted. The rough wooden shelves on both sides of the store were filled from floor to ceiling with cans of fruits and vegetables, jars of pickles and olives, and special imported canned fish. A large refrigerator case against one wall was always humming loudly from the effort of keeping milk, cream, and several cases of soda and beer cool at all times. At the end of the store was the main counter with its cold cuts, freshly made salads, and its gleaming white metal scale on top. Stacked beside the scale today were baskets of fresh rolls and breads which gave off an aroma that contained a mixture of onion, caraway seed, and pumpernickel. Behind the scale was the friendly face of Mr. Rubino, who was in his store seven days a week, fourteen hours or more each day. He was always ready with a smile or a friendly comment, or even a sample piece of cheese or smoked meat as a friendly gesture for his "growing customers," as he referred to us kids in the neighborhood.

The three terms defined above are essential for the skills you will be developing in this chapter. These skills are:

* How to create a topic sentence with a *dominant impression*
* How to support the topic sentence with details that use *sensory images* allowing the reader to imagine what is being described
* How to put the details in a logical *order*, which in descriptive writing is usually some kind of *spatial order*

Working with description: Selecting the dominant impression

When you use a number of specific, sensory images as you write a description, you should do more than simply write a series of sentences that deal with a single topic. You should also create a dominant impression in your reader's mind. Each individual sentence that you write is part of a picture that becomes clear when the reader finishes the paragraph.

For example, when you describe a place, the dominant impression you create might be one of warmth, friendliness, or comfort; or it could be one of formality or elegance. When you write a description of a person, your reader could receive the dominant impression of a positive, efficient individual who is outgoing and creative, or of a person who appears to be cold, distant, or hostile. All the sentences in the paragraph should support the dominant impression you have chosen.

Picking a dominant impression is essential in writing any descriptive paragraph. Here is a short list of possible dominant impressions for you to use as a guide while you work through this unit.

Dominant impressions for descriptions of place				
crowded	cozy	inviting	cheerful	dazzling
romantic	restful	dreary	drab	uncomfortable
cluttered	ugly	tasteless	unfriendly	gaudy
stuffy	eerie	depressing	spacious	sunny

Dominant impressions for descriptions of people				
creative	angry	independent	proud	withdrawn
tense	shy	aggressive	generous	sullen
silent	witty	pessimistic	responsible	efficient
snobbish	placid	bumbling	bitter	easygoing

Selecting the dominant impression

EXERCISE 1

Each of the following places could be the topic for a descriptive paragraph. Fill in each blank to the right of the topic with an appropriate dominant impression. Use the guide above if you need help. Remember, there is no single right answer.

Topic | **Dominant impression**

1. A high school gym on prom night _____
2. Your barber or hairdresser's shop _____
3. The room where you are now sitting _____
4. The grocery store nearest you _____
5. A hardware store _____
6. The post office on Saturday morning _____
7. An overcrowded waiting room _____
8. San Francisco in the spring _____
9. The home of your best friend _____
10. The kitchen in the morning _____

<u>**EXERCISE 2**</u>   **Selecting the dominant impression**

Each of the following persons could be the topic for a descriptive paragraph. Fill in each blank to the right of the topic with an appropriate dominant impression. Use the guide at the top of the page if you need help. Remember, there is no one right answer.

Topic   **Dominant impression**

1. An actor or actress being interviewed
    on television   _____

2. An old woman in a nursing home   _____

3. A librarian   _____

4. A bank clerk on a busy day   _____

5. A farmer   _____

6. A politician running for office   _____

7. A cab driver   _____

8. A shoe salesperson   _____

9. A bride   _____

10. A soldier just discharged from the service   _____

Revising vague dominant impressions

Certain words in the English language have become so overused that they no longer have any specific meaning for a reader. Careful writers avoid these words because they are almost useless in descriptive writing. Here is a list of the most commonly overused words:

> good, bad
>
> nice, fine, okay
>
> normal, typical
>
> interesting
>
> beautiful

The following paragraph is an example of the kind of writing that results from the continued use of vague words:

> I had a typical day. The weather was nice and my job was interesting. The food for lunch was okay; supper was really good. After supper I saw my girl-friend, who is really beautiful. That's when my day really became fun.

Notice that all of the details in the paragraph are vague. The writer has told us what happened, but we cannot really see any of the details that are mentioned. This is because the writer has made the mistake of using words that have lost much of their meaning.

On a separate piece of paper rewrite this vague paragraph you have just read. Replace the vague words with details that are more specific.

The next group of exercises will give you practice in recognizing and eliminating overused words.

Revising vague dominant impressions

In each of the spaces provided, change the underlined word to a more specific dominant impression. An example has been done for you. You might want to work in groups to think of words that are more specific.

> **Vague:**   The tablecloth was beautiful.
>
> **Revised:**   The tablecloth was of white linen with delicate blue embroidery.

1. The sky was beautiful. _____
2. The water felt nice. _____
3. Walking along the beach was fun. _____
4. The storm was bad. _____
5. The parking lot was typical. _____
6. The main street is interesting. _____
7. The dessert tasted good. _____
8. My brother is normal. _____
9. Our house is fine. _____
10. My job is okay. _____

Revising vague dominant impressions

In each of the spaces provided, change the underlined word to a more specific dominant impression. Working in groups may be helpful.

1. It was a really nice date. _____
2. The window display was beautiful. _____
3. The boat ride was fine. _____
4. The circus was fun. _____
5. The lemonade was awful. _____
6. The play was bad. _____
7. His new suit looked okay. _____
8. The dance class was fine. _____
9. Her new watch was nice. _____
10. It was a good lecture. _____

Working with description: Sensory images

One of the basic ways all good writers communicate experiences to their readers is by using sense impressions. We respond to writing that makes us see an object, hear a sound, touch a surface, smell an odor, or taste a flavor. When a writer uses one or more of these sensory images in a piece of writing, we tend to pay more attention to what the writer is saying, and we tend to remember the details of what we have read.

For example, if you come across the word *door* in a sentence, you might or might not pay attention to it. However, if the writer tells you it was a *brown wooden door* that was rough to the touch and that creaked loudly when it opened, you would hardly be able to forget it. The door would stay in your mind because the writer used sensory images to make you aware of it.

PRACTICE The following sentences are taken from the description of Mr. Rubino's delicatessen, a description that you read on page 278. Notice how in each sentence the writer uses at least one sensory image to make the details of that sentence remain in your mind. As you read each of the sentences, identify what physical sense the writer appeals to when a sensory image is used.

1. A large refrigerator case against one wall was always humming loudly from the effort of keeping milk, cream, and several cases of soda and beer cool at all times.

   Physical senses: _____

   _____

2. Stacked on top of the counter were baskets of fresh rolls and breads which gave off an aroma that contained a mixture of onion, caraway seed, and pumpernickel.

   Physical senses: _____

   _____

3. He was always ready with a sample piece of cheese or smoked meat as a friendly gesture.

   Physical senses: _____

   _____

When you use sensory images, you will stimulate the readers' interest, and these images will stay in their minds.

EXERCISE 5 Recognizing sensory images

The following paragraph contains examples of sensory images. Find the images and list them in the spaces provided.

I knew how a newspaper office should look and sound and smell—I worked in one for thirteen years. The paper was the *New York Herald Tribune*, and its city room, wide as a city block, was dirty and disheveled. Reporters wrote on ancient typewriters that filled the air with clatter; copy editors labored on coffee-stained desks over what the reporters had written. Crumpled balls of paper littered the floor and filled the wastebaskets—failed efforts to write a good lead or a decent sentence. The walls were grimy—every few years they were painted over in a less restful shade of eye-rest green—and the atmosphere was hazy with the smoke of cigarettes and cigars. At the very center the city editor, a giant named L. L. Engelking, bellowed his displeasure with the day's work, his voice a rumbling volcano in our lives. I thought it was the most beautiful place in the world.

FROM WILLIAM ZINSSER,
Writing with a Word Processor

Sensory images

Sight: _____

_____

Sound: _____

_____

Smell: _____

_____

Recognizing sensory images

The following paragraph contains examples of sensory images. Find the images and list them in the spaces provided.

The lake ice split with a sound like the crack of a rifle. Thick slabs of ice broke apart, moving ponderously, edge grinding against edge, up-thrusting in jagged peaks, the green-gray water swirling over half-submerged floes. In an agony of rebirth, the splitting and booming of the ice reverberated across the thawing land. Streams raced toward the lake, their swift currents carrying fallen branches and undermining overhanging banks of earth and softened snow. Roads became mires of muck and slush, and the meadows of dried, matted grass oozed mud.

FROM NAN SALERNO,
Shaman's Daughter

Sensory images

Sight: _____

_____

Sound: _____

_____

Touch: _____

_____

Recognizing sensory images

The following paragraph contains examples of sensory images. Find the images and list them in the spaces provided.

> In the waiting room there were several kerosene stoves, placed about to warm the shivering crowd. The stoves were small black chimneys with nickel handles. We stood around them rubbing hands and watching our clothes steam. An American lady, in a slicker, like the men, and rubber boots up to her knees kept bringing bowls of soup and shiny tin cups with hot coffee. Whatever she said to us and whatever we said to her neither understood, but she was talking the language of hot soup and coffee and kindness and there was perfect communication.

> FROM ERNESTO GALARZA,
> *Barrio Boy*

Sensory images

Sight: _____

_____

Sound: _____

_____

Touch: _____

_____

Taste: _____

_____

Smell: _____

_____

Creating sensory images

Each of the following topic sentences contains an underlined word that names a physical sense. For each topic sentence, write three sentences that give examples of sensory images. For example, in the first sentence the sensory image of sound in the vicinity of a hospital could be explained by writing sentences that describe ambulance sirens, doctors being called over loudspeaker systems, and the voices of people in the waiting room.

1. I knew I was walking past the hospital emergency room from the sounds I could hear.

   Three sentences with sensory images:

   a. _____

   _____

   b. _____

   _____

   c. _____

   _____

2. I can't help stopping in the bakery every Sunday morning because the <u>smells</u> are so good.

    Three sentences with sensory images:

    a. _____

    _____

    b. _____

    _____

    c. _____

    _____

3. The best part of my vacation last year was the <u>sight</u> that greeted me when I got up in the morning.

    Three sentences with sensory images:

    a. _____

    _____

    b. _____

    _____

    c. _____

    _____

Creating sensory images

EXERCISE 9

Each of the following topic sentences contains an underlined word that names a physical sense. For each topic sentence, write three sentences that give examples of sensory images.

1. It is a luxury to wear clothing made with natural fibers because the <u>feeling</u> is quite different from polyesters.

    Three sentences with sensory images:

    a. _____

    _____

    b. _____

    _____

    c. _____

    _____

2. I knew the garbage strike had gone on for a long time when I had to <u>hold my nose</u> walking down some streets.

    Three sentences with sensory images:

    a. _____

    _____

    b. _____

    _____

    c. _____

    _____

3. A lake in the summertime is a relaxing place to be because the <u>sounds</u> you hear all day are so subdued.

Three sentences with sensory images:

a. _____

_____

b. _____

_____

c. _____

_____

EXERCISE 10   Creating sensory images

Each of the following topic sentences contains an underlined word that names a physical sense. For each topic sentence, write three sentences that give examples of sensory images.

1. Going to a disco is an overwhelming experience because of the different sounds you <u>hear</u> there.

Three sentences with sensory images:

a. _____

_____

b. _____

_____

c. _____

_____

2. My friend Bill says he loves the <u>feel</u> of the chocolate, the nuts, and the coconut when he eats that candy bar.

Three sentences with sensory images:

a. _____

_____

b. _____

_____

c. _____

_____

3. I could <u>see</u> that the old woman standing on the corner was very poor.

Three sentences with sensory images:

a. _____

_____

b. _____

_____

c. _____

_____

Coherence in description: Putting details in space order

In descriptive paragraphs, the writer often chooses to arrange supporting details according to space. With this method, you place yourself at the scene and then use a logical order such as moving from nearby to farther away, right to left, or top to bottom. Often you move in such a way that you save the most important detail until last in order to achieve the greatest effect.

In the paragraph on the delicatessen given on page 278, the writer first describes the ceilings and walls of the store, then proceeds to the shelves and large refrigerator, and ends by describing the main counter of the deli with its owner, Mr. Rubino, standing behind it. By ordering the details in this way, the reader is led from the edges of the room to focus on what is most important—Mr. Rubino behind his counter. A description of a clothes closet might order the details differently. Perhaps the writer would begin with the shoes standing on the floor and finish with the hats and gloves arranged on the top shelf, an arrangement that goes from the ground up.

Here is a paragraph from Ernesto Galarza's autobiography, *Barrio Boy*. The writer is describing the one-room apartment where he and his family lived in Mazatlán, Mexico.

> The floor was of large square bricks worn smooth and of grey mortar between. The ceiling was the underside of the tile resting on beams that pointed from back to front. Families who had lived there before had left a helter-skelter of nails, bolts, and pegs driven into the walls. The kerosene lamp hung from a hook on the center beam.

Notice that the writer begins with a description of the floor, then gives us an idea of what the ceiling is like, and ends with a detailed picture of the walls. We are able to follow the writer through the description because there is a plan and a sense of logic. No matter which method of space order you choose in organizing details in a descriptive paragraph, be sure the results allow your reader to see the scene in a logical order.

Working for coherence: Using space order

EXERCISE 11

Each of the following topic sentences is followed by four or more descriptive sentences that are not in order. Put these descriptive sentences in order by placing a number (1, 2, 3, 4, or 5) in the space provided before each sentence.

1. The Statue of Liberty, now completely restored, is a marvel to visitors from all over the world.

   (*Order the material from the bottom to top.*)

   _____ With current restoration finished, the crown continues to be used as a place where visitors can get a good view of New York Harbor.

   _____ The granite base of the statue was quarried and cut many miles from New York City and then taken by boat to Bedloe's Island, where the statue was built.

   _____ The torch has been repaired and will now be illuminated by outside lights, not lights from inside the torch itself.

   _____ The seven spikes that rise above the crown represent the seven seas of the world.

   _____ The body was covered with sheets of copper that was originally mined on an island off the coast of Norway.

2. The young woman was a teen of the nineties.

   (*Order the material from top to bottom.*)

   _____ She wore an oversized sweater that she had borrowed from her father.

   _____ Her shoes were white tennis sneakers.

   _____ From her ears dangled silver and turquoise earrings.

   _____ Her short blond hair was clean and styled attractively.

   _____ The black cotton stretch pants flattered her slim figure.

3. My aunt's kitchen is a very orderly place.

   (*Order the material from near to far.*)

   _____ As usual, in the center of the table sits a vase with a fresh yellow daffodil.

   _____ Nearby on the refrigerator, a magnet holds the week's menu.

   _____ Sitting at the kitchen table, I am struck by the freshly pressed linen tablecloth.

   _____ Looking across the room through the stained glass doors of her kitchen cupboards, I can see neat rows of dishes, exactly eight each, matching the colors of the tablecloth and wallpaper.

EXERCISE 12 Working for coherence: Using space order

Each of the following topic sentences could be expanded into a fully developed paragraph. In the spaces provided, give the appropriate supporting details for the topic sentence. Be sure to give your supporting details in a particular order. That is, the details should go from top to bottom, from outside to inside, from close to far, or around the area you are describing.

1. The airport terminal was as busy inside as it was outside.

   a. _____

   _____

   b. _____

   _____

   c. _____

   _____

   d. _____

   _____

2. The student lounge is a quiet and relaxing place in our school.

   a. _____

   _____

   b. _____

   _____

   c. _____

   _____

d. _____
_____

3. The motel lobby was obviously once very beautiful, but it was beginning to look shabby.

    a. _____
    _____

    b. _____
    _____

    c. _____
    _____

    d. _____
    _____

Working for coherence: Using space order

Each of the following topic sentences could be expanded into a fully developed paragraph. In the spaces provided, give the appropriate supporting details for the topic sentence. Be sure to give your supporting details in a particular order. That is, the details should go from top to bottom, from outside to inside, from close to far, or around the area you are describing.

1. The shopping mall was supposed to be restful, but the noise and the bright lights gave me a headache.

    a. _____
    _____

    b. _____
    _____

    c. _____
    _____

    d. _____
    _____

2. The pizza shop is so tiny that people are not likely to stay and eat.

    a. _____
    _____

    b. _____
    _____

    c. _____
    _____

    d. _____
    _____

3. The bus was filled with a strange assortment of people.

a. _____

_____

b. _____

_____

c. _____

_____

d. _____

_____

Writing the descriptive paragraph step by step

To learn a skill with some degree of ease, it is best to follow a step by step approach so that various skills are isolated. This will ensure that you are not missing a crucial point or misunderstanding a part of the whole. There certainly are other ways to go about writing an effective paragraph, but here is one method you can use to achieve successful results. You will learn that writing, like most skills, can be developed by using a logical process.

Steps for writing the descriptive paragraph

1. Study the given topic, and then plan your topic sentence, especially the dominant impression.
2. List at least ten details that come to your mind when you think about the description you have chosen.
3. Then choose the five or six most important details from your list. Be sure these details support the dominant impression.
4. Put your list in order.
5. Write one complete sentence for each of the details you have chosen from your list.
6. Write a concluding statement that offers some reason for describing this topic.
7. Finally, copy your sentences into standard paragraph form.

EXERCISE 14 **Writing the descriptive paragraph step by step**

The following exercise will guide you through the construction of a descriptive paragraph. Start with the suggested topic. Use the seven steps to help you work through each stage of the writing process.

Topic: A place you have lived

1. Topic sentence: _____

_____

2. Make a list of possible supporting details.

   a. _____

   b. _____

   c. _____

   d. _____

   e. _____

   f. _____

   g. _____

   h. _____

   i. _____

   j. _____

3. Circle the five or six details you believe are the most important for the description.

4. Put your selected details in order by numbering them.

5. Using your final list, write at least one sentence for each detail you have chosen.

   a. _____
   _____

   b. _____
   _____

   c. _____
   _____

   d. _____
   _____

   e. _____
   _____

   f. _____
   _____

   g. _____
   _____

6. Write a concluding statement. _____
   _____
   _____

7. Copy your sentences into standard paragraph form.

EXERCISE 15   Writing the descriptive paragraph step by step

The following exercise will guide you through the construction of a descriptive paragraph. Start with the suggested topic. Use the seven steps to help you work through each stage of the writing process.

Topic: A person you admire

1. Topic sentence: _____

   _____

2. Make a list of possible supporting details.

   a. _____

   b. _____

   c. _____

   d. _____

   e. _____

   f. _____

   g. _____

   h. _____

   i. _____

   j. _____

3. Circle the five or six details you believe are the most important for the description.

4. Put your selected details in order by numbering them.

5. Using your final list, write at least one sentence for each detail you have chosen.

   a. _____

   _____

   b. _____

   _____

   c. _____

   _____

   d. _____

   _____

   e. _____

   _____

   f. _____

   _____

   g. _____

   _____

6. Write a concluding statement. _____

_____

_____

_____

7. Copy your sentences into standard paragraph form.

Writing the descriptive paragraph step by step

The following exercise will guide you through the construction of a descriptive paragraph. Start with the suggested topic. Use the seven steps to help you work through each stage of the writing process.

   Topic: An ideal gift for a child

1. Topic sentence: _____

_____

2. Make a list of possible supporting details.

   a. _____

   b. _____

   c. _____

   d. _____

   e. _____

   f. _____

   g. _____

   h. _____

   i. _____

   j. _____

3. Circle the five or six details you believe are the most important for the description.

4. Put your selected details in order by numbering them.

5. Using your final list, write at least one sentence for each detail you have chosen.

   a. _____

   _____

   b. _____

   _____

   c. _____

   _____

d. _____

_____

e. _____

_____

f. _____

_____

g. _____

_____

6. Write a concluding statement. _____

_____

_____

_____

7. Copy your sentences into standard paragraph form.

On your own: Writing descriptive paragraphs from model paragraphs

A description of a home

Assignment 1   Write a paragraph in which you describe a house or room that you remember clearly. Choose your dominant impression carefully and then make your sensory images support that impression. In your description you may want to include the person who lives in the house or room. Notice in the model paragraph from Charles Chaplin's *My Autobiography* the importance of the last sentence, in which the writer gives his paragraph added impact by naming the person who lives in the house he has described.

> ### Model paragraph
>
> It was dark when we entered his bungalow, and when we switched on the light I was shocked. The place was empty and drab. In his room was an old iron bed with a light bulb hanging over the head of it. A rickety old table and one chair were the other furnishings. Near the bed was a wooden box upon which was a brass ashtray filled with cigarette butts. The room allotted to me was almost the same, only it was minus a grocery box. Nothing worked. The bathroom was unspeakable. One had to take a jug and fill it from the bath tap and empty it down the flush to make the toilet work. This was the home of G. M. Anderson, the multimillionaire cowboy.

Ten suggested topics

1. A student's apartment
2. A vacation cottage
3. A dormitory
4. The house of your dreams
5. Your bedroom
6. A kitchen
7. The messiest room you ever saw
8. The strangest room you ever saw
9. A house you will never forget
10. A house that did not fit the character of the person living there

A description of a person

Describe a person whose appearance made a deep impression on you. If you saw this person only once, indicate the details that made him or her stay in your mind. If you choose to describe a person with whom you are more familiar, select the most outstanding details that will help your reader have a single, dominant impression. In the model paragraph, Scott Russell Sanders remembers the men from his rural and working class childhood in Tennessee.

Assignment 2

Model paragraph

The bodies of the men I knew were twisted and maimed in ways visible and invisible. The nails of their hands were black and split, the hands tattooed with scars. Some had lost fingers. Heavy lifting had given many of them finicky backs and guts weak from hernias. Racing against conveyor belts had given them ulcers. Their ankles and knees ached from years of standing on concrete. Anyone who had worked for long around machines was hard of hearing. They squinted, and the skin of their faces was creased like the leather of old work gloves. There were times, studying them, when I dreaded growing up. Most of them coughed, from dust or cigarettes, and most of them drank cheap wine or whiskey, so their eyes looked bloodshot and bruised. The fathers of my friends always seemed older than the mothers. Men wore out sooner. Only women lived into old age.

Ten suggested topics

1. An elderly relative
2. A hard-working student
3. An outstanding athlete
4. A loyal friend
5. An overworked waitress
6. A cab driver
7. A fashion model
8. A gossipy neighbor
9. A street vendor
10. A rude salesperson

A description of a time of day

Assignment 3   Write a paragraph in which you describe the sights, sounds, and events of a particular time of day in a place you know well. In the model paragraph that follows, the writer has chosen to describe an especially busy time of day, the morning, when activity can be frantic in a household.

Model paragraph

I remember the turmoil of mornings in our house. My brothers and sisters rushed about upstairs and down trying to get ready for school. Mom would repeatedly tell them to hurry up. Molly would usually scream down from her bedroom, "What am I going to do? I don't have any clean underwear!" Amy, often in tears, sat at the kitchen table still in her pajamas trying to do her math. Paul paced back and forth in front of the mirror angrily combing his unruly hair which stuck up in all directions while Roland threatened to punch him if he didn't find the pen he had borrowed the night before. Mother was stuffing sandwiches into bags while she sighed, "I'm afraid there isn't anything for dessert today." No one heard her. Then came the yelling up the stairs, "You should have left ten minutes ago." One by one, these unwilling victims were packed up and pushed out the door. Mother wasn't safe yet. Somebody always came back frantic and desperate. "My flute, Mom, where's my flute, quick! I'll get killed if I don't have it today." Every crisis apparently meant the difference between life and death. Morning at our house was like watching a troop preparing for battle. When they had finally gone, I was left in complete silence while my mother slumped on a chair at the kitchen table. She paid no attention to me.

Ten suggested topics
1. A Saturday filled with errands
2. The dinner hour at my house
3. Lunchtime in a cafeteria
4. A midnight raid on the refrigerator
5. Christmas morning
6. TGIF (Thank God It's Friday)
7. Getting ready to go out on a Friday night
8. My Sunday morning routine
9. Coming home from school or work
10. Watching late-night movies

A description of a place

Write a paragraph in which you describe a place you know well or remember clearly. The model paragraph that follows is from *The Airtight Cage*, a classic study by Joseph Lyford of an urban neighborhood in a state of change.

Assignment 4

> **Model paragraph**
>
> The wreckers would put a one-story scaffold in front of the building to protect automobiles and pedestrians, then begin at the top, working down story by story, gutting the rooms, ripping out woodwork, electrical wiring, plumbing, and fixtures. Once this was done, the men would hammer the shell of the house with sledges. Sections of brick wall would shudder, undulate for a second and dissolve into fragments that fell in slow motion. When the fragments hit the ground, the dust rocketed several feet into the air. The heaps of brick and plaster, coils and stems of rusty pipe attracted children from all over the area. On weekends and after 4 p.m. on weekdays, they would scamper from building to building, dancing in the second-, third-, and fourth-story rooms where fronts and backs had been knocked out, bombing each other with bricks and bits of concrete. Sometimes when they were dashing in and out of clouds of smoke and dust, with ruined buildings in the background, the children looked as if they were taking a town over under heavy artillery fire. The city eventually assigned a guard to stop the children but apparently there were too many of them to handle and the pandemonium continued.

1. A large department store
2. A sports stadium
3. A coffee shop
4. A pizza parlor
5. A shoe store
6. A night spot
7. A lively street corner
8. A college bookstore
9. A gymnasium
10. A medical clinic

Ten suggested topics

A description of a time of year

Assignment 5   Write a paragraph in which you describe a particular time of year. Make sure that all of the details you choose relate specifically to that time of year. In the model paragraph that follows, from "Boyhood in Jamaica" by Claude McKay, the writer remembers springtime on his native island.

Model paragraph

Most of the time there was hardly any way of telling the seasons. To us in Jamaica, as elsewhere in the tropics, there were only two seasons—the rainy season and the dry season. We had no idea of spring, summer, autumn, and winter like the peoples of northern lands. Springtime, however, we did know by the new and lush burgeoning of grasses and the blossoming of trees, although we had blooms all the year round. The mango tree was especially significant of spring, because it was one of the few trees that used to shed its leaves. Then, in springtime, the new leaves sprouted—very tender, a kind of sulphur brown, as if they had been singed by fire. Soon afterwards the white blossoms came out and we knew that we would be eating juicy mangoes by August.

Ten suggested topics

1. A winter storm
2. A summer picnic
3. Summer in the city
4. A winter walk
5. Jogging in the spring rain
6. Sunbathing on a beach
7. Signs of spring in my neighborhood
8. The woods in autumn
9. Ice skating in winter
10. Halloween night

Working Together

Writing a Character Sketch

The following personal advertisement appeared in a local newspaper:

> Young man seeks neat, responsible roommate to share off-campus apartment for next academic year. Person must be a nonsmoker and respect a vegetarian who cooks at home. Furniture not needed, but CD player would be welcome!

Personal habits have a way of causing friction between people who share the same living space. For this reason, finding the right roommate in a college dormitory, finding the right person with whom to share an apartment, or finding the right long-term companion can be very difficult.

   Divide into groups. Develop a random list of habits that can become problems when people share living space. Then, working together, group the items on your list into categories with general headings. For instance, one general heading might be called *eating patterns.*

Portfolio Suggestions

1. Imagine that you must write a paragraph or two in which you provide a character description of yourself for an agency that will match you up with a roommate. As you write, be sure you include information about your hobbies, habits, attitudes, and any other personal characteristics that could make a difference in the kind of person the agency will select for you.

2. Imagine that you must write a paragraph or two in which you provide a character sketch of the person you would like the agency to find for you.

3. Write your own description of what you imagine would be the "roommate from Hell."

Developing Paragraphs: Process

What is process?

> *Process* is the method that explains how to do something or that shows how something works. There are two kinds of process writing: *directional* and *informational*. A process that is directional actually shows you, step by step, how to do something; a process that is informational is not intended to be carried out.

Your daily life is filled with activities that involve process. For example, if you wanted to show someone how to brew a perfect cup of coffee, you would take the person through each step of the process, from selecting and grinding the coffee beans to pouring the finished product. Instructions on a test, directions on how to get to a wedding reception, or your favorite spaghetti recipe are a few examples of the kinds of process writing you see and use regularly. You can find examples of directional process writing everywhere you look, in newspapers, magazines, and books, as well as on the containers and packages of products you use every day.

On the other hand, a process that is *informational* tells you how something is or was done for the purpose of informing you about the process. For example, in a history course it might be important to understand how a general planned his strategy during the Civil War. Of course, you would not use this strategy yourself. The purpose is for information.

The following paragraph describes the various steps the writer and public speaker Malcolm X went through in the process of his self-education. Notice that each step is given in its proper sequence. Words such as *first*, *next*, and *finally* can be used to show that a writer is developing an idea by using process. In the paragraph, the words that signal the *steps* or *stages* of the process have been italicized:

When Malcolm X was in prison, he became very frustrated because he could not express his thoughts in letters written to his family and friends. Nor could he read well enough to be able to get the meaning from a book. He decided upon a program to change this situation. *First*, he got hold of a dictionary along with some paper and pencils. He was astounded at how many words there were. Not knowing what else to do, he turned to the first page and *began* by copying words from the page. It took him the entire day. *Next*, he read what he had written aloud, over and over again. He was excited to be learning words he never knew existed. *The next morning*, he reviewed what he had forgotten and *then* copied the next page. He found he was learning about people, places, and events from history. This process *continued until* he had filled a tablet with all the A's and *then* all the B's. *Eventually*, Malcolm X copied the entire dictionary!

Working with process: Don't overlook any one of the steps

The writer of the process essay is almost always more of an authority on the subject than the person reading the essay. In giving directions or information on how something was done or is to be done, it is possible to leave out a step that you think is so obvious that it is not worth mentioning. The reader, on the other hand, does not necessarily fill in the missing step as you did. An important part of process writing, therefore, is understanding your reader's level of ability. All of us have been given directions that, at first, seemed very clear. However, when we actually tried to carry out the process, something went wrong. A step in the process was misunderstood or missing. The giver of the information either assumed we would know certain parts of the process or didn't stop to think through the process completely. The important point is that directions must be complete and accurate. Here is one further consideration: If special equipment is required in order to perform the process, the directions must include a clear description of the necessary tools.

EXERCISE 1   Is the process complete?

In each of the following processes, figure out what important step or steps of information have been omitted. Imagine yourself going through the process using only the information provided.

How to make a Swedish spice cake
1. Butter an 8-inch tube pan and sprinkle with 2 Tbsp. of fine dry bread crumbs.
2. Cream ½ cup of butter; add 1 cup of firmly packed brown sugar and cream until light and fluffy.
3. Beat 2 egg yolks in a small bowl until light and add to the creamed mixture.
4. Sift together 1½ cups all purpose flour, 1 tsp. baking power, 2 tsp. ground cardamon, and 2 tsp. of ground cinnamon.
5. Add the dry ingredients to the creamed ingredients mixing alternately with ½ cup of light cream.
6. Beat egg whites stiff and fold into batter.
7. Turn in prepared pan, bake, and serve unfrosted.

Missing step or steps: _____

_____

_____

_____

How to plan a wedding

1. Make an appointment with the minister or other authority involved, to set a date for the wedding.
2. Discuss plans with both families as to the budget available for the wedding; this will determine the size of the party and where it is to be held.
3. Reserve the banquet hall as much as eight months in advance.
4. Choose members of the wedding party and ask them whether they will be able to participate in the ceremony.
5. Begin to choose the clothing for the wedding party, including your own wedding gown or suit.
6. Enjoy your wedding!

Missing step or steps: _____

_____

_____

_____

Is the process complete?

EXERCISE 2

In each of the following processes, figure out what important step or steps of information have been omitted. Imagine yourself going through the process using only the information provided.

How to prepare for an essay exam

1. Read the chapters as they are assigned well in advance of the test.
2. Take notes in class.
3. Ask the teacher what format the test will take if the teacher has not described the test.
4. Get a good night's sleep the night before.
5. Bring any pens or pencils that you might need.
6. Arrive at the classroom a few minutes early in order to get yourself settled and to keep yourself calm.

Missing step or steps: _____

_____

_____

_____

How to wrap a present

1. Gather all the materials needed: box for gift, wrapping paper, tape, scissors, and ribbon.
2. Measure the amount of paper needed and cut off excess.
3. Place box top side down on paper.
4. Bring one long side of wrapping paper up and tape it to the box.
5. Bring the other long side of the paper up over the box to the far edge. Pull tight. Fold the paper under so that it fits exactly along the far edge of the box. Tape securely.
6. Tie ribbon, make bow, and attach the card.

You can see that illustrations with directions like these would be very helpful.

Missing step or steps: _____

_____

_____

_____

Coherence in process: Order in logical sequence

When you are working with process, it is important not only to make sure the steps in the process are complete but also to present the steps in the right sequence. For example, if you are describing the process of cleaning a mixer, it is important to point out that you must first unplug the appliance before you actually remove the blades. The importance of this step is clear when you realize that a person could lose a finger if this part of the process were missing. Improperly written instructions have caused serious injuries and even death.

EXERCISE 3   Coherence in process: Order in logical sequence

The following steps describe the process of refinishing hardwood floors. Put the steps into their proper sequence.

_____ Keep sanding until you expose the hard wood.

_____ Apply a coat of polyurethane finish.

_____ When the sanding is done, clean the floor thoroughly with a vacuum sweeper to remove all the sawdust.

_____ Allow the finish to dry for three days before waxing and buffing.

_____ Take all furnishings out of the room.

_____ Do the initial sanding with a coarse sandpaper on the sanding machine.

_____ The edger and hand sander are used after the machine sanding to get to those hard-to-reach places.

_____ Put the second coat of polyurethane finish on the following day, using a brush or a roller.

_____ Change the machine to a fine sandpaper for the final sanding.

_____ Any nails sticking out from the floor should be either pulled out or set below the surface of the boards before you start the sanding machine.

Coherence in process: Order in logical sequence

The following steps describe the process of making a filing system that works. Put the steps into their proper sequence.

_____ When your mind begins to blur, stop filing for that day.

_____ Now label the file folder and slip the piece of paper in.

_____ Gather together all materials to be filed so that they are all in one location.

_____ Alphabetize your file folders and put them away into your file drawer, and you are finished for that session.

_____ Add to these materials a wastebasket, folders, labels, and a pen.

_____ Pick up the next piece of paper and go through the same procedure, the only variation being that this new piece of paper might fit into an existing file, rather than one with a new heading.

_____ Pick up an item on the top of the pile and decide whether this item has value for you. If it does not, throw it away. If it does, go on to the next step.

_____ Finally, to maintain your file once it is established, each time you consult a file folder, riffle through it quickly in order to throw out material no longer useful.

_____ If the piece of paper is worth saving, ask yourself the question, "What is this paper about?"

Transitions for process

Writers of process, like writers of narration, usually order their material by time sequence. Although it would be tiresome to use "and then" for each new step, a certain number of transitions are necessary for the process to read smoothly and coherently. Here is a list of transitions frequently used for a process paragraph.

Transitions		
the first step	while you are . . .	the last step
in the beginning	as you are . . .	the final step
to start with	next	finally
to begin with	then	at last
first of all	the second step	eventually
	after you have . . .	

EXERCISE 5   **Using transitions to go from a list to a paragraph**

Select one of the four processes given on pages 302–303. Use this list to write a process paragraph that includes transitional devices to make the paragraph smooth and coherent.

_____

_____

_____

_____

_____

_____

_____

_____

_____

_____

_____

_____

EXERCISE 6   **Using transitions to go from a list to a paragraph**

Select one of the four processes listed on pages 302–303. Use this list to write a process paragraph that includes transitional devices to make the paragraph smooth and coherent.

_____

_____

_____

_____

_____

_____

_____

_____

_____

_____

_____

_____

_____

_____

Writing the process paragraph step by step

To learn a skill that has so many different demands, the best approach is to work step by step so that one aspect can be worked on at a time. This will ensure that you are not missing a crucial point or misunderstanding a part of the whole. There certainly are other ways to go about writing an effective paragraph, but here is one logical method you can use to achieve results.

Steps for writing the process paragraph
1. After you have chosen your topic and controlling idea, plan your topic sentence.
2. List as many steps or stages in the process as you can.
3. Eliminate any irrelevant steps; add equipment needed or explain any special circumstances of the process.
4. Put the steps in order.
5. Write at least one complete sentence for each of the steps you have chosen from your list.
6. Write a concluding statement that says something about the results of completing the process.
7. Finally, copy your sentences into standard paragraph form.

Writing the process paragraph step by step

EXERCISE 7

This exercise will guide you through the construction of a complete process paragraph. Start with the topic suggested below. Use the seven steps to help you work through each stage of the writing process.

   Topic: How to lose weight

Perhaps no topic has filled more bookstores or magazine pages than the "lose ten pounds in two days" promise. The wide variety of diet plans boggles the mind. Here is your chance to add your own version.

1. Topic sentence: _____

_____

2. Make a list of possible steps.

   a. _____

   b. _____

   c. _____

   d. _____

   e. _____

   f. _____

   g. _____

   h. _____

   i. _____

   j. _____

3. Eliminate any irrelevant steps; add equipment needed or explain any special circumstances.

4. Put your steps in order by numbering them.

5. Using your final list, write at least one sentence for each step you have chosen.

    a. _____

    _____

    b. _____

    _____

    c. _____

    _____

    d. _____

    _____

    e. _____

    _____

    f. _____

    _____

    g. _____

    _____

6. Write a concluding statement. _____

    _____

    _____

7. On a separate piece of paper, copy your sentences into standard paragraph form.

EXERCISE 8   **Writing the process paragraph step by step**

This exercise will guide you through the construction of a complete process paragraph. Start with the topic suggested below. Use the seven steps to help you work through each stage of the writing process.

Topic: How to pick a college

Sometimes an individual goes through an agonizing process before he or she is finally seated in a college classroom. The factors that go into selecting a college can be extremely complicated. Give advice to a prospective college student on how to go about finding the right college.

1. Topic sentence: _____

    _____

2. Make a list of possible steps.

    a. _____

    b. _____

    c. _____

    d. _____

e. _____

f. _____

g. _____

h. _____

i. _____

j. _____

3. Eliminate any irrelevant steps; add equipment needed or explain any special circumstances.

4. Put your steps in order by numbering them.

5. Using your final list, write at least one sentence for each step you have chosen.

a. _____
   _____

b. _____
   _____

c. _____
   _____

d. _____
   _____

e. _____
   _____

f. _____
   _____

g. _____
   _____

6. Write a concluding statement. _____
   _____
   _____

7. On a separate piece of paper, copy your sentences into standard paragraph form.

Writing the process paragraph step by step

EXERCISE 9

This exercise will guide you through the construction of a complete process paragraph. Start with the topic suggested below. Use the seven steps to help you work through each stage of the writing process.

   Topic: How to manage a budget

Imagine you are the expert who has been hired by a couple to help them sort out their money problems. They bring in a reasonable salary, but still they are always spending more than they earn.

1. Topic sentence: _____

   _____

2. Make a list of possible steps.

   a. _____

   b. _____

   c. _____

   d. _____

   e. _____

   f. _____

   g. _____

   h. _____

   i. _____

   j. _____

3. Eliminate any irrelevant steps; add equipment needed or explain any special circumstances.

4. Put your steps in order by numbering them.

5. Using your final list, write at least one sentence for each step you have chosen.

   a. _____

   _____

   b. _____

   _____

   c. _____

   _____

   d. _____

   _____

   e. _____

   _____

   f. _____

   _____

   g. _____

   _____

6. Write a concluding statement. _____

   _____

   _____

7. On a separate piece of paper, copy your sentences into standard paragraph form.

On your own: Writing process paragraphs from model paragraphs

Directional: How to accomplish a physical task

Assignment 1

Write a paragraph in which you describe the process of doing a physical task of some kind, or the process of doing a task in order to accomplish something else. For example, you might have learned how to antique an old piece of furniture in order to save money, or you might have learned how to drive so that you would be in a better position to get a job. The following paragraph shows the correct process for making a common beverage, one used by millions of people every day: the ordinary cup of tea.

> ### Model paragraph
>
> Making a good cup of tea is exquisitely simple. First, heat the teapot by filling it with water that has just come to a boil. Discard this water, and place 1 teaspoon of loose tea per cup in the teapot (the exact amount may vary according to taste). Pour in fresh water that has just come to a boil, 6 ounces for each cup of tea. Allow the tea to steep for 3 to 5 minutes; then, pour it through a strainer into a cup or mug. A pound of loose tea will yield about 200 cups of brewed tea. Using a tea bag eliminates the strainer, but it is still best to make the tea in a teapot so the water stays sufficiently hot. The typical restaurant service, a cup of hot water with the tea bag on the side, will not produce the best cup of tea because the water is never hot enough when it reaches the table and because the tea should not be dunked into the water; the water should be poured over the tea. Tea in a pot often becomes too strong, but that problem can be dealt with by adding boiling water.

Ten suggested topics

1. How to move from one city to another
2. How to install your own telephone
3. How to install a stereo system
4. How to lay a carpet
5. How to make homemade ice cream
6. How to prepare a package for mailing
7. How to pack a suitcase
8. How to furnish an apartment inexpensively
9. How to wallpaper a room
10. How to care for a lawn

Informational: How something scientific works

Assignment 2   Write a paragraph in which you describe a scientific process. You could tell how a simple radio works, or you could describe how a snake sheds its skin. The following paragraph gives a description of a modern scientific process that increases the world's supply of drinking water. After you have chosen a topic, look for specific information in encyclopedias, textbooks, or other sources to help you explain the process.

> **Model paragraph**
>
> The Anse method of converting sea water to fresh water is a cheap and efficient way to produce drinkable water from the sea. First, you cover an area of water with a sheet of black plastic. Air-filled channels in the plastic keep it raised slightly above the water. Underneath this plastic is another sheet of plastic that floats on the water; this plastic has small holes that allow sea water to seep up between the two layers of plastic. The heat of the sun, striking the upper layer of the plastic, causes the water to evaporate, leaving the salt behind. The hot air, filled with water, is then forced through a pipe and into an underground collection chamber by wind that is channeled between the plastic sheets by air ducts built on top of the plastic. When the hot air enters the collection chamber, the water in the air condenses, leaving fresh water on the bottom of the submerged chamber. This fresh water can then be pumped out of the chamber and used.

Ten suggested topics
1. How leather is made
2. How metamorphosis happens
3. How an airplane flies
4. How stars are formed
5. How an eclipse occurs
6. How the human heart works
7. How a bee makes honey
8. How a camera works
9. How a piano works
10. How a book is produced

Directional: How to care for your health

Assignment 3   Write a paragraph in which you show steps you could take for your mental or physical health. Concern for health and physical fitness is enjoying great popularity, bringing in big profits to health-related magazines, health clubs, health-food producers, and sports equipment manufacturers. The following paragraph tells us how to get a good night's sleep.

Model paragraph

The process of getting a good night's sleep depends on several factors. First, the conditions in your bedroom must be correct. Be sure that the room temperature is around sixty-five degrees and that the room is as quiet as possible. Next, pay attention to your bed and how it is furnished. A firm mattress is best and wool blankets are better than blankets made of synthetic material. In addition, pillows that are too soft can cause stiffness of the neck and lead to a poor night's sleep. Also, keep in mind that what you eat and how you eat are part of the process of preparing for bed. Do not go to bed hungry, but do not overeat, either. Avoid candy bars or cookies; the sugar they contain acts as a stimulant. Finally, do not go to bed until you are sleepy; do something relaxing until you are tired.

Ten suggested topics

1. How to plan a healthful diet
2. How to care for someone who is ill
3. How to plan a daily exercise program
4. How to choose a sport that is suitable for you
5. How to live to be one hundred
6. How to pick a doctor
7. How to make exercise and diet foods fun
8. How to stop eating junk food
9. How to deal with depression
10. How to find a spiritual side to life

Informational: How something in the world of nature functions

Write a paragraph in which you show how an important task is accomplished. The task may be something that is frequently done in human society, or that occurs in the world of nature. The following paragraph, which describes how a mosquito bites a human, is an example of this kind of process.

Assignment 4

Model paragraph

On six long legs, she puts down so lightly that you feel nothing. Sensors on her feet detect the carbon dioxide that your skin exhales. Down comes the long proboscis; up go the long back legs, as though to balance it. The little soft lobes at the tip of the proboscis are spread to test the surface. It will do. A sudden contraction of the legs with the weight of the body behind it bends the proboscis backward in an arc while the six sharp blades it has unsheathed are thrust into your skin. Two of the blades are tipped with barbs. These work alternately, shove and hold, shove and hold, pulling the insect's face down and carrying their fellows deeper into your skin.

Ten suggested topics

1. How cheese is made
2. How to repair a lamp
3. How a school yearbook is produced
4. How people obtain a divorce
5. How Madame Curie discovered radium
6. How the ancient Egyptians built the pyramids
7. How a bill becomes a law
8. How penicillin was discovered
9. How Henry Ford mass-produced the automobile
10. How glass is made

Directional: How to write school assignments

Assignment 5

Your writing in school takes many forms. Write a paragraph in which you show the process of writing a specific assignment related to school. The following paragraph, adapted from Donald Murray's *Write to Learn*, shows the several steps you need to follow in the writing of a term paper.

Model paragraph

Doing a term paper involves both careful research on a topic and a methodical approach to the writing of the material. First, consult the important and up-to-date books and articles related to your subject. Next, find out the style of writing that your instructor wants; also find out details about length, organization, footnoting, and bibliography that will be part of the presentation of your paper. Then write a draft of the paper as quickly as you can, without using notes or bibliography; this will help you see your ideas and how they can be further developed. Before you go any further, review what you have written to see if you have begun to develop a point of view about your subject or an attitude toward your topic. Finally, write a draft of your paper that includes all of the important information about your subject, a draft that includes your footnotes and your bibliography.

Ten suggested topics

1. How to prepare an oral report
2. How to write a resume
3. How to write a letter of application (for a school or for a job)
4. How to write a science experiment
5. How to write a book review
6. How to revise an essay
7. How to take classroom notes
8. How to take notes from a textbook
9. How to write a letter home, asking for money
10. How to write a story for the school newspaper

Working Together

Building a Team

Working well in groups or teams is important, not only in many college situations, but also increasingly in the workplace. Group work, however, may have its problems if not approached with a careful understanding of how groups work. Appoint one person in your class to direct the discussion and then choose another person to put on the board the main ideas that come out of the discussion. Your class may want to consider some of the following issues often encountered when people work in groups:

1. How important is it that everybody first understands the task?
2. How can you avoid a situation where one person seems to be doing all the work?
3. What can be done about the person who dominates all the discussions?
4. What can be done about the person who is very shy?
5. What can be done about the person who comes to class with an "attitude"?
6. How can you be sure the group meeting does not end up with people chatting and not focusing on the task?
7. How do you avoid personality conflicts?
8. How can you avoid disagreements later on about what decision were made during the meeting?
9. What procedure should be followed when the group meets?

Portfolio Suggestion

Use the material from the classroom discussion to write a process essay. In your essay, give the procedure to be followed when a team meets to work on a project. Even though you are giving general rules to be followed, it might be helpful to give an example of a project that could be assigned to a group of workers doing a particular job, such as a group of teachers who are meeting to design a new curriculum for a course, or a group of magazine writers who are trying to decide on a theme for the next issue of their magazine.

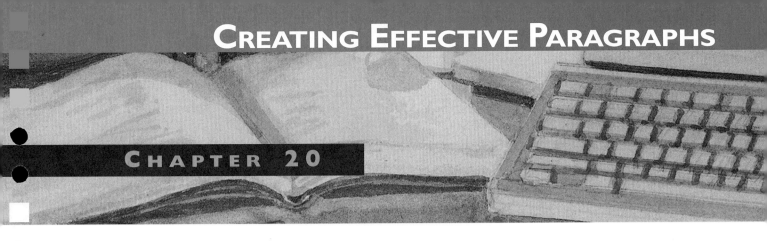

Developing Paragraphs: Comparison or Contrast

What is comparison or contrast?

One method of developing a subject in writing is to compare it to another item to show its similarities or to contrast it with another item to show how it differs. This method is used when we need to demonstrate our understanding of a complex subject and make some conclusion that is usually judgmental.

Placing one item next to another and pointing out the similarities is called a **comparison;** pointing out the differences, is called a **contrast.** The entire process of looking at both similarities and differences, however, is often referred to as **comparison.** In this chapter, we will distinguish between the two terms.

> **Comparison** or **contrast** in writing is the careful look at the similarities and/or differences between people, objects or ideas, usually in order to make some conclusion or judgment about what is being compared or contrasted.

We use comparison or contrast in a variety of ways every day. In the grocery store, we consider similar products before we decide to buy one of them; we listen to two politicians on television and think about the differences between their positions before we vote for one of them; and we read college catalogues and talk to our friends before we make a final choice as to which school we should attend.

When we compare or contrast two items, we want to be able to see very clearly the points of comparison or contrast so that we may judge which item is better or worse than the other. The process of comparison gives us a deeper understanding of the subject and enables us to make well-researched decisions rather than being at the mercy of a clever salesperson or being convinced by a good price or some other feature that might strike us at first glance.

Let's think about the selection of a word processing program, an expensive purchase that many individuals and companies will make. A shopper must consider price, availability of help for installing and troubleshooting, compatibility with available computers, specific features that differentiate the package from other programs available, how "user-friendly" the program is, what the specific needs are now and what they might be in the future, and how current or popular the program is among other software users. Also, it is a good idea to seek out advice from others who are more expert on the available programs. All of this research is basically comparison and contrast. Especially with such a complex and expensive purchase as computer software, we can see that comparison and contrast becomes not only a useful tool, but an essential one.

Working with comparison or contrast: Choosing the two-part topic

The problem with writing a good comparison or contrast paragraph usually centers on the fact that you now have a two-part topic. This demands very careful attention to the topic sentence. While you must be careful to choose two subjects that have enough in common to make them comparable, you must also not choose two things having so much in common that you cannot possibly handle all the comparable points in one paragraph or even ten paragraphs. For example, a student trying to compare the French word *chaise* with the English word *chair* might be able to come up with only two sentences of material. With only a dictionary to consult, it is unlikely that the student would find enough material for several points of comparison. On the other hand, contrasting the United States with Europe would present such an endless supply of points to compare that the tendency would be to give only general facts that your reader would already know. When the subject is too broad, the writing is often too general. A better two-part topic might be to compare traveling by train in Europe with traveling by train in the United States.

Once you have chosen a two-part topic that you feel is not too limiting and not too broad, you must remember that a good comparison or contrast paragraph should devote an equal or nearly equal amount of space to each of the two parts. If the writer is only interested in one of the topics, the danger is that the paragraph will end up being very one-sided.

Here's an example of a one-sided contrast:

While American trains go to only a few towns, are infrequent, and are often shabby and uncomfortable, the European train is much nicer.

The following example is a better written contrast that gives attention to both topics:

While American trains go to only a few large cities, run very infrequently, and are often shabby and uncomfortable, European trains go to virtually every small town, are always dependable, and are clean and attractive.

EXERCISE 1 Evaluating the two-part topic

Study the following topics and decide whether each topic is *too broad* for a paragraph, or whether it is *suitable* as a topic for a paragraph of comparison or contrast. Mark your choice in the appropriate space to the right of each topic.

Topic	Too broad	Suitable
1. Australia and England	_____	_____
2. Indian elephants and African elephants	_____	_____
3. California champagne and French champagne	_____	_____
4. Wooden furniture and plastic furniture	_____	_____
5. Wood and plastic	_____	_____
6. Paperback books and hardcover books	_____	_____
7. Mothers and fathers	_____	_____
8. Taking photographs with a flash and taking photographs using available light	_____	_____
9. Doctors and lawyers	_____	_____
10. Trains and airplanes	_____	_____

Working with comparison or contrast

EXERCISE 2

Each of the suggested comparison or contrast topics below is followed by a more specific topic that has not been completed. Complete each of these specific topics by supplying details of your own. Each topic you complete should be one that you could develop as an example of comparison or contrast.

1. Compare two friends:

   My friend _____ with my friend _____

2. Compare two kinds of coats:

   _____ coats with _____ coats

3. Compare two kinds of diets:

   The _____ diet and the _____ diet

4. Compare two kinds of floors:

   _____ floors with _____ floors

5. Compare two kinds of entertainment:

   Watching _____ with looking at _____

6. Compare two kinds of rice:

   _____ rice with _____ rice

7. Compare two places where you can study:

   Studying in the _____ with studying in the _____

8. Compare the wedding customs of two groups:

   What _____ do at a wedding with what _____ do at a wedding

9. Compare two textbooks:

   A textbook that has _____ with a textbook that contains _____

10. Compare two politicians:

    A local politician who _____ with a national politician who _____

<u>EXERCISE 3</u> **Working with comparison or contrast**

Each of the suggested comparison or contrast topics below is followed by a more specific topic that has not been completed. Complete each of these specific topics by supplying details of your own. Each topic you complete should be one that you could develop as an example of comparison or contrast.

1. Compare two kinds of popular board games people play:

   Playing _____ with playing _____

2. Compare two ways of looking at movies:

   Watching movies on _____ with going to _____

3. Compare two careers:

   A career in _____ with a career as a _____

4. Compare two ways of paying for a purchase:

   Using _____ to buy something, with using _____ to buy something

5. Compare two different lifestyles:

   Living the life of a _____ with living as a _____

6. Compare two places to go swimming:

   Swimming in a _____ with swimming in a _____

7. Compare a no-frills product with the same product sold under a standard brand name (such as no-frills corn flakes with Kellogg's corn flakes):

   A no-frills _____ with _____

8. Compare two popular magazines:

   _____ with _____

9. Compare two hobbies:

   Collecting _____ with _____

10. Compare two kinds of tests given in school:

    The _____ kind of test with the _____ kind of test

Coherence in comparison or contrast: Two approaches to ordering material

The first method for ordering material in a paragraph of comparison or contrast is known as the ***point-by-point method.*** When you use this method, you compare a point of one topic with a point of the other topic. For example, here is a paragraph from Julius Lester's *All Is Well.* In the paragraph, the writer uses the point-by-point method to compare the difficulties of being a boy with the difficulties of being a girl:

> Now, of course, I know that it was as difficult being a girl as it was a boy, if not more so. While I stood paralyzed at one end of a dance floor trying to find the courage to ask a girl for a dance, most of the girls waited in terror at the other, afraid that no one, not even I, would ask them. And while I resented having to ask a girl for a date, wasn't it also horrible to be the one who waited for the phone to ring? And how many of those girls who laughed at me making a

fool of myself on the baseball diamond would have gladly given up their places on the sidelines for mine on the field?

Notice how, after the opening topic sentence, the writer uses half of each sentence to describe a boy's situation growing up and the other half of the same sentence to describe a girl's experience. This technique is effective in such a paragraph, and it is most often used in longer pieces of writing in which many points of comparison are made. This method helps the reader keep the comparison or contrast carefully in mind at each point.

The second method for ordering material in a paragraph of comparison or contrast is known as the ***block method.*** When you use this approach, you present all of the facts and supporting details about your first topic, and then you give all of the facts and supporting details about your second topic. Here, for example, is another version of the paragraph you studied above, but this time it is written according to the block method:

> Now, of course, I know that it was as difficult being a girl as it was being a boy, if not more so. I stood paralyzed at one end of the dance floor trying to find the courage to ask a girl for a dance. I resented having to ask a girl for a date, just as I often felt foolish on the baseball diamond. On the other hand, most of the girls waited in terror at the other end of the dance floor, afraid that no one, not even I, would ask them to dance. In addition, it was a horrible situation for the girls who had to wait for the phone to ring. And how many of those girls who waited on the sidelines would have traded places with me on the baseball diamond?

Notice how the first half of this version presents all of the details about the boy, while the second part of the paragraph presents all of the information about the girls. This method is often used in shorter pieces of writing because with a shorter piece it is possible for the reader to keep the blocks of information in mind.

Looking at the two paragraphs in outline form will help you see the shape of their development.

Point-by-point method

"Now, of course, I know that it was as difficult being a girl as it was a boy, if not more so."   *Topic sentence*

First point, *first topic:* "While I stood paralyzed at one end of a dance floor trying to find the courage to ask a girl for a dance . . . "

First point, *second topic:* " . . . most of the girls waited in terror at the other, afraid that no one, not even I, would ask them."

Second point, *first topic:* "And while I resented having to ask a girl for a date, . . . "

Second point, *second topic:* " . . . wasn't it also horrible to be the one who waited for the phone to ring?"

Third point, *first topic:* "And how many of those girls who laughed at me making a fool of myself on the baseball diamond . . . "

Third point, *second topic:* " . . . would have gladly given up their places on the sidelines for mine on the field?"

Block method

Topic sentence "Now, of course, I know that it was as difficult being a girl as it was a boy, if not more so."

> *First topic, points one, two, and three:*
> "I stood paralyzed at one end of the dance floor trying to find the courage to ask a girl for a dance. I resented having to ask a girl for a date, just as I often felt foolish on the baseball diamond."
>
> *Second topic, points one, two, and three:*
> "On the other hand, most of the girls waited in terror at the other end of the dance floor, afraid that no one, not even I, would ask them to dance. In addition, it was a horrible situation for the girls who had to wait for the phone to ring. And how many of those girls who waited on the sidelines would have traded places with me on the baseball diamond?"

You will want to choose one of these methods before you write a comparison or contrast assignment. Keep in mind that although the block method is most often used in shorter writing assignments, such as a paragraph, you will have the chance to practice the point-by-point method as well.

EXERCISE 4 ## Working for coherence: Recognizing the two approaches to ordering material

Each of the following passages is an example of comparison or contrast. Read each paragraph carefully and decide whether the writer has used the point-by-point method or the block method. Also indicate whether the piece emphasizes similarities or differences. Indicate your choices in the spaces provided after each example.

1. Female infants speak sooner, have larger vocabularies, and rarely demonstrate speech defects. (Stuttering, for instance, occurs almost exclusively among boys.) Girls exceed boys in language abilities, and this early linguistic bias often prevails throughout life. Girls read sooner, learn foreign languages more easily, and, as a result, are more likely to enter occupations involving language mastery. Boys, in contrast, show an early visual superiority. They are also clumsier, performing poorly at something like arranging a row of beads, but excel at other activities calling on total body coordination. Their attentional mechanisms are also different. A boy will react to an inanimate object as quickly as he will to a person. A male baby will often ignore the mother and babble to a blinking light, fixate on a geometric figure, and, at a later point, manipulate it and attempt to take it apart.

   _____ Point-by-Point   _____ Block

   _____ Similarities   _____ Differences

2. Each man had, to begin with, the great virtue of utter tenacity and fidelity. Grant fought his way down the Mississippi Valley in spite of acute personal discouragement and profound military handicaps. Lee hung on in the trenches at Petersburg after hope itself had died. In each man there was an indomitable quality . . . the born fighter's refusal to give up as long as he can still remain on his feet and lift his two fists. Daring and resourcefulness they had, too; the ability to think faster and move faster than the enemy. These were the qualities which gave Lee the dazzling campaigns of Second Manassas and Chancellorsville and won Vicksburg for Grant.

   _____ Point-by-Point   _____ Block

   _____ Similarities   _____ Differences

3. I first realized that the act of writing was about to enter a new era five years ago when I went to see an editor at *The New York Times*. As I was ushered through the vast city room I felt that I had strayed into the wrong office. The place was clean and carpeted and quiet. As I passed long rows of desks, I saw that almost every desk had its own computer terminal and its own solemn occupant—a man or a woman typing at the computer keyboard or reading what was on the terminal screen. I saw no typewriters, no paper, no mess. It was a cool and sterile environment; the drones at their machines could have been processing insurance claims or tracking a spacecraft in orbit. What they didn't look like were newspaper people, and what the place didn't look like was a newspaper office. I knew how a newspaper office should look and sound and smell—I worked in one for thirteen years. The paper was the *New York Herald Tribune*, and its city room, wide as a city block, was dirty and disheveled. Reporters wrote on ancient typewriters that filled the air with clatter; copy editors labored on coffee-stained desks over what the reporters had written. Crumpled balls of paper littered the floor and filled the wastebaskets—failed efforts to write a good lead or a decent sentence. The walls were grimy—every few years they were painted over in a less restful shade of eye-rest green—and the atmosphere was hazy with the smoke of cigarettes and cigars. At the very center the city editor, a giant named L. L. Engelking, bellowed his displeasure with the day's work, his voice a rumbling volcano in our lives. I thought it was the most beautiful place in the world.

_____ Point-by-Point _____ Block

_____ Similarities _____ Differences

4. We went fishing the first morning. I felt the same damp moss covering the worms in the bait can, and saw the dragonfly alight on the tip of my rod as it hovered a few inches from the surface of the water. It was the arrival of this fly that convinced me beyond any doubt that everything was as it always had been, that the years were a mirage and there had been no years. The small waves were the same, chucking the rowboat under the chin as we fished at anchor, and the boat was the same boat, the same color green and the ribs broken in the same places, and under the floor-boards the same freshwater leavings and debris—the dead helgramite, the wisps of moss, the rusty discarded fishhook, the dried blood from yesterday's catch. We stared silently at the tips of our rods, at the dragonflies that came and went. I lowered the tip of mine into the water, tentatively, pensively dislodging the fly, which darted two feet away, poised, darted two feet back, and came to rest again a little farther up the rod. There had been no years between the ducking of this dragonfly and the other one—the one that was part of memory. I looked at the boy, who was silently watching his fly, and it was my hands that held his rod, my eyes watching. I felt dizzy and didn't know which rod I was at the end of.

_____ Point-by-Point _____ Block

_____ Similarities _____ Differences

5. The streets are littered with cigarette and cigar butts, paper wrappings, particles of food, and dog droppings. How long before they become indistinguishable from the gutters of medieval towns when slop pails were emptied from the second-story windows? Thousands of New York women no longer attend evening services in their churches. They fear assault as they walk the few steps from bus or subway station to their apartment houses. The era of the medieval footpad has returned, and, as in the Dark Ages, the cry for help brings no assistance, for even grown men know they would be cut down before the police could arrive.

_____ Point-by-Point _____ Block

_____ Similarities _____ Differences

EXERCISE 5   **Using the point-by-point and block methods for comparison or contrast**

Passage Number Three, given on page 323, uses the block method to make its points of contrast. Rewrite the material using the point-by-point approach.

EXERCISE 6   **Using the point-by-point and block methods for comparison or contrast**

Use the list below to write a comparison or contrast paragraph on life in the city compared with life in a suburban area. Review the list provided and add to it any of your own ideas. Omit any you do not wish to use. Then, selecting either the block method or the point-by-point method, write a comparison or contrast paragraph.

Topic sentence: If I could move back to the city from the suburbs, I know I would be happy.

The following points provide details that relate to living in the city and living in a suburban community:

Topic I Advantages of the city	Topic II Disadvantages of the suburbs
A short ride on the bus or subway gets you to work.	Commuting to work from the suburb to the city is often long and exhausting.
Men are as visible as women in the neighborhood.	Because most men in the suburbs work in the city, few of them are active in the suburban community.
Variety in the architecture and ethnic diversity	Sameness of people and streets is monotonous.
Families and single people	Mostly families
Local shopping for nearly everything	Mostly highway shopping
Mingle with people walking in the neighborhood daily	Little walking, use cars to go everywhere

Notice that the writer who created this list emphasized the disadvantages of the suburbs, in contrast to the advantages of the city. No mention was made, for example, of crime in the city. A writer could create another list, this time from the point of view of a person who prefers the suburbs.

Working for coherence: Using transitions

A number of words and phrases are useful to keep in mind when writing the comparison or contrast paper. Some of them are used in phrases, some in clauses.

Common transitions		
Transitions for Comparison	**Transitions for Contrast**	
similar to	on the contrary	though
similarly	on the other hand	unlike
like	in contrast with	even though
likewise	in spite of	nevertheless
just like	despite	however
just as	instead of	but
furthermore	different from	otherwise
moreover	whereas	except for
equally	while	and yet
again	although	still
also		
too		
so		

Notice the different uses of *like* and *as:*
Like is a preposition and is used in the prepositional phrase *like me.*

My sister is just *like* me.

As is a subordinate conjunction and is used in the clause below with a subject and a verb.

My sister sews every evening, *as* does her older daughter.

Using transitions in comparisons and contrasts

Each of the following examples is made up of two sentences. Read both sentences and decide whether the idea being expressed is one of comparison or contrast. Next, combine the two sentences by using a transition you have chosen from the list at the top of the page. Then write your new sentence on the lines provided. You may reword your new sentence slightly in order to make it grammatically correct. An example has been done for you.

Mr. Johnson is a teacher.

His wife is a teacher.

First you decide that the two sentences show a comparison. Then you combine the two by using an appropriate transition:

Mr. Johnson is a teacher just like his wife.

or

Mr. Johnson is a teacher; his wife is too.

1. Dr. Rappole has a reputation for excellent bedside manners.

   Dr. Connolly is very withdrawn and speaks so softly that it is almost impossible to understand what he has said.

   Your combined sentence: _____

   _____

   _____

2. In the United States, interest in soccer has become apparent only in recent years.

   Soccer has always been immensely popular in Brazil.

   Your combined sentence: _____

   _____

   _____

3. Hemingway's book *Death in the Afternoon* deals with the theme of man against nature.

   The same writer's novel *The Old Man and the Sea* deals with the theme of man against nature.

   Your combined sentence: _____

   _____

   _____

4. Amy is carefree and fun-loving, with little interest in school.

   Janet, Amy's sister, is so studious and hard-working that she is always on the honor roll.

   Your combined sentence: _____

   _____

   _____

5. The apartment had almost no furniture, was badly in need of painting, and felt chilly even though I was wearing a coat.

   The other apartment was attractively furnished, had been freshly painted, and was warm enough so that I had to take off my coat.

   Your combined sentence: _____

   _____

   _____

EXERCISE 8   **Using transitions in comparisons and contrasts**

First, identify each of the following examples as comparison or contrast. Then combine the two sentences by using a transition from the list on page 325. Finally, write your new sentence on the lines provided.

1. Oprah Winfrey's daytime talk show deals with current controversial issues that are of importance to society.

   David Letterman's program gives people light entertainment in the evening.

   Your combined sentence: _____

   _____

   _____

2. Shakespeare's *Romeo and Juliet* is a famous love story that takes place in Italy.

   West Side Story is a modern-day version of Shakespeare's love story that takes place in New York City.

   Your combined sentence: _____

   _____

   _____

3. The French Revolution was directed by the common people.

   The Russian Revolution was directed by an elite group of thinkers.

   Your combined sentence: _____

   _____

   _____

4. Some scientists believe that dinosaurs became extinct because they ran out of food.

   Some scientists think that dinosaurs were victims of radiation from a meteor from outer space.

   Your combined sentence: _____

   _____

   _____

5. The Museum of Modern Art in New York City shows paintings, photographs, movies, and many other forms of twentieth-century art.

   The Metropolitan Museum of Art in New York City contains sculptures, paintings, and other forms of art that date from the beginning of recorded history.

   Your combined sentence: _____

   _____

   _____

Using transitions in comparisons and contrasts

EXERCISE 9

First, identify each of the following examples as comparison or contrast. Then combine the two sentences by using a transition from the list on page 325. Finally, write your new sentence on the lines provided.

1. A ballet dancer trains for years in order to master all aspects of dancing.

   A football player puts in years of practice in order to learn the game from every angle.

   Your combined sentence: _____

   _____

   _____

2. The University of Chicago is a large urban university that has the resources of a big city as part of its attraction for faculty and students.

   Fredonia State College is a small rural college that has beautiful surroundings as part of its attraction.

   Your combined sentence: _____

   _____

   _____

3. Ice cream, a popular dessert for many years, has many calories and added chemicals to give it more flavor.

   Tofuti is a dessert made of processed soybeans that is low in calories and contains no harmful additives.

   Your combined sentence: _____

   _____

   _____

4. Nelson Rockefeller gave much of his time and money for education and the arts.

   Andrew Carnegie set up a famous foundation to support learning and artistic achievement.

   Your combined sentence: _____

   _____

   _____

5. *A Soldier's Play* is a play that has a single setting for all of its action.

   A Soldier's Story, a film based on the play, is a movie that is able to use many different settings to present all of its action.

   Your combined sentence: _____

   _____

   _____

Writing the comparison or contrast paragraph step by step

To learn a skill that has so many different demands, the best approach is to work step by step so that one aspect can be worked on at a time. This will ensure that you are not missing a crucial point or misunderstanding a part of the whole. There certainly are other ways to go about writing an effective paragraph, but here is one logical method you can use to achieve results.

Steps for writing the comparison or contrast paragraph

1. After you have chosen your two-part topic, plan your topic sentence.
2. List all your ideas for points that could be compared or contrasted.
3. Then choose the three or four most important points from your list.
4. Decide whether you want to use the point-by-point method or the block method of organizing your paragraph.
5. Write at least one complete sentence for each of the points you have chosen from your list.
6. Write a concluding statement that summarizes the main points, makes a judgment, or emphasizes what you believe is the most important point.
7. Finally, copy your sentences into standard paragraph form.

Writing the comparison or contrast paragraph step by step

This exercise will guide you through the construction of a comparison or contrast paragraph. Start with the suggested topic. Use the seven steps to help you work through each stage of the writing process.

Topic: Compare or contrast how you spend your leisure time with how your parents or a friend spends leisure time.

1. Topic sentence: _____

_____

2. Make a list of possible comparisons or contrasts.

   a. _____

   b. _____

   c. _____

   d. _____

   e. _____

   f. _____

   g. _____

   h. _____

   i. _____

   j. _____

3. Circle the three or four comparisons or contrasts that you believe are most important and put them in order.

4. Choose either the point-by-point method or the block method.

5. Using your final list, write at least one sentence for each comparison or contrast you have chosen.

   a. _____

   _____

   b. _____

   _____

   c. _____

   _____

   d. _____

   _____

   e. _____

   _____

   f. _____

   _____

   g. _____

   _____

6. Write a concluding statement. _____

_____

_____

7. On a separate piece of paper, copy your sentences into standard paragraph form.

EXERCISE 11   **Writing the comparison or contrast paragraph step by step**

This exercise will guide you through the construction of a comparison or contrast paragraph. Start with the suggested topic. Use the seven steps to help you work through each stage of the writing process.

Topic: Compare or contrast going to work with going on to college immediately after high school.

1. Topic sentence: _____

_____

2. Make a list of possible comparisons or contrasts.

a. _____

b. _____

c. _____

d. _____

e. _____

f. _____

g. _____

h. _____

i. _____

j. _____

3. Circle the three or four comparisons or contrasts that you believe are most important and put them in order.

4. Choose either the point-by-point method or the block method.

5. Using your final list, write at least one sentence for each comparison or contrast you have chosen.

a. _____

_____

b. _____

_____

c. _____

_____

d. _____

_____

e. _____

_____

f. _____

_____

g. _____

_____

6. Write a concluding statement. _____

_____

_____

7. On a separate piece of paper, copy your sentences into standard paragraph form.

Writing the comparison or contrast paragraph step by step

EXERCISE 12

This exercise will guide you through the construction of a comparison or contrast paragraph. Start with the suggested topic. Use the seven steps to help you work through each stage of the writing process.

Topic: Compare or contrast the styles of two television personalities (or two public figures often in the news).

1. Topic sentence: _____

_____

2. Make a list of possible comparisons or contrasts.

a. _____

b. _____

c. _____

d. _____

e. _____

f. _____

g. _____

h. _____

i. _____

j. _____

3. Circle the three or four comparisons or contrasts that you believe are most important and put them in order.

4. Choose either the point-by-point method or the block method.

5. Using your final list, write at least one sentence for each comparison or contrast you have chosen.

   a. _____
   _____

   b. _____
   _____

   c. _____
   _____

   d. _____
   _____

   e. _____
   _____

   f. _____
   _____

   g. _____
   _____

6. Write a concluding statement. _____
   _____
   _____

7. On a separate piece of paper, copy your sentences into standard paragraph form.

On your own: Writing comparison or contrast paragraphs

Contrasting two different perceptions toward a topic

Write a paragraph in which you contrast two perceptions toward a topic. The following paragraph contrasts the Disney film depiction of the Pocahontas story with
what we know to be more historically correct about the real Pocahontas.

Assignment 1

> ### Model paragraph
>
> The Disney version of the Pocahontas story is not an accurate portrayal of
> what we know to be true. A seventeenth-century portrait of Pocahontas re-
> veals her to be buxom, full-faced, and strong, not the Barbie-like glamour
> girl of Disney. John Smith, too, is portrayed inaccurately in the film. Far
> from the young blond heroic figure shown in the movie, John Smith was in
> actuality a bearded and weathered-looking man of thirty when he met Poca-
> hontas. The dramatic version of romance and rescue is another historical
> inaccuracy of the Disney film. Most historians contend that the supposed
> "rescue" of John Smith was in fact a farce. The Powhatans, historians claim,
> may have been adopting Smith into their tribe through a ritual that required
> a little play acting. So, while Pocahontas may have rescued Smith, the cir-
> cumstances of that rescue may have been very different from the film's de-
> piction. Furthermore, there is no historical evidence to support a romance
> between Pocahontas and John Smith as the movie shows. The unfortunate
> reality was that Pocahontas was taken captive by the English and forced to
> marry an English tobacco planter named John Rolfe. The ending of the film
> is certainly the final blow to what we know to be fact. Pocahontas did not, as
> Disney suggests, stay in North America while John Smith sailed into the dis-
> tance toward his native England. Instead, she traveled to England with
> Rolfe, her new husband. On the return trip to her native North America, at
> the young age of twenty-two, Pocahontas fell ill, probably with smallpox,
> and died.

Compare or contrast two perceptions you have had of the same topic. Choose
from one of the topics suggested below or a topic you think of yourself.

1. A sports figure's public image, versus his or her private personality
2. A politician's promises before an election with those after an election
3. A "friend" before you win the lottery and after
4. Attitudes toward smoking twenty years ago contrasted with attitudes today
5. A person's reputation in the past with his or her reputation today
6. An actor or musician on television or stage with the same actor offstage
7. Baseball years ago and baseball now
8. Attitudes toward AIDS when the virus was first discovered contrasted with
   attitudes toward the disease today
9. Traditional portrayal of Native Americans (in old films, for example) with
   portrayals today
10. How a member of your family acts at home, contrasted with how that same
    person acts in public

Comparing two cultures

Assignment 2   Write a paragraph in which you compare two cultures, or an aspect of culture that may be observed in two societies. The following paragraph was written by Brenda David, an American teacher who worked with schoolchildren in Milan, Italy, for several years.

Model paragraph

All young children, whatever their culture, are alike in their charm and innocence—in being a clean slate on which the wonders and ways of the world are yet to be written. But during the three years I worked in a school in Milan, I learned that American and Italian children are different in several ways. First, young American children tend to be active, enthusiastic, and inquisitive. Italian children, on the other hand, tend to be passive, quiet, and not particularly inquisitive. They usually depend on their parents to tell them what to do. Second, American children show their independence while their Italian counterparts are still looking to their parents and grandparents to tell them what to do or not do. Third, and most important to those who question the influence of environment on a child, the American children generally surpass their Italian schoolmates in math, mechanical, and scientific abilities. But American children are overshadowed by their Italian counterparts in their language, literature, art, and music courses. Perhaps the differences, which those of us at the school confirmed in an informal study, were to be expected. After all, what priority do Americans give to the technological skills? And what value do Italians—with the literature of poets and authors like Boccaccio, the works of Michelangelo, and the music of the world-famous LaScala opera at Milan—place on the cultural arts?

Ten suggested topics   Compare or contrast:

1. Mexican cooking with Chinese cooking
2. Marriage customs in Africa and in the United States
3. Attitudes toward women's roles in Saudi Arabia and in the United States
4. Folk dancing in two countries
5. Raising children in China and raising them in the United States
6. Urban people with small-town people
7. The reputation of a place with the reality of the place as you found it
8. The culture of your neighborhood with the general culture of our society
9. The culture you live in now with the culture in which your parents were raised
10. Medical care in our society with the medical care of another society

Comparing a place then and now

Write a paragraph in which you compare the appearance of a place you knew when   *Assignment 3*
you were growing up with the appearance of that same place now. The following
paragraph compares a small city as it was some years ago and how it appeared to the
writer on a recent visit.

> ### Model paragraph
>
> As I drove up Swede Hill, I realized that the picture I had in my mind all
> these years was largely a romantic one. It was here that my father had
> boarded, as a young man of eighteen, with a widow who rented rooms in her
> house. Now the large old wooden frame houses were mostly two-family
> homes; no single family could afford to heat them in the winter. The porches
> which had once been beautiful and where people had passed their summer
> evenings had peeling paint and were in poor condition. No one now stopped
> to talk; the only sounds to be heard were those of cars whizzing past. The
> immigrants who had come to this country and worked hard to put their chil-
> dren through school were now elderly and mostly alone, since their educated
> children could find no jobs in the small upstate city. From the top of the hill
> I looked down fondly upon the town built on the hills and noticed that a new
> and wider highway now went through the town. My father would have liked
> that; he would not have had to complain about Sunday drives on Foote Av-
> enue. In the distance I could see the large shopping mall which now had most
> of the business in the surrounding area and which had forced several local
> businesses to close. Now the center of town no longer hummed with activity,
> as it once had. My town was not the same place I had known, and I could see
> that changes were taking place that would eventually transform the entire
> area.

Compare or contrast a place as it appears now with how it appeared some years ago: *Ten suggested topics*

1. A barber shop or beauty salon
2. A house of worship
3. A local "corner store"
4. A friend's home
5. Your elementary school
6. A local bank
7. A downtown shopping area
8. A restaurant or diner
9. An undeveloped place such as an open field or wooded area
10. A favorite local gathering place

Comparing two approaches to a subject

Assignment 4 Write a paragraph in which you compare two ways of considering a particular topic. The following paragraph compares two approaches to the art of healing—the traditional medical approach and the approach that involves less dependence on chemicals and more reliance on the body's natural defense system.

Model paragraph

Natural healing is basically a much more conservative approach to health care than traditional medical practice. Traditional medical practice aims for the quick cure by means of introducing substances or instruments into the body which are highly antagonistic to whatever is causing the disease. A doctor wants to see results, and he or she wants you to appreciate the fact that traditional medicine is what is delivering those results to you. Because of this desire for swift, decisive victories over disease, traditional medicine tends to be dramatic, risky, and expensive. Natural healing takes a slower, more organic approach to the problem of disease. It first recognizes that the human body is superbly equipped to resist disease and heal injuries. But when disease does take hold or an injury occurs, the first instinct in natural healing is to see what might be done to strengthen that natural resistance and those natural healing agents so that they can act against the disease more effectively. Results are not expected to occur overnight, but neither are they expected to occur at the expense of the body, which may experience side effects or dangerous complications.

Ten suggested topics Compare or contrast:

1. Retiring or working after age sixty-five
2. Owning your own business or working for someone else
3. Two views on abortion
4. Two attitudes toward divorce
5. Two political viewpoints
6. Your lifestyle today and five years ago
7. Mothers who stay home and those who work away from home
8. Buying U.S.-made products or buying foreign-made goods
9. Two attitudes on the "right to die" issue
10. Two attitudes toward religion

Comparing male attitudes and female attitudes

Assignment 5

Some observers believe that males share similar attitudes toward certain subjects, while females seem to have a similar way of thinking on certain other topics. Some observers believe that such conclusions are nothing more than stereotypes and that people should not be divided in this way. The following paragraph reports that recent studies indicate a possible biological basis for some of the differences between males and females.

Model paragraph

Recent scientific research has shown that differences in behavior between males and females may have their origins in biological differences in the brain. Shortly after birth, females are more sensitive than males to certain types of sounds, and by the age of five months a female baby can recognize photographs of familiar people, while a boy of that age can rarely accomplish this. Researchers also found that girls tend to speak sooner than boys, read sooner than they do, and learn foreign languages more easily than boys do. On the other hand, boys show an early visual superiority over girls and they are better than girls at working with three-dimensional space. When preschool girls and boys are asked to mentally work with an object, the girls are not as successful as the boys. In this case, as in several others, the girls are likely to give verbal descriptions while the boys are able to do the actual work in their minds.

In a paragraph, compare or contrast what you believe are male and female attitudes on one of the following topics:

Ten suggested topics

1. Cooking
2. Sports
3. The nursing profession
4. Child care
5. The construction trade
6. Military careers
7. A career in science
8. Hobbies
9. Friendship
10. Clothing

Working Together

Advertising Then and Now

Study these two advertisements, the first dating from 1933 and the other a current example. Discuss with your classmates how each ad reflects its time and how each appeals to its intended market.

ALWAYS TIRED ? *Check your coffee... stale or fresh?*

IF you're feeling let-down, check your coffee. *Fresh* coffee puts new life into you—for work or play. But *stale* coffee develops a rancid oil, and, science says, stale coffee often causes headaches, depression, "nerves."

That's why Chase & Sanborn give you *Dated* Coffee. At your grocer's you will find the actual date of delivery on every pound. No can of *Dated* Coffee can stay on your grocer's shelf more than 10 days. You *know* it's fresh.

Copyright, 1933, by Standard Brands Inc.

Woman's Home Companion September 1933

Can it taste this good at home?

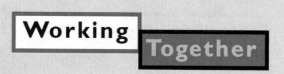

Continued

Prepare to write a comparison and contrast paragraph by working together to find points of comparison and contrast. Use the chart provided below.

Points to Compare or Contrast	1933 Coffee Ad	1998 Coffee Ad
Point 1		
Point 2		
Point 3		
Point 4		
Point 5		

Portfolio Suggestion

Write a paragraph that compares the two ads. Use the information that your class developed in the chart. Each person will have to decide which method of development to use, the block method or the point-by-point method.

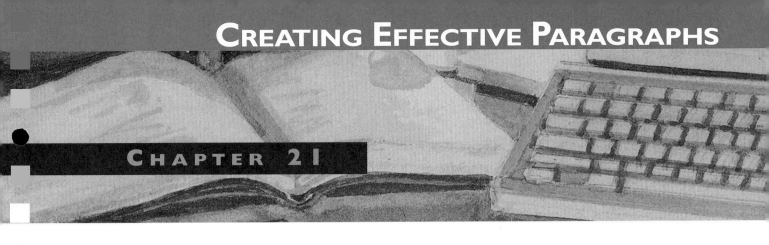

Developing Paragraphs: Cause and Effect

**S
T
E
P**

4

What is cause and effect?

People have always looked at the world and asked the questions, "Why did this happen?" or "What will be the result?" Ancient societies created beautiful myths and legends to explain the origin of the universe and our place in it, while modern civilization has emphasized scientific methods of observation to find the cause of a disease or to determine why the planet Mars appears to be covered by canals. When we examine the spiritual or physical mysteries of our world, we are trying to discover the connections or links between events. In this chapter, we will refer to connections between events as *causal relationships.*

Causal relationships are part of our daily lives and provide a way of understanding the cause, result, or consequence of a particular event. The search for cause or effect is a bit like detective work. Probing an event is a way of searching for clues to discover what caused an event or what result it will have in the future.

For example, we might ask the question, "Why did the car break down just after it came back from the garage?" as a way of searching for the cause of the car's new problem. Or we might ask, "What will be the side effects of taking a certain medicine?" This search for connections can be complex. Often the logical analysis of a problem reveals more than one possible explanation. Sometimes the best one can do is find possible causes or probable effects. In the exercises that follow, you will be asked to search for causes, effects, and connections which are causal relationships.

PRACTICE   Become familiar with the causal relationship by thinking through a few typical situations signaled by the following expressions:

1. If . . . . then

   If you _____ , **then** you will _____

   _____ .

2. The cause or reason . . . . the result, consequence, or effect

   Because I _____ , the **result** was that I _____

   _____ .

3. The problem . . . . the solution _____

   _____ could be **solved** by _____ .

EXERCISE 1   **Finding causes and effects in paragraphs**

Below are two paragraphs about the same topic: headaches. One paragraph considers causes and the other looks at some of the effects recurring headaches have on people's lives. In each case, list the causal relationships suggested in the paragraph.

1. CAUSE: Explaining WHY

   Headaches can have several causes. Many people think that the major cause of headache is nervous tension, but there is strong evidence that suggests diet and environment as possible factors. Some people get headaches because they are dependent on caffeine. Other people may be allergic to salt, or they may have low blood sugar. Still other people are allergic to household chemicals including polishes, waxes, bug killers, and paint. If they can manage to avoid these substances, their headaches tend to go away. When a person has recurring headaches, it is worthwhile to look for the underlying cause, especially if the result of that search is freedom from pain.

What causes a headache?

1. _____

2. _____

   a. _____

   b. _____

   c. _____

3. _____

   a. _____

   b. _____

   c. _____

   d. _____

2. EFFECT: Understanding or predicting RESULTS, CONSEQUENCES, EFFECTS, SOLUTIONS

Recurring headaches can have several disruptive effects on a person's life. Severe headaches are more than temporary inconveniences. In many cases, these headaches make a person nauseous to the point that he or she must go to bed. Sleep is often interrupted because of the pain. This worsens the physical and emotional state of the sufferer. For those who try to maintain a normal lifestyle, drugs are often relied on to get through the day. Such drugs, of course, can have other negative side effects. Productivity on a job can certainly be reduced, even to the point of regular absences. Finally, perhaps the most distressing aspect of all this is the seemingly unpredictable occurrence of these headaches. The interruption to a person's family life is enormous: cancelling plans in the last minute and straining relationships with friends and family. It is no wonder that many of these people feel discouraged and even depressed.

What are some of the effects of headaches?

1. _____

2. _____

3. _____

4. _____

5. _____

Separating the cause from the effect

EXERCISE 2

In each sentence, separate the cause, problem, or reason from the effect, solution or result. Remember the cause is not necessarily given first.

1. More than half of the mothers with children under one year of age work outside the home which has resulted in the unprecedented need for daycare in this country.

   cause _____

   _____

   effect _____

   _____

2. In 1995, two-thirds of all preschool children had mothers who worked, and four out of five school-age children had working mothers, facts that led to increased strains on the daycare system.

   cause _____

   _____

   effect _____

   _____

3. In one national survey, over half the working mothers reported that they had either changed jobs or cut back on their hours in order to be more available to their children.

problem _____

_____

solution _____

_____

4. Many mothers who work do so only when their children are in school, while other mothers work only occasionally during the school year because they feel their children need the supervision of a parent.

cause _____

_____

effect _____

_____

5. Many mothers experience deep emotional crises as a result of their need to combine the financial obligations of their home with their own emotional needs as parents.

problem _____

_____

result _____

_____

Working with cause and effect: Recognizing relationships and connections between events

Avoid these common errors in logic
1. Do not confuse coincidence or chronological sequence with evidence.
2. Look for underlying causes beneath the obvious ones and for far-reaching effects beyond the ones that first come to mind. Often what appears to be a single cause or a single effect is a much more complex problem.

Here is an example of a possible error in logic:

> Every time I try to write an essay in the evening, I have trouble getting to sleep. Therefore, writing must prevent me from sleeping.

In this case, writing may indeed be a stimulant that prevents the person from sleeping. However, if the person is serious about finding the cause of insomnia, he or she must observe whether any other *factors* may be to blame. For instance, if the person is drinking several cups of coffee while writing each evening, this could be a more likely cause of why the person is not sleeping.

Looking for the causal relationship

Study each of the following situations. In each case, if the sequence of events is merely coincidental or chronological, put a "T" for "time" in the space provided. If the relationship is most likely causal, put a "C." Be able to explain your answers in class.

_____ 1. Every time I carry my umbrella, it doesn't rain. I am carrying my umbrella today; therefore, it won't rain.

_____ 2. We put the fertilizer on the grass. A week later the grass grew two inches and turned a deeper green.

_____ 3. On Tuesday morning, I walked under a ladder. On Wednesday morning, I walked into my office and was told I had lost my job.

_____ 4. The child grew up helping her mother cook. In adulthood, she became a famous chef.

_____ 5. Tar and nicotine from cigarettes damage the lungs. People who smoke cigarettes increase their chances of dying from lung cancer.

_____ 6. A political scandal was exposed in the city on Friday. On Saturday night, only twenty-four hours later, a power blackout occurred in the city.

_____ 7. Increasing numbers of tourists came to the island last year. The economy of the island reached new heights.

_____ 8. Many natural disasters have occurred this year. The world must be coming to an end.

_____ 9. The factory in a certain town decided to relocate to another country. The town officials invited different industries to consider moving to the town.

_____ 10. A woman sings beautifully. She must have an equally beautiful personality.

Underlying causes

Below are five topics. For each topic, give a possible immediate or direct cause and then give a possible underlying cause. Discuss your answers in class. An example has been done for you.

Causes for a Disease

Immediate or direct cause: contact with a carrier of the disease

Underlying cause: weakened immune system due to poor nutrition

1. Causes for being selected out of several candidates for a position

   Immediate cause _____

   Underlying cause _____

2. Causes for immigrants coming to the United States

   Immediate cause _____

   Underlying cause _____

3. Causes for spanking a child

Immediate cause _____

Underlying cause _____

4. Causes for an unreasonable fear you have

Immediate cause _____

Underlying cause _____

5. Causes for a bad habit you have

Immediate cause _____

Underlying cause _____

EXERCISE 5 **Immediate or long-term effects**

Below are five topics. For each topic give an immediate effect and then give a possible long-term effect. Discuss your answers in class. An example has been done for you.

Possible Effects of Using Credit Cards

Immediate effect: money available on the spot for purchases

Long-term effect: greater cost due to interest payments

1. Effects of horror movies on young children

Immediate effect _____

Long-term effect _____

2. Effects of tuition increases in four year colleges

Immediate effect _____

Long-term effect _____

3. Effects of increased carjackings on people's driving habits

Immediate effect _____

Long-term effect _____

4. Effects of a microwave oven on how a family lives

Immediate effect _____

Long-term effect _____

5. Effects of having a family member with special needs

Immediate effect _____

Long-term effect _____

Working for coherence: Using transitions

Several transitions and expressions are particularly useful when writing about causes or effects. You will need to feel comfortable using these words and expressions, and you will need to know what punctuation is required.

Common transitions
common transitions for *cause*:
because
caused by
results from
the reason is that . . . + a complete sentence
since
common transitions for *effect*:
accordingly
as a result, resulted in
consequently
for this reason
so, so that
then, therefore, thus

Using transitional words and expressions of cause

EXERCISE 6

Use each of the following words or phrases in a sentence that demonstrates your understanding of its use for expressing **causal** relationships.

1. to be caused by

   _____

   _____

2. because (of)

   _____

   _____

3. resulted from

   _____

   _____

4. the reason is that + clause (subject and verb)

   _____

   _____

5. since

   _____

   _____

Using transitional words and expressions for effect

Use each of the following words or phrases in a complete sentence to demonstrate your understanding of how the word or phrase is used to point to an effect.

1. accordingly

_____

_____

2. as a result

_____

_____

3. results in

_____

_____

4. consequently

_____

_____

5. for this reason

_____

_____

6. so

_____

_____

7. therefore

_____

_____

Writing the cause or effect paragraph step by step

To learn a skill that has so many different demands, the best approach is to work step by step so that one aspect can be worked on at a time. This will ensure that you are not missing a crucial point or misunderstanding a part of the whole. There certainly are other ways to go about writing an effective paragraph, but here is one logical method you can use to achieve results.

Steps for writing the cause or effect paragraph

1. After you have chosen your topic, plan your topic sentence.
2. Brainstorm by jotting down all possible causes or effects. Ask others for their thoughts. Do research if necessary. Consider long-range effects or underlying causes.
3. Then choose the three or four best points from your list.
4. Decide on the best order for these points. (One way to organize them is from least important to most important.)
5. Write at least one complete sentence for each of the causes or effects you have chosen from your list.
6. Write a concluding statement.
7. On a separate piece of paper or at the computer, copy your sentences into standard paragraph form.

Writing the causal paragraph step by step

EXERCISE 8

This exercise will guide you through the causal paragraph. Start with the suggested topic. Use the seven steps to help you work through each stage of the writing process.

Topic: Why do so few Americans want to learn a second language?

1. Topic sentence: _____

_____

2. Make a list of possible causes. (Consider underlying causes.)

a. _____
b. _____
c. _____
d. _____
e. _____

3. Cross out any points that may be illogical or merely coincidental.

4. Put your list in order.

5. Using your final list, write at least one sentence for each of the causes you have found.

a. _____

_____

b. _____

_____

c. _____

_____

d. _____

_____

6. Write a concluding statement. _____

_____

_____

_____

7. On a separate piece of paper, copy your sentences into standard paragraph form.

Writing the effect paragraph step-by-step

This exercise will guide you through the effect paragraph. Start with the suggested topic. Use the seven steps to help you work through each stage of the writing process.

Topic: What are the effects of teenagers having part-time jobs after school?

1. Topic sentence: _____

_____

2. Make a list of possible causes. (Consider underlying causes.)

a. _____

b. _____

c. _____

d. _____

e. _____

3. Cross out any points that may be illogical or merely coincidental, or the result of only time sequence.

4. Put your list in order.

5. Using your final list, write at least one sentence for each of the causes you have found.

a. _____

_____

b. _____

_____

c. _____

_____

d. _____

_____

6. Write a concluding statement. _____

_____

_____

_____

7. On a separate piece of paper, copy your sentences into standard paragraph form.

On your own: Writing cause and effect paragraphs from model paragraphs

The causes of a social problem

Write a paragraph about the causes of a social problem that is of concern to you. *Assignment 1*
The following paragraph looks at possible causes for placing an elderly relative in a
nursing home.

> **Model paragraph**
>
> Industrialized societies have developed homes for the elderly who are un-
> able to care for themselves. In spite of much criticism, these homes have a
> growing percentage of our nation's elderly. Why do some people feel forced
> into placing parents into a nursing home? The most immediate cause is that
> following some serious illness, there is often no place for the elderly person
> to go where he or she can be cared for. In the family of today, it is often the
> case that both partners work outside the home so no one is home during the
> day to care for the person. Hiring a nurse to be in the home every day is be-
> yond the budget of nearly every family. Even when a family member can be
> home to care for the elderly person, the problems can be overwhelming. The
> older person can be too heavy for one or even two to manage. Bathing, par-
> ticularly, can be dangerous in these circumstances. In addition, many elderly
> people have to be watched very carefully because of their medical condition.
> Many families do not have the proper training to meet these needs. Finally,
> elderly people who may be senile and difficult can often intrude on a family's
> life to the point that a caregiver may never be able to leave the house or get a
> proper night's rest. Perhaps a better system of visiting nursing care could
> help some families keep their loved ones in their homes longer.

1. The causes of homelessness *Ten suggested topics*
2. The causes of prostitution
3. The causes of teenage runaways
4. The causes of high school dropouts
5. The causes of divorce
6. The causes of child abuse
7. The causes of tax cheating
8. The causes of high stress among college students
9. The causes of long life
10. The causes of the increase in childless couples

The causes that led to a particular historical event

Assignment 2   Write a paragraph about the causes that led to a particular event in history. The following model paragraph describes the causes that led to the French Revolution.

> **Model paragraph**
>
> Several reasons can account for the outbreak of the French Revolution in eighteenth century France. First was people's widespread feeling of resentment against the nobility and the clergy, groups that paid almost no taxes. The nobility held all the highest posts in the government, and the clergy had the right to impose new taxes on the people, facts that added to the people's resentment. In addition, the upper classes used lawyers to rediscover old laws that led to even more oppression of the lower classes. Secondly, people from the middle class who had been successful in business found themselves cut off from higher positions by the nobles, who wanted to restrict the number of people in the upper class. Thirdly, the rising economic situation at the end of the eighteenth century led to even more discontent as clergy and nobles, unable by law to enter commerce or industry, increased their pressure for tax money on the lower classes. Finally, the most immediate cause of the revolution was the French government's growing financial crisis, beginning in 1789. Because France had helped the American colonies in their struggle against England during the American Revolution, the French government could not balance its budget. The combination of social and economic injustice, along with the inability of the French upper classes to change, eventually led to the explosive situation known to history as the French Revolution.

Ten suggested topics

1. Causes for the growing disenchantment with the British royal family.
2. Causes for the growth of the Civil Rights Movement in the 1960s in the United States
3. Causes for the Gulf War in 1991
4. Causes for the reductions in the United States military budget in the 1990s
5. Causes for the victory (or loss) of a particular political candidate in a recent election
6. Causes for the increase in white-collar crime
7. Causes for the growth of the feminist movement starting in the 1970s in the United States
8. Causes for the Depression of 1929
9. Causes for the rise in Neo-Nazism in Germany in 1992
10. Causes for the loss of many jobs in the early 1990s in the United States

The effects of a substance or activity on the human body

Write a paragraph about what happens to the human body when it uses a substance or engages in some activity. The following model paragraph is from Norman Taylor's *Plant Drugs That Changed the World*.

Assignment 3

Model paragraph

The ordinary cup of coffee, of the usual breakfast strength, contains about one and a half grains of caffeine (100 mg.). That "second cup of coffee" hence means just about three grains of caffeine at one sitting. Its effects upon the nervous system, the increased capacity for thinking, its stimulating effects on circulation and muscular activity, not to speak of its sparking greater fluency—these are attributes of the beverage that few will give up. If it has any dangers, most of us are inclined to ignore them. But there is no doubt that excessive intake of caffeine at one time, say up to seven or eight grains (*i.e.*, 5 or 6 cups), has harmful effects such as restlessness, nervous irritability, insomnia, and muscular tremor. The lethal dose in man is unknown, for there are no records of it. Experimental animals die in convulsions after overdoses and from such studies it is assumed that a fatal dose of caffeine in man may be about 150 grains (*i.e.*, one-half ounce). That would mean about one hundred cups of coffee!

---

1. The effects of alcohol on the body
2. The effects of regular exercise
3. The effects of overeating
4. The effects of a strict diet
5. The effects of fasting
6. The effects of drug abuse
7. The effects of sunburn
8. The effects of allergies
9. The effects of a sedentary lifestyle
10. The effects of vitamins

Ten suggested topics

The effects of a community disaster

Assignment 4   Select a community or area disaster that you have personally experienced or heard about. This could include a severe climactic condition or a man-made disaster. Describe the effects it had on yourself or the people involved. The following model paragraph looks at the causes for the loss of life in the sinking of a supposedly unsinkable ship on its maiden voyage over 80 years ago.

> **Model paragraph**
>
> One of the most tragic events of the twentieth century was the sinking of the British ship *Titanic* in the Atlantic Ocean on April 15, 1912, with the loss of over 1500 lives. The immediate cause of this terrible loss of life was a large iceberg that tore a three hundred foot gash in the side of the ship, flooding five of its watertight compartments. Some believe that the tragedy took place because the crew members did not see the iceberg in time, but others see a chain of different events that contributed to the tragedy. First was the fact that the ship was not carrying enough lifeboats for all of its passengers: It had enough boats for only about half of the people on board. Furthermore, the ship's crew showed a clear lack of caring about the third class or "steerage" passengers, who were left in their cramped quarters below decks with little or no help as the ship went down. It has often been said that this social attitude of helping the wealthy and neglecting the poor was one of the real causes of the loss of life that night. Indeed, some of the lifeboats that were used were not filled to capacity when the rescue ships eventually found them. Finally, the tragedy of the Titanic was magnified by the fact that some ships nearby did not have a radio crew on duty and therefore missed the distress signals sent by the Titanic. Out of all this, the need to reform safety regulations on passenger ships became obvious.

Ten suggested topics

1. The effects of a hurricane
2. The effects of a power blackout on a town
3. The effects of a flood or other extensive water damage on a home or community
4. The effects of a long dark winter or other lengthy bad weather
5. The effects of a bus, train, or taxi strike on a community
6. The effects of a major fire to a downtown block
7. The effects of the loss of small businesses in a community
8. The effects of the loss of an important community leader
9. The effects of increased budget demands and decreased services in communities
10. The effects of civil unrest in a city neighborhood.

Rosa Parks on a city bus

Planning the Cause/Effect Essay

Read the following excerpt taken from an article on the life of Rosa Parks, the Alabama woman who showed incredible courage during the earliest years of the civil rights struggle.

The incident that changed Parks' life occurred on Thursday, December 1, 1955, as she was riding home on the Cleveland Avenue bus from her job at Montgomery Fair, a downtown department store where she worked as an assistant tailor. The first ten seats on the city buses, which were always reserved for whites, soon filled up. She sat down next to a man in the front of the section designated for blacks, when a white male got on and looked for a seat. In such situations, the black section was made smaller. The driver, who was white, requested that the four blacks move. The others complied, but Parks refused to surrender her seat, so the driver called the police. Parks had been evicted from a bus twelve years earlier by the same driver, but this time it was different. In a *Black Women Oral History Project* interview, she said, "I didn't consider myself breaking any segregation laws . . . because he was extending what we considered our section of the bus." And in *Black Women* she explained, "I felt just resigned to give what I could to protest against the way I was being treated."

At this time there had been fruitless meetings with the bus company about the rudeness of the drivers and other issues—including trying to get the bus line extended farther into the black community, since three-quarters of the bus riders were from there. In the previous year three black women, two of them teenagers, had been arrested for defying the seating laws on the Montgomery buses. The community had talked many times about a citywide demonstration, such as boycotting the bus line, but it never developed. The Women's Political Council already had a network of volunteers in place and had preprinted flyers; they needed only a time and place for a meeting.

About six o'clock that evening, Parks was arrested and sent to jail. She was later released on a one-hundred-dollar bond, and her trial was scheduled for December 5. Parks agreed to allow her case to become the focus for a struggle against the system of segregation. On December 2, the Women's Political Council distributed more than 52,000 flyers throughout Montgomery calling for a one-day bus boycott on the day of Parks's trial. There was a mass meeting of more than 7,000 blacks at the Holt Street Baptist Church. The black community formed the Montgomery Improvement Association and elected Martin Luther King, Jr., president. The success of the bus boycott on December 5 led to its continuation. In the second month it was almost one hundred percent effective, involving 30,000 black riders. When Parks was tried, she was found guilty and fined ten dollars plus court costs of four dollars. She refused to pay and appealed the case to the Montgomery Circuit Court.

Following her release from jail, Parks went back to work but later lost her job, as did her husband. At home, the couple had to deal with threatening telephone calls. Rosa Parks devoted her time to arranging rides in support of the boycott. Blacks were harassed and intimidated by the authorities in

Working Together

Continued

Montgomery, and there was an attempt to break up their carpools. Parks served for a time on the board of directors of the Montgomery Improvement Association, and often was invited elsewhere to speak about the boycott.

On February 1, 1956, in an attempt to have the Alabama segregation laws declared unconstitutional, the Montgomery Improvement Association filed a suit in the United States District Court in the names of four women and on behalf of all who had suffered indignities on the buses. On June 2 the lower court declared segregated seating on the buses unconstitutional. The Supreme Court upheld the lower court order that Montgomery buses must be integrated, and on December 20, 1956, the order was served on Montgomery officials. After 381 days of boycotting, resulting in extreme financial loss to the bus company, segregation and other discriminatory practices were outlawed on the city buses. Parks's refusal to give up her seat on a bus was the beginning of the civil rights movement of the 1950s and 1960s. Her action marked the beginning of a time of struggle by black Americans and their supporters as they sought to become an integral part of America.

With the notoriety surrounding her name, Parks was unable to find employment in Montgomery. Her husband became ill and could not work, so Parks, her husband, and mother moved to Detroit in 1957 to join Parks's brother. Since Raymond did not have a Michigan barber's license, he worked in a training school for barbers. In 1958 Parks accepted a position at Hampton Institute in Virginia for one year, after which she returned to Detroit and worked as a seamstress. She continued her efforts to improve life for the black community, working with the Southern Christian Leadership Conference in Detroit. In 1965 Parks became a staff assistant in the Detroit office of United States Representative John Conyers; she retired in 1988.

The entire class should listen as the excerpt is read out loud. Divide into groups. Then, work together to make two lists: immediate effect and long-term effects of the decision Rosa Parks made on December 1, 1955, in Montgomery, Alabama.

Come together as a class and check to see if each group has the same items on the list of immediate effects and the same items on the list of long-term effects.

Portfolio Suggestion

Since Rosa Parks took her historic stand in 1955, many changes have taken place in the area of civil rights in our society. Write an essay in which you detail several of these changes. You may want to do some research on the topic.

Another idea for an essay would be to look at the effects of current laws or social pressures on one of the following groups:

- Women.
- A particular religious group.
- A particular ethnic group.
- The elderly.

CHAPTER 22

Developing Paragraphs: Definition and Classification

What is definition?

> You define a term in order to explain its meaning or significance. The starting point for a good definition is to group the word into a larger *category* or *class.*

For example, the trout is a kind of fish; a doll is a kind of toy; a shirt is an article of clothing. Here is a dictionary entry for the word *family.*

> **family** (fam´e -le, fam´le) *n., pl.* **-lies.** *Abbr.* **fam.** 1. The most instinctive, fundamental social or mating group in man and animal, especially the union of man and woman through marriage and their offspring; parents and their children. 2. One's spouse and children. 3. Persons related by blood or marriage; relatives; kinfolk. 4. Lineage; especially, upper-class lineage. 5. All the members of a household; those who share one's domestic home.

To what larger category does the word *family* belong? The family, according to this entry, is a kind of *social group.*

> Once the word has been put into a larger class, the reader is ready to understand the *identifying characteristics* that make it different from other members in the class.

What makes a *trout* different from a *bass*, a *doll* different from a *puppet*, a *shirt* different from a *sweater?* Here a definition can give examples. The dictionary definition of *family* identifies the family as a married man and woman and their children. Four additional meanings provide a suggestion of some variations.

When you write a paragraph or an essay that uses definition, the dictionary entry is only the beginning. In order for your reader to understand a difficult term or idea, you will need to expand this definition into what is called **extended definition.** It is not the function of a dictionary to go into great depth. It can only provide the basic meanings and synonyms.

> Extended definition, however, seeks to analyze a concept so that the reader will have a more complete understanding.

For instance, you might include a historical perspective. When or how did the concept begin? How did the term change or evolve over the years, or how do different cultures understand the term? You will become involved in the word's connotations. **Extended definition,** or **analysis** as it is sometimes called, uses more than one method to arrive at an understanding of a term.

The following paragraph, taken from *Sociology: An Introduction* by John E. Conklin, is the beginning of a chapter on the family. The author's starting point is very similar to the dictionary entry.

> In every society, social norms define a variety of relationships among people, and some of these relationships are socially recognized as family or kinship ties. A *family* is a socially defined set of relationships between at least two people who are related by birth, marriage, or adoption. We can think of a family as including several possible relationships, the most common being between husband and wife, between parents and children, and between people who are related to each other by birth (siblings, for example) or by marriage (a woman and her mother-in-law, perhaps). Family relationships are often defined by custom, such as the relationship between an infant and godparents, or by law, such as the adoption of a child.

The author began this definition by putting the term into a larger class. *Family* is one type of social relationship among people. The writer then identifies the people who are members of this group. Family relationships can be formed by marriage, birth, adoption, or custom, as with godparents. The author does not stop here. The extended definition explores the functions of the family, conflicts in the family, the structure of the family, and the special characteristics of the family.

The writer could also have defined *family* by **negation.** That is, he could have described what a family is *not:*

A family is not a corporation.

A family is not a formal school.

A family is not a church.

When a writer defines a concept using negation, the definition should be completed by stating what the subject *is:*

A family is not a corporation, but it is an economic unit of production and consumption.

A family is not a formal school, but it is a major center for learning.

A family is not a church, but it is where children learn their moral values.

Working with definition: Class

Define each of the following terms by placing it in a larger class. Keep in mind that when you define something by class, you are placing it in a larger category so that the reader can see where it belongs. Use the dictionary if you need help. An example has been done for you.

> Chemistry is *one of the branches of science* that deals with a close study of the natural world.

1. Mythology is _____

2. Nylon is _____

3. An Amoeba is _____

4. A Tricycle is _____

5. Cabbage is _____

6. Democracy is _____

7. Asbestos is _____

8. A Piccolo is _____

9. Poetry is _____

10. A University is _____

Working with definition: Distinguishing characteristics

Using the same terms as in Exercise 1, give one or two identifying characteristics that differentiate your term from other terms in the same class. An example is done for you.

> Chemistry studies the structure, properties, and reactions of matter.

1. Mythology _____

   _____

2. Nylon _____

   _____

3. An Amoeba _____

   _____

4. A Tricycle _____

   _____

5. Cabbage _____

   _____

6. Democracy _____

   _____

7. Asbestos _____

   _____

8. A Piccolo _____

_____

9. Poetry _____

_____

10. A University _____

_____

EXERCISE 3 **Working with definition: Example**

Help define each of the following terms by providing one example. Examples always make writing more alive. An example has been done for you.

Term: Chemistry

Example: Chemistry studies an element like hydrogen. This element is the simplest in structure of all the elements, with only one electron and proton; it is colorless, highly flammable, the lightest of all gases, and the most abundant element in the universe.

1. Mythology

_____

_____

2. Friendship

_____

_____

3. Philanthropist

_____

_____

4. Planet

_____

_____

5. Gland

_____

_____

6. Greed

_____

_____

7. Volcano

_____

_____

8. Patriotism

_____

_____

9. Terrorism

_____

_____

10. Equality

_____

_____

Working with definition: Negation

Define each of the following terms by using negation to construct your definition. Keep in mind that such a definition is not complete until you have also included what the topic is that you are defining.

1. A _disability_ _____

   but it _____

2. The _perfect car_ _____

   but it _____

3. _Drugs_ are not _____

   but they are _____

4. _Freedom_ is not _____

   but it _____

5. A _good job_ _____

   but it _____

6. _Exercise_ _____

   but it _____

7. A _university_ is not _____

   but it is _____

8. A _legislator_ _____

   but he or she _____

9. The _ideal pet_ is not _____

   but it _____

10. A _boring person_ is not _____

    but he or she is _____

Writing a paragraph using definition

Here is a list of topics for possible paragraph assignments. For each topic that you choose to write about, develop a complete paragraph of definition by using one or more of the techniques you have studied—*class, identifying characteristics, example,* and *negation*—as well as any further analysis, historical or cultural, that will help the reader.

Ten Suggested Topics

1. Photosynthesis
2. Ecology
3. Symphony
4. Football
5. Paranoia
6. Courage
7. Algebra
8. Democracy
9. Masculinity or femininity
10. Justice

What is classification?

> *Classification* is the placing of items into separate categories for the purpose of helping us to think about these items more clearly. This can be extremely useful and even necessary when large numbers of items are being considered.

In order to classify things properly, you must always take the items you are working with and put them into *distinct categories,* making sure that each item belongs in only one category. For example, if you wanted to classify motorcycles into imported motorcycles, U.S.-made motorcycles, and used motorcycles, this would not be an effective use of classification because an imported motorcycle or a U.S.-made motorcycle could also be a used motorcycle. When you classify, you want each item to belong in only one category.

A classification should also be *complete.* For example, if you were classifying motorcycles into the two categories of new and used, your classification would be complete because any item can only be new or used. Finally, a classification should be *useful.* If you are thinking of buying a motorcycle, or if a friend is thinking of buying one, then it might be very useful to classify them in this way because you or your friend might save a great deal of money by deciding to buy a used machine.

The following paragraph is taken from Judith Viorst's essay "Friends, Good Friends—and Such Good Friends" and shows the writer classifying different kinds of friends.

There are medium friends, and pretty good friends, and very good friends indeed, and these friendships are defined by their level of intimacy. And what we'll reveal at each of these levels of intimacy is calibrated with care. We might tell a medium friend, for example, that yesterday we had a fight with our husband. And we might tell a pretty good friend that this fight with our husband made us so mad that we slept on the couch. And we might tell a very good friend that the reason we got so mad in that fight that we slept on the couch had something to do with that girl who works in his office. But it's only to our very best friends that we're willing to tell all, to tell what's going on with that girl in his office.

In this paragraph, the writer gives us four distinct types of friends, beginning with "medium friends," going on to "pretty good friends" and "very good friends," and ending with "very best friends." Her classification is complete because it covers a full range of friendships, and of course it is useful because people are always interested in the types of friends they have.

Working with classification: Finding the basis for a classification

EXERCISE 5

For each of the following topics, pick three different ways that topic could be classified. You may find the following example helpful.

Topic: Ways to choose a vacation spot

Basis for classification: By price (first class, medium price, economy), by its special attraction (the beach, the mountains, the desert, etc.), by the accommodations (hotel, motel, cabin, trailer)

1. Topic: Cars

   Ways to divide the topic: _____

   _____

2. Topic: Houses

   Ways to divide the topic: _____

   _____

3. Topic: Neighborhoods

   Ways to divide the topic: _____

   _____

4. Topic: Religions

   Ways to divide the topic: _____

   _____

5. Topic: Soft drinks

   Ways to divide the topic: _____

   _____

6. Topic: Dating

   Ways to divide the topic: _____

   _____

7. Topic: Floor coverings

   Ways to divide the topic: _____

   _____

8. Topic: Medicines

   Ways to divide the topic: _____

   _____

9. Topic: Snack foods

   Ways to divide the topic: _____

   _____

10. Topic: Relatives

    Ways to divide the topic: _____

    _____

EXERCISE 6   **Working with classification: Making distinct categories**

First pick a basis for classifying each of the following topics. Then break it down into distinct categories. Divide the topic into as many distinct categories as you think the classification requires.

Keep in mind that when you divide your topic, each part of your classification must belong to only one category. For example, if you were to classify cars, you would not want to make *sports cars* and *international cars* two of your categories because several kinds of sports cars are also international cars.

1. Clothing stores

   Distinct categories:

   _____   _____   _____

   _____   _____   _____

2. Television commercials

   Distinct categories:

   _____   _____   _____

   _____   _____   _____

3. College sports

   Distinct categories:

   _____   _____   _____

   _____   _____   _____

4. Doctors

   Distinct categories:

   _____   _____   _____

   _____   _____   _____

5. Hats

   Distinct categories:

   _____   _____   _____

   _____   _____   _____

6. Courses in the English department of your college

   Distinct categories:

   _____   _____   _____

   _____   _____   _____

7. Pens

   Distinct categories:

   _____   _____   _____

   _____   _____   _____

8. Dances

   Distinct categories:

   _____   _____   _____

   _____   _____   _____

9. Mail

   Distinct categories:

   _____   _____   _____

   _____   _____   _____

10. Music

    Distinct categories:

    _____   _____   _____

    _____   _____   _____

Writing a paragraph using classification

Here is a list of topics for possible paragraph assignments using classification. As you plan your paragraph, keep in mind the following points. Does the classification help to organize the material? Are you sure the classification is complete and that no item could belong to more than one category? Is there some purpose for your classifying the items as you did? (For example, will it help someone make a decision or understand a concept?)

1. Parents
2. Governments
3. Dogs
4. Careers
5. Parties
6. Summer jobs
7. Movies
8. Classmates
9. Co-workers
10. Restaurants

Ten Suggested Topics

What Is a Hero?

Some words or ideas are hard to define, either because they are controversial or because there are so many differences of opinion that people find it hard to agree on a single definition. One such idea is the concept of *heroism*.

Working together as a class, make a list of ten people you believe are heroes or heroines. What has each of them done to deserve the title of hero or heroine? Once you have decided on your examples, note the qualities shared by these people. In your view, do these qualities define *heroism?* Finally, develop a single sentence to define the term. After working out a definition in the class, you may want to look up what a dictionary definition says. How close is the classroom definition to the dictionary definition? Which one do you like better?

Portfolio Suggestion

Using the definition you and your classmates agreed upon, look up some famous historical figures in an encyclopedia. Your choices could come from any period of history, from the ancient world (Cleopatra or Alexander the Great) to our own time (Mother Teresa, Martin Luther King, Jr., or Amelia Earhart). Examine these persons' lives and then make judgment about these persons based on your definition. According to your definition, are they true heroes or heroines?

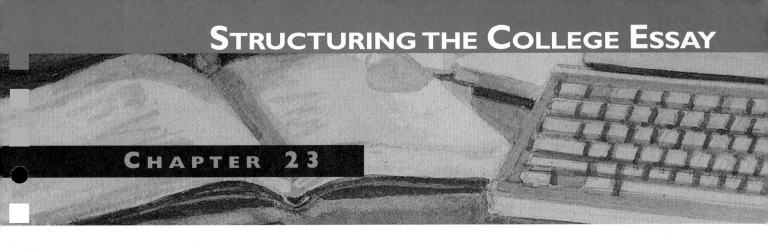

CHAPTER 23

Moving from the Paragraph to the Essay

When you learned to write a well-developed paragraph in Step 4, you were creating the basic support paragraph for essay writing. An essay is a longer piece of writing, usually five or more paragraphs, in which you can develop a topic in much more depth than you could in a single paragraph. This longer piece of writing is usually called a college essay, composition, theme, or paper. Such writing is an important part of almost every course, not only the English composition class.

You learned in Step 4 that the paragraph with its topic sentence and supporting details must have an organization that is both unified and coherent. The essay must have the same characteristics. Furthermore, since the essay develops a topic at greater length or depth, making all the parts work together becomes an added challenge.

What kinds of paragraphs are in an essay?

In addition to the support paragraphs that you studied in Step 4, the essay has two new kinds of paragraphs:

1. The **introductory paragraph** is the first paragraph of the essay. Its purpose is to be so inviting that the reader will not want to stop reading. In most essays, this introduction contains a **thesis statement.**
2. **Support paragraphs** (sometimes called **body paragraphs**) provide the evidence that shows your thesis is valid. An essay must have at least three well-developed support paragraphs. (You have studied these kinds of paragraphs in Step 4.) One paragraph must flow logically into the next. This is accomplished by the careful use of **transitional expressions.**

3. The **concluding paragraph** is the last paragraph of the essay. Its purpose is to give the reader a sense of coming to a satisfying conclusion. The reader should have the feeling that everything has been said that needed to be said.

Before you begin to write your own college essays, study this chapter to become familiar with these special essay features:

- Thesis statement
- Introductory paragraph
- Transitions between body paragraphs
- Concluding paragraph

What is a thesis?

> A *thesis* is a statement of the main idea of an essay.

The thesis states what you are going to explain, defend, or prove about your topic. It is usually placed at the end of the introductory paragraph.

How to recognize the thesis statement

A thesis statement is always expressed in a complete sentence, and it usually presents a viewpoint about a topic that can be defended or explained in the essay that follows.

Be careful not to confuse a title or a simple fact with a thesis. Remember that a **title** is usually a phrase, not a complete sentence. A **fact** is something known for certain—it can be verified. A fact does not give a personal viewpoint.

Thesis: Most children at five years of age should not be in school more than half a day.

or

Schools should offer parents the option of an all-day kindergarten program which would benefit the children as well as the working mother.

Title: The Disadvantages of All-Day Kindergarten

or

The Advantages of All-Day Kindergarten

Fact: Nearly all kindergartens in the United States offer only a half day of instruction.

PRACTICE Read each of the following statements. If you think the statement is a thesis, write TH on the blank line. If you think the statement is a title, mark T. If you think the statement is a fact, mark F.

_____ 1. In the United States, kindergarten is not compulsory.

_____ 2. Children should begin learning to read in kindergarten.

_____ 3. Putting a child into kindergarten before he or she is ready can have several unfortunate effects on that child.

_____ 4. Learning to read in Kindergarten

_____ 5. In some European countries, children do not begin formal schooling until the age of seven.

Recognizing the thesis statement

EXERCISE 1

Identify each of the following as (T) a _title_, (TH) a _thesis_, or (F) a _fact_ that could be used to support a thesis.

_____ 1. The personal interview is the most important step in the employment process.

_____ 2. Looking for a job

_____ 3. Sixty percent of all jobs are obtained through newspaper advertisements.

_____ 4. The best time to begin a foreign language is in grade school.

_____ 5. The importance of learning a foreign language

_____ 6. In the 1970s, the number of students studying foreign languages declined dramatically.

_____ 7. Most Americans doing business with Japan do not know a word of Japanese.

_____ 8. Working and studying at the same time

_____ 9. Many students in community colleges have part-time jobs while they are going to school.

_____ 10. Working a part-time job while going to school puts an enormous strain on a person.

Recognizing the thesis statement

EXERCISE 2

Identify each of the following as (T) a _title_, (TH) a _thesis_, or (F) a _fact_ that could be used to support a thesis.

_____ 1. It is estimated that approximately 2 grizzly bears live in Yellowstone National Park.

_____ 2. The survival of grizzly bears in our country should be a top priority.

_____ 3. When bears are young cubs, there are twice as many males as females.

_____ 4. Only about 60 percent of bear cubs survive the first few years of life.

_____ 5. Bears, a precious natural resource

_____ 6. The average life span of a bear today is only five or six years.

_____ 7. The sad plight of the American grizzly bear

_____ 8. Five actions need to be taken to save the grizzly bear from extinction.

_____ 9. To save the grizzly bear, we need laws from Congress, the cooperation of hunters and campers, and an educated general public.

_____ 10. A decision to save the grizzly bear

EXERCISE 3 **Recognizing the thesis statement**

Identify each of the following as (T) a *title*, (TH) a *thesis*, or (F) a *fact* that could be used to support a thesis.

_____ 1. Tons of ancient material have been taken out of Russell Cave.

_____ 2. The opening of the cave is 107 feet wide and 26 feet high.

_____ 3. People lived in this cave more than nine thousand years ago.

_____ 4. Russell Cave in Jackson County, Alabama, should be preserved as an important source of information about the ancient people of North America.

_____ 5. The way ancient people lived

_____ 6. All kinds of articles, from fish hooks to human skeletons, have been found in Russell Cave.

_____ 7. Learning about the diet of an ancient people of North America

_____ 8. An archaeologist discovers Russell Cave

_____ 9. Some of the theories previously held about life in North America thousands of years ago must now be changed because of the discoveries made in Russell Cave.

_____ 10. Russell Cave is the oldest known home of human beings in the southeastern United States.

Writing the effective thesis statement

An effective thesis statement has the following parts:

1. **A topic that is not too broad:** Broad topics must be narrowed in scope. You can do this by *limiting the topic* (changing the term to cover a smaller part of the topic), or *qualifying the topic* (adding phrases or words to the general term that will narrow the topic).

   Broad topic: Swimming

   Limited topic: Floating (*Floating* is a kind of swimming, more specialized than the term *swimming*.)

   Qualified topic: Swimming for health two hours a week (The use of the phrase *for health two hours a week* narrows the topic down considerably. Now the topic concentrates on the fact that the *time* and the *reason* spent swimming are important parts of the topic.)

   There are a number of ways to narrow a topic in order to make it fit into a proper essay length, as well as make it fit your experience and knowledge.

2. **A controlling idea that you can defend:** The controlling idea is what you want to show or prove about your topic; it is your attitude about that topic. Often the word is an adjective such as *beneficial*, *difficult*, or *maddening*.

   Learning to float at the age of twenty was a *terrifying* experience.

   Swimming two hours a week brought about a *dramatic change* in my health.

3. **An indication of what strategy of development is to be used:** (Often you can use words such as the following: *description, steps, stages, comparison, contrast, causes, effects, reasons, advantages, disadvantages, definition, analysis, persuasion.*)

   Although not all writers include the strategy in the thesis statement, they must always have in mind what major strategy they plan to use to prove their thesis. Professional writers often use more than one strategy to prove their thesis. However, in this book you are asked to develop your essays by using one major strategy at a time. By working in this way, you can concentrate on understanding and developing the skills needed for each specific strategy.

Study the following thesis statement:

> Although a date with the right person is marvelous, going out with a group can have many advantages.

Now look back and check the parts of this thesis statement.

General topic:	Going out
Qualified topic:	Going out in a group (as opposed to a single date)
Controlling idea:	To give the advantages of going out in a group
Strategy of development:	Contrast between the single date and the group date

Writing the thesis statement

EXERCISE 4

Below are four topics. For each one, develop a thesis sentence by (1) limiting or qualifying the general topic, (2) choosing a controlling idea (what you want to explain or prove about the topic), and (3) selecting a strategy that you could use to develop that topic. An example is done for you.

General topic: Senior citizens

a. *Limit or qualify the subject:*

   Community services available to the senior citizens in my town

b. *Controlling idea:*

   To show the great variety of programs

c. *Strategy for development* (narration, process, cause and effect, definition and analysis, comparison or contrast, classification, argument):

   Classify the services into major groups

Thesis statement:

   The senior citizens of Ann Arbor, Michigan, are very fortunate to have three major kinds of programs available that help them deal with health, housing, and leisure time.

1. Miami (or another city with which you are familiar)

   a. Limit or qualify the subject:

   _____

   b. Controlling idea:

   _____

c. Strategy for development (narration, process, cause and effect, definition and analysis, comparison or contrast, classification, or argument):

_____

Thesis statement:

_____

_____

_____

2. Female vocalist

a. Limit or qualify the subject:

_____

b. Controlling idea:

_____

c. Strategy for development (narration, process, cause and effect, definition and analysis, comparison or contrast, classification, or argument):

_____

Thesis statement:

_____

_____

_____

3. Shopping

a. Limit or qualify the subject:

_____

b. Controlling idea:

_____

c. Strategy for development (narration, process, cause and effect, definition and analysis, comparison or contrast, classification, or argument):

_____

Thesis statement:

_____

_____

_____

4. The library

a. Limit or qualify the subject:

_____

b. Controlling idea:

_____

c. Strategy for development (narration, process, cause and effect, definition and analysis, comparison or contrast, classification, or argument):

_____

Thesis statement:

_____

_____

_____

Writing the thesis statement

Below are five topics. For each one, develop a thesis sentence by (1) limiting or qualifying the general topic, (2) choosing a controlling idea (what you want to explain or prove about the topic), and (3) selecting a strategy that you could use to develop that topic. Review the example in Exercise 4 (page 371).

1. Television

   a. Limit or qualify the subject:

   _____

   b. Controlling idea:

   _____

   c. Strategy for development (narration, process, example, cause and effect, definition and analysis, comparison or contrast, classification, or argument):

   _____

   Thesis statement:

   _____

   _____

   _____

2. Soccer (or another sport)

   a. Limit or qualify the subject:

   _____

   b. Controlling idea:

   _____

   c. Strategy for development (narration, process, example, cause and effect, definition and analysis, comparison or contrast, classification, or argument):

   _____

   Thesis statement:

   _____

   _____

   _____

3. Math (or another field of study)

    a. Limit or qualify the subject:

    _____

    b. Controlling idea:

    _____

    c. Strategy for development (narration, process, example, cause and effect, definition and analysis, comparison or contrast, classification, or argument):

    _____

Thesis statement:

_____

_____

_____

4. Hobbies

    a. Limit or qualify the subject:

    _____

    b. Controlling idea:

    _____

    c. Strategy for development (narration, process, example, cause and effect, definition and analysis, comparison or contrast, classification, or argument):

    _____

Thesis statement:

_____

_____

_____

5. Clubs

    a. Limit or qualify the subject:

    _____

    b. Controlling idea:

    _____

    c. Strategy for development (narration, process, example, cause and effect, definition and analysis, comparison or contrast, classification, or argument):

    _____

Thesis statement:

_____

_____

_____

Ways to write an effective introductory paragraph

> An *introduction* has one main purpose: to "grab" your readers' interest so that they will keep reading.

There is no one way to write an introduction. However, since many good introductions follow the same common patterns, you will find it helpful to look at a few examples of the more typical patterns. When you are ready to create your own introductions, you can consider trying out some of these patterns.

1. *Begin with a general subject that can be narrowed down into the specific topic of your essay.* Here is an introduction to an essay about a family making cider on their farm:

   The number of children who eagerly help around a farm is rather small. Willing helpers do exist, but many more of them are five years old than fifteen. In fact, there seems to be a general law that says as long as a kid is too little to help effectively, he or she is dying to. Then, just as they reach the age when they really could drive a fence post or empty a sap bucket without spilling half of it, they lose interest. Now it's cars they want to drive, or else they want to stay in the house and listen for four straight hours to The Who. There is one exception to this rule. Almost no kid that I have ever met outgrows an interest in cidering.

   From Noel Perrin,
   "Falling for Apples"

2. *Begin with specifics (a brief anecdote, a specific example or fact) that will broaden into the more general topic of your essay.* Here is the introduction to an essay on the place of news programs in our lives:

   Let me begin with a confession. I am a news addict. Upon awakening I flip on the *Today* show to learn what events transpired during the night. On the commuter train which takes me to work, I scour *The New York Times,* and find myself absorbed in tales of earthquakes, diplomacy and economics. I read the newspaper as religiously as my grandparents read their prayerbooks. The sacramental character of the news extends into the evening. The length of my workday is determined precisely by my need to get home in time for Walter Cronkite. My children understand that my communion with Cronkite is something serious and cannot be interrupted for light and transient causes. What is news, and why does it occupy a place of special significance for so many people?

   From Stanley Milgram,
   "Confessions of a News Addict"

3. *Give a definition of the concept that will be discussed.* Here is the introduction to an essay about the public's common use of two addictive drugs, alcohol and cigarettes:

   Our attitude toward the word "drug" depends on whether we are talking about penicillin or heroin or something in-between. The unabridged three-volume Webster's says a drug is "a chemical substance administered to prevent or cure disease or enhance physical and mental welfare" or "a substance affecting the structure or function of the body." Webster's should have added "mind," but they probably thought that was part of the body. Some substances that aren't drugs, like placebos, affect "the structure or function of the body," but they work because we *think* they're drugs.

FROM ADAM SMITH,
"Some American Drugs Familiar to Everybody"

4. *Make a startling statement:*

Man will never conquer space. Such a statement may sound ludicrous, now that our rockets are already 1 million miles beyond the moon and the first human travelers are preparing to leave the atmosphere. Yet it expresses a truth which our forefathers knew, one we have forgotten—and our descendants must learn again, in heartbreak and loneliness.

FROM ARTHUR C. CLARKE,
"We'll Never Conquer Space"

5. *Start with an idea or statement that is a widely held point of view. Then surprise the reader by stating that this idea is false or that you hold a different point of view:*

Tom Wolfe has christened today's young adults as the "me" generation, and the 1970s—obsessed with things like consciousness expansion and self-awareness—have been described as the decade of the new narcissism. The cult of "I," in fact, has taken hold with the strength and impetus of a new religion. But the joker in the pack is that it is all based on a false idea.

FROM MARGARET HALSEY,
"What's Wrong with 'Me, Me, Me'?"

6. *Start with a familiar quotation or a quotation by a famous person:*

"The very hairs of your head," says Matthew 10:30, *"are all numbered."* There is little reason to doubt it. Increasingly, everything tends to get numbered one way or another, everything that can be counted, measured, averaged, estimated or quantified. Intelligence is gauged by a quotient, the humidity by a ratio, pollen by its count, and the trends of birth, death, marriage and divorce by rates. In this epoch of runaway demographics, society is as often described and analyzed with statistics as with words. Politics seems more and more a game played with percentages turned up by pollsters, and economics a learned babble of ciphers and indexes that few people can translate and apparently nobody can control. Modern civilization, in sum, has begun to resemble an interminable arithmetic class in which, as Carl Sandburg put it, "numbers fly like pigeons in and out of your head."

FROM FRANK TRIPPETT,
"Getting Dizzy by the Numbers"

7. *Give a number of descriptive images that will lead to the thesis of your essay.* Here is the opening of a lengthy essay about the importance of sports in our lives:

I cannot remember when I was not surrounded by sports, when talk of sports was not in the air, when I did not care passionately about sports. As a boy in Chicago in the late Forties, I lived in the same building as the sister and brother-in-law of Barney Ross, the welterweight champion. Half a block away, down near the lake, the Sullivan High School football team worked out in the spring and autumn. Summers the same field was given over to baseball and men's softball on Sundays. A few blocks to the north was the Touhy Avenue Fieldhouse, where basketball was played, and lifeguards trained, and behind which, in a softball field frozen over in winter, crack-the-whip, hockey, and speed skating took over. To the west, a block or so up Morse Avenue, was the

Morse Avenue "L" Recreations, a combined pool hall and bowling alley. Life, in short, was games.

FROM JOSEPH EPSTEIN,
"Obsessed with Sport:
On the Interpretation of a Fan's Dreams"

8. *Ask a question that you intend to answer.* Many essays you will read in magazines and newspapers use a question in the introductory paragraph to make the reader curious about the author's viewpoint. Some writing instructors prefer that students do not use this method. Check with your instructor for his or her viewpoint. Here is an example of such an introduction:

> Suppose there were no critics to tell us how to react to a picture, a play, or a new composition of music. Suppose we wandered innocent as the dawn into an art exhibition of unsigned paintings. By what standards, by what values would we decide whether they were good or bad, talented or untalented, successes or failures? How can we ever know that what we think is right?

FROM MARYA MANNES,
"How Do You Know It's Good?"

9. *Use classification to indicate how your topic fits into the larger class to which it belongs, or how your topic can be divided into categories that you are going to discuss.* Here is how Aaron Copland began an essay on listening to music:

> We all listen to music according to our separate capacities. But, for the sake of analysis, the whole listening process may become clearer if we break it up into its component parts, so to speak. In a certain sense we all listen to music on three separate planes. For lack of a better terminology, one might name these: the sensuous plane, the expressive plane, the sheerly musical plane. The only advantage to be gained from mechanically splitting up the listening process into these hypothetical planes is the clearer view to be had of the way in which we listen.

FROM AARON COPLAND,
What to Listen For in Music

What *not* to say in your introduction

1. *Avoid telling your reader that you are beginning your essay:*

   In this essay I will discuss . . .

   I will talk about . . .

   I am going to prove . . .

2. *Don't apologize:*

   Although I am not an expert . . .

   In my humble opinion . . .

3. *Do not refer to later parts of your essay:*

   By the end of this essay you will agree . . .

   In the next paragraph you will see . . .

4. *Don't use trite expressions.* Since they have been so overused, they will lack interest. Using such expressions shows that you have not taken the time to use your own words to express your ideas. The following are some examples of trite expressions:

   busy as a bee

   you can't tell a book by its cover

   haste makes waste

Using transitions to move the reader from one idea to the next

Successful essays help the reader understand the logic of the writer's thinking by using transitional expressions when needed. Usually this occurs when the writer is moving from one point to the next. It can also occur whenever the idea is complicated. The writer may need to summarize the points so far; the writer may need to emphasize a point already made; or the writer may want to repeat an important point. The transition may be a word, a phrase, a sentence, or even a paragraph.

- Here are some of the transitional expressions that might be used to help the reader make the right connections:

    1. To make your points stand out clearly:

the first reason	second, secondly	finally
first of all	another example	most important
in the first place	even more important	all in all
	also, next	in conclusion
	then	to summarize

    2. To show an example of what has just been said:

        for example

        for instance

    3. To show the consequence of what has just been said:

        therefore

        as a result

        then

    4. To make a contrasting point clear:

        on the other hand

        but

        contrary to current thinking

        however

    5. To admit a point:

        of course

        granted

    6. To resume your argument after admitting a point:

        nevertheless

        even though

        nonetheless

        still

    7. To call the reader's attention to your organization:

        Before attempting to answer these questions, let me . . .

        In our discussions so far, we have seen that . . .

        At this point, it is necessary to . . .

        It is beyond the scope of this paper to . . .

- A more subtle way to link one idea to another in an essay is to repeat a word or phrase from the preceding sentence. Sometimes instead of the actual word, a pronoun will take the place of the word.

8. To repeat a word or phrase from a preceding sentence:

> I have many memories of my childhood in Cuba. These *memories* include the aunts, uncles, grandparents, and friends I had to leave behind.

9. To use a pronoun to refer to a word or phrase from a preceding sentence:

> Like all immigrants, my family and I have had to build a new life from almost nothing. *It* was often difficult, but I believe the struggle made us strong.

Finding transitional expressions

EXERCISE 6

Below are the first three paragraphs of an essay on African art. Circle all the transitional expressions including repeated words that are used to link one sentence to another or one idea to the next.

Like language and social organization, art is essential to human life. As embellishment and as creation of objects beyond the requirements of the most basic needs of living, art has accompanied man since prehistoric times. Because of its almost unfailing consistency as an element of many societies, art may be the response to some biological or psychological need. Indeed, it is one of the most constant forms of human behavior.

However, use of the word *art* is not relevant when we describe African "art" because it is really a European term that at first grew out of Greek philosophy and was later reinforced by European culture. The use of other terms, such as *exotic art, primitive art, art sauvage,* and so on, to delineate differences is just as misleading. Most such terms are pejorative—implying that African art is on a lower cultural level. Levels of culture are irrelevant here, since African and European attitudes toward the creative act are so different. Since there is no term in our language to distinguish between the essential differences in thinking, it is best then to describe standards of African art.

African art attracts because of its powerful emotional content and its beautiful abstract form. Abstract treatment of form describes most often—with bare essentials of line, shape, texture, and pattern—intense energy and sublime spirituality. Hundreds of distinct cultures and languages and many types of people have created over one thousand different styles that defy classification. Each art and craft form has its own history and its own aesthetic content. But there are some common denominators (always with exceptions).

Ways to write an effective concluding paragraph

A concluding paragraph has one main purpose: to give the reader the sense of reaching a satisfying ending to the topic discussed. Students often feel they have nothing to say at the end. A look at how professional writers frequently end their essays can ease your anxiety about writing an effective conclusion. You have more than one possibility. Here are some of the most frequently used patterns for ending an essay:

1. *Come full circle. That is, return to the material in your introduction.* Finish what you started there. Remind the reader of the thesis. Be sure to restate the main idea using a different wording. Here is the conclusion to an essay "Confessions of a News Addict." (The introductory paragraph appears on page 375.)

   Living in the modern world, I cannot help but be shaped by it, suckered by the influence and impact of our great institutions. *The New York Times, CBS,* and *Newsweek* have made me into a news addict. In daily life I have come to accept the supposition that if *The New York Times* places a story on the front page, it deserves my attention. I feel obligated to know what is going on. But sometimes, in quieter moments, another voice asks: If the news went away, would the world be any worse for it?

2. *Summarize by repeating the main points.* This example is the concluding paragraph to an essay on African art. (The first three paragraphs appear on page 379.)

   In summary, African art explains the past, describes values and a way of life, helps man relate to supernatural forces, mediates his social relations, expresses emotions, and enhances man's present life as an embellishment denoting pride or status as well as providing entertainment such as with dance and music.

3. *Show the significance of your thesis by making predictions, giving a warning, giving advice, offering a solution, suggesting an alternative, or telling the results.* This example is the concluding paragraph to "Falling for Apples." (The introductory paragraph appears on page 375.)

   This pleasure goes on and on. In an average year we start making cider the second week of September, and we continue until early November. We make all we can drink ourselves, and quite a lot to give away. We have supplied whole church suppers. One year the girls sold about ten gallons to the village store, which made them some pocket money they were prouder of than any they ever earned from baby-sitting. Best of all, there are two months each year when all of us are running the farm together, just like a pioneer family.

4. *End with an anecdote that illustrates your thesis.* This example is the concluding paragraph to the essay "Obsessed with Sport . . . " (The introductory paragraph appears on pages 376–377.)

   When I was a boy I had a neighbor, a man who, after retirement, had a number of strokes. An old man and a young boy, we had in common a love of sports, which, when we met on the street, was our only topic of conversation. He once inspected a new glove of mine, and instructed me to rub it down with neat's-foot-oil, place a ball firmly in the pocket, wrap string tightly around the glove, and leave it like that for the winter. I did, and it worked. After his last stroke but one, he seldom left his house. Afternoons he spent in a chair in his bedroom, a blanket over his lap, listening to Cub games over the radio. It was while listening to a ball game that he quietly died. I cannot imagine a better way.

What *not* to say in your conclusion

1. Do not introduce a new point.
2. Do not apologize.
3. Do not end up in the air, leaving the reader feeling unsatisfied. This sometimes happens if the very last sentence is not strong enough.

A note about titles

Be sure to follow the standard procedure for writing your title.

1. Capitalize all words except articles (*the, a, an*) and prepositions.
2. Do not underline the title or put quotation marks around it.
3. Try to think of a short and catchy phrase (three to six words). Often writers wait until they have written a draft before working on a title. There may be a phrase from the essay that will be perfect. If you still cannot think of a clever title after you have written a draft, choose some key words from your thesis statement.
4. Center the title at the top of the page, and remember to leave about an inch of space between the title and the beginning of the first paragraph.

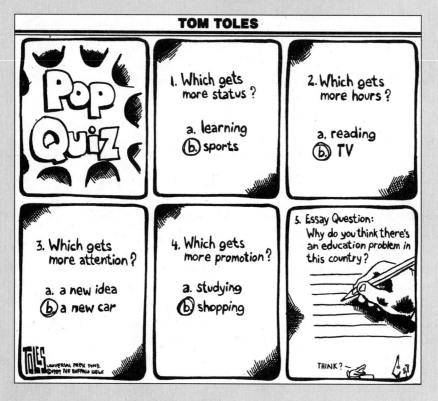

Planning the Parts of an Essay

The cartoon uses the technique of a multiple choice quiz to suggest some of the possible reasons why education in America is in trouble. As a class, discuss each of the four areas of concern raised by the cartoonist. What do you think is the *thesis* for this cartoon?

Break into groups of five or six. Work together to produce a five or six paragraph essay using the organization and content suggested by Tom Toles. Use any ideas that were presented in the class discussion or in your group. Assign each person in your group to one of the following paragraphs:

Introductory Paragraph

Four paragraphs of support

1. Learning vs. sports
2. Reading vs. television
3. A new idea vs. a new car
4. Studying vs. shopping

Concluding Paragraph

Before you write, review the basic content for each paragraph so that each group member understands what should be in his or her paragraph.

Portfolio Suggestion

Keep this group essay effort in your portfolio. How well did the members of your group succeed in helping each other build one unified essay? Many people in their jobs are expected to work with their colleagues to produce annual reports, write-ups of experiments, or brochures that advertise their products or services. Seek to improve your ability to work with others in school and on the job.

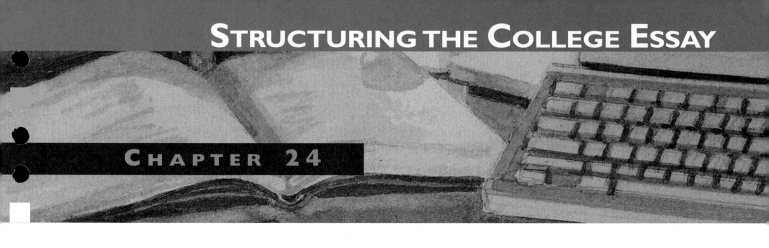

CHAPTER 24

Watching a Student Essay Take Form

It's an exciting experience for most writers to see a beginning thought or inspiration evolve into a fully developed essay. In this chapter, you will follow a student writer as she works through the sequence of steps, from the initial assignment to the final proofreading of her essay.

The sequence of steps in the writing process are given here so you can review them before you study the student's development of her essay.

Steps in the writing process
1. Find a topic and controlling idea for the thesis statement.
2. Gather the information using brainstorming techniques or research.
3. Select and organize material.
4. Write the rough draft.
5. Revise the rough draft for greater clarity of ideas. (Many writers work on several drafts before a satisfactory final version is reached.)
6. Edit the revised draft for correctness. (Correct errors such as misspellings or faulty grammar.)
7. Prepare the final typed copy, print it out, and proofread.

As you follow the student's progress through this chapter, you should maintain a critical attitude. That is, you should be prepared to analyze how well the student succeeds in producing a finished essay. Ask yourself what you might have done with the same topic. You may eventually want to write your own essay on the same topic, but with a very different controlling idea.

S
T
E
P

5

Choosing a topic and a controlling idea for the thesis statement

The student's first task is to think over what topic would be appropriate and what approach should be taken. This leads the writer in the direction of developing a tentative thesis—the sentence that states the main idea—for the entire essay. Although not all essays come right out and state the thesis directly, the writer must always have a main idea if the writing is to be focused. A reader should never have to wonder what your main idea is.

In this case, the student has been asked to write an essay about a social issue using cause or effect as the method of development. Having this assignment from the beginning is helpful because it gives the student a good sense of direction. With the help of several members of the class, she begins by making a list of possible topics on social issues that come to mind.

The causes of children failing in school

The causes of children succeeding in school

The effects of dishonesty in business

The causes of couples choosing to have small families

The effects of growing up in a large city

The effects of consumerism on the environment

The effects on the family when both parents work

The effects of being an only child

The topic she chooses is important because her success will depend on selecting a topic that is of interest to her. Writing on a topic that you don't care about will not produce a very creative result.

The student reviews the list, talks over the ideas with others and finds herself responding most directly to the topic of families with two wage earners. Although she doesn't work at present and her mother never worked outside the home, she intends to find a job as soon as she finishes her education. She has been thinking about the changes that going to work might mean for her family, particularly her husband. Not only is the topic of real interest to her, but she suspects most people in her class, many of whom are young mothers, will also have a strong interest in the topic.

Once a student knows the subject for the essay, there still is the question about what the point should be for this essay. Many students may find it difficult to figure this out before they actually do some brainstorming and see what material they have to develop. In this case, the instructor has already asked the students in the class to develop their essay by discussing the causes or the effects. This limits how our student can handle the material. Her main form of development will not be to tell a story about a friend who works (narration). She will not contrast a woman who works outside the home to a woman who stays at home (comparison and contrast); she will not give advice on how a woman can manage a job and a family at the same time (process). Although writing often can combine methods of development, she will focus on the *effects* on the family when both parents work.

Gathering information using brainstorming techniques

Here is what the student listed when she thought about her topic, *Working Parents:*

no time to cook

more microwavable dinners

more fast food

no hot meals for children

nobody at home for deliveries

hard to get to bank and to medical appointments

grocery shopping on weekends

no time to entertain

dads have to do more household chores—more than just take out the garbage

dads may be resentful

some marriages could fail

moms have to clean house at night

mom not home for children's emergencies

Some writers like to cluster their ideas when they brainstorm. *Clustering* is a *visual map* of your ideas rather than a *list*. Had the student clustered her ideas, they might have looked like this:

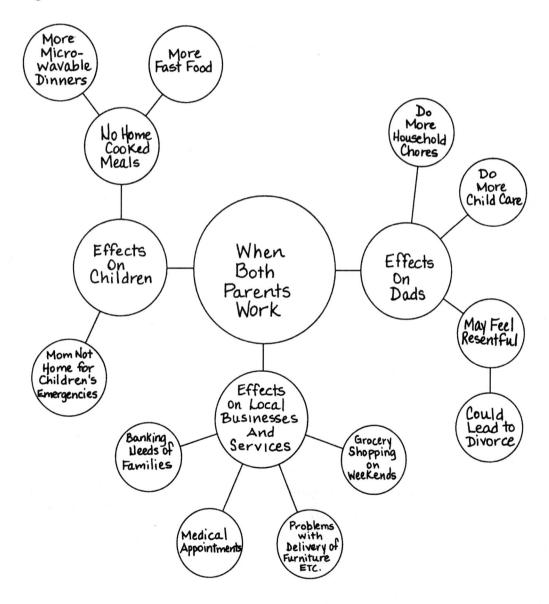

You might want to try both ways of generating ideas to see which approach works better for you.

Selecting and organizing the material

When the student has listed as many ideas as she can think of and has also asked her classmates for their ideas, she then looks over the list to see how she might group the words, phrases, or ideas into sections. Perhaps some ideas should be crossed out and not used at all. Maybe other ideas could be further developed. The student must also remember that once she starts to write, some creative flow may also direct her writing away from the exact outline she has developed by this point. That is fine. The outline is useful if it keeps the focus of the essay in mind.

Many instructors require the student to write a tentative thesis statement and an outline at this point so the instructor can verify that the student is on the right track.

Here is the outline the student wrote:

Topic:	Parents who work outside the home
Method of Development:	Discuss the effects on the family
Tentative Thesis:	When economic needs force both parents to work, the effects on the family are noticeable.

I. Introductory paragraph: Economy makes it necessary for both parents to work

II. Support paragraphs: Effects on the family

    A. Effects on children

        1. No hot meals

        2. No sympathetic ear

    B. Effects on local businesses and services

        1. Medical appointments

        2. Banking and other businesses

        3. Grocery shopping

    C. Effects on dads

        1. More household chores

        2. More child care

        3. More meal preparation

    D. Effects on family eating habits

        1. More convenience foods

        2. More microwavable foods

III. Concluding paragraph: Effects on marriage

    A. Dads could feel threatened

    B. Dads could feel resentful

Writing the rough draft

This student went to the computer lab where she knew she could work without interruption. With her outline and brainstorming list in front of her, she wrote the first draft of her essay. At this point, she was not concerned about a polished piece of work. The writer's goal was to get all her thoughts written down as a first draft. When she finished this rough draft, she not only saved it on a diskette of her own, she also printed out her draft so she could take the hard copy (actual printed pages) with her for later review. At that time, she would be ready to consider making revisions.

Read the student's rough draft and discuss your first impressions of it with your classmates. What are the strengths and weaknesses of this draft?

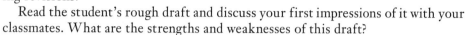

When Both Parents Work

1   The economy today has made it necessary for both parents to work. Rising prices have made two-income families the norm. What has been the effect?

2   The most noticeable change for most families is that Mom is no longer home during the day. She is not there to fix hot lunches or to soothe scraped knees and bruised egos.

3   Another effect of Mom's absence from the home is that businesses are discovering that she is no longer available to let meter readers in, accept furniture deliveries, take children to the doctor and dentist, or take care of banking needs. Just as many supermarkets have changed to a twenty-four-hour selling day, retail stores and service industries are beginning to realize that they must also adapt if they want to keep the working woman's business.

4   Even when Mom comes home in the evening, life is still not normal. Housecleaning is becoming a shared activity, when it gets done at all. Dad's duties are no longer confined to mowing the lawn and taking out the garbage, he is now expected to do lots of other things.

5   It's always a pleasure to see fathers taking their children out on weekends. Sometimes they are trying to give their wives a break, so they take the children out for a few hours or even for an entire day. This is a positive experience for the children, for they will remember these as happy hours spent with the exclusive attention of one parent.

6   So now we have Dad helping with the household chores and with the children. What about meals? Again, Dad may be asked to help out. But many men (and women) still feel the kitchen is the woman's domain. The idea that women belong in the kitchen is a popular one. Enter time-saving appliances, such as the microwave oven and convenience foods such as boil-in-the-bag frozen entrees. Mom simply doesn't have the time or the energy to prepare traditional meals. Instant meals are no longer considered a luxury and the food industry is cashing in on the demand. Even old standby items on the grocery shelves now proclaim that they are microwavable. A fact that is not hurting their sales one bit.

7   How does the family feel about Mom as a late bloomer? Dad may feel somewhat threatened, especially if he was raised to believe that a womans place is in the home. He may resent her working even more when the financial need is severe. Because he feels it announces to the world that he cannot provide for his family. In marriages that are not solid to begin with, this perceived loss of dominance by the husband may lead to divorce.

Revising the rough draft for greater clarity of ideas

When the student has left the rough draft for a day or more and then returns to make revisions, she must consider what needs to be changed. Some of the questions that follow should help in the revision process. Go through these questions with your classmates and discuss what revisions need to be made. Remember that at this stage the writer should be concerned about the ideas and the organization of the ideas, not how a word is spelled or where a comma belongs.

1. Is the essay unified? Does she stick to the topic? Does any material need to be cut?

2. Does she repeat herself anywhere? If so, what needs to be cut?

3. Does the essay make sense? Can you follow her logic? If any spot is confusing, how could she make her idea clear? Sometimes the use of transitional expressions such as *another effect*, *the most important effect*, or *the second effect* will help show the writer is moving to the next point.

4. Are the paragraphs roughly the same length? If you see one sentence presented as a paragraph, you know something is wrong.

5. Does the essay follow essay form? Is there an introductory paragraph with the thesis statement? Are there at least three supporting paragraphs in the body of the essay? Is there a concluding paragraph?

6. Are there places where more specific details could be added to develop an idea further or to add more interest?

7. Could the introduction, conclusion, or title be more creative?

Now let's look at what the student's writing instructor suggested. Here is the rough draft again with the instructor's comments written in the margins. Notice that no corrections of punctuation, spelling, or grammar have yet been considered. See if you agree with the instructor's comments. Think about what other comments you would have added if you had been the instructor.

When Both Parents Work

You might be able to think of a more catchy title.

Introductory paragraph needs more development. You might tell us more about the economy.

¶2 Is anyone available for this? More development please!

¶4 What exactly does Dad do now? Be more specific. Give examples.

¶5 is not relevant to this essay, is it? Omit it in your next draft or revise it.

¶3 good specific details

In ¶6, which two sentences say the same thing?

1　The economy today has made it necessary for most women to work. What has been the effect?

2　The most noticeable change for most families is that Mom is no longer home during the day. She is not there to fix hot lunches or to soothe scraped knees and bruised egos.

3　Another effect of Mom's absence from the home is that businesses are discovering that she is no longer available to let meter readers in, accept furniture deliveries, take children to the doctor and dentist, or take care of banking needs. Just as many supermarkets have changed to a twenty-four-hour selling day, retail stores and service industries are beginning to realize that they must also adapt if they want to keep the working woman's business.

4　Even when Mom comes home in the evening, life is still not normal. Housecleaning is becoming a shared activity, when it gets done at all. Dad's duties are no longer confined to mowing the lawn and taking out the garbage, he is now expected to do lots of other things.

5　It's always a pleasure to see fathers taking their children out on weekends. Sometimes they are trying to give their wives a break, so they take the children out for a few hours or even for an entire day. This is a positive experience for the children, for they will remember these as happy hours spent with the exclusive attention of one parent.

6　So now we have Dad helping with the household chores and with the children. What about meals? Again, Dad may be asked to help out. But many men (and women) still feel the kitchen is the woman's domain. The idea that women belong in the kitchen is a popular one. Enter time-saving appliances, such as the microwave oven and convenience foods such as boil-in-the-bag frozen entrees. Mom simply doesn't have the time or the energy to prepare traditional meals. Instant meals are no longer considered a luxury and the food industry is cashing in on the demand. Even old standby items on the grocery shelves now proclaim that they are microwavable. A fact that is not hurting their sales one bit.

7   How does the family feel about Mom as a late bloomer? Dad may feel somewhat threatened, especially if he was raised to believe that a womans place is in the home. He may resent her working even more when the financial need is severe. Because he feels it announces to the world that he cannot provide for his family. In marriages that are not solid to begin with, this perceived loss of dominance by the husband may lead to divorce.

¶ 7 presents another effect. It is not a conclusion to the essay.

In your concluding ¶, you might look to the future for more positive solutions or summarize all your points.

Editing the revised draft for correctness

Until now, the student has been concerned with the content and organization of the essay. After the student is satisfied with these revisions, it is time to look at the sentences themselves for errors such as faulty grammar, misspelling, incorrect punctuation, and inappropriate diction.

Now she should take each sentence by itself, perhaps starting with the last sentence and working backwards. (This will help her focus on the correctness of the sentences and words themselves rather than on the ideas.) She should concentrate on any weaknesses that usually cause problems for her. Many of the errors we make are unconscious and therefore hard for us to spot. Some attention from another student may be helpful and may lead to finding some of her particular errors.

When you edit your draft, look for problems such as those suggested in the following list:

1. Sentence level errors: run-ons and fragments, often corrected by use of the proper punctuation.
2. Misspellings.
3. Lack of understanding about when to use the comma.
4. Possessives: *dog's* collar, but *its* collar.
5. Diction: wordiness, use of slang, informal language or abbreviated forms, wrong word.
6. Grammar errors: subject-verb agreement, parallel structure, pronoun consistency.

Here is the fourth paragraph from the student's revised draft. The student has responded to the instructor's comments and has added more specific details along with examples. Edit the paragraph for correctness, finding at least one mistake from each of the problem areas just listed.

Even when Mom comes home in the evening, life is still not normal. Housecleaning is becoming a shared activity, when it gets done at all. Dads duties are no longer confined to mowing the lawn and taking out the garbage, he is now expected to vacuum wash dishes bathe children fold laundry—chores that no self-respecting man of a generation ago would have done. Has Dad's ego suffered? Maybe. But possibly, just possibly, his sense of being part of a family unit, not just the bread winner and disciplinarian, have increased. Because he is now forced to deal with his kids on a less exalted level, he may find that he is closer to them and they to him. Certainly, both parent and kid will be effected by this more active fathering.

Preparing the final copy

Read the student's final version which she has typed, printed, and proofread. Compare it to the rough draft. Did the student make the changes suggested by the instructor? In what ways has the essay improved? What criticisms do you still have?

Goodbye, Mom's Apple Pie

1 Inflation. Stagflation. Recession. No matter what you call the current state of our economy, virtually all of us have been touched by its effects. Rising prices and the shrinking dollar have made two-income families, once a rarity, now almost the norm. Besides fattening the family pocketbook (if only to buy necessities), how else has this phenomenon changed our lives?

2 The most noticeable change for most families is that Mom is no longer home during the day. She is not there to fix hot lunches or to soothe scraped knees and bruised egos. So who does? The answer, unfortunately, often is "No one." Countless numbers of children have become "latchkey children," left to fend for themselves after school because there aren't enough dependable, affordable babysitters or after-school programs for them. Some children are able to handle this early independence quite well and may even become more resourceful adults because of it, but many are not. Vandalism, petty thievery, alcohol and drug abuse may all be products of this unsupervised life, problems that society in general must deal with eventually. Some companies (although too few) have adapted to this changing lifestyle by instituting on-site childcare facilities and/or "flextime" schedules for working mothers and fathers. Schools have begun to provide low-cost after-school activities during the schoolyear, and summer day camps are filling the need during those months.

3 Another effect of Mom's absence from the home is that businesses are discovering that she is no longer available to let meter readers in, accept furniture deliveries, take children to the doctor and dentist, or take care of banking needs. Just as many supermarkets have changed to a twenty-four-hour selling day, retail stores and service industries are beginning to realize that they must also adapt if they want to keep the working woman's business.

4 Even when Mom comes home in the evening, life is still not normal. Housecleaning is becoming a shared activity, when it gets done at all. Dad's duties are no longer confined to mowing the lawn and taking out the garbage. He is now expected to vacuum, wash dishes, bathe children, fold laundry—chores that no self-respecting man of a generation ago would have done. Has Dad's ego suffered? Maybe. But possibly, just possibly, his sense of being part of a family unit, not just the breadwinner and disciplinarian, has increased. Because he is now forced to deal with his children on a less exalted level, he may find that he is closer to them and they to him. Certainly, both parent and child will be affected by this more active fathering.

5 So now we have Dad helping with the household chores and with the children. What about meals? Again, Dad may be asked to help out, but many men (and women) still feel the kitchen is the woman's domain. Enter time-saving appliances, such as the microwave oven and convenience foods such as boil-in-the-bag frozen entrees. Mom simply doesn't have the time or the energy to prepare traditional meals, including apple pie and home-baked bread. Instant meals are no longer considered a luxury and the food industry is cashing in on the demand. Even old standby items on the grocery shelves now proclaim that they are microwavable, a fact that is not hurting their sales one bit. However, even with quickie meals Mom is sometimes just too

tired to cook. At those times fast-food restaurants enjoy the family's business. They offer no fuss, no muss, and someone to clean up after the meal. And "clean up" the restaurants have. At a time when food prices were rising almost daily and supermarket sales were dropping, fast-food restaurants were enjoying even higher sales. Maybe part of the reason was that women were beginning to realize that their time was valuable too, and if food prices were high anyway, they reasoned, they might as well eat out and not have to spend their few precious hours at home in the kitchen.

6   How does the family feel about Mom as a late bloomer? Dad may feel somewhat threatened, especially if he was raised to believe that a woman's place is in the home. He may resent her working even more when the financial need is severe because he feels it announces to the world that he cannot provide for his family. Sometimes in marriages that are not solid to begin with, this perceived loss of dominance by the husband may even lead to divorce.

7   Yes, the two-income family has played havoc with our lifestyles but it hasn't been all bad. There are problems that must be solved, changes that are difficult to accept, priorities that must be rearranged. However, with increased pressure from the growing number of two-income families, these problems will be addressed. Hopefully, society in general and individual families in particular will find even better ways to deal with these changes regarding how we raise our children, how we care for our homes, and how we view our marriages and ourselves.

Working Together

Outlining an Essay

1. Imagine yourself in the following situation: you and your classmates are guidance counselors in a high school. You have been asked to produce a brochure that will be entitled, "When a Young Person Quits School." This brochure is intended for students who are thinking of dropping out of school. You and the other counselors meet to brainstorm on the topic. Divide into groups. Each group will choose a method of brainstorming: clustering, mapping, or listing. Work for 15 minutes or so, and then come together again as a class. Discuss what brainstorming method you chose and then on the board make a final grouping of the ideas for this topic.

2. In groups, or as a class, use the information gathered in the brainstorming activity above to construct an outline for the brochure "When a Young Person Quits School." Organize the information into main points and supporting details. Use the traditional framework (shown below) to construct your outline. *Roman numerals* (I, II, etc.) indicate main sections or different paragraphs of the piece of writing. *Capital letters* (A, B, etc.) indicate supporting points that will be contained in those sections.

I. _____

   A. _____

   B. _____

II. _____

   A. _____

   B. _____

   C. _____

   D. _____

Working Together

Continued

III. _____

    A. _____

    B. _____

Portfolio Suggestion

Gather a few brochures from different offices on campus. (Five or six may be sufficient.) Study them carefully. What are the differences among the brochures? What makes one brochure more attractive, more effective, more impressive than another? Write an article that gives advice on how to produce an effective brochure.

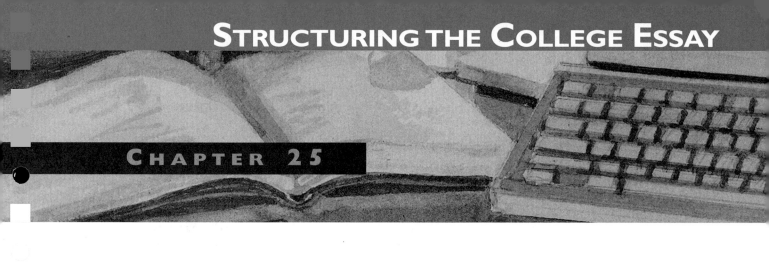

Writing an Essay Using Examples, Illustrations, or Anecdotes

Exploring the topic: The fear of AIDS

One of our most serious medical situations today is the widespread menace of the AIDS virus, along with all the suffering the disease has caused. In this chapter, you will be working on an essay that emphasizes the use of *example*. As you answer the following questions, and as you read the selection in this chapter, you will be preparing to write an essay of your own, complete with examples that will illustrate and support the points you are making.

1. Based upon what you have read and what you have heard, do most people act reasonably or unreasonably when it comes to AIDS? Can you think of any other illnesses that carry this level of fear? Explain.

   _____

   _____

   _____

   _____

S
T
E
P

5

2. Based upon your discussions with others, do you believe most people know the proper precautions to take when it comes to protection against AIDS?

_____

_____

_____

_____

3. Some people in our society have different attitudes toward AIDS victims, depending on the circumstances under which those victims contracted the disease. How widespread are these attitudes? Are these attitudes fair or unfair?

_____

_____

_____

_____

4. Scientists are working continually to find a cure for AIDS. What evidence is there that they may eventually be successful? Some people are critical of the amount of money being spent to fight this illness when the same resources could be spent fighting other diseases. What is your opinion on this question?

_____

_____

_____

_____

Reading a model essay to discover examples, illustrations, and anecdotes

AIDS: An Epidemic of Fear

MARGARET O. HYDE AND
ELIZABETH H. FORSYTH, M.D.

The cure for AIDS remains to be found. The disease is an epidemic that has caused widespread misery and death. In the following essay, two prominent writers on medical subjects show us another aspect of the disease we know as AIDS: the pervasive fear that accompanies the very mention of its name and the immediate unthinking reaction some people have when they find themselves near someone who has been stricken by the virus.

1   Some people are so frightened by AIDS that they shun all homosexuals. Many customers have changed hairdressers because they suspected that the ones they frequented were gay. They now insist on women doing their hair. Actresses have refused to be made up by men who might be homosexual. One couple visiting New Orleans was so concerned about the numerous gay waiters in the French Quarter restaurants that they stopped going out to eat. They bought food in supermarkets and ate it in their hotel room. A woman who was given a book purchased at a gay-lesbian book store called the store and asked if she could safely open the package without getting AIDS. Even people who do not think they know a homosexual person have expressed fear of the disease.

All of these people were acting on unfounded fears.

2 The epidemic of fear has been evident in many places. Some television technicians refused to work on a program in which an AIDS patient was to be interviewed. Fourteen people asked to be excused from jury duty in the trial of a man who had AIDS and was accused of murder. The sheriff's deputies who had to walk with this murder suspect were so concerned about contracting the disease that they wore rubber gloves and other protective clothing when they escorted him into the courtroom.

3 There have been reports that funeral homes refused to handle the bodies of AIDS patients without using elaborate precautions. In one case, it was alleged that a funeral home charged a family an extra two hundred dollars for the gloves and gowns used to handle an AIDS patient's body, and another funeral home tried to sell a family an expensive "germ-free" coffin. A Baltimore man, Don Miller, who is concerned about the rights of homosexuals, reported that he called ninety-nine funeral homes to see what response they gave when he told them he had AIDS and was making funeral arrangements in advance. Ten refused to deal with him, and about half of them said they would require special conditions such as no embalming and/or a sealed casket. Some groups have been working toward establishing guidelines for embalming and burying people who had AIDS.

4 Children with AIDS and those whose parents have AIDS have been the victims of the epidemic of fear that spread throughout the country. Prospective foster parents often shy away from children whose mothers died from infectious diseases because of AIDS, even though the children do not have the disease. For example, one little boy lived at Jackson Memorial Hospital in Miami, Florida, for two years after he was born because his mother had AIDS before she died. He showed no indication of having the virus.

5 While some babies die quickly after birth, others live well into school age. In a number of places, hospitals have begun day care programs for children with AIDS, and a California monastery has opened its doors to unwanted infants born with AIDS who might otherwise have to spend their lives in hospitals. For many children with AIDS, life outside the hospital is one in which they are shunned by friends, neighbors, and even relatives because of the fear that still surrounds the disease.

6 Controversies about whether or not children with AIDS should be permitted to attend school have reached far and wide. The case of Ryan White of Russiaville, Indiana, was well publicized. A hemophiliac, he contracted AIDS from a blood transfusion he received in December 1984. At one point, Ryan was forced to monitor classes at home by telephone because of a restraining order obtained by parents of the other children. In the fall of 1986, Ryan started school with his class for the first time in two years, after the parents who fought his return dropped their lawsuit because of legal costs. Ryan's school had been picketed in the past, but by 1986, some students just took the attitude that they did not mind his being in school as long as he did not sit near them. Ryan was assigned his own bathroom and was given disposable utensils in the cafeteria, even though scientists believe this precaution to be unnecessary. School staff members were instructed in handling any health emergencies that arose.

7 In New York City, when school opened in late August of 1985, the fear of AIDS created a great deal of excitement. Whether or not a child who had AIDS could attend public school in New York City was determined by a panel made up of health experts, an educator, and a parent. One child with AIDS had been attending school for three years and was identified only as a second grader. The child was said to have been born with AIDS but was in good health, the disease being in remission. She had received all the inoculations necessary for school admission, and had recovered from a case of chicken pox, managing to fight off this childhood illness uneventfully.

8 In Hollywood, many people were near hysteria after Rock Hudson's announcement that he was suffering from AIDS. Some actresses who had kissed

people with AIDS were especially concerned, while others refused to work with anyone considered to be gay. After one actor became sick, make-up artists burned the brushes they had used on him. But Hollywood stars have been outstanding in their support of care for persons with AIDS and research on AIDS. Shortly before he died, Rock Hudson sent a brief message to a benefit dinner, "I am not happy that I am sick. I am not happy that I have AIDS. But if that is helping others, I can, at least, know that my own misfortune has had some positive worth."

9 Only through education and further research can one strike a balance between fear of the disease, sensible precautions, and concern for people who suffer from AIDS. Fear makes people "block out" information. We need more campaigns which emphasize the lack of danger from casual contact since polls show that people are simply not listening.

Analyzing the writers' strategies

1. In the first paragraph of the essay, the writers choose a variety of examples to introduce their subject. Examine each sentence of the paragraph and underline each example. How do these different examples show the variety of the AIDS experience in our society?

2. One of the points the writers make throughout their essay is that AIDS is a nationwide problem. Review each paragraph and note the area of the country mentioned in the paragraph. How do the contents of the different paragraphs confirm the idea that AIDS is a widespread problem?

3. Throughout the essay, the writers use a number of short examples. They also use extended examples. Review the essay and find at least two paragraphs that contain several short examples. Then find at least two paragraphs that each contain one more fully developed example.

4. One method writers use to make their work more memorable is to be very specific when they use examples. Choose one paragraph in the essay and judge each example in that paragraph. How have the writers made a good example even better by being specific?

5. Can you find an anecdote in this essay? (An anecdote tells a brief story in order to illustrate a point.)

Writing an essay using examples, illustrations, or anecdotes

Of the many ways writers choose to support their ideas, none is more useful or appreciated than the *example.* All of us have ideas in our minds, but these ideas will not become real for our readers until we use examples to make our concepts clear, concrete, and convincing. Writers who use good examples will be able to hold the attention of their readers.

> *Example,* one of the methods for developing a writer's ideas, provides one or more instances of the idea, either briefly or in some detail, in order to clarify, make concrete, or convince readers of the more general idea or point.

The following terms are closely related:

Example:	a specific instance of something being discussed
Extended example:	an example which is developed at some length, often taking up one or more complete paragraphs
Illustration:	an example used to clarify or explain
Anecdote:	a brief story used to illustrate a point

Choose a topic and controlling idea for the thesis statement

Suggested topics for writing

Here is a list of possible topics that could lead to an essay using example as the main method of development. The section that follows this list will help you work through the various stages of the writing process.

1. Doctors I Have Encountered
2. The Quality of Medical Care
3. Crises Children Face
4. What Makes a Class Exciting
5. Features to Look for When Buying a _____
6. The World's Worst Habits
7. The Lifestyles of College Students Today
8. The Increasing Problem of Homelessness
9. People I Have Admired
10. The Top Five Best Recording Artists

Using this list or ideas of your own, jot down two or three topics that appeal to you.

_____

_____

_____

From these topics, select the one you think would give you the best opportunity for writing. About which one do you feel strongest? About which one are you the most expert? Which one is most likely to interest your readers? Which one is best suited to being developed into a college essay containing examples?

Selected Topic: _____

Your next step is to decide what your controlling idea should be. What is the point you want to make about the topic you have chosen? For instance, if you choose to write about "Doctors I Have Encountered," your controlling idea may be "compassionate," or it may be "egotistical."

Controlling idea: _____

Now put your topic and controlling idea together into your thesis statement.

Thesis statement: _____

_____

Gather the information (use brainstorming techniques)

Take at least fifteen minutes to jot down every example you can think of that you could use in your essay. If your topic is not of a personal nature, you might form a group to help each other think of examples, anecdotes, and illustrations. Later, you may want to refer to material from magazines or newspapers if you feel your examples need to be improved. If you do use outside sources, be sure to take notes, checking the correct spelling of names and the accuracy of dates and facts.

_____

_____

_____

_____

_____

_____

_____

_____

_____

_____

_____

Select and organize material

Review your list of examples, crossing out any ideas that are not useful. Do you have enough material to develop three body paragraphs? This might mean using three extended examples, some anecdotes, or several smaller examples that could be organized into three different groups. Decide the order in which you want to present your examples. Do you have any ideas for how you might want to write the introduction? On the lines that follow, show your plan for organizing your essay. You may want to make an outline that will show major points with supporting details under each major point.

_____

_____

_____

_____

_____

_____

_____

_____

_____

_____

_____

Write the rough draft

Now you are ready to write your rough draft. Approach the writing with the attitude that you are going to write down all your thoughts on the subject without worrying about mistakes of any kind. It is important that your mind is relaxed enough to allow your thoughts to flow freely, even if you do not follow your plan exactly. Just get your thoughts on paper. You are free to add ideas, drop others, or rearrange the order of your details at any point. Sometimes a period of freewriting leads to new ideas, ideas that could be better than the ones you had in your brainstorming session. Once a writer has something on paper, he or she usually feels a great sense of relief, even though it is obvious there are revisions ahead.

Coherence in the example essay

Keep in mind that in a paragraph with several examples, the order of these examples usually follows some logical progression. This could mean that you would start with the less serious and then move to the more serious, or you might start with the simpler one and move to the more complicated. If your examples consist of events, you might begin with examples from the more distant past and move forward to give examples from the present day. Whatever logical progression you choose, you will find it helpful to signal your examples by using some of transitional expressions that follow.

Transitional expressions in essays using examples
the following illustration
to illustrate this
as an illustration
for example
for instance
specifically
an example of this is
such as
one such case
a typical case
To prove my point, listen what happened to me
Let me tell you a story.

Guidelines for revising the essay using examples

As you work on your rough draft, you may revise alone, with a group, with a peer tutor, or directly with your instructor. Here are some of the basic questions you should consider at this most important stage of your work:

1. Does the rough draft satisfy the conditions for the essay form? Is there an introductory paragraph? Are there at least three well-developed paragraphs in the body of the essay? Do each of these paragraphs have at least one example? Is there a concluding paragraph? Remember that one sentence is not usually considered an acceptable paragraph. (Many journalistic pieces do not follow this general rule because they often have a space limitation and are not expected to develop every idea.)

2. Have you used *example* as your major method of development? Could you make your examples even better by being more specific or by looking up statistics or facts that would lend more authority to your point of view? Could you quote an expert on the subject?

3. What is the basis for the ordering of your examples? Whenever appropriate, did you use transitions to signal the beginning of an example?

4. Is any important part missing? Are there any parts that seem irrelevant or out of place?

5. Are there expressions or words that need to be better chosen? Is there any place where you have been repetitious?

6. Find at least two verbs (usually some form of the verb "to be") that could be replaced with more descriptive verbs. Add at least two adjectives that will provide better sensory images for the reader.

7. Find at least one place in the draft where you can add a sentence or two that will make an example better.

8. Can you think of a more effective way to begin or end?

9. Show your draft to two other readers and ask each one to give you at least one suggestion for improvement.

Prepare the final copy, print, and proofread it

The typing of the final version should follow the traditional rules for an acceptable submission.

Checklist for the final copy

Use only 8½-by-11 inch paper (never paper torn out of a spiral bound notebook).

Type on one side of the paper only.

Double space.

Leave approximately 1½-inch margins on each side of the paper.

Center the title at the top of the page. Do not put quotation marks around the title and do not underline it.

Do not hyphenate a word at the end of a line unless you are willing to consult a dictionary to check on the acceptable division of the word into syllables.

You may put your name, the date, and the title of your paper on a separate title page. Ask your instructor for specific advice on what information to include.

Indent each paragraph five spaces.

Leave two spaces after each period.

If your paper is more than one page, number the pages and staple the pages together so they will not get lost.

Do not forget to make a copy before you submit the paper.

Note: In most cases, college teachers will not accept handwritten work. However, if you are submitting handwritten work, you must be sure to write on every other line and have good legible handwriting. Begin today to learn to type on the computer. You will be at a disadvantage if you cannot use the current technology.

Once you have typed your final version and printed it out, an important step still remains. This step can often mean the difference of an entire letter grade. You must *proofread* your paper. Even if you have used a spellcheck feature available on your word processing program, there still could be errors in your paper. The spellcheck feature only finds groupings of letters that are not words. For example, if you typed the word *van* when you meant to type *ban*, the spellcheck would not catch this error.

The secret of good proofreading is to look at each word and sentence construction by itself without thinking about the paper's contents.

Checklist for proofreading

Study each sentence: One way to proofread is to read backwards, starting with the last sentence and examining every sentence, one at a time. First, check that the sentence is really complete and not a fragment or a run-on. Then check the punctuation. Go on to the next sentence and do the same. In this way, you will develop a critical eye for spotting any problems with sentence level errors.

Study each word: Read the paper again, this time studying each word in every sentence. Look at the letters of the words. Have you transposed any letters or have you left off an ending such as the *-ed* or the *-s?* If there are any words you are not sure how to spell, do not forget to check for the correct spelling. Is there any word you have omitted?

Working Together

Brainstorming for Examples

Topic: Why do some employees fail to get ahead in their jobs?

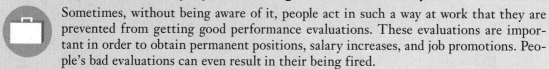

Sometimes, without being aware of it, people act in such a way at work that they are prevented from getting good performance evaluations. These evaluations are important in order to obtain permanent positions, salary increases, and job promotions. People's bad evaluations can even result in their being fired.

Work in groups for at least twenty minutes to develop a list of examples that illustrate this kind of behavior. Your list should be made up of things workers do that make their employers (and their fellow workers) think less of them.

Then come together as a class and share your lists. Put the examples on the board. Can class members think of specific incidents they have observed that would illustrate these examples?

Portfolio Suggestion

Use this list to write an essay in which you incorporate some of the examples provided by members of your class. If you wish, you could do more research on this work-related topic in order to develop your essay into a longer research paper.

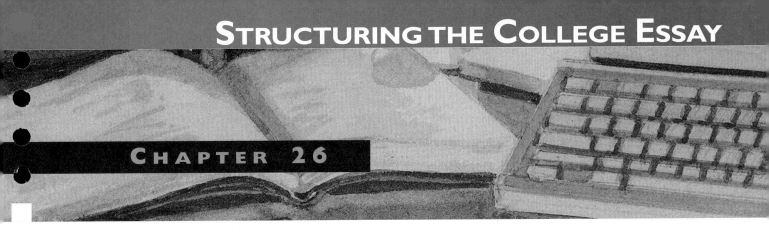

Writing an Essay Using Narration

Exploring the topic: A painful childhood memory

For most of us, childhood holds a mixture of happy and painful memories. The memory that the author Audré Lorde writes about in the selection you are about to read is the humiliation and agony of being the target of racist practices. The essay you will write in this chapter will be a narrative essay, based on a painful experience you have had as a child, perhaps an incident in which you were treated unfairly. As you answer the following questions, and as you read the narrative selection, think about what childhood experience you might want to choose.

1. What are some of the painful experiences that nearly all children go through?

   _____

   _____

   _____

   _____

2. What are some of the painful experiences that only some children are forced to endure?

   _____

   _____

   _____

   _____

3. How has society tried to protect children from cruel and unjust treatment?

_____

_____

_____

4. How can individuals survive injustices that they have suffered?

_____

_____

_____

Reading a model essay to discover narrative elements

The Fourth of July

AUDRÉ LORDE

Audré Lorde (1934–1992) was born and raised in New York City. Her career included teaching at the City University of New York (CUNY), autobiographical writing, and the creation of some memorable poetry. In 1991, she was named the official poet for New York State.

The following selection, taken from her 1982 memoir *Zami: A New Spelling of My Name,* tells us the story of a trip the thirteen-year-old Audré took with her family to Washington, D.C. The account also provides us with a portrait of the state of our nation in the late 1940s.

1   The first time I went to Washington, D.C., was on the edge of the summer when I was supposed to stop being a child. At least that's what they said to us all at graduation from the eighth grade. My sister Phyllis graduated at the same time from high school. I don't know what she was supposed to stop being. But as graduation presents for us both, the whole family took a Fourth of July trip to Washington, D.C., the fabled and famous capital of our country.

2   It was the first time I'd ever been on a railroad train during the day. When I was little, and we used to go to the Connecticut shore, we always went at night on the milk train, because it was cheaper.

3   Preparations were in the air around our house before school was even over. We packed for a week. There were two very large suitcases that my father carried, and a box filled with food. In fact, my first trip to Washington was a mobile feast; I started eating as soon as we were comfortably ensconced in our seats, and did not stop until somewhere after Philadelphia. I remember it was Philadelphia because I was disappointed not to have passed by the Liberty Bell.

4   My mother had roasted two chickens and cut them up into dainty bite-size pieces. She packed slices of brown bread and butter and green pepper and carrot sticks. There were little violently yellow iced cakes with scalloped edges called "marigolds," that came from Cushman's Bakery. There was a spice bun and rock-cakes from Newton's, the West Indian bakery across Lenox Avenue from St. Mark's School, and iced tea in a wrapped mayonnaise jar. There were sweet pickles for us and dill pickles for my father, and peaches with the fuzz still on them, individually wrapped to keep them from bruising. And, for neatness, there were piles of napkins and a little tin box with a washcloth dampened with rosewater and glycerine for wiping sticky mouths.

5   I wanted to eat in the dining car because I had read all about them, but my

mother reminded me for the umpteenth time that dining car food always cost too much money and besides, you never could tell whose hands had been playing all over that food, nor where those same hands had been just before. My mother never mentioned that Black people were not allowed into railroad dining cars headed south in 1947. As usual, whatever my mother did not like and could not change, she ignored. Perhaps it would go away, deprived of her attention.

6   I learned later that Phyllis's high school senior class trip had been to Washington, but the nuns had given her back her deposit in private, explaining to her that the class, all of whom were white, except Phyllis, would be staying in a hotel where Phyllis "would not be happy," meaning, Daddy explained to her, also in private, that they did not rent rooms to Negroes. "We will take you to Washington, ourselves," my father had avowed, "and not just for an overnight in some measly fleabag hotel."

7   American racism was a new and crushing reality that my parents had to deal with every day of their lives once they came to this country. They handled it as a private woe. My mother and father believed that they could best protect their children from the realities of race in America and the fact of american racism by never giving them name, much less discussing their nature. We were told we must never trust white people, but *why* was never explained, nor the nature of their ill will. Like so many other vital pieces of information in my childhood, I was supposed to know without being told. It always seemed like a very strange injunction coming from my mother, who looked so much like one of those people we were never supposed to trust. But something always warned me not to ask my mother why she wasn't white, and why Auntie Lillah and Auntie Etta weren't, even though they were all that same problematic color so different from my father and me, even from my sisters, who were somewhere in-between.

8   In Washington, D.C., we had one large room with two double beds and extra cot for me. It was a back-street hotel that belonged to a friend of my father's who was in real estate, and I spent the whole next day after Mass squinting up at the Lincoln Memorial where Marian Anderson had sung after the D.A.R. refused to allow her to sing in their auditorium because she was Black. Or because she was "Colored," my father said as he told the story. Except that what he probably said was "Negro," because for his times, my father was quite progressive.

9   I was squinting because I was in that silent agony that characterized all of my childhood summers, from the time school let out in June to the end of July, brought about by my dilated and vulnerable eyes exposed to the summer brightness.

10   I viewed Julys through an agonizing corolla of dazzling whiteness and I always hated the Fourth of July, even before I came to realize the travesty such a celebration was for Black people in this country.

11   My parents did not approve of sunglasses, nor of their expense.

12   I spent the afternoon squinting up at monuments to freedom and past presidencies and democracy, and wondering why the light and heat were both so much stronger in Washington, D.C., than back home in New York City. Even the pavement on the streets was a shade lighter in color than back home.

13   Late that Washington afternoon my family and I walked back down Pennsylvania Avenue. We were a proper caravan, mother bright and father brown, the three of us girls step-standards in-between. Moved by our historical surroundings and the heat of the early evening, my father decreed yet another treat. He had a great sense of history, a flair for the quietly dramatic and the sense of specialness of an occasion and a trip.

14   "Shall we stop and have a little something to cool off, Lin?"

15   Two blocks away from our hotel, the family stopped for a dish of vanilla ice cream at a Breyer's ice cream and soda fountain. Indoors, the soda fountain was dim and fan-cooled, deliciously relieving to my scorched eyes.

16   Corded and crisp and pinafored, the five of us seated ourselves one by one at

Marian Anderson
internationally famous African-American singer

the D.A.R.
The Daughters of the American Revolution

corolla
the petals of a flower

avowed
promised

mottled
*having spots of
different colors*

the counter. There was I between my mother and father, and my two sisters on the other side of my mother. We settled ourselves along the white mottled marble counter, and when the waitress spoke at first no one understood what she was saying, and so the five of us just sat there.

17   The waitress moved along the line of us closer to my father and spoke again. "I said I kin give you to take out, but you can't eat here. Sorry." Then she dropped her eyes looking very embarrassed, and suddenly we heard what it was she was saying all at the same time, loud and clear.

18   Straight-backed and indignant, one by one, my family and I got down from the counter stools and turned around and marched out of the store, quiet and outraged, as if we had never been Black before. No one would answer my emphatic questions with anything other than a guilty silence. "But we hadn't done anything!" This wasn't right or fair! Hadn't I written poems about Bataan and freedom and democracy for all?

19   My parents wouldn't speak of this injustice, not because they had contributed to it, but because they felt they should have anticipated it and avoided it. This made me even angrier. My fury was not going to be acknowledged by a like fury. Even my two sisters copied my parents' pretense that nothing unusual and anti-American had occurred. I was left to write my angry letter to the president of the united states all by myself, although my father did promise I could type it out on the office typewriter next week, after I showed it to him in my copybook diary.

20   The waitress was white, and the counter was white, and the ice cream I never ate in Washington, D.C., that summer I left childhood was white, and the white heat and the white pavement and the white stone monuments of my first Washington summer made me sick to my stomach for the whole rest of that trip and it wasn't much of a graduation present after all.

Analyzing the writer's strategies

1. Explain how the first paragraph establishes the setting for the story by telling us *who*, *what*, *where*, *when*, and *why*.

2. Narration uses transitions of time to move the story along. Go through the story and find these transitions.

3. Go through the story and find the places where the author uses quotations to set off the exact words a person used. Who are the persons Audré Lorde has chosen to quote, and why do you think she selected those people?

4. Throughout the story, Audré Lorde provides a number of details that reveal how her family lived. Choose five details and explain how each detail reveals something about their lives.

5. Point out each instance in the selection where the writer mentions her problems with eyesight. How does her difficulty in *seeing* relate to her ability to *see* (in the sense of understanding) the injustice she and her family have suffered?

Writing the essay using narration

Narration is the oldest and best-known form of verbal communication. It is, quite simply, the telling of a story.

Choose a story and a point for that story

1. A terrible classroom experience
2. A parent who wasn't sensitive
3. The pain of growing up being shy
4. The pain of not fitting in
5. The difficulty of moving to a new neighborhood
6. Losing a loved one
7. The pain of being in a family that doesn't get along together
8. A time of loneliness
9. An accident that affected my childhood
10. Having to endure discrimination

Using the above list of suggested topics to start you thinking, jot down two or three powerful memories you have from your own childhood. These are possible topics for your writing.

_____

_____

_____

From these two or three topics, select the one you think would give you the best opportunity for writing an interesting story. Which one do you feel strongest about? Which one is most likely to interest your readers? Which topic is most suitable for a college essay?

_____

_____

_____

Selected topic: _____

Good narration should have a point. Think about your story. What is the point you could make by telling this story? In a story, a writer does not always come right out and state the point of the story, but the reader should understand the point by the time he or she reaches the end.

Point of your story: _____

_____

_____

The introductory paragraph for a story usually sets the scene. What will be the time (time of year, time of day), place, and mood that you would like to set in your introductory paragraph?

Time: _____

Place: _____

Mood: _____

Gather the information (use brainstorming techniques)

Take at least fifteen minutes to jot down the sequence of events for your story as you remember it. Try to remember the way things looked at the time, how people reacted (what they did, what they said), and what you thought as the event was happening. If you can go to the actual spot where the event took place, you might go there and take notes of the details of the place. Later on you can sort through the material and pick out what you want to use.

_____

_____

_____

_____

_____

_____

_____

_____

_____

_____

_____

_____

Select and organize material

Review your brainstorming list and cross out any details that are not appropriate. Prepare to build on the ideas that you like. Put these remaining ideas into an order that will serve as your temporary guide.

_____

_____

_____

_____

_____

_____

_____

_____

_____

_____

_____

_____

Write the rough draft

Find a quiet place where you will not be interrupted for at least one hour. With the plan for your essay in front of you, sit down and write the story that is in your mind. Do not try to judge what you are putting down as right or wrong. What is important is that you let your mind relax and allow the words to flow freely. Do not worry if you find yourself not following your plan exactly. Keep in mind that you are free to add parts, drop sections of the story, or rearrange details at any point. Sometimes just allowing your thoughts to take you wherever they will lead results in new ideas. You may like these inspirations better than your original plan. Writing a rough draft is a little like setting out on an expedition; there are limitless possibilities, so it is important to be flexible.

Keep in mind that in a narrative essay, details are usually ordered according to a *time sequence.* One way to make the time sequence clear is to use transitional words that will signal a time change.

Transitional expressions for narration

A few carefully chosen transitional words will help the reader move smoothly from one part of a story to the next. Here are some examples:

in December of 1980 . . .	after a little while
the following month	then
soon afterward	meanwhile
at once	next, the next day
suddenly	several weeks passed
immediately	later, later on
now, by now	at the same time
in the next month	finally

Revise the rough draft

As you work on your rough draft, you may work alone, with a group, with a peer tutor, or directly with your instructor. If you are working on a computer, making changes is so easy that you will feel encouraged to explore alternatives. Working on a computer to insert or delete material is a simple matter, unlike making changes using traditional pen and paper.

Here are some of the basic questions you should consider when the time comes to revise your narration:

1. Does the rough draft satisfy the conditions for the essay form? Is there an introductory paragraph? Are there at least three well-developed paragraphs in the body of the essay? Is there a concluding paragraph? Remember that one sentence is not a developed paragraph. One exception to this rule is when you use dialogue. When you write a story, you often include the conversation between two people. In this case, the writer makes a new paragraph each time a different person speaks. This often means that one sentence could be a separate paragraph.

2. Is your essay a narration? Does it tell the story of one particular incident that takes place in a specific time and location? Sometimes writers make the mistake of talking about incidents in a general way, and commenting on the meaning of the incidents. Be careful. This would not be considered a narration. You must be a story teller. Where does the action take place? Can the reader see it? What time of day, week, or season is it? What is your main character in the story doing?

3. Have you put the details of the essay in a certain time order? Find the expressions you have used that show the time sequence.

4. Can you think of any part of the story that is missing and should be added? Is there any material that is irrelevant and should be omitted?

5. Are there sentences or paragraphs that seem to be repetitious?

6. Find several places where you can substitute stronger verbs or nouns. Add adjectives to give the reader better sensory images.

7. Find at least three places in your draft where you can add details. Perhaps you might add an entire paragraph that will more fully describe the person or place that is central to your story.

8. Can you think of a more effective way to begin or end?

9. Does your story have a point? If a person just told you everything he did on a certain day, that would not be a good story. A good story needs to have a point.

10. Show your rough draft to at least two other readers and ask for suggestions.

Prepare the final copy, print, and proofread it

The typing of the final version should follow the traditional rules for an acceptable submission.

Checklist for the final copy

Use only 8½-by-11 inch paper (never paper torn out of a spiral bound notebook).

Type on one side of the paper only.

Double space.

Leave approximately 1½-inch margins on each side of the paper.

Center the title at the top of the page. Do not put quotation marks around the title and do not underline it.

Do not hyphenate a word at the end of a line unless you are willing to consult a dictionary to check on the acceptable division of the word into syllables.

You may put your name, the date, and the title of your paper on a separate title page. Ask your instructor for specific advice on what information to include.

Indent each paragraph five spaces.

Leave two spaces after each period.

If your paper is more than one page, number the pages and staple the pages together so they will not get lost.

Do not forget to make a copy before you submit the paper.

Note: In most cases, college teachers will not accept handwritten work. However, if you are submitting handwritten work, you must be sure to write on every other line and have good legible handwriting. Begin today to learn to type on the computer. You will be at a disadvantage if you cannot use the current technology.

Once you have typed your final version and printed it out, an important step still remains. This step can often mean the difference of an entire letter grade. You must *proofread* your paper. Even if you have used a spellcheck feature available on your word processing program, there still could be errors in your paper. The spellcheck feature only finds groupings of letters that are not words. For example, if you typed the word *van* when you meant to type *ban*, the spellcheck would not catch this error.

The secret of good proofreading is to look at each word and sentence construction by itself without thinking about the paper's contents.

Checklist for proofreading

Study each sentence: One way to proofread is to read backwards, starting with the last sentence and examining every sentence, one at a time. First, check that the sentence is really complete and not a fragment or a run-on. Then check the punctuation. Go on to the next sentence and do the same. In this way, you will develop a critical eye for spotting any problems with sentence level errors.

Study each word: Read the paper again, this time studying each word in every sentence. Look at the letters of the words. Have you transposed any letters or have you left off an ending such as the *-ed* or the *-s?* If there are any words you are not sure how to spell, do not forget to check for the correct spelling. Is there any word you have omitted?

Working Together

Reading Stories Out Loud

Everyone loves a good story, and children are especially fond of being read to by an older person. In this chapter, everyone has already written at least one piece that could be called a narrative or a story. For this Working Together, divide into groups of five or six students; each person should read his or her narrative out loud to the others. As you listen to the narratives, remember to give each person the same careful attention as you would want to have.

After everyone has had a turn reading, attach a full-sized piece of paper to each essay. Pass the essays around. Each person in the group will now respond to the essay by writing a few sentences on the full-sized piece of paper. Use these questions as your guide:

1. In your opinion, what part of the story did you find most interesting?

2. Was there any part or detail that you found confusing?

3. What is one part you would have liked the writer to explain in more detail?

4. What do you think was the point of the story?

Portfolio Suggestion

Keep in your portfolio all the narratives you have worked on in this chapter. These may be the beginning of a series of stories you could write to capture the memories of your own childhood. You will be surprised how much you can recall when you actually focus on writing about these past events.

CHAPTER 27

Writing an Essay Using Process

Exploring the topic: Following and giving instructions

It is your sister's birthday. You have bought her a gift that tells you that "some assembly is required." You follow the instructions carefully as you try to put the item together, but something is wrong. No matter what you try, it does not work. You feel frustrated and angry and rip up the instructions in disgust.

At one time or another, all of us have found ourselves in such a situation. When we do, we understand the misery caused by poorly written instructions. Providing directions or instructions takes careful thought. These writers must be able to put themselves in the shoes of the persons following the directions. These readers may have no special skills for performing the procedure. Careful writers must be sensitive to those places in the directions where the readers could go wrong. Clarity and accuracy are absolutely essential.

1. Think of a time when you had to put something together, but you were not given good directions. Describe the process that was involved and what happened when you tried to accomplish it.

   _____

   _____

   _____

   _____

   _____

2. When people write instructions or give directions, what do they often leave out? Looking back on the situation you described above, why do you think you were not able to assemble the item?

_____

_____

_____

_____

_____

3. Recall a time when you had to explain a process to someone. You might have had to show someone how to get somewhere, or you might have had to write a detailed description of how you performed a science experiment in a chemistry class. What was the process? Was it hard to explain? Why or why not?

_____

_____

_____

_____

_____

4. What was your worst experience in trying to follow a process? You could have been trying to work something out yourself, or you could have been trying to follow someone else's directions. How did you overcome your difficulty?

_____

_____

_____

_____

_____

_____

Reading a model essay to discover steps in a process

How to Short-Cook Vegetables

GAYELORD HAUSER

Some of the most commonly seen examples of process writing occur in books and articles on cooking. In order to be understood, a writer describing a process like cooking must be clear, accurate, and complete. In the following selection, the famous nutritionist and health expert Gayelord Hauser first gives background information on the right approach to cooking vegetables and then takes us through the actual process of cooking them.

1   In lean vegetable cookery, just remember that the quicker vegetables are prepared and cooked, the better your family will like them. Also, the less is the loss of vitamins B, C, P. These vitamins, like salt, dissolve in water; therefore we never pour off any vegetable water. Better still, we short-cook vegetables in such a way that all the goodness and nutrients remain. I have said it a thousand and one times and I'll say it again—when vegetables are cooked half an hour or more in pots full of water, you'd be wiser to throw out the dead

vegetables and drink the water they were cooked in, for that's where the precious vitamins and minerals have gone.

2 Any vegetable can be short-cooked in a matter of minutes. All you need is a heavy cooking utensil, preferably heavy enamelware, and one of those handy vegetable cutters, or "snitzlers" as they are called. Or use an ordinary shredder (the coarse one). Or cut vegetables into thin slivers. Do your shredding or slivering as quickly as possible to prevent vitamin C loss.

3 Have your cooking pot piping hot; use a small one so it will be filled to the top; the less space for air, the better. In the bottom of the pot have three tablespoons of water; when this boils and the pot is filled with steam, put in your cut-up vegetables and cover the pot tightly. Let the vegetables cook on low flame for two minutes; then shake the pot (without lifting the lid) so there is no possible chance of sticking. After about four minutes, remove the cover and taste of the vegetable slivers; if it is soft but still a bit chewy, as the vegetables are in Chinese restaurants, it is at its best. Now all you add is a sprinkle of vegetable salt, some herbs, and a bit of vegetable oil; or, if you prefer, you may use half vegetable oil and half butter as

my Italian students do. Such short-cooked vegetables have a wonderful, natural flavor and keep their attractive color. When you use vegetable salt last, the juices are not extracted during cooking.

4 For *extra* lean short-cooking, here is a trick: Instead of water, we steam the sliced vegetables in flavorsome broth—left-over "pot likker," Hauser broth, canned or dehydrated vegetable broth, or chicken or beef broth made with bouillon cubes. Cooked this way, with the addition of vegetable salt and sprinkled with herbs, short-cooked vegetables can be enjoyed without the addition of extra fat. You'll be amazed how soon you and your family will begin to like, and even prefer, the nutty flavor of these vegetables short-cooked *extra* lean.

5 Here are three easily remembered pointers for successful vegetable cookery: (1) do not peel; just wash thoroughly, or scrub with a vegetable brush; (2) boil or bake whole vegetables in their skins; (3) short-cook sliced or shredded vegetables in the smallest amount of water or broth, and add a bit of vegetable salt *after* they are done. If your family insists on a "buttery" taste, add a pat of sunbutter just before serving.

Analyzing the writer's strategies

1. What is the writer's purpose, as he states it in the first paragraph?

2. Often a process requires specialized tools. What paragraph in the Hauser selection describes the needed cooking utensils? What are those utensils?

3. Which paragraph describes the process? How many steps are there in the process? Make a list of the steps and number each of them.

4. What is the author's purpose in writing paragraph 4?

5. How does the writer's last paragraph provide a useful conclusion to the essay?

Writing the essay using process (how to . . .)

> *Process* is one method of development that shows a step-by-step progression in the accomplishment of a goal. It can be directional (explaining how to do something readers might try themselves), or it can be strictly informational (explaining how something was done or how something works, with no expectation that the readers will actually try the process).

The "how to" section of every library and bookstore is usually a busy area. People come to find books that will help them perform thousands of different tasks—from plumbing to flower arranging. If you want to learn how to cook Chinese dishes, assemble a child's bicycle, start your own business, or even remodel your bathroom, you can find a book that will tell you how to do it. Thousands of books and articles have been written that promise to help people accomplish their goals in life. What do you think are the best selling "how to" books in America? Perhaps you have guessed the answer: how to lose weight! In the essay that you write, be sure to choose a process with which you are already familiar.

Choose a topic and the purpose of the information for the thesis statement

1. How to get good grades in college
2. How to do well in a job interview
3. How to plan a budget
4. How to buy a used car
5. How to study for a test
6. How to change a tire
7. How to redecorate a room
8. How to buy clothes on a limited budget
9. How to find the right place to live
10. How to make new friends

Using the above list of ten topics or using ideas of your own, jot down two or three processes with which you are familiar.

_____

_____

_____

_____

From these two or three topics, select the one you think would give you the best opportunity for writing. Which process do you feel strongest about? Which one is most likely to interest your readers? For which topic do you have the most first-hand experience?

Selected topic: _____

Your next step is to decide your purpose in writing. Which of the two types of process writing will you be doing? Do you want to give directions on how to carry out each step in a process so that your readers can do this process themselves? For instance, would you provide directions on how to change a tire, perhaps suggesting that your readers keep these directions in the glove compartments of their cars? On the other hand, do you want to provide information as to how a certain process works because you think your readers might find the process interesting? For instance, you might explain the process involved in getting an airplane off the ground. Not many of us understand how this works, and very few of us will actually ever pilot a plane. Perhaps you know a lot about an unusual process that might amuse or entertain readers.

Directional _____ or informational _____

Now put your topic and controlling idea together into your thesis statement.

Thesis statement: _____

_____

Gather the information (use brainstorming techniques)

Take at least fifteen minutes to list as many steps or stages in the process as you can. If the process is one that others in your class or at home already know, consult with them for any additional steps that you may have overlooked. You may also need to think of the precise vocabulary words associated with the process (such as the names of tools used for building or repairing something). The more specific you can be, the more helpful and interesting the process will be for your readers. List the steps or stages in the process:

_____

_____

_____

_____

_____

_____

_____

_____

_____

_____

_____

_____

_____

_____

Select and organize material

Review your brainstorming list and ask yourself if you now have a complete list. Have you left out any step that someone who is unfamiliar with this process might need to know? Is there some extra information you could provide along the way that would be helpful and encouraging? Do you have a special warning about something that the reader should *not* do? You might consider telling your readers exactly where in the process most people are likely to make mistakes.

Make an outline giving each stage a heading. Underneath each heading, list all of the different ideas or vocabulary words that you should keep in mind as you begin to write. In a process essay, the most essential elements for judging its success are the order, the accuracy, and the completeness of all the steps.

_____

_____

_____

_____

_____

_____

_____

_____

_____

_____

_____

_____

_____

Write the rough draft

Follow your outline and write your rough draft, keeping in mind that this outline is only a guide. As you write, you will find yourself reevaluating the logic of your ideas, a perfectly natural step that may involve making some changes from your outline. You may think of some special advice that would help the reader, and if you do, feel free to add these details. Your main goal is to get the process down on paper as completely and accurately as possible.

Achieving coherence in the process essay

When you buy a product and read the instructions that go with it, the form of writing in those instructions usually consists of a list of numbered items, each telling you what to do. In an essay, you do not usually number the steps. Instead, you can signal the movement from one step to another by changing to a new paragraph and/or by using a transitional expression. As in other methods for developing ideas, *process* has its own special words and expressions that can be used to signal movement from one step to the next.

Transitional expressions for process		
the first step	while you are	the last step
in the beginning	as you are	the final step
to start with	next	finally
to begin with	then	at last
first of all	the second step	eventually
	after you have	

Revise the rough draft

A space of time is very helpful to allow you to think about your written ideas; this allows you to judge your work more objectively than you can immediately after writing. Therefore, if you can put aside your draft for a day or two before you need to revise it, your work will benefit.

When you revise, you may work alone, with a group, with a peer tutor, or directly with your instructor. Here are some of the basic questions you should consider during this most important stage of your work:

1. Does the rough draft satisfy all the conditions for the essay form? Is there an introductory paragraph? Are there at least three well-developed paragraphs in the body of the essay? Have you written a concluding paragraph? Remember that a single sentence is not a developed paragraph.

2. Does the essay describe the process, one that is either directional or informational?

3. Are the steps in the process in the correct order? In a process essay, the sequence of the steps is crucial. A step that is placed out of order could result in a disaster of major proportions.

4. Are the directions accurate and complete? Check more than once that no important piece of information has been left out. Have you considered the points where some special advice might be helpful? Are there any special tools that would be useful?

5. Is any of the material not relevant?

6. Are there sentences or words that seem to be repetitious?

7. Find several places where you can substitute more specific verbs, nouns or adjectives. Always try to use vocabulary that is appropriate for the process being described.

8. Can you think of a more effective way to begin or end?

9. Does the essay flow logically from one idea to the next? Could you improve this flow with better use of transitional expressions?

10. Show your draft to at least two other readers and ask for suggestions.

Prepare the final copy, print, and proofread it

The typing of the final version should follow the traditional rules for an acceptable submission.

Checklist for the final copy

Use only 8½-by-11 inch paper (never paper torn out of a spiral bound notebook).

Type on one side of the paper only.

Double space.

Leave approximately 1½-inch margins on each side of the paper.

Center the title at the top of the page. Do not put quotation marks around the title and do not underline it.

Do not hyphenate a word at the end of a line unless you are willing to consult a dictionary to check on the acceptable division of the word into syllables.

You may put your name, the date, and the title of your paper on a separate title page. Ask your instructor for specific advice on what information to include.

Indent each paragraph five spaces.

Leave two spaces after each period.

If your paper is more than one page, number the pages and staple the pages together so they will not get lost.

Do not forget to make a copy before you submit the paper.

Note: In most cases, college teachers will not accept handwritten work. However, if you are submitting handwritten work, you must be sure to write on every other line and have good legible handwriting. Begin today to learn to type on the computer. You will be at a disadvantage if you cannot use the current technology.

Once you have typed your final version and printed it out, an important step still remains. This step can often mean the difference of an entire letter grade. You must *proofread* your paper. Even if you have used a spellcheck feature available on your word processing program, there still could be errors in your paper. The spellcheck feature only finds groupings of letters that are not words. For example, if you typed the word *van* when you meant to type *ban*, the spellcheck would not catch this error.

The secret of good proofreading is to look at each word and sentence construction by itself without thinking about the paper's contents.

Checklist for proofreading

Study each sentence: One way to proofread is to read backwards, starting with the last sentence and examining every sentence, one at a time. First, check that the sentence is really complete and not a fragment or a run-on. Then check the punctuation. Go on to the next sentence and do the same. In this way, you will develop a critical eye for spotting any problems with sentence level errors.

Study each word: Read the paper again, this time studying each word in every sentence. Look at the letters of the words. Have you transposed any letters or have you left off an ending such as the -*ed* or the -*s?* If there are any words you are not sure how to spell, do not forget to check for the correct spelling. Is there any word you have omitted?

DEAR ABBY

Dear Abby: I work for a cable television company as a computer operator. Lately, every morning when I sign in on my computer I find suggestive messages from the man I relieve from the night shift.

I am a single mother. I am also dating another man and have no interest in this co-worker. Should I report him to my supervisor? Someone in my office suggested that I file a sexual harassment charge. —Harassed

**ABIGAIL
VAN BUREN**

Sexual Harassment in the Workplace

Being harassed at work can create very complicated issues on the job. In many cases, it comes down to one person's word against that of another. In addition, the person in the less powerful position is often afraid to report a more powerful person to outside authorities. Fear of losing one's job is a strong incentive to remain silent. However, a person should not have to endure unacceptable behavior. Consider the specific example described in the letter to Dear Abby. Divide into groups and discuss the following questions concerning the woman who wrote the letter:

a) Should she confront the man who is harassing her?

b) Should she go to her supervisor? Should she have told her co-workers about the problem?

c) Should she share her problem with the man she is dating?

d) Should she avoid the problem and quit her job?

e) How important is evidence for a person in this situation? How and when should she gather documentation for a possible formal action?

f) Does she need a lawyer? Does she need to consider the consequences of a formal action?

Portfolio Suggestion

Write a process essay in which you outline the steps a person should take if he or she is being harassed on the job.

The discussion of this issue may remind you of other problems that arise in the workplace. If so, you may want to start gathering ideas on some of these other problems that are of interest to you. Your examination of these issues could relate directly to other subject areas you might study, such as psychology, sociology, business ethics, or business management.

CHAPTER 28

Writing an Essay Using Comparison or Contrast

Exploring a topic: Computers and the human brain

Computer technology is advancing so rapidly that scientists are already discussing the possibility of creating *artificial intelligence*—a computer that will be able to duplicate the thinking process of the human mind. Scientists in this country and abroad are making progress in designing such a computer. While many people are skeptical that any machine could ever replace a person's mind, many jobs are certainly changing or disappearing because of the work that computers are now able to do.

1. What are some of the jobs computers can already do better and faster than human beings can?

   _____

   _____

   _____

2. What are some of the jobs you have to do now that you would like a computer to do for you? How many of these jobs do you think a computer will take over in your lifetime?

   _____

   _____

   _____

S
T
E
P

5

425

3. Do you think a computer could ever be programmed to be as creative as the human mind? Why or why not?

_____

_____

_____

4. In your opinion, what are the dangers in the sophisticated computer technology we see today?

_____

_____

_____

Reading a model essay to discover how a writer uses comparison or contrast to develop a topic

The Computer and the Brain

ISAAC ASIMOV

In the following selection from his book *Please Explain*, science writer Isaac Asimov compares the workings of the modern computer with the workings of the human mind.

1   The difference between a brain and a computer can be expressed in a single word: complexity.

mammalian
having the characteristics of animals that produce milk for their young

2   The large **mammalian** brain is the most complicated thing, for its size, known to us. The human brain weighs three pounds, but in that three pounds are ten billion neurons and a hundred billion smaller cells. These many billions of cells are interconnected in a vastly complicated network that we can't begin to unravel as yet.

intricacy
having complex parts

3   Even the most complicated computer man has yet built can't compare in **intricacy** with the brain. Computer switches and components number in the thousands rather than in the billions. What's more, the computer switch is just an on-off device, whereas the brain cell is itself possessed of a tremendously complex inner structure.

4   Can a computer think? That depends on what you mean by "think." If solving a mathematical problem is "thinking," then a computer can "think" and do so much faster than a man. Of course, most mathematical problems can be solved quite mechanically by repeating certain straightforward processes over and over again. Even the simple computers of today can be geared for that.

5   It is frequently said that computers solve problems only because they are "programmed" to do so. They can only do what men have them do. One must remember that human beings also can only do what they are "programmed" to do. Our genes "program" us the instant the fertilized ovum is formed, and our potentialities are limited by that "program."

6   Our "program" is so much more enormously complex, though, that we might like to define "thinking" in terms of the creativity that goes into writing a great play or composing a great symphony, in conceiving a brilliant scientific theory or a profound ethical judgment. In that sense, computers certainly can't think and neither can most humans.

7   Surely, though, if a computer can be made complex enough, it can be as creative as we. If it could be made as complex as a human brain, it could be the equivalent of a human brain and do whatever a human brain can do.

8 To suppose anything else is to suppose that there is more to the human brain than the matter that composes it. The brain is made up of cells in a certain arrangement and the cells are made up of atoms and molecules in certain arrangements. If anything else is there, no signs of it have ever been detected. To duplicate the material complexity of the brain is therefore to duplicate everything about it.

9 But how long will it take to build a computer complex enough to duplicate the human brain? Perhaps not as long as some think. Long before we approach a computer as complex as our brain, we will perhaps build a computer that is at least complex enough to design another computer more complex than itself.

This more complex computer could design one still more complex and so on and so on and so on.

10 In other words, once we pass a certain critical point, the computers take over and there is a "complexity explosion." In a very short time thereafter, computers may exist that not only duplicate the human brain—but far surpass it.

11 Then what? Well, mankind is not doing a very good job of running the earth right now. Maybe, when the time comes, we ought to step gracefully aside and hand over the job to someone who can do it better. And if we don't step aside, perhaps Supercomputer will simply move in and push us aside.

Analyzing the writer's strategies

1. An essay of comparison usually emphasizes the similarities between two subjects, while an essay of contrast emphasizes the differences. With this in mind, is the essay you have just read an essay of comparison or contrast?

2. How does this essay help to explain why a human can still beat a computer in a game of chess?

3. Does the writer provide an equal number of details that relate to both computers and the human brain or does he concentrate mostly on one part of the two-part topic? Go through the essay and underline each comparison or contrast that is made.

4. Specifically, how does the writer demonstrate the complexity of a computer and the complexity of the human brain?

5. Study the conclusion. How serious is the author's final suggestion?

Writing the essay using comparison and contrast

> *Comparison* or *Contrast,* a method for developing ideas, is the careful look at the similarities and/or differences between people, objects, or ideas, usually in order to make some conclusion or judgment.

Choose a topic and controlling idea for the thesis statement

1. High school classes and college classes
2. Studying with a friend or studying alone
3. Male and female stereotypes
4. Your best friend in childhood with your best friend now
5. Using public transportation versus using a car
6. Our current president with any previous chief executive

7. Two items you have compared when shopping
8. Two apartments or houses where you have lived
9. Cooking dinner at home versus eating out
10. Watching television versus reading a book

Using the above list of ten topics or using ideas of your own, jot down a few two-part topics that appeal to you.

_____

_____

_____

From your list of two-part topics, select the one you think would give you the best opportunity for writing. Which one of these do you feel most strongly about? Which one is most likely to interest your readers? For which topic do you have the greatest first-hand experience?

Selected topic: _____

Your next step is to decide what your controlling idea should be. What is your main purpose in comparing or contrasting these two topics? Do you want to show that although people think two topics are similar, they actually differ in important ways? Do you want to show one topic is better in some ways than the other topic? Do you want to analyze how something has changed over the years (a "then-and-now" essay)?

Controlling idea: _____

At this point, combine your two-point topic and controlling idea into one thesis statement.

Thesis statement: _____

_____

Gather the information (use brainstorming techniques)

Take at least fifteen minutes to brainstorm (use listing or clustering) as many comparison or contrasting points as you can on your chosen topic. You will probably want to think of at least three or four points. Under each point, brainstorm as many details as come to mind. For instance, if you are comparing two friends and the first point concerns the interests you have in common, recall as much as you can about the activities you share together. If you are brainstorming a topic that other classmates or family members might know something about, ask them to help you think of additional points to compare. If any special vocabulary comes to mind, jot that down as well. The more specific you can be, the more helpful and interesting you will make your comparison or contrast for your readers.

Points that could be compared or contrasted:

_____

_____

_____

_____

_____

_____

_____

_____

_____

_____

_____

_____

_____

Select and organize material

As a method of developing ideas, comparison or contrast involves a two-part topic. For instance, you might compare the school you attend now with a school you attended in the past. Often we need to make choices or judgments, and we can make better decisions if we can compare and/or contrast the two items in front of us. Since this is a two-part topic, there is a choice in organizing the essay:

1. **The block method:** This is when you write entirely about one item or idea, and then in a later paragraph or paragraphs you write entirely about the other topic. If you choose this method, you must be sure to bring up the same points and keep the same order as when you discussed the first topic.

2. **The point-by-point method:** This is when you discuss one point and show both topics relating to this in one paragraph. Then, in a new paragraph, you discuss the second point and relate it to both topics, and so forth.

Which method will be best for the topic you have selected—the block method or the point-by-point method?

At this stage, review your brainstorming list and ask yourself if you have a list that is complete. Have you left out any point that might need to be considered? Do you have at least three points, and do you have enough material to develop both parts of the topic? You do not want the comparison or contrast to end up one-sided with all the content about only one part of the topic.

Make an outline, choosing one of the formats below, depending on whether you selected the block method or point-by-point method.

The example shown is the contrast between high school classes and college classes.

Outline for Block Method

I. Topic 1		High School Classes
A. First Point		meet 5 days a week
B. Second Point		daily homework
C. Third Point		no research papers
D. Fourth Point		disciplinary problems in the class
II. Topic 2		College Classes
A. First Point		meet only 2 or 3 days a week
B. Second Point		long term assignments
C. Third Point		research papers required
D. Fourth Point		no discipline problems

Outline for point-by-point method

I.	First Point	How often classes meet
	A. Topic 1	high school classes
	B. Topic 2	college classes
II.	Second Point	Homework
	A. Topic 1	high school classes
	B. Topic 2	college classes
III.	Third Point	Research papers
	A. Topic 1	high school classes
	B. Topic 2	college classes
IV.	Fourth Point	Discipline
	A. Topic 1	high school classes
	B. Topic 2	college classes

_____

_____

_____

_____

_____

_____

_____

_____

_____

_____

_____

_____

_____

_____

_____

_____

_____

_____

_____

_____

Write the rough draft

Follow your outline and write your rough draft. Remember the outline is a guide. Most writers find new ideas occur to them at this time, so if you have new thoughts, you should feel free to explore these ideas along the way. As you write, you will be constantly re-evaluating the logic of your ideas.

Coherence in the comparison or contrast essay

As in other methods of developing ideas, the comparison and contrast essay has its particular words and expressions which can be used to signal the movement from one point to the next.

Common transitional expressions		
Transitions for Comparison	**Transitions for Contrast**	
similar to	on the contrary	though
similarly	on the other hand	unlike
like	in contrast with	even though
likewise	in spite of	nevertheless
just like	despite	however
just as	instead of	but
furthermore	different from	otherwise
moreover	whereas	except for
equally	while	and yet
again	although	still
also		
too		
so		

Revise the rough draft

If you can have an interval of time between the writing of the rough draft and your work on revising it, you will be able to look at your work with a greater objectivity. Ideally, you should put aside your first draft for a day or two before you approach it again for revision.

When you revise, you may work alone, with a group, with a peer tutor, or directly with your instructor. Here are some of the basic questions you should consider during this most important stage of your work:

1. Does the rough draft satisfy the conditions for the essay form? Is there an introductory paragraph? Are there at least three well-developed paragraphs in the body of the essay? Is there a concluding paragraph? Remember that one sentence is not a developed paragraph.

2. Does the essay compare or contrast a two-part topic and come to some conclusion about the comparison or contrast?

3. Did you use either the point-by-point method or the block method to organize the essay?

4. Is any important point omitted? Is any of the material included irrelevant?

5. Are there sentences or paragraphs that are repetitious?

6. Find several places where you can substitute more specific verbs, nouns or adjectives. Try to use the vocabulary appropriate for the topic being discussed.

7. Can you think of a more effective way to begin or end?

8. Does the essay flow logically from one idea to the next? Could you improve this flow with better use of transitional devices?

9. Show your draft to at least two other readers and ask for suggestions.

Prepare the final copy, print, and proofread it

The typing of the final version should follow the traditional rules for an acceptable submission.

Checklist for the final copy

Use only 8½-by-11 inch paper (never paper torn out of a spiral bound notebook).

Type on one side of the paper only.

Double space.

Leave approximately 1½-inch margins on each side of the paper.

Center the title at the top of the page. Do not put quotation marks around the title and do not underline it.

Do not hyphenate a word at the end of a line unless you are willing to consult a dictionary to check on the acceptable division of the word into syllables.

You may put your name, the date, and the title of your paper on a separate title page. Ask your instructor for specific advice on what information to include.

Indent each paragraph five spaces.

Leave two spaces after each period.

If your paper is more than one page, number the pages and staple the pages together so they will not get lost.

Do not forget to make a copy before you submit the paper.

Note: In most cases, college teachers will not accept handwritten work. However, if you are submitting handwritten work, you must be sure to write on every other line and have good legible handwriting. Begin today to learn to type on the computer. You will be at a disadvantage if you cannot use the current technology.

Once you have typed your final version and printed it out, an important step still remains. This step can often mean the difference of an entire letter grade. You must *proofread* your paper. Even if you have used a spellcheck feature available on your word processing program, there still could be errors in your paper. The spellcheck feature only finds groupings of letters that are not words. For example, if you typed the word *van* when you meant to type *ban*, the spellcheck would not catch this error.

The secret of good proofreading is to look at each word and sentence construction by itself without thinking about the paper's contents.

Checklist for proofreading

Study each sentence: One way to proofread is to read backwards, starting with the last sentence and examining every sentence, one at a time. First, check that the sentence is really complete and not a fragment or a run-on. Then check the punctuation. Go on to the next sentence and do the same. In this way, you will develop a critical eye for spotting any problems with sentence level errors.

Study each word: Read the paper again, this time studying each word in every sentence. Look at the letters of the words. Have you transposed any letters or have you left off an ending such as the *-ed* or the *-s?* If there are any words you are not sure how to spell, do not forget to check for the correct spelling. Is there any word you have omitted?

The Top Ten Sources of Calories in the American Diet

Whole Milk

Cola

Margarine

White Bread

Rolls
(commercial ready-to-serve)

Sugar

2% Milk

Ground Beef
(broiled medium)

Wheat Flour

Pasteurized Process American Cheese

SOURCE:
U.S. DEPARTMENT OF AGRICULTURE

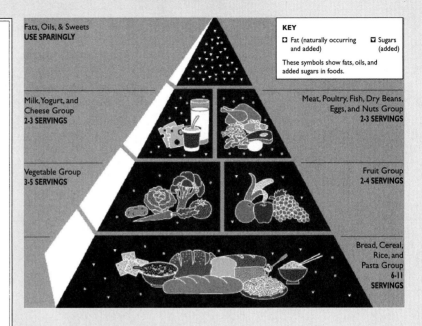

KEY
☐ Fat (naturally occurring and added)   ☑ Sugars (added)

These symbols show fats, oils, and added sugars in foods.

Fats, Oils, & Sweets
USE SPARINGLY

Milk, Yogurt, and Cheese Group
2-3 SERVINGS

Meat, Poultry, Fish, Dry Beans, Eggs, and Nuts Group
2-3 SERVINGS

Vegetable Group
3-5 SERVINGS

Fruit Group
2-4 SERVINGS

Bread, Cereal, Rice, and Pasta Group
6-11 SERVINGS

Using Outside Sources

Topic: Comparing the ideal diet with your real diet

The two charts show (1) the well-known food pyramid that the U.S. Government has developed and (2) to the left, a dietary chart provided by the U.S. Department of Agriculture. The first source tells us what we should be eating according to government research. The second tells us what the diets of most Americans are really like.

Divide into groups and discuss how you could plan an essay on the topic of people's eating habits using the information in these charts as well as facts about your own diet. Consider the following questions as you plan your presentation of information:

1. First outline your own diet. You might list typical foods eaten at each meal of the day or you might be very scientific and make an exact list of everything eaten for one week to see what patterns emerge. Don't forget to include snacks.

2. What do you think the ideal diet should look like?

3. Is your own diet closer to the ideal, or is it closer to the diet of most Americans?

Discuss these issues with other members of your group. Take notes on information gained from the ideas of others.

Portfolio Suggestion

Write your own outline on how you might compare the ideal diet with that of your own actual diet. Will you use the block method or the point by point method? Then, using your outline, compose an essay that examines your own diet and compares it to what you should be eating.

Three related subjects that may be of interest to you for future writing projects include:

- Why don't most people follow a healthier diet?
- What are some of the results of poor eating habits?
- How can parents instill in their children healthy eating habits?

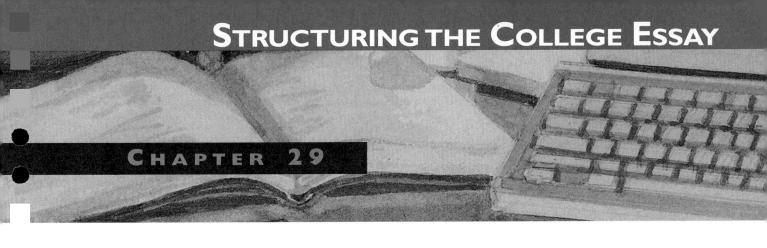

CHAPTER 29

Writing an Essay Using Persuasion

What is persuasion?

From one point of view, all writing is persuasion since the main goal of any writer is to convince a reader to see, think, or believe in a certain way. There is, however, a more formal understanding of persuasive writing. Anyone who has ever been a member of a high school debate team knows there are techniques that the effective speaker or writer uses to present a case successfully. Learning how to recognize these techniques of persuasion and discovering how to use them in your own writing is the subject of this chapter.

> An essay of **persuasion** presents evidence intended to convince the reader that the writer's viewpoint is valid.

Guide to writing the persuasive essay

1. **State a clear thesis.** Use words such as *must*, *ought*, or *should*. Study the following three sample thesis statements:

   The United States must reform its prison system.

   All states ought to have the same legal drinking age.

   We should not ban all handguns.

Words and phrases that signal parts of an argument

To signal the thesis of an argument

  I agree (disagree) that

  I support (do not support) the idea that

  I am in favor of (not in favor of)

  I propose

  _____ must be (must not be) changed

  _____ should be (should not be) adopted

To signal a reason

  because, just because, since, for

  in the first place

  in view of

  can be shown

  The first reason is . . .

  An additional reason is . . .

  Another reason is . . .

  The most convincing piece of evidence is . . .

To suggest another way to think about something

  Most people assume that . . .

  One would think that . . .

  We have been told that . . .

  Popular thought is that . . .

  Consider the case of . . .

  There is no comparison between . . .

To signal a conclusion

  therefore, thus, consequently, so

  as a result

  We can conclude that . . .

  This proves that . . .

  This shows that . . .

  This demonstrates that . . .

  This suggests that . . .

  This leads to the conclusion that . . .

  It follows that . . .

---

2. **Give evidence or reasons for your beliefs.** Your evidence is the heart of the essay. You must show the wisdom of your logic by providing the best evidence available.

3. **Use examples.** Well-chosen examples are among the best types of evidence for an argument. People can identify with a specific example from real life in a way that is not possible with an abstract idea. Without examples, essays of persuasion would be flat, lifeless, and unconvincing.

4. **Use opinions from recognized authorities to support your points.** One of the oldest methods of supporting an argument is to use one or more persons of authority to support your particular position. People will usually believe what well-known experts claim. However, be sure that your expert is someone who is respected in the area you are discussing. For example, if you are arguing that we must end ocean dumping, your argument will be stronger if you quote a

respected scientist who can accurately predict the consequences of this approach to waste disposal. A famous movie star giving the same information might be more glamorous and get more attention, but he or she would not be as great an authority as the scientist.

5. **Answer your critics in advance.** When you point out, beforehand, what your opposition is likely to say in answer to your argument, you will be writing from a position of strength. You are letting your reader know that there is another side to the argument you are making. By pointing out this other side and then answering its objections in advance, you are strengthening your own position.

6. **Point out the results.** Here, you help your reader see what will happen if your argument is (or is not) believed or acted upon as you think it should be. You should be very specific and very rational when you point out results, making sure that you avoid exaggerations of any kind. For example, if you are arguing against the possession of handguns, it would be an exaggeration to say that if we don't ban handguns, "everyone will be murdered."

As in other methods of developing the essay, the essay using persuasion has its own special words that signal parts of the argument. The chart at the top of page 436 can help you choose transitional expressions that will move you from one part of your argument to the next.

Be careful not to fall into the following traps, both of which are poor ways to try to win over an opponent to your position:

1. Appeals to fear or pity:

    If we don't double the police force this year, a child in our neighborhood might be killed.

2. Sweeping or false generalizations:

    All women belong in the kitchen.

It's Time We Helped Patients Die

DR. HOWARD CAPLAN

Howard Caplan is a medical doctor who specializes in geriatrics, that branch of medicine that deals with the care of older people. He is also the medical director of three nursing homes in Los Angeles, California.

As you read Dr. Caplan's essay, look for all of the elements of an effective argument. Where does the writer give his thesis statement? Where are his major examples? At what point does he use authorities to support his point of view? In addition, look for the paragraphs where he answers those who do not agree with him and be sure to find that section of the essay where he predicts the future of euthanasia, commonly known as "mercy killing." As you read the essay, do you see any weaknesses in the writer's argument?

1   For three years, the husband of one of my elderly patients watched helplessly as she deteriorated. She'd burst an *aneurysm* and later had an *astrocytoma* removed from her brain. Early in the ordeal, realizing that she'd never recover from a vegetative state, he'd pleaded with me to pull her *nasogastric* tube.

2   I'd refused, citing the policy of the convalescent hospital. I told him I could do it only if he got a court order. But he couldn't bring himself to start such proceedings, although the months dragged by with no signs of improvements in his wife's condition. He grieved as her skin broke down and she developed terrible bedsores. She had to have several courses of antibiotics to treat the infections in them, as well as in her bladder, which had an indwelling catheter.

3   Finally I got a call from a lawyer who said he'd been retained by the family to

aneurysm
a sac formed by the swelling of a vein or artery

astrocytoma
a tumor made up of nerve cells

nasogastric
relating to a tube inserted through the nose and into the stomach

aphasic triplegic
a person who has lost the ability to express or comprehend language, and who has paralysis of three limbs

force me to comply with the husband's wishes.

4 "I'm on your side," I assured him. "But you'll have to get that court order just the same."

5 I went on to suggest—though none too hopefully—that we ask the court to do more than just let the patient starve to death. "If the judge will agree to let her die slowly, why won't he admit that he wants death to happen? Let's ask for permission to give her an injection and end her life in a truly humane manner."

6 The lawyer had no answer except to say, "Aw, come on, Doc—that's euthanasia!"

7 Frankly, I'd have been surprised at any other reaction. Although most states have enacted living-will laws in the past decade, none has yet taken the next logical step—legalizing euthanasia. But I believe it's time they did. Ten years of practice in geriatrics have convinced me that a proper death is a humane death, either in your sleep or being *put* to sleep.

8 I see appropriate patients every day in the extended-care facilities at which I practice. About 50 of the 350 people under my care have already ended their biographical lives. They've reached the stage in life at which there's no more learning, communicating, or experiencing pleasure. They're now simply existing in what is left of their biological lives.

9 Most of these patients are the elderly **demented**. A typical case is that of a woman in her 80s or 90s, who speaks only in gibberish and doesn't recognize her family. She has forgotten how to eat, so she has a feeding tube coming from her nose. She is incontinent, so she has an indwelling catheter. She can no longer walk, so she is tied into a wheelchair. She's easily agitated, so she gets daily doses of a major tranquilizer. Why shouldn't I, with the concurrence of her family and an independent medical panel, be allowed to quickly and painlessly end her suffering?

demented
having lost normal brain function

10 I think of another patient, a woman in her 50s, with end-stage multiple sclerosis, unable to move a muscle except for her eyeballs and her tongue. And younger patients: I have on my census a

anesthesiologist
a medical specialist who administers anesthesia, or pain killers, to people about to undergo operations

man in his early 40s, left an **aphasic triplegic** by a motorcycle accident when he was 19. For nearly a quarter of a century, while most of us were working, raising children, traveling, reading, and otherwise going about our lives, he's been vegetating. His biographical life ended with that crash. He can't articulate—only make sounds to convey that he's hungry or wet. If he were to become acutely ill, I would prefer not to try saving him. I'd want to let pneumonia end it for him.

11 Of my remaining 300 patients, there are perhaps 50 to 100 borderline functional people who are nearing the end of their biographical lives and—were euthanasia legal—would probably tell me: "I'm ready to go. My bags are packed. Help me."

12 Anyone who's had front-line responsibility for the elderly has been asked if there wasn't "something you can give me" to end life. Such requests are made by patients who clearly see the inevitability of their deterioration and dread having to suffer through it. For these people, there is no more pleasure, let alone joy—merely misery. They want out.

13 What is their fate? Chances are they'll be referred for psychiatric consultation on the grounds that they must be seriously depressed. The psychiatrist, usually decades younger than the patient, does indeed diagnose depression and recommends an antidepressant.

14 But if such patients lived in the Netherlands, odds are they'd get assistance in obtaining a release from the slow dying process to which our modern technology condemns them. While euthanasia is not yet legal there, it's openly practiced. On a segment of the CBS show "60 Minutes" not long ago, I heard a Dutch **anesthesiologist** describe how doctors in his country help 5,000 terminal patients slip away peacefully each year. Isn't that a promising indication of how well euthanasia would work in this country?

15 I realize that there are those who vigorously oppose the idea. And there are moral issues to confront—how much suffering is too much, the one-in-several-million chance that a person

given no hope of improving will beat the odds. But it's time for society to seriously reconsider whether it is immoral to take the life of someone whose existence is nothing but irreversible suffering. Euthanasia ought to be treated the same way the abortion issue has been treated: People who believe it a sin to take a life even for merciful reasons would not be forced to do so. What I'm pleading for is that doctors and their patients at least have the choice.

16 I doubt that we'll get congressional action on such an emotionally charged issue during my lifetime. Action may have to come at the state level. Ideally, legislatures should permit each hospital and each nursing home to have a panel that would approve candidates for euthanasia. Or it might be more practical to have one panel serve several hospitals and nursing homes in a geographic area. Made up of one or two physicians and a lawyer or judge, plus the attending doctor, the panel would assess the attending's findings and recommendations, the patient's wishes, and those of the immediate family. This would ensure that getting a heart-stopping injection was truly in the patient's best interests, and that there was no ulterior motive—for example, trying to hasten an insurance payout. Needless to say, members of the board would be protected by law from liability claims.

17 Then, if the patient had made it known while of sound mind that under certain circumstances he wanted a deadly substance administered, the process would be easy for everyone. But in most cases, it would be up to the attending to raise the question of euthanasia with the patient's relatives.

18 I'd start with those who've been part of the patient's recent life. If there are relatives who haven't seen the patient for years, it really shouldn't be any of their business. For instance, I'd try involving a son who's just kept in touch by phone. I'd say to him, "If you really want to stop this from happening, then you'd better come out here to see firsthand what's going on."

19 However, if he said, "Well, I can't really get away, Doctor, but I violently disagree," my answer would be, "Well,

not violently enough. Everyone here can see what shape your mother's in. We're quite sure what she'd want if she could tell us, and we're going to help her."

20 Before any of this can happen, though, there's going to have to be widespread public education. The media will have to do a better job of discussing the issues than it has with living wills. Among my patients who are nearing death, there aren't more than a half-dozen with living wills attached to their charts. Patients' families often haven't even heard of them, and even when large institutions encourage families to get these things taken care of while the patient is still alert, it's hardly ever done.

21 Not knowing about living wills, unaware of no-code options, many families plunge their loved ones—and themselves—into unwanted misery. How many rapidly deteriorating patients are rushed from a nursing home to a hospital to be intubated, simply because that's the facility's rigid policy? How many families impoverish themselves to keep alive someone who's unaware of himself and his surroundings?

22 For that matter, how many people themselves suffer heart attacks or ulcers—not to mention divorces or bankruptcies—from the stresses involved in working to pay where Medicare and Medicaid leave off?

23 Every day in my professional life, I encounter illogical, irrational, and inhumane regulations that prevent me, and those with whom I work, from doing what we know in our souls to be the right thing. Before high technology, much of this debate was irrelevant. There was little we could do, for example, when a patient **arrested**. And what we could do rarely worked.

arrested
died

24 But times have changed. Now we have decisions to make. It helps to understand that many of the elderly infirm have accepted the inevitability—and, indeed, the desirability—of death. We who are younger must not mistake this philosophical position for depression. We need to understand the natural acceptance of death when life has lost its meaning.

25 About 28 percent of our huge Medicare budget is spent providing care

during the last year of life. Far too little of that money goes to ensure that dying patients' last months are pain-free and comfortable. Far too much is wasted on heroic, pain-inducing measures that can make no difference. It's time to turn that ratio around—and to fight for the right to provide the ultimate assistance to patients who know their own fight to prolong life is a losing one.

Analyzing the writer's strategies

Because Dr. Caplan deals with a very sensitive subject, many people might find his position to be dangerous and even frightening. Even before we examine his essay, the title of the piece and the writer's medical background gain our attention. When a doctor writes on matters of life and death, we tend to pay more attention than we ordinarily might; the fact that Dr. Caplan works so closely with older people tends to give his views even more authority. For example, the facts and figures he gives in paragraphs eight and eleven go a long way toward strengthening his point of view. In addition, the writer uses both his own experience and his close observation of people in other countries to convince us that his stand on this controversial topic is a valid one.

The writer's position is also supported by the fact that he is so precise in paragraphs three to seven, when he deals with the law; almost from the beginning, Dr. Caplan is seen as a careful and caring professional. We notice too that in paragraphs twelve and thirteen he points out what happens under our present system, and in paragraphs sixteen to eighteen he gives practical suggestions that would help put his own system into operation. Finally, we see that in paragraph fifteen he pays attention to the other side's arguments and then answers those same arguments.

It is clear that Dr. Caplan's argument is carefully written and complete; it has all of the parts needed for a good argument. After you have studied each part of the essay, are you able to find any weaknesses in the writer's presentation?

Responding to the writer's argument

Take a position either for or against one of the following topics and write an argumentative essay supporting your position. Use the "Guide to Writing the Persuasive Essay" (pages 435–437) to help construct the essay. Be sure to include all of the important points needed for a good argument.

1. All medical care should be free in our society.
2. Doctors should not be burdened by outrageously high malpractice insurance payments.
3. If a person wishes to commit suicide, for any reason, society should not try to interfere with that decision.
4. Doctors should always work to preserve life; they must never cooperate in any effort to end a life.
5. New medical technology has created more problems than it has solved.
6. Permitting euthanasia would create a dangerous precedent that could easily lead to government-sponsored murder of people it considers "undesirable."
7. People should always leave instructions (a living will) as to what should be done if they are terminally ill and are unable to respond to their surroundings.
8. A person's family has the responsibility to support decisions for life, not death, when a person is gravely ill, no matter how much money and effort it might cost that family.
9. In the case of a hopeless medical situation, no human being—including the person who is ill—has the right to make decisions that would lead to immediate death (euthanasia).

10. A husband or wife who helps a terminally ill spouse die should not be prosecuted by the law since the decision for euthanasia was made out of love, not from a desire to commit murder.

Using research material to write the persuasive essay

EXERCISE 1

Who would make the life-and-death decisions if mercy killings were to be permitted? The following pieces of information are on this controversial topic of mercy killing. Use this information as the basis for your own essay on the topic. You may select as many of the items as you want, or you may adapt the items to agree with your own way of thinking. After selecting the material to be used, be sure to organize your major points before starting the rough draft.

1. The idea of suicide has been rejected by society for many centuries.
2. Some societies discourage suicide by enacting strict laws against it.
3. In the famous Karen Anne Quinlan case, when the life-support system was turned off, she remained alive for nearly ten years.
4. As our technical ability to extend life increases, the pressure on us to make life and death decisions will also increase.
5. If we had laws that encouraged mercy killing, we would not have the lives of such people as Helen Keller to show the world what handicapped people can do.
6. The general reaction to mercy killing will change as people realize that life should not always go on no matter what the cost may be.
7. In 1973 the American Medical Association stated that "mercy killing . . . is contrary to the policy of the American Medical Association."
8. The worst tragedy in life is to live without dignity.
9. Years ago, people seldom spoke openly about suicide; now there are organizations that openly advocate it.
10. A very common form of mercy killing occurs when parents and doctors agree not to give retarded newborn children needed medical attention, eventually causing their deaths.

A View of Affirmative Action in the Workplace

MICHAEL GNOLFO

Michael Gnolfo lives and works in New York City. After being out of school for over fifteen years, he graduated from the City University of New York (CUNY). The following essay combines essay writing skills that one learns in college, along with the kind of perceptions that come only from someone who has had considerable experience in the workplace.

1   Affirmative action is by definition any plan or program that promotes the employment of women and of members of minority groups. This has come about to right all the wrongs suffered by these groups in the past. It is intended to be a positive force for civil rights.

2   Directly or indirectly, because of Affirmative Action women and minorities have increasingly found more opportunity where none existed for them. Traditional role separation is disappearing. Society is realizing an untapped wealth of talent and business is reaping a whirlwind of benefits from this new diversity.

3   Jobs that were traditionally male dominated have had major inroads by women. Bus drivers, construction workers, telephone technicians and pilots now count women among their numbers as do the management staffs of many

corporations. The reverse is also true. Men have increasingly entered such fields as nursing, secretarial sciences and flight attendants which have been traditionally female occupations. It seems that no barriers exist to an individual with the skills to perform a job.

zealous
strongly committed

altruism
unselfish concern for others

4   While all of this is good and the proper course to pursue, there are problems. We can all agree that the protection and promotion of one group in society is wrong. So, when does a program designed to promote fairness become discriminatory? When capable people are neglected at the expense of less capable or similarly capable politically correct/connected candidates. A glaring example of this is the New York City Police exam and requirements. A comparison of physical requirements from today versus thirty years ago reveals a less demanding test of strength and physique. The requirements were relaxed to allow lesser physical candidates to pass. Minority candidates with lower written test marks are also taken over other candidates if a certain percentage of those minorities are not represented on the force. We are legislating mediocrity at best. What is more desirable, a competent organization or a gender/racially correct structure?

dearth
a lack
CEOs
chief executive officers

abhorrent
loathsome; repellent

5   Private business is doing just the same. It is especially true in any large company that is contractually obligated to the government or is regulated by

it. Those not included in Affirmative Action become less likely to be successful despite qualification. They are fast becoming a new oppressed minority. Companies are **zealous** in their adherence to Affirmative Action not out of **altruism** but of fear of loss of contract or stiffer regulation. Remember that while there has been much progress by minorities in business there is a **dearth** of minority **CEOs** in the major corporations and that says so much about the reality of Affirmative Action.

6   The time is right for another step in the evolution of American society. We all realize the positive contributions of the groups protected by Affirmative Action. They have been valuable additions to our society. But abuses have now surfaced. Let's not make the same mistakes we made before. We need a Positive Fairness principle to replace Affirmative Action. Qualification and achievement should be the deciding factors in society and business. Quotas are **abhorrent**. Discrimination is bad, be it directed toward a race, gender, religion or anyone for any reason. Affirmative Action is becoming a racist, sexist instrument that is quickly turning into a tool of those who would replace one form of dominance with another. Contrary to the belief of feminists, the best man for the job is not a WOMAN but the most qualified individual.

Analyzing the writer's strategies

Michael Gnolfo's essay begins with a definition of Affirmative Action. Defining the key terms is an essential part of being certain that all readers are starting with the same understanding of the topic. He then points out the positive results of Affirmative Action. These introductory paragraphs are there to establish the writer's careful and fair attitude. He understands that all readers need to acknowledge first that Affirmative Action has a worthy goal: to make up for society's past conduct of discrimination. He then provides examples of how women and minorities have found more opportunities in careers that traditionally hired only males or only whites. He agrees that society has benefited from this new opportunity for new varieties of talent.

With this positive view in place, he then presents the problems. Using a detailed example of how the New York City Police Department changed the standards of its exams and requirements, he asks his central question: "So, when does a program designed to promote fairness become discriminatory?" His fifth paragraph suggests that businesses have only adhered to Affirmative Action by following the letter of the law, not the spirit of the policy, since so few CEOs are women or minorities.

The last paragraph finally gives us Michael Gnolfo's thesis: "We need a Positive Fairness principle to replace Affirmative Action." The best person for the job should be the one most qualified.

Responding to the writer's argument

Take a position either for or against one of the following topics and write an argumentative essay supporting your position. You may quote Michael Gnolfo or use any of his examples along with your own. Use the "Guide to Writing the Persuasive Essay" (pages 435–437) to help construct the essay. Be sure to include all of the important points needed for an effective argument.

1. Argue your opinion to Michael Gnolfo's question, "When does a program designed to promote fairness become discriminatory?"
2. Argue your opinion to Michael Gnolfo's question, "What is more desirable, a competent organization or a gender/racially correct structure?"
3. Argue: We will always need Affirmative Action because there will always be people who act unfairly towards others.
4. Argue: Treating one group differently than another is always wrong. Therefore, Affirmative Action is always wrong.
5. Argue: Affirmative Action is a present day form of injustice that tries to make up for past injustice.
6. Michael Gnolfo's argument sounds reasonable, but he has forgotten to mention some important points that change the outcome of the argument.

Using research material to write the persuasive essay

EXERCISE 1

Should there be a national law that more strictly regulates the possession and use of guns? The following pieces of information are on this controversial topic of *gun control*. Use this information as the basis for your own essay on the topic. You may select as many of the items as you want, or you may adapt the items to agree with your own way of thinking. After selecting the material to be used, be sure to organize your major points before starting the rough draft.

1. More than half of the people who kill themselves each year do so with handguns.
2. More than half of the murders committed in the United States each year are committed with handguns.
3. Robert Digrazia, the chief of police of Montgomery County, Maryland, states that "No private citizen, whatever his claim, should possess a handgun."
4. Anybody can purchase machine guns by mail order.
5. There are forty million handguns in this country, and every year two and a half million more handguns are sold.
6. Since 1963, guns have killed over 400,000 Americans.
7. There are over 20,000 state and local gun laws on the books, but they are obviously ineffective.
8. It has been estimated that simply to track down and register all of the handguns in this country would cost four or five billion dollars.
9. The state of California has a law which requires a jail sentence for a person who is convicted of a gun-related felony.
10. Members of the National Rifle Association often assert that people, not guns, kill people.

Writing the persuasive essay: Additional topics

Choose one of the fifteen topics listed and write an essay of at least five paragraphs. Use the six points discussed on pages 435–437 and repeated below as a guide for your writing.

- Write a strong thesis statement.
- Give evidence for your beliefs.
- Provide examples for each of your reasons.
- Use at least one authority to support your thesis.
- Admit that others may have a different point of view.
- Indicate the results, predictions, or your solution in the conclusion.

Essay topics   Argue for or against:

1. Legalized prostitution
2. Gambling casinos
3. Stricter immigration laws
4. Prayer in the public schools
5. Abortion
6. Tax exemption for religious organizations
7. Capital punishment
8. Single-parent adoption
9. Continuation of the manned space program
10. Females playing on male sports teams
11. Required courses in college
12. Tenure for teachers
13. Expense accounts for business people
14. Canceling a driver's license for drunk driving
15. Random drug testing in the workplace

EXERCISE 2   **Using research material to write the persuasive essay**

The following pieces of information are on the controversial topic of *violence in the movies and on television.* To what extent is the violence we see in films and on television programs responsible for the degree of violence in our society? Use this information as the basis for your own essay on the topic. You may select as many of the items as you want, or you may adapt the items to agree with your way of thinking. As you study the list, decide which of your paragraphs could make use of these facts or opinions.

1. The National Coalition on Television Violence estimates that up to half of all violence in our country comes from the violent entertainment we are exposed to every day.

2. In 1984, violence in Hollywood movies contained an average of 28.5 violent acts per hour.

3. Hollywood spends over $300 million dollars each year advertising movies that are extremely violent.

4. Three Surgeons General of the United States have publicly declared that violence is a serious health problem that contributes to the violence and rape in our society.

5. Sixty-six percent of Americans interviewed think that violent entertainment increases crime in the streets.

6. Television violence has increased by 65 percent since 1980.

7. Mark Fowler, the former head of the Federal Communications Commission (FCC), stated openly that he did not want an investigation of the whole question of violence in the media.

8. Horror, slasher, and violent science fiction movies have increased from 6 percent of box office receipts in 1970 to over 30 percent today.

9. In some years, more than half of the films produced by Hollywood have content that is intensely violent.

10. Over 900 research studies on violent entertainment give overwhelming evidence that violent films and other programs are having a harmful effect on the American people.

Using research material to write the persuasive essay   EXERCISE 3

To what extent can a society permit its people to read, write, and say whatever they want? The following pieces of information are on this controversial topic of *censorship and free speech*. Use this information as the basis for your own essay on the topic. You may select as many of the items as you want, or you may adapt the items to agree with your own way of thinking. After selecting the material to be used, be sure to organize your major points before starting the rough draft.

1. In Anchorage, Alaska, the *American Heritage Dictionary* was banned from the schools.

2. In 1961, the American Nazi leader George Lincoln Rockwell was denied the right to speak in New York City, but the courts upheld his right to express his views.

3. Such literary works as D.H. Lawrence's *Lady Chatterly's Lover*, James Joyce's *Ulysses*, and J.D. Salinger's *The Catcher in the Rye*, have been denounced as pornographic.

4. The Supreme Court has stated that the government may prohibit materials that "portray sexual conduct in a patently offensive way."

5. In ancient Rome, the Censor was a powerful official who judged people's morals and who could even remove government officials from office.

6. *MS* magazine was banned from a number of high school libraries because it was judged to be obscene.

7. The researcher and writer Gay Talese believes that we should not allow law enforcement officials "to deny pornography to those who want it."

8. Jerry Falwell, the founder of Moral Majority, has stated that "basic values such as morality, individualism, respect for our nation's heritage, and the benefits of the free-enterprise system have, for the most part, been censored from today's public-classroom textbooks."

9. In 1983, when the United States invaded the Caribbean island of Grenada, newspaper and television reporters were not told there would be an invasion. When they did find out, they were not permitted to go to the island and report on the invasion.

10. Some psychologists believe that being able to enjoy pornography helps people deal with their frustrations without having to commit criminal or anti-social acts.

Working Together

Analyzing a Newspaper Editorial

The following editorial appeared in the *Chicago Tribune* on June 18, 1995.

Where have all the fathers gone?

Merc
The Chicago Mercantile Exchange

1   Today is Father's Day, so let's talk about dads. Not the ones who cheer their sons and daughters at baseball and soccer games or the ones who fix dinner for the family every night or the ones who come home dead tired after a day at the Merc or McDonald's but still have time for a little family conversation.

2   No, let's talk about the invisible dads, the ones who don't marry mom, don't support their kids and don't hang around for hugs, kisses and helping with homework. There are millions of them in the United States, and their numbers are growing.

3   In 1950, 14 of every 1,000 unmarried women had babies. By 1992, 45 of every 1,000 did. In fact, almost one-third of the children born in the United States in 1992 were born to unwed parents, a 54 percent increase over 1980, according to figures released this month by the National Center for Health Statistics.

4   And though the figures generally are compiled in terms of unmarried women and the resulting handwringing is done in the name of unwed mothers, the facts of life are that for every one of those unmarried mothers there is an unmarried father.

5   The moms are a lot more visible though, because in the overwhelming number of cases, they are the ones raising the kids. So who's the real problem here? And why should we care?

6   We *must* care because the social and financial costs of children growing up in households without fathers is immense. Many of the country's most troublesome social problems—poverty, poor performance in schools, gang activity, juvenile crime, mounting welfare costs—have their roots in families where a father has abdicated responsibility for his children.

7   Women who do not marry before having their first child are three times more likely to wind up on welfare for 10 years or more than those who do marry. And census figures indicate that an intact mother-father household has a far

better chance for financial security than a single-parent family.

8 Moreover, children who have little or no contact with their fathers are robbed of a crucial role model for fashioning their own lives.

9 What's to be done? For starters, parents, grandparents, churches and schools must hammer home the lesson that a man who conceives a child without marrying and being prepared to support the child for 18 years unfairly burdens his family and his community. He must understand that his action will be met by community disapprobation, not the respect and awe of his peers.

10 And while government can't legislate morality, it can encourage responsibility. Legislators should make that a priority by providing tax incentives for couples to marry and by requiring every woman to name her child's father on the birth certificate. Law enforcement officers can (and are beginning to) go after the fathers for child support.

11 Fatherhood, like motherhood, is its own reward—as most dads have found. Sadly, for the others, the invisible ones, it is a gift foolishly squandered.

Read the editorial out loud. Then divide into groups and discuss the following questions:

1. What is the thesis of the editorial?

2. What supporting evidence for the thesis is given in the editorial?

3. Were any outside sources used to support the thesis? If so, indicate the sources.

4. Does the editor say what will or will not happen if nothing is done?

5. Does the editorial propose a solution to the problem?

6. Does the editorial seem reasonable to you?

7. State whether or not you believe this is an effective argument.

When the members of your group are satisfied with the answers to these questions, each person should write his or her own answer (in compete sentences, of course) to each question. Your instructor will want to collect these answers at the end of the class period, so be sure to allow twenty minutes for students to write their own answers to these questions.

Portfolio Suggestion

For many readers, the editorial page is the best part of the newspaper. It is on this paper that writers argue, passionately at times, about issues that are of great importance to them. Look at the editorial section of a newspaper at least once a week and clip editorials that are about subjects that interest you. This is one way to gradually develop a feeling for argumentative or persuasive writing. You can learn from editorials that are outrageous in their points of view as well as from those that are logical and convincing.

On this subject of the deadbeat dad, you might want to use one of the following ideas for a piece of writing to add to your portfolio:

1. Write a letter to a "vanished" father. Try to persuade him to become involved in the lives of his children.

2. Imagine you have gathered ten of these "vanished" fathers in a room. What do you think would be some of their arguments for not participating in the raising of their children?

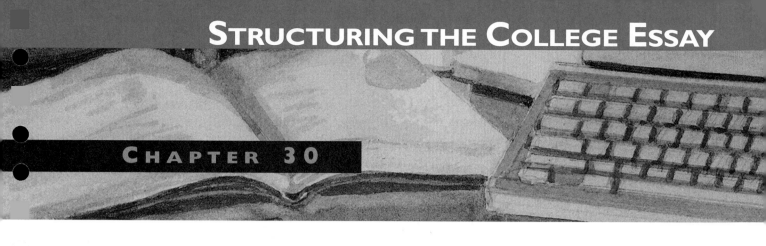
CHAPTER 30

Writing Under Pressure

Most people prefer to do their writing when they are not under the pressure of a time limit. However, many situations demand that a piece of writing be finished by a certain time. One situation is the writing of a story for a newspaper that constantly works under a very tight deadline. Another pressured situation is writing an essay exam that must be handed in by the end of a class period. This chapter will review some of the techniques for writing successful essays under pressure.

How to write well under pressure

The first rule of doing well in any test is to come to the test well rested and well prepared. Research proves that reviewing notes and reading assignments systematically throughout the semester is much more effective than cramming for a test the night before. You'll be greatly satisfied if you learn to use your time efficiently and wisely.

Coming to an exam well prepared

1. Study the textbook chapters and your notes. In your textbook, review headings and bolded words as well as information you have highlighted or underlined. Look for both chapter reviews and summaries at the ends of chapters. If you have already made an outline, study that too.

2. Avoid having to face any surprises when the exam is distributed. When the test is first announced in class, ask if it will include material from the textbook in addition to notes taken in class. Also, find out the format of the test. How many essay questions will there be, and how many points is each question worth? How much time will you have to complete the test?

3. Form a study group if you can. One way a study group can work is the following: each person comes to the study group prepared to present at least one major question that he or she thinks the instructor will ask and then provides the information that will be needed for answering that question. The

other students take notes and add whatever additional information they can. Each person in turn presents a different question along with the information needed for the answer. Members of the group can quiz each other on the information that is to be covered by the exam. For an essay exam, some material needs to be memorized. If you are unable to be part of a study group, you should still try to predict what questions will be on the exam. Prepare an outline for study and then memorize your outline.

Remember that an essay test, unlike a multiple-choice test, requires more than simply recognizing information. In an essay exam, you must be able to recall ideas and specific details and present them quickly in your own words. This ability to memorize both concepts and factual information is quite demanding.

Strategies for answering timed in-class essay questions

The smart test taker does not begin to answer the first question immediately. Instead, he or she takes a few moments to look over the test and form a strategy for the best way to tackle it. The following pointers will help you become "test smart."

1. When you receive the exam, *read over each essay question twice*. How many points is each question worth? The way in which you budget your time will depend heavily on the importance of each question. A well-written test should tell you how many points each question is worth. If, for example, one essay question is worth 50 points, you should spend approximately half your time planning and answering this question. However, if the test consists of ten shorter essay questions and you have a class period of 100 minutes, you should spend no more than ten minutes on each question, keeping a careful watch on your time. Tests composed of several shorter essays can be disastrous to people who do not watch their time. Students often write too much for the first four or five questions and then panic because they have very little time left to answer the final questions.

2. When you read an essay question, ask yourself *what method of development is being asked for*. We all know stories of people who failed tests because they misunderstood the question.

3. *Use key words from the test question itself* to compose your thesis statement, which in a test should be your first sentence. Don't try to be too clever on a test. State your points as directly and clearly as possible.

4. Answer the question by stating your basic point and then *use as many specific details as you have time or knowledge to give*. The more specific names, dates, and places (all spelled correctly) that you can provide the more points will be added to your grade.

5. Since a question can have more than one part, be sure you *answer all the parts*. Check over the question to be sure your answer includes all parts.

Study the question to determine exactly what is being asked for.

Sample essay question   What were the changes that contributed to the rise of the feminist movement in the 1960s in the United States? Be specific.

If the question given were one of ten short essay questions on a ninety-minute final examination, the following answer would probably be adequate.

Sample essay question answer   The feminist movement grew out of many changes happening in the 1960s in the United States. In 1961, the President's Commission on the Status of Women documented discrimination against women in the work force. The result of the Commission's report was a growing public awareness which soon led to the enactment of two pieces of legislation: the Equal Pay Act of 1963 and the Civil Rights Act of 1964. In addition, the development of the birth-control pill brought the discussion of sexuality out into the open. It also lowered the birth rate, leaving more women looking to the world of work. A high divorce rate as well as delayed marriages further contributed to more women being concerned with feminist issues. Finally, in 1966 the National Organization for Women was formed which encouraged women to share their experiences with each other and to organize in an effort to lobby for legislative change.

Notice that the first sentence uses the key words from the question to state the thesis. The answer gives not one but four examples of the changes that were taking place in the 1960s. Moreover, the answer is very specific, naming legislation or an organization and giving dates whenever significant. Can you spot the transitional expressions the writer uses to signal the movement from one example to the next?

Frequently used terms in essay questions

Definition: A definition is the precise meaning of a word or term. When you define something in an essay you usually write an *extended definition*, in which you select an appropriate example or examples to illustrate the meaning of a term.

Comparison or Contrast: When you *compare* two people or things, you point out the similarities between them. When you *contrast* two items, you point out the differences. Sometimes you may find yourself using both comparison and contrast in an essay.

Narration: Narration is the telling of a story by the careful use of a sequence of events. The events are usually (but not always) told in chronological order.

Summary: When you write a summary, you are supplying the main ideas of a longer piece of writing.

Discussion: This is a general term that encourages you to analyze a subject at length. Inviting students to discuss some aspect of a topic is a widely used method of asking examination questions.

Classification: When you *classify* items of any kind, you place them into separate groups so that large amounts of material can be more easily understood.

Cause and Effect: When you deal with causes, you answer the question *why*; when you deal with effects you show *results* or *consequences*.

Methods of development

EXERCISE 1

Each of the following college essay questions deals with the single topic of computers. Use the above list of explanations to decide which method of development is being called for in each case. In the space provided after each question, identify the method being required.

1. Trace the development of the computer, beginning in 1937. Be sure to include all significant developments discussed in class.

   Method of development: _____

2. Choose two of the word processing programs practiced in class and discuss the similarities and differences you encountered. What in your opinion were the advantages and disadvantages of each?

   Method of development: _____

3. Explain the meaning of each of the following terms: *hard disk*, *memory*, *directory*, *menu*, and *software*.

Method of development: _____

4. We have discussed many of the common business applications for the computer. Select ten applications and group them according to the functions they perform.

Method of development: _____

5. Discuss the problems that have resulted in the typical office as a result of computer technology.

Method of development: _____

EXERCISE 2 **Methods of development/parts of a question**

Each of the following is an example of an essay question that could be asked in different college courses. In the spaces provided after each question, indicate: (a) what method of development (definition, comparison or contrast, narration, summary, or discussion) is being called for; (b) how many parts there are to the question. This indicates how many parts there will be in your answer.

1. What does the term *sociology* mean? Include in your answer at least four different meanings the term *sociology* has had since this area of study began.

Method of development: _____

The different parts of the question: _____

_____

_____

2. Compare and contrast the reasons the United States entered the Korean War with the reasons it entered the Vietnam War.

Method of development: _____

The different parts of the question: _____

_____

_____

3. Trace the history of our knowledge of the planet Jupiter, from the time it was first discovered until the present day. Include in your answer at least one nineteenth-century discovery and three of the most recent discoveries that have been made about Jupiter through the use of unmanned space vehicles sent near that planet.

Method of development: _____

The different parts of the question: _____

_____

_____

4. In view of the dramatic increase in cases of contagious diseases, describe the types of precautions now required for medical personnel. What changes are likely to be required in the future?

   Method of development: _____

   The different parts of the question: _____

   _____

   _____

5. Explain the three effects of high temperatures on space vehicles as they reenter the earth's atmosphere.

   Method of development: _____

   The different parts of the question: _____

   _____

   _____

6. What was the complete process of restoring the Statue of Liberty to its original condition? Include in your answer six different aspects of the restoration, from the rebuilding of the inside supports to the treatment of the metal surface.

   Method of development: _____

   The different parts of the question: _____

   _____

   _____

7. Trace the history of the English language from its beginning to the present day. Divide the history of the language into at least three different parts, using Old English, Middle English, and Modern English as your main divisions.

   Method of development: _____

   The different parts of the question: _____

   _____

   _____

8. Discuss the events that led up to World War II. Be sure to include both the political and social problems of the time that directly and indirectly led to the war.

   Method of development: _____

   The different parts of the question: _____

   _____

   _____

9. Summarize the four theories that have been proposed as to why dinosaurs became extinct sixty-five million years ago.

   Method of development: _____

   The different parts of the question: _____

   _____

   _____

10. Define the term *monarchy* and discuss the relevance or irrelevance of this form of government in today's world.

Method of development: _____

The different parts of the question: _____

_____

_____

Using the thesis statement in timed in-class essay questions

One of the most effective ways to begin an essay answer is to write a thesis statement. Your thesis statement should include the important parts of the question and should also give a clear indication of the approach you intend to take in your answer. Writing your opening sentence in this way gives you a real advantage: as your professor begins to read your work, it is clear what you are going to write about and how you are going to treat your subject.

For example, suppose you were going to write an essay on the following topic:

Agree or disagree that a woman president could handle the demands of the most stressful job in the country.

An effective way to write your opening sentence would be to write the following thesis sentence:

I agree that a woman president could handle the demands of the most stressful job in the country.

The reader would then know that this was indeed the topic you had chosen and would also know how you intended to approach that topic.

EXERCISE 3   **Writing thesis statements**

Rewrite each of the following essay questions in thesis statement form. Read each question carefully and underline the important words or phrases in it. Then decide on the approach you would take in answering that question. An example has been done for you.

Essay question: How does one learn another language?

Thesis statement: The process of learning another language is complicated but usually follows four distinct stages.

1. Essay Questions: Discuss Thorstein Veblen's theory of the leisure class.

   Thesis statement: _____

   _____

2. Essay Question: What are the effects of television violence on children?

   Thesis statement: _____

   _____

3. Essay Question: Trace the development of portrait painting from the Middle Ages to today.

   Thesis statement: _____

   _____

4. Essay Question: What are the major causes for the economic crisis facing the African nations today?

   Thesis statement: _____

   _____

5. Essay Question: What have we recently learned from ocean exploration, and what remains to be done?

   Thesis statement: _____

   _____

6. Essay Question: What are the problems when a couple adopts a child from one culture and raises that child in another culture?

   Thesis statement: _____

   _____

7. Essay Question: In what ways does the new Japan differ from the old Japan?

   Thesis statement: _____

   _____

8. Essay Question: What four countries depend on tourism for the major part of their national income and why is this so?

   Thesis statement: _____

   _____

9. Essay Question: What factors should a college use when judging the merits of a particular student for admission?

   Thesis statement: _____

   _____

10. Essay Question: What is Alzheimer's disease, its sequence of characteristic symptoms, and the current methods of treatment?

    Thesis statement: _____

    _____

    _____

Working Together

Preparing for Tests

The following information is taken from a computer textbook. The material is found at the end of the final chapter in the book.

Chapter Title: Computers—The Future and You

Review of Key Points

- We are gradually becoming an information-based society rather than an agricultural or industrial one; the reduction of "information float" will accelerate this movement.
- Careers in computer-related fields have a bright future with an expanding need for workers.
- The seven major areas in computer careers are operations, analysis and programming, information management, repair and service, sales and marketing, instruction, and engineering.
- Computers will continue to become smaller and faster through the increase in the number of transistors on each chip and the eventual use of gallium arsenide and photonic switches.
- Internal and external storage capacities will also continue to grow, with internal capacities on personal computers possibly exceeding 1 Mbyte.
- The use of video disks for external storage appears to a strong possibility in the near future.
- Supercomputers will continue to grow more powerful through the use of parallel processing and pipelining.

- The markets for mainframe computers and personal computers are growing at about the same rate. The use of minicomputers may decline in the future.
- The use of robots in assembly line operations is expected to grow dramatically in the future, with negative effects on some human workers.
- Software will have to become easier to use if new users are to be enticed into the computer market.
- "Softer" software will include voice input, natural languages, expert systems, and other forms of artificial intelligence.
- Telecommunications may be the most rapidly expanding computer-related field in the future.
- Electronic funds transfer makes it unnecessary to leave the home or office to handle financial matters.

—Patrick G. McKeown, *Living with Computers*

Working Together

Continued

1. After you have read through the review material, divide into groups. Each group should do the following:

   a. Construct four essay questions that you believe would be fair questions for a test covering the material in the chapter.

   b. From the "Review of Key Points," make a list of key terms in this chapter. (Students would have to memorize the definitions of these terms in order to be prepared for a test on this material.)

2. Come together as a class and put some of these questions on the board to be analyzed. Use the following checklist to analyze the questions:

   a. Does the question seem to be fair? (Some questions might be too vague or too general to be a fair test of what the student has learned.)

   b. How many parts does the question have?

   c. Does the question call for a specific method of development (for example, definition and analysis)?

   d. What are the key terms that should be used in the answer?

   e. What would be an effective opening sentence for the answer?

Portfolio Suggestion

Write about test anxiety. What can be done to help students who feel under pressure at exam time? In one paragraph, discuss what students can do to help themselves. In another paragraph, discuss what teachers can do to help students reduce their level of anxiety. In a third paragraph, suggest what the college could do to help students who become unusually tense when taking exams.

Irregular Verbs

Alphabetical listing of principal parts of irregular verbs

Base Form	Past Tense	Past Participle
arise	arose	arisen
bear	bore	borne
beat	beat	beat or beaten
become	became	become
begin	began	begun
bend	bent	bent
bet	bet	bet
bind	bound	bound
bite	bit	bitten, bit
bleed	bled	bled
blow	blew	blown
break	broke	broken
breed	bred	bred
bring	brought	brought
build	built	built
burst	burst	burst
buy	bought	bought
cast	cast	cast
catch	caught	caught
choose	chose	chosen
cling	clung	clung
come	came	come
cost	cost	cost

Base Form	Past Tense	Past Participle
creep	crept	crept
cut	cut	cut
deal	dealt	dealt
dig	dug	dug
dive	dived, dove	dived
do	did	done
draw	drew	drawn
drink	drank	drunk
drive	drove	driven
eat	ate	eaten
fall	fell	fallen
feed	fed	fed
feel	felt	felt
fight	fought	fought
find	found	found
fit	fit	fit
flee	fled	fled
fling	flung	flung
fly	flew	flown
forbid	forbade, forbad	forbidden
forget	forgot	forgotten
forgive	forgave	forgiven
freeze	froze	frozen
get	got	gotten
give	gave	given
go	went	gone
grind	ground	ground
grow	grew	grown
hang	hung, hanged	hung, hanged
have	had	had
hear	heard	heard
hide	hid	hidden
hit	hit	hit
hold	held	held
hurt	hurt	hurt
keep	kept	kept
kneel	knelt	knelt
know	knew	known
lay (to put)	laid	laid
lead	led	led
leave	left	left
lend	lent	lent
let	let	let
lie (to recline)	lay	lain

Base Form	Past Tense	Past Participle
lose	lost	lost
make	made	made
mean	meant	meant
meet	met	met
mistake	mistook	mistaken
pay	paid	paid
plead	pled	pled
prove	proved	proved, proven
put	put	put
quit	quit	quit
read	*read	*read
ride	rode	ridden
ring	rang	rung
rise	rose	risen
run	ran	run
say	said	said
see	saw	seen
seek	sought	sought
sell	sold	sold
send	sent	sent
set	set	set
sew	sewed	sewn, sewed
shake	shook	shaken
shave	shaved	shaved, shaven
shed	shed	shed
shine	shone	shone
shoot	shot	shot
show	showed	shown, showed
shrink	shrank, shrunk	shrunk, shrunken
shut	shut	shut
sing	sang	sung
sink	sank	sunk
sit	sat	sat
slay	slew	slain
sleep	slept	slept
slide	slid	slid
sling	slung	slung
slink	slunk	slunk
slit	slit	slit
sow	sowed	sown, sowed
speak	spoke	spoken
speed	sped, speeded	sped, speeded

---

*Pronunciation changes in past and past participle forms.

Base Form	Past Tense	Past Participle
spend	spent	spent
spin	spun	spun
spit	spat	spat
split	split	split
spread	spread	spread
spring	sprang	sprung
stand	stood	stood
steal	stole	stolen
stick	stuck	stuck
sting	stung	stung
stink	stank, stunk	stunk
stride	strode	stridden
strike	struck	struck
string	strung	strung
swear	swore	sworn
sweep	swept	swept
swim	swam	swum
swing	swung	swung
take	took	taken
teach	taught	taught
tear	tore	torn
tell	told	told
think	thought	thought
throw	threw	thrown
wake	woke, waked	woken, waked
wear	wore	worn
weave	wove	woven
weep	wept	wept
wet	wet	wet
win	won	won
wind	wound	wound
wring	wrung	wrung
write	wrote	written

Parts of Speech

Words can be divided into categories called *parts of speech.* Understanding these categories will help you work with language more easily, especially when it comes to revising your own writing.

Nouns

A *noun* is a word that names persons, places, or things.

Common Nouns	Proper Nouns
officer	Michael Johnson
station	Grand Central Station
magazine	*Newsweek*

Nouns are said to be *concrete* if you can see or touch them.

window
paper
river

Nouns are said to be *abstract* if you cannot see or touch them. These words can be concepts, ideas, or qualities.

meditation
honesty
carelessness

To test for a noun, it may help to ask these questions.

- Can I make the word plural? (Most nouns have a plural form.)
- Can I put the article *the* in front of the word?
- Is the word used as the subject or object of the sentence?

Pronouns

A ***pronoun*** is a word used to take the place of a noun. Just like a noun, it is used as the subject or object of a sentence.

Pronouns can be divided into several classes. Here are some of them:

	Pronouns					

Note: Personal pronouns have three forms depending on how they are used in a sentence: as a subject, object, or possessive.

Personal Pronouns

	Subjective		Objective		Possessive	
	Singular	*Plural*	*Singular*	*Plural*	*Singular*	*Plural*
1st person	I	we	me	us	my (mine)	our (ours)
2nd person	you	you	you	you	your (yours)	your (yours)
3rd person	he	they	him	them	his (his)	their (theirs)
	she		her		her (hers)	
	it		it		its (its)	

Relative Pronouns	**Demonstrative Pronouns**	**Indefinite Pronouns**			
who, whom, whose	this	*Singular*			
which	that	everyone	someone	anyone	no one
that	these	everybody	somebody	anybody	nobody
what	those	everything	something	anything	nothing
whoever		each	another	either	neither
whichever		*Singular* or *Plural* (depending on meaning)			
whatever		all	more	none	
		any	most	some	
		Plural			
		both	few	many	several

Adjectives

> An *adjective* is a word that modifies a noun or pronoun. Adjectives usually come before the nouns they modify, but they can also come in the predicate.

The adjective comes directly in front of the noun it modifies:

The *unusual* package was placed on my desk.

The adjective occurs in the predicate but refers back to the noun it modifies:

The package felt *cold*.

Verbs

> A *verb* is a word that shows action or expresses being. It can also change form in order to show the time (past, present, or future) of that action or being.

Verbs can be divided into three classes:

1. *Action Verbs*

> *Action verbs* tell us what the subject is doing and when the subject does the action.

The action takes place in the present:

The athlete *runs* five miles every morning.

The action takes place in the past:

The crowd *cheered* for the oldest runner.

2. *Linking Verbs*

> A *linking verb* joins the subject of a sentence to one or more words that describe or identify the subject.

The linking verb *was* identifies *He* with the noun *dancer:*

   He *was* a dancer in his twenties.

The linking verb *seemed* describes *She* as *disappointed:*

   She *seemed* disappointed with her job.

Common linking verbs
be (am, is, are, was, were, have been)

act	grow
appear	look
become	seem
feel	taste

3. *Helping Verbs* (also called "auxiliaries")

> A *helping verb* is any verb used before the main verb.

The helping verb could show the **tense** of the verb:

   It *will* rain tomorrow.

The helping verb could show the **passive voice:**

   The new civic center *has been* finished.

The helping verb could give a **special meaning** to the verb:

   Annie Lennox *may be* singing here tonight.

Common helping verbs
can, could
may, might, must
shall, should
will, would
forms of the irregular verbs *be, have,* and *do*

Adverbs

> An **adverb** is a word that modifies a verb, an adjective, or another adverb. It often ends in -ly, but a better test is to ask yourself if the word answers one of the questions *how, when,* or *where.*

The adverb could modify a **verb:**

The student walked *happily* into the classroom.

The adverb could modify an **adjective:**

It will be *very* cold tomorrow.

The adverb could modify another **adverb:**

Winter has come *too* early.

Here are some adverbs to look out for:

Common adverbs	
Adverbs of Frequency	**Adverbs of Degree**
often	even
never	extremely
sometimes	just
seldom	more
always	much
ever	only
	quite
	surely
	too
	very

Prepositions

> A *preposition* is a word used to relate a noun or pronoun to some other word in the sentence. The preposition with its noun or pronoun is called a *prepositional phrase*.

The letter is *from* my father.

The envelope is addressed *to* my sister.

Read through the following list of prepositions several times so that you will be able to recognize them. Your instructor may ask you to memorize them.

Common prepositions			
about	below	in	since
above	beneath	inside	through
across	beside	into	to
after	between	like	toward
against	beyond	near	under
along	by	of	until
among	down	off	up
around	during	on	upon
at	except	outside	with
before	for	over	within
behind	from	past	without

Conjunctions

> A *conjunction* is a word that joins or connects other words, phrases, or clauses.

A conjunction connecting *two words:*

Sooner *or* later, you will have to pay.

A conjunction connecting *two phrases:*

The story was on the radio *and* in the newspaper.

A conjunction connecting *two clauses:*

Dinner was late *because* I had to work overtime.

Conjunctions	
Coordinating Conjunctions	**Subordinating Conjunctions**

Coordinating Conjunctions
and
but
or
nor
for (meaning *because*)
yet
so

Correlative Conjunctions
either . . . or
neither . . . nor
both . . . and
not only . . . but also

Subordinating Conjunctions

after	provided that
although	since
as, as if, as though	unless
because	until
before	when, whenever
how	where, wherever
if, even if	while

Adverbial Conjunctions (also known as *conjunctive adverbs*)

To add an idea:	furthermore
	moreover
	likewise
To contrast:	however
	nevertheless
To show results:	consequently
	therefore
To show an alternative:	otherwise

Interjections

> An *interjection* is a word that expresses a strong feeling and is not connected grammatically to any other part of the sentence.

Oh, I forgot my keys.

Well, that means I'll have to sit here all day.

Study the context

Since one word can function differently or have different forms or meanings, you must often study the context in which the word is found to be sure of its part of speech.

for functioning as a preposition:

The parent makes sacrifices *for* the good of the children.

for functioning as a conjunction meaning *because:*

The parent worked two jobs, *for* her child needed a good education.

Summer Reading

MICHAEL DORRIS

Important events from childhood never fade from our minds, and if we are able to write them down, they acquire an even greater reality. In writing the following essay, Michael Dorris has achieved this greater reality. Long after this memorable summer from his adolescence, the Native American professor and writer looks back on a debt that was repaid in an unexpected way, one that profoundly changed his life.

1   When I was fourteen, I earned money in the summer by mowing lawns, and within a few weeks I had built up a regular clientele. I got to know people by the flowers they planted that I had to remember not to cut down, by the things they lost in the grass or stuck in the ground on purpose. I reached the point with most of them when I knew in advance what complaint was about to be spoken, which particular request was most important. And I learned something about the measure of my neighbors by their preferred method of payment: by the job, by the month—or not at all.

2   Mr. Ballou fell into the last category, and he always had a reason why. On one day he had no change for a fifty, on another he was flat out of checks, on another, he was simply out when I knocked on his door. Still, except for the money part, he was a nice enough old guy, always waving or tipping his hat when he'd see me from a distance. I figured him for a thin retirement check, maybe a work-related injury that kept him from doing his own yard work. Sure, I kept a running total, but I didn't worry about the amount too much. Grass was grass, and the little that Mr. Ballou's property comprised didn't take long to trim.

3   Then, one late afternoon in mid-July, the hottest time of the year, I was walking by his house and he opened the door, motioned me to come inside. The hall was cool, shaded, and it took my eyes a minute to adjust to the muted light.

4   "I owe you," Mr. Ballou began, "but . . ."

5   I thought I'd save him the trouble of thinking up a new excuse. "No problem. Don't worry about it."

6   "The bank made a mistake in my account," he continued, ignoring my words. "It will be cleared up in a day or two. But in the meantime I thought perhaps you could choose one or two volumes for a down payment."

7   He gestured toward the walls and I saw that books were stacked everywhere. It was like a library, except with no order to the arrangement.

8   "Take your time," Mr. Ballou encouraged. "Read, borrow, keep. Find something you like. What do you read?"

9   "I don't know." And I didn't. I generally read what was in front of me, what I could snag from the paperback rack at the drugstore, what I found at the library, magazines, the back of cereal boxes, comics. The idea of consciously seeking out a special title was new to me, but, I realized, not without appeal—so I browsed through the piles of books.

10   "You actually read all of these?"

11   "This isn't much," Mr. Ballou said. "This is nothing, just what I've kept, the ones worth looking at a second time."

12   "Pick for me, then."

13   He raised his eyebrows, cocked his head, regarded me appraisingly as though measuring me for a suit. After a moment, he nodded, searched through a stack, and handed me a dark red hardbound book, fairly thick.

14   "*The Last of the Just*," I read. "By André Schwarz-Bart. What's it about?"

15   "You tell me," he said. "Next week."

16   I started after supper, sitting outdoors on an uncomfortable kitchen chair. Within a few pages, the yard, the summer, disappeared, the bright oblivion of adolescence temporarily lifted, and I was plunged into the aching tragedy of the Holocaust, the extraordinary clash of

clientele
customers

appraisingly
with judgment

muted
soft

oblivion
total forgetfulness

good, represented by one decent man, and evil. Translated from French, the language was elegant, simple, overwhelming. When the evening light finally failed I moved inside, read all through the night.

intermission
a period between events

17 To this day, thirty years later, I vividly remember the experience. It was my first voluntary encounter with world literature, and I was stunned by the undiluted power a novel could contain. I lacked the vocabulary, however, to translate my feelings into words, so the next week, when Mr. Ballou asked, "Well?" I only replied, "It was good."

18 "Keep it, then," he said. "Shall I suggest another?"

19 I nodded, and was presented with the paperback edition of Margaret Mead's *Coming of Age in Samoa*.

20 To make two long stories short, Mr. Ballou never paid me a dime for cutting his grass that year or the next, but for fifteen years I taught anthropology at Dartmouth College. Summer reading was not the innocent pastime I had assumed it to be, not a breezy, instantly forgettable escape in a hammock (though I've since enjoyed many of those, too). A book, if it arrives before you at the right moment, in the proper season, at a point of intermission in the daily business of things, will change the course of all that follows.

Questions for Critical Thinking

1. The author uses narration to develop his idea about the importance of reading. Summarize the story.

2. Review paragraphs two through six in the essay and decide why Mr. Ballou could not (or would not) pay Michael Dorris. Do you think he did not have enough money, or was he unwilling to spend money on something other than books?

3. What were the author's reading habits before his encounter with Mr. Ballou? What do you think his reading habits were after this summer experience?

4. The second book Mr. Ballou gave the author was Margaret Mead's *Coming of Age in Samoa*, a very important book on the study of social and cultural development of people—anthropology. In the next sentence, Michael Dorris tells us that "for fifteen years I taught anthropology at Dartmouth College." What connection does the writer want us to make?

5. When is it appropriate or acceptable for a person to repay a financial debt not with money but with some other form of repayment, either in goods or services? When is it not a good idea to try to settle a debt in this way?

6. In the first paragraph, the writer indicates he received no payment from some of his customers, and in the concluding paragraph returns to the idea that Mr. Ballou never gave him any money for mowing his lawn. The writer did, nevertheless, get paid. Explain.

Writing in Response

1. This story is about an adolescent who had a summer job. Write an essay in which you discuss the lessons that young people can learn by having the responsibility of part-time jobs while they are growing up.

2. Write an essay in which you talk about the people in your neighborhood and the personalities you have observed through the years you have lived there. What lessons did they teach you or what help did they offer you? You could use description, narration, example, and/or cause and effect to develop your ideas.

3. Michael Dorris concludes his essay by noting that if you come across a book "at the right moment," it could change the direction of your life. Write an essay about something that happened to you that changed your life in an important way.

My Daughter Smokes

ALICE WALKER

Not every part of the heritage a family passes from one generation to another is necessarily a positive inheritance. In the following autobiographical essay, prize-winning writer Alice Walker tells of an undesirable tradition in her family, a tradition that fortunately may be at an end.

1   My daughter smokes. While she is doing her homework, her feet on the bench in front of her and her calculator clicking out answers to her algebra problems. I am looking at the half-empty package of Camels tossed carelessly close at hand. Camels. I pick them up, take them into the kitchen, where the light is better, and study them—they're filtered, for which I am grateful. My heart feels terrible. I want to weep. In fact, I do weep a little, standing there by the stove holding one of the instruments, so white, so precisely rolled, that could cause my daughter's death. When she smoked Marlboros and Players I hardened myself against feeling so bad; nobody I knew ever smoked these brands.

2   She doesn't know this, but it was Camels that my father, her grandfather, smoked. But before he smoked "ready-mades"—when he was very young and very poor, with eyes like lanterns—he smoked Prince Albert tobacco in cigarettes he rolled himself. I remember the bright-red tobacco tin, with a picture of Queen Victoria's consort, Prince Albert, dressed in a black frock coat and carrying a cane.

3   The tobacco was dark brown, pungent, slightly bitter. I tasted it more than once as a child, and the discarded tins could be used for a number of things: to keep buttons and shoelaces in, to store seeds, and best of all, to hold worms for the rare times my father took us fishing.

4   By the late forties and early fifties no one rolled his own anymore (and few women smoked) in my hometown, Eatonton, Georgia. The tobacco industry, coupled with Hollywood movies in which both hero and heroine smoked like chimneys, won over completely people like my father, who were hopelessly addicted to cigarettes. He never looked as dapper as Prince Albert, though; he continued to look like a poor, over-weight, overworked colored man with too large a family; black, with a very white cigarette stuck in his mouth.

5   I do not remember when he started to cough. Perhaps it was unnoticeable at first. A little hacking in the morning as he lit his first cigarette upon getting out of bed. By the time I was my daughter's age, his breath was a wheeze, embarrassing to hear; he could not climb stairs without resting every third or fourth step. It was not unusual for him to cough for an hour.

6   It is hard to believe there was a time when people did not understand that cigarette smoking is an addiction. I wondered aloud once to my sister—who is perennially trying to quit—whether our father realized this. I wondered how she, a smoker since high school, viewed her own habit.

7   It was our father who gave her her first cigarette, one day when she had taken water to him in the fields.

8   "I always wondered why he did that," she said, puzzled, and with some bitterness.

9   "What did he say?" I asked.

10   "That he didn't want me to go to anyone else for them," she said, "which never really crossed my mind."

11   So he was aware it was addictive, I thought, though as annoyed as she that he assumed she would be interested.

12   I began smoking in eleventh grade, also the year I drank numerous bottles of terrible sweet, very cheap wine. My friends and I, all boys for this venture, bought our supplies from a man who ran a segregated bar and liquor store on the outskirts of town. Over the entrance there was a large sign that said colored. We were not permitted to drink there, only to buy. I smoked Kools, because my sister did. By then I thought her toxic darkened lips and gums glamorous.

perennially
continually, regularly

consort
the spouse of a king or queen

pungent
sharp and penetrating

chronic
lasting a long time

However, my body simply would not tolerate smoke. After six months I had a chronic sore throat. I gave up smoking, gladly. Because it was a ritual with my buddies—Murl, Leon, and "Dog" Farley—I continued to drink wine.

13   My father died from "the poor man's friend," pneumonia, one hard winter when his bronchitis and emphysema had left him low. I doubt he had much lung left at all, after coughing for so many years. He had so little breath that, during his last years, he was always leaning on something. I remember once, at a family reunion, when my daughter was two, that my father picked her up for a minute—long enough for me to photograph them—but the effort was obvious. Near the very end of his life, and largely because he had no more lungs, he quit smoking. He gained a couple of pounds, but by then he was so emaciated no one noticed.

empathy
identifying with another very closely

14   When I travel to Third World countries I see many people like my father and daughter. There are large billboards directed at them both: the tough, "take-charge," or dapper older man, the glamorous, "worldly" young woman, both puffing away. In these poor countries, as in American ghettos and on reservations, money that should be spent for food goes instead to the tobacco companies; over time, people starve themselves of both food and air, effectively weakening and addicting their children, eventually eradicating themselves. I read in the newspaper and in my gardening magazine that cigarette butts are so toxic that if a baby swallows one, it is likely to die, and that the boiled water from a bunch of them makes an effective insecticide.

15   My daughter would like to quit, she says. We both know the statistics are against her; most people who try to quit smoking do not succeed.*

cajole
to gently urge repeatedly

16   There is a deep hurt that I feel as a mother. Some days it is a feeling of futility. I remember how carefully I ate

_____

*Three months after reading this essay my daughter stopped smoking.

when I was pregnant, how patiently I taught my daughter how to cross a street safely. For what, I sometimes wonder; so that she can wheeze through most of her life feeling half her strength, and then die of self-poisoning, as her grandfather did?

17   But, finally, one must feel empathy for the tobacco plant itself. For thousands of years, it has been venerated by Native Americans as a sacred medicine. They have used it extensively—its juice, its leaves, its roots, its (holy) smoke—to heal wounds and cure diseases, and in ceremonies of prayer and peace. And though the plant as most of us know it has been poisoned by chemicals and denatured by intensive mono-cropping and is therefore hardly the plant it was, still, to some modern Indians it remains a plant of positive power. I learned this when my Native American friends, Bill Wahpepah and his family, visited with me for a few days and the first thing he did was sow a few tobacco seeds in my garden.

18   Perhaps we can liberate tobacco from those who have captured and abused it, enslaving the plant on large plantations, keeping it from freedom and its kin, and forcing it to enslave the world. Its true nature suppressed, no wonder it has become deadly. Maybe by sowing a few seeds of tobacco in our gardens and treating the plant with the reverence it deserves, we can redeem tobacco's soul and restore its self-respect.

19   Besides, how grim, if one is a smoker, to realize one is smoking a slave.

20   There is a slogan from a battered women's shelter that I especially like: "Peace on earth begins at home." I believe everything does. I think of a slogan for people trying to stop smoking: "Every home a smoke-free zone." Smoking is a form of self-battering that also batters those who must sit by, occasionally cajole or complain, and helplessly watch. I realize now that as a child I sat by, through the years, and literally watched my father kill himself; surely one such victory in my family, for the rich white men who own the tobacco companies, is enough.

Questions for Critical Thinking

1. What do you think is the writer's thesis? Consider the title and the first sentence. Is this a case of a thesis where the attitude about the topic is unstated but the writer can assume that readers would understand from the very beginning what a mother's attitude would be?

2. In this essay, how many family members' stories are told?

3. Narration involves a story usually with a sequence of events. This essay uses elements of narration to develop the main point. What is the sequence of events Alice Walker has chosen for this essay?

4. In order to achieve coherence, writers need to use transitions of time in narrative pieces. Review the essay and underline all the transitional expressions you can find.

5. In the final paragraph of her essay, Alice Walker quotes the slogan "Peace on earth begins at home," and she adds, "I believe everything does." Make a list with your classmates of the kinds of problems that can be solved in the home. What if any are the problems that cannot be solved in the home and for which government intervention is needed?

6. When Alice Walker remembers the Prince Albert tobacco tin, with its picture of the elegant royal prince, she observes that her father "never looked as dapper as Prince Albert . . ." Examine advertisements for widely used products that you consider harmful or dangerous. In your view, how far away are these advertising images from the reality you know to be true about the product?

Writing in Response

1. Alice Walker describes a bad habit that links the generations of her family. Look at your own family. Looking back on your parents or grandparents, and then considering yourself or your own children, what habit (bad or good) can you observe going through more than one generation? Write an essay in which you trace your own family history in terms of this habit.

2. Alice Walker tells us in a footnote that three months after reading her essay, her daughter stopped smoking. Do you think Alice Walker's essay played any part in her daughter's success in quitting? Write an essay in which you deal with the issue of a bad habit. You might choose from the following:

   How you were able to break a bad habit

   How you helped someone else break a bad habit

   Advice to someone trying to break a bad habit

3. Write an essay in which you discuss the possibility that some products being sold on the market today may be judged harmful in the future. Your essay could include discussions of a number of products, or you could choose to concentrate on one product and discuss its future in detail.

4. Alice Walker gave up cigarettes because her throat hurt, but she continued to drink wine as a "ritual" with her "buddies." Write an essay in which you discuss the ways in which teenagers are tempted by peer pressure to engage in harmful activities. How do some teenagers resist this pressure? Give examples or a story from your own experience or observation.

The Paterson Public Library

JUDITH ORTIZ COFER

Places and events that shape our childhoods can create mixed memories for us as adults. For Judith Ortiz Cofer, growing up in Paterson, New Jersey, had both a positive and a negative impact on her life. As you read these recollections of her childhood, think how you might write about your childhood.

1 It was a Greek temple in the ruins of an American city. To get to it I had to walk through neighborhoods where not even the carcasses of rusted cars on blocks nor the death traps of discarded appliances were parted with, so that the yards of the borderline poor, people who lived not in a huge building, as I did, but in their own decrepit little houses, looked like a reversed archaeological site, incongruous next to the pillared palace of the Paterson Public Library.

incongruous
not fitting in; not in harmony

2 The library must have been built during Paterson's boom years as the model industrial city of the North. Enough marble was used in its construction to have kept several Michelangelos busily satisfied for a lifetime. Two roaring lions, taller than a grammar school girl, greeted those brave enough to seek answers there. Another memorable detail about the façade of this important place to me was the phrases carved deeply into the walls—perhaps the immortal words of Greek philosophers—I could not tell, since I was developing astigmatism at that time and could only make out the lovely geometric designs they made.

façade
the face of a building

astigmatism
a defect of the eye, resulting in blurred vision

harbored
held a feeling

3 All during the school week I both anticipated and feared the long walk to the library because it took me through enemy territory. The black girl Lorraine, who had chosen me to hate and terrorize with threats at school, lived in one of the gloomy little houses that circled the library like beggars. Lorraine would eventually carry out her violence against me by beating me up in a confrontation formally announced through the school grapevine so that for days I lived with a panic that has rarely been equaled in my adult life, since now I can get grown-ups to listen to me, and at that time disasters had to be a fait accompli for a teacher or a parent to get

fait accompli
something already done

involved. Why did Lorraine hate me? For reasons neither one of us fully understood at the time. All I remember was that our sixth grade teacher seemed to favor me, and her way of showing it was by having me tutor "slow" students in spelling and grammar. Lorraine, older and bigger than myself, since she was repeating the grade, was subjected to this ritual humiliation, which involved sitting in the hallway, obviously separated from the class—one of us for being smart, the other for the opposite reason. Lorraine resisted my efforts to teach her the basic rules of spelling. She would hiss her threats at me, addressing me as *You little spic*. Her hostility sent shudders through me. But baffling as it was, I also accepted it as inevitable. She would beat me up. I told my mother and the teacher, and they both reassured me in vague adult terms that a girl like Lorraine would not dare get in trouble again. She had a history of problems that made her a likely candidate for reform school. But Lorraine and I knew that the violence she harbored had found a target: me—the skinny Puerto Rican girl whose father was away with the navy most of the time and whose mother did not speak English; I was the perfect choice.

4 Thoughts like these occupied my mind as I walked to the library on Saturday mornings. But my need for books was strong enough to propel me down the dreary streets with their slush-covered sidewalks and the skinny trees of winter looking like dark figures from a distance: angry black girls waiting to attack me.

5 But the sight of the building was enough to reassure me that sanctuary was within reach. Inside the glass doors was the inexhaustible treasure of books, and I made my way through the stacks

like the beggar invited to the wedding feast. I remember the musty, organic smell of the library, so different from the air outside. It was the smell of an ancient forest, and since the first books that I read for pleasure were fairy tales, the aroma of transforming wood suited me as a prop.

6 With my pink library card I was allowed to check out two books from the first floor—the children's section. I would take the full hour my mother had given me (generously adding fifteen minutes to get home before she sent my brother after me) to choose the books I would take home for the week. I made my way first through the world's fairy tales. Here I discovered that there is a Cinderella in every culture, that she didn't necessarily have the white skin and rosy cheeks Walt Disney had given her, and that the prince they all waited for could appear in any color, shape, or form. The prince didn't even have to be a man.

7 It was the way I absorbed fantasy in those days that gave me the sense of inner freedom, a feeling of power and the ability to fly that is the main reward of the writer. As I read those stories I became not only the characters but their creator. I am still fascinated by the idea that fairy tales and fables are part of humankind's collective unconscious—a familiar theory that acquires concreteness in my own writing today, when I discover over and over that the character I create or the themes that recur in my poems and in my fiction are my own versions of the "types" I learned to recognize very early in my life in fairy tales.

8 There was also violence in these stories: villains decapitated in honorable battle, goblins and witches pursued, beaten, and burned at the stake by heroes with magic weapons, possessing the supernatural strength granted to the self-righteous in folklore. I understood those black-and-white duels between evil and justice. But Lorraine's blind hatred of my person and my knee-liquefying fear of her were not so clear to me at that time. It would be many years before I learned about the politics of race, before I internalized the awful reality of the struggle for territory that underscored the lives of blacks and Puerto Ricans in Paterson during my childhood. Each job given to a light-skinned Hispanic was one less job for a black man; every apartment leased to a Puerto Rican family was one less place available to blacks. Worst of all, though the Puerto Rican children had to master a new language in the schools and were often subjected to the scorn and impatience of teachers burdened with too many students making too many demands in a classroom, the blacks were obviously the ones singled out for "special" treatment. In other words, whenever possible they were assigned to special education classes in order to relieve the teacher's workload, mainly because their black English dialect sounded "ungrammatical" and "illiterate" to our white Seton Hall University and City College—educated instructors. I have on occasion become angry at being treated like I'm mentally deficient by persons who make that prejudgment upon hearing an unfamiliar accent. I can only imagine what it must have been like for children like Lorraine, whose skin color alone put her in a pigeonhole she felt she had to fight her way out of every day of her life.

9 I was one of the lucky ones; as an insatiable reader I quickly became more than adept at the use of the English language. My life as a navy brat, moving with my family from Paterson to Puerto Rico every few months as my father's tours of duty demanded, taught me to depend on knowledge as my main source of security. What I learned from books borrowed from the Greek temple among the ruins of the city I carried with me as the lightest of carry-on luggage. My teachers in both countries treated me well in general. The easiest way to become a teacher's pet, or *la favorita*, is to ask the teacher for books to read—and I was always looking for reading material. Even my mother's romantic novels by Corín Tellado and her *Buenhogar* (Spanish *Good Housekeeping* magazine) were not safe from my insatiable word hunger.

10 Since the days when I was stalked by Lorraine, libraries have always been an adventure for me. Fear of an ambush is

collective unconscious
according to Carl Jung, a part of the human memory all people share

decapitated
beheaded

no longer the reason why I feel my pulse quicken a little when I approach a library building, when I enter the stacks and inhale the familiar smell of old leather and paper. It may be the memory of the danger that heightens my senses, but it is really the expectation that I felt then and that I still feel now about books. They contained most of the information I needed to survive in two languages and in two worlds. When adults were too busy to answer my endless questions, I could always *look it up;* when I felt unbearably lonely, as I often did during those early gypsy years traveling with my family, I read to escape and also to connect: you can come back to a book as you cannot always to a person or place you miss. I read and reread favorite books until the characters seemed like relatives or friends I could see when I wanted or needed to see them.

11 I still feel that way about books. They represent my spiritual life. A library is my sanctuary, and I am always at home in one. It is not surprising that in recalling my first library, the Paterson Public Library, I have always described it as a temple.

12 Lorraine carried out her threat. One day after school, as several of our classmates, Puerto Rican and black, circled us to watch, Lorraine grabbed a handful of my long hair and forced me to my knees. Then she slapped my face hard enough that the sound echoed off the brick walls of the school building and ran off while I screamed at the sight of blood on my white knee socks and felt the throbbing on my scalp where I would have a bald spot advertising my shame for weeks to come.

13 No one intervened. To this crowd, it was one of many such violent scenes taking place among the adults and the children of people fighting over a rapidly shrinking territory. It happens in the jungle and it happens in the city. But another course of action other than "fight or flight" is open to those of us lucky enough to discover it, and that is channeling one's anger and energy into the development of a mental life. It requires something like obsessiveness for a young person growing up in an environment where physical labor and physical endurance are the marks of a survivor—as is the case with minority peoples living in large cities. But many of us do manage to discover books. In my case, it may have been what anthropologists call a cultural adaptation. Being physically small, non-English-speaking, and always the new kid on the block. I was forced to look for an alternative mode to survival in Paterson. Reading books empowered me.

14 Even now, a visit to the library recharges the batteries in my brain. Looking through the card catalog reassures me that there is no subject that I cannot investigate, no world I cannot explore. Everything that is is mine for the asking. Because I can read about it.

Questions for Critical Thinking

1. This narrative selection begins with two paragraphs of description. Underline each sensory image that makes the opening vivid. Point out how the neighborhood was in sharp contrast to the library.

2. Although the writer clearly sees Lorraine as her enemy, she also shows a great deal of sympathy for her. Point out where in the essay Judith Ortiz Cofer shows her sympathetic feelings toward Lorraine. What reasons does she give for Lorraine's attitude toward her?

3. The author directs much of the essay to an analysis of what reading has meant to her through the years. She describes it as her spiritual life. Review the essay and mark each place where the writer introduces a benefit of reading. Why did she read as a child? What does reading mean to her now? Why do you think some children develop such a great interest in reading and others do not?

4. Narration usually includes a sequence of events with transitional expressions of time that help the reader move through the narrative. Find these transitional expressions of time and underline them.

Writing in Response

1. Write a description of a place that offered safety and security to you during your childhood.

2. Cofer tells us in her essay that books gave her a way to survive in her childhood neighborhood in Paterson. In fact, being able to explore her library and read on her own empowered her. In your own writing, discuss the importance that a book, poem, or story has had in your life. It could even be a short quotation or verse from a special book you have read that has empowered you or helped you to adapt or survive a difficult situation.

3. Many Americans have a complex identity; that is, they must exist in two worlds, sometimes with two languages. Write an essay in which you discuss the advantages or disadvantages of living in two cultures.

4. Write an essay in which you discuss the violence that we see in many schools today. Give what you believe are the causes for this increased level of violence in schools. To what degree is intolerance a factor?

Sleepless in El Paso

LEO N. MILETICH

Along with the different habits and lifestyles of today's society has come a change in the level of comfort we enjoy: places are noisier and more crowded, and in this regard, we often find ourselves wishing for a little less. Leo N. Miletich finds himself looking back to a quieter time and wishing he could have now what most people took for granted then.

1   Stephen Foster's words to "Beautiful Dreamer," "Sounds of the rude world, heard in the day/Lulled by the moonlight have all passed away," belong in another time. On a recent evening, un-lulled by the moonlight, the city streets department ripped up nine blocks of pavement around my apartment building between 9:30 P.M. and 6 A.M. Compared with what I usually hear at night, the steady roar of heavy equipment was actually soothing.

2   Night noise to Stephen Foster was an occasional steamboat whistle, or the rattle of a passing buckboard; "life's busy throng" came to a halt for him after dark. Of that I'm envious: Foster didn't have my neighbors. The world has grown ruder.

3   I've had to share common apartment walls with numerous people for most of my life. The experience has often left me feeling that if the human race were a club, I'd turn in my membership.

4   Some neighbors use car horns in lieu of doorbells; other residents have barking dogs. A number of people can't seem to hear music unless the beat is vibrating the walls and rattling the windows;

and there are those dysfunctional couples who debate by smashing crockery against the walls (passing observation: small apartments contribute to domestic discord). There are helpful souls who keep their televisions so loud that I have no need to use the sound on mine if we're on the same channel.

5   Growing up, I had to keep my voice down, use an earphone for the radio and stereo, place the TV away from any shared wall, step lightly on the stairs and ease the door closed, all in an effort not to disturb the neighbors. And the neighbors did the same. It was a cardinal rule of apartment living. It was called courtesy and consideration—the neighborly thing to do. What ever happened to that? Do parents ever say, "Don't slam that door" to their children anymore?

6   My next-door neighbors slam doors at all hours of the day or night. These are heavy iron-framed security screen doors that when slammed reverberate through my place like cannon shots. The kids slam them. Their parents slam. People who visit slam them. I find this crashing incomprehensible.

dysfunctional
not able to function

cardinal
of greatest importance

in lieu of
in place of

7   There's a college kid down the block with a boom car. When he cranks it up, the bass alone sounds like there's a rumbling Sherman tank in my bathroom, a rolling thunderstorm overhead. When he adds music (and "Beautiful Dreamer" is not on his playlist), it can be heard for three blocks in any direction, especially at midnight. The vibrations alone have been known to set off car alarms as he drives past. I hope his ears bleed at night.

8   In the next building is a 13-year-old girl who likes to blast her stereo at a pulse-pounding level so that it's clearly audible in my place even with the doors and windows closed. I knocked on her front door late one night and found myself facing not a bunch of drugged-out crazoids, as I'd feared, but her middle-aged parents. They seemed distressed and intimidated. They said they couldn't do a thing about the rock music pounding away in the next room, that the girl refused to use her earphones. I was getting a headache just standing at the door. Always in favor of compromise, I suggested unplugging the stereo and tossing it in the dumpster. Instead, the mother pulled me inside the sonic maelstrom, pleading with me to reason with the girl. At my approach, the teenager bolted down the hallway, locked herself in the bathroom (slamming the door) and screamed at us for disturbing her.

9   And friends wonder why I never wanted children.

10   I've tried seeing things in a wider perspective. I'm sure the people in my paternal grandparents' war-torn, ancestral homeland of Croatia would love to exchange the sound of artillery and snipers for the sound of stereos and televisions, just as people in squalid public-housing areas would cheer the sound of music and sitcoms over the sounds of screams, gunfire and sirens in the street. To the hearing impaired, I'm a fortunate man. But intellectualizing this problem doesn't prevent my yawning all day and nodding off on the bus.

11   The people currently sharing a thin, hollow bedroom wall with me have been disrupting my sleep for nearly three years through simple, inconsiderate acts that have the cumulative effect of being profoundly irritating. Apart from the door slamming, I have music throbbing through the wall (which, like a drum, seems to amplify low-frequency sounds). Voices chatter throughout the night. If something needs fixing or building in the apartment, no neighborly inhibitions prevail because of the hour. I've been awakened at 1 A.M. by hammering and sawing.

12   I've tried explaining, in a friendly manner, how thin the wall is and how I have this peculiar habit of needing to sleep at night. I've also tried the time-honored method of noise reduction by pounding on the wall when the decibels reach impossible limits. The return response from next door is to pound right back and increase the volume. I've tried earplugs and sound machines that simulate rain, trains and waves. Nothing can drown out the late-night conversation or the sudden thumps, bumps and rattles in the middle of the night. I might as well be living next to poltergeists.

13   When I mentioned to my landlord that professional torturers use sleep deprivation as a way to break people, he was unfazed; after all, he doesn't live here. One day, in response to my last complaint, the landlord's son uttered what must be the defining attitude for this closing decade of the 20th century: "It's the '90s: People don't give a s---."

14   That, I thought, should be on a T shirt or a bumper sticker. Or maybe it should be the title of Newt's next book.

15   Bob Dole and the Christian Coalition might think about giving up their fruitless attack on sex and violence in our pop culture and start concentrating on the real-world aural terrorists who stress out our nights. Make consideration a campaign issue, rudeness an etiquette crime. If presidential candidates have a need for a campaign promise that's sure to win votes, they should forget the chicken-in-every pot cliché (or is it now a gun in every car?). Guarantee everyone in America a good night's sleep on a regular basis.

simulate
imitate closely

poltergeists
ghosts that reveal themselves through noise

maelstrom
a strong, almost violent situation or atmosphere

unfazed
undisturbed

Questions for Critical Thinking

1. The sentence that states the main idea for this essay is not the first sentence, but it does occur somewhere in the first two paragraphs. Which sentence states the main idea?

2. In his opening two paragraphs, the writer uses an example from the past to compare to his life in the present. Identify this example from the past and explain why it is appropriate for the writer to use.

3. What were the rules of courtesy the author observed as a boy (paragraph 5)? To what extent do you think these rules have changed?

4. Go through the essay and mark each time the author gives a specific example of something that disrupts his sleep. Notice how often the writer uses young people in his examples. Is the author being fair to young people?

5. To achieve humor, a writer often exaggerates. Can you find any examples of such exaggeration in the essay?

6. What word in paragraph 15 is a word associated with a negative meaning? Why would the author use such a word?

Writing in Response

1. Write about the kinds of problems neighbors cause each other. Provide examples from your own experience or reading.

2. Write an article that could be for a magazine. The article could advise people what to do when their neighbors bother them.

3. Write a letter to noisy neighbors, asking them for some consideration.

4. What changes in courtesy have you observed since your own childhood? What changes have you heard about from parents or other adults? What rules of courtesy would you like to see observed?

5. What are some of the advantages and disadvantages of living in an apartment? If you have lived in both a private house and an apartment, compare both experiences.

Talking to People

LARRY KING

As one of the most recognized interviewers in America today, Larry King has had extensive experience presenting famous people to millions of viewers. In the following selection, the interviewer turns writer as he shares some of the techniques he has found to be effective after many years in the business of interviewing.

1   My first rule of conversation is this: I never learn a thing while I'm talking. I realize every morning that nothing *I* say today will teach me anything, so if I'm going to learn a lot today, I'll have to do it by listening.

2   As obvious as this sounds, you run across proof every day that people simply do not listen. Tell your family or friends your plane will arrive at eight and before the conversation ends they'll ask, "What time did you say your plane is coming in?" And try to estimate the number of times you have heard someone say, "I forgot what you told me."

3   If you don't listen any better than that to someone, you cannot expect them to listen any better to you. I try to remember the signs you see at railroad crossings in small towns and rural areas: "Stop—Look—Listen." Show the people you talk to that you're interested in what they're saying. They will show you the same.

4   To be a good talker, you must be a good listener. This is more than just a matter of showing an interest in your conversation partner. Careful listening makes you better able to respond—to be a good talker when it's your turn. Good follow-up questions are the mark of a good conversationalist.

5   When I watch Barbara Walters' interviews I'm often disappointed, because I think she asks too many "so what" questions, like "If you could come back, what would you like to be?" In my opinion Barbara would be much better if she asked less frivolous questions and better follow-ups, logical extensions of the answer to her previous question. That comes from listening.

6   I was pleased by something Ted Koppel said to *Time* magazine a few years ago. "Larry listens to his guests," he said. "He pays attention to what they say. Too few interviewers do that." Even though I'm known as a "talking head," I think my success comes first and foremost from listening.

7   When I interview guests on the air, I make notes ahead of time about the kinds of questions I will ask them. But often I'll hear something in one of their responses that leads me into an unexpected question—and a surprising answer.

8   Example: When Vice President Dan Quayle was my guest during the 1992 presidential campaign, we talked about the laws governing abortion. He said it made no sense at all for his daughter's school to require his or his wife's permission for their daughter to miss a day of school, but not to get an abortion. As soon as he said that, I was curious about Quayle's personal angle on this political topic. So I asked what his attitude would be if his daughter said she was going to have an abortion. He said he would support her in whatever decision she made.

9   Quayle's reply made news. Abortion was a white-hot issue in that campaign, and here was President Bush's very conservative running mate, the national Republican spokesman for his conservative wing's unalterable opposition to abortion, suddenly saying he would support his daughter if she decided to have one.

10   Regardless of your views on that issue, the point here is that I got the response from Quayle because I wasn't just going through a list of questions. I was listening to what he was saying. That was what led me to the newsworthy answer.

11   The same thing happened when Ross Perot came on my show on February 20, 1992, and denied several times that he was interested in running for president. I kept hearing that his denials were less than complete, and when I put the question differently near the end of the show—bang! Perot said he'd run if his supporters succeeded in registering him on the ballot in all fifty states.

12   All of that happened not because of what I said, but because of what I *heard*. I was listening.

13   The late Jim Bishop, the popular writer, columnist, and author, was another New Yorker who spent a lot of time in Miami when I was there. He told me once that one of his pet peeves was people who ask you how you are but then don't listen to your answer. One man in particular was a repeat offender on this subject, so Jim decided to test just how poor a listener this fellow was.

14   The man called Jim one morning and began the conversation the way he always did: "Jim, how are ya?"

15   Jim says, "I have lung cancer."

16   "Wonderful. Say, Jim . . . "

17   Bishop had proved his point.

18   Dale Carnegie put it effectively in his book *How to Win Friends and Influence People*, which has now sold fifteen million copies: "To be interesting, be interested."

19   He added, "Ask questions that other persons will enjoy answering. Encourage them to talk about themselves and their accomplishments. Remember that the people you are talking to are a hundred times more interested in themselves and their wants and problems than they are in you and your problems. A person's toothache means more to that person than a famine in China which kills a million people. A boil on one's neck interests one more than forty earthquakes in Africa. Think of that the next time you start a conversation."

Questions for Critical Thinking

1. What is the thesis of this essay? Do you agree with the author?

2. How does Larry King prepare for the questions he asks in his interviews?

3. Review the essay and count the various examples that Larry King provides in order to develop his point of view. Are examples more interesting when you recognize the names of the persons mentioned?

4. Study the conclusion. What makes it so effective?

Writing in Response

1. Write a paragraph in which you describe a person who either is or is not a good listener. The more examples you give, the better your paragraph will be.

2. In paragraph two, Larry King says that "People simply do not listen." Write a narrative piece about a time when you did or did not "listen" to someone else, with memorable results!

3. In paragraph five, Larry King is critical of Barbara Walters' work as an interviewer. Choose an interviewer you have either heard on radio or seen on television and write your own analysis of that person's work. Specifically, why are you critical of this person's approach, or what is it that you admire about his or her presentation?

4. Who is the best or worst talk show host you have seen on television? Write an essay in which you discuss the talk show format. You might want to compare different shows, you might want to classify talk shows, or you might want to give several examples to develop a particular point of view about talk shows.

How to Try to Wash a Dog

CHRISTOPHER BILLOPP

Some of the duties of daily life can be pleasant, but we face other stresses reluctantly and must simply endure them. The following essay, which originally appeared in the *Richmond Times-Dispatch,* shows two "partners" coming together for a stressful event that both realize they can no longer avoid.

1   The time inevitably comes in the life of your dog when you must decide whether he is to cease being a house dog or whether to give him a bath. The time will be apparent when your wife issues an ultimatum that you do something about the dog immediately, or either he or she moves out.

2   A dog knows instinctively when a bath is in the air. He cannot be deceived into thinking you are going to take him for a walk or to chase a rabbit. He will be found with his tail between his legs at the far end of the lawn or under a bed or sofa where he has sought sanctuary.

3   If your dog is small he may be bathed in the tub left over from the last baby. But at best such quarters are cramped. The ideal place, unquestionably, is the commodious family bathtub. However, it will prove difficult to sell a wife on the idea that the same tub can serve for both man and beast. She may, perhaps, be persuaded to compromise on your placing the baby's tub inside the family tub.

4   That much accomplished, next in order is locating the dogsoap and a towel without affording an opportunity for the dog to escape or your wife to change her mind. If you act with dispatch you may be so fortunate as to assemble dog, tub, water and soap within reach of each other. Your dog will look at you reproachfully as dogs do when a grave injustice is being done them. Your course is to look back at him just as reproachfully. That may convince him the operation

commodious
roomy

ultimatum
final statement of terms

affording
giving

with dispatch
quickly

preliminary to
before

indisputable
undeniable

hurts you more than it does him, even if there is less chance of your getting soap in your eyes.

5   In fact, once a dog is well lathered he may derive a certain satisfaction out of being clean. But he will never let on for fear you will make baths a regular practice. In this respect he gives you more credit than you deserve.

6   The water will soon afford indisputable proof that your dog needed the bath. He should now be rinsed with clean water. But how can you remove the dirty water from the tub without removing the dog? That is obviously impossible. So, in spite of promises to your wife, it will be necessary to stand the dog in the family tub, "just for a moment," while you empty the water from the baby's tub. After all, merely standing him in the family tub is not washing him there. And it is not your fault if he seizes the opportunity to shake.

7   You should now go through the form of drying him with the towel preliminary to his doing his own drying on the best living-room rug or down in the coal bin, while you remain behind to remove tell-tale footprints from the bathtub and other damaging evidence before your wife arrives on the scene of the crime.

Questions for Critical Thinking

1. This essay presents an amusing account of a common duty, that of caring for a pet. In the course of a week, what are some of the duties you must perform on a regular basis? Make a list of these duties and compare your list with those of your classmates.

2. According to the author, what are the different stages in the process of washing a dog? If you have a dog, would you make any changes in the description of these stages?

3. Why do you think the author keeps referring to his wife? What purpose does she serve in the story? What is her attitude about the dog?

4. Not all writers are able to communicate the humor of a situation, and what is funny to one person may not amuse another person at all. Take a poll in your class. How many people found this essay humorous and why? How many did not? Do you have to have a pet in order to appreciate this essay?

Writing in Response

1. Caring for a pet (or a baby) involves many jobs beyond a "simple" bath. Explain a process that is related to the care of a pet (or child) of your own.

2. Sometimes it is easier to do a job by yourself rather than have help from a friend or family member. Describe a process that became more difficult for you to complete because of the "help" you received from someone who tried to advise or assist you.

3. If we maintain our things, they will often last longer. Explain a process you follow faithfully, in order to maintain something you value.

Neat People vs. Sloppy People

SUZANNE BRITT JORDAN

Sometimes we learn about our vices and virtues best when we are told about them in a humorous way. This is what Suzanne Britt Jordan does in the following essay, as she invites us to look for ourselves in one of two groups: those who are organized and those who can only hope to be.

1   I've finally figured out the difference between neat people and sloppy people. The distinction is, as always, moral. Neat people are lazier and meaner than sloppy people.

2   Sloppy people, you see, are not really sloppy. Their sloppiness is merely the unfortunate consequence of their extreme moral *rectitude*. Sloppy people carry in their mind's eye a heavenly vision, a precise plan, that is so stupendous, so perfect, it can't be achieved in this world or the next.

3   Sloppy people live in Never-Never Land. Someday is their *métier*. Someday they are planning to alphabetize all their books and set up home catalogues. Someday they will go through their wardrobes and mark certain items for tentative mending and certain items for passing on to relatives of similar shape and size. Someday sloppy people will make family scrapbooks into which they will put newspaper clippings, postcards, locks of hair, and the dried corsage from their senior prom. Someday they will file everything on the surface of their desks, including the cash receipts from coffee purchases at the snack shop. Someday they will sit down and read all the back issues of *The New Yorker*.

4   For all these noble reasons and more, sloppy people never get neat. They aim too high and wide. They save everything, planning someday to file, order, and straighten out the world. But while these ambitious plans take clearer and clearer shape in their heads, the books spill from the shelves onto the floor, the clothes pile up in the hamper and closet, the family mementos accumulate in every drawer, the surface of the desk is buried under mounds of paper and the unread magazines threaten to reach the ceiling.

5   Sloppy people can't bear to part with anything. They give loving attention to every detail. When sloppy people say they're going to tackle the surface of the desk, they really mean it. Not a paper will go unturned; not a rubber band will go unboxed. Four hours or two weeks into the excavation, the desk looks exactly the same, primarily because the sloppy person is meticulously creating new piles of papers with new headings and scrupulously stopping to read all the old book catalogs before he throws them away. A neat person would just bulldoze the desk.

6   Neat people are bums and clods at heart. They have cavalier attitudes toward possessions, including family heirlooms. Everything is just another dust-catcher to them. If anything collects dust, it's got to go and that's that. Neat people will toy with the idea of throwing the children out of the house just to cut down on the clutter.

7   Neat people don't care about process. They like results. What they want to do is get the whole thing over with so they can sit down and watch the rasslin' on TV. Neat people operate on two unvarying principles: Never handle any item twice, and throw everything away.

8   The only thing messy in a neat person's house is the trash can. The minute something comes to a neat person's hand, he will look at it, try to decide if it has immediate use and, finding none, throw it in the trash.

9   Neat people are especially vicious with mail. They never go through their mail unless they are standing directly over a trash can. If the trash can is beside the mailbox, even better. All ads, catalogs, pleas for charitable contributions, church bulletins and money-saving coupons go straight into the trash can without being opened. All letters from home, postcards from Europe, bills and paychecks are opened, immediately

rectitude
correctness

métier
French for "a person's specialty"

responded to, then dropped in the trash can. Neat people keep their receipts only for tax purposes. That's it. No sentimental salvaging of birthday cards or the last letter a dying relative ever wrote. Into the trash it goes.

10 Neat people place neatness above everything, even economics. They are incredibly wasteful. Neat people throw away several toys every time they walk through the den. I knew a neat person once who threw away a perfectly good dish drainer because it had mold on it. The drainer was too much trouble to wash. And neat people sell their furniture when they move. They will sell a La-Z-Boy recliner while you are reclining in it.

11 Neat people are no good to borrow from. Neat people buy everything in expensive little single portions. They get their flour and sugar in two-pound bags. They wouldn't consider clipping a coupon, saving a leftover, reusing plastic non-dairy whipped cream containers or rinsing off tin foil and draping it over the unmoldy dish drainer. You can never borrow a neat person's newspaper to see what's playing at the movies. Neat people have the paper all wadded up and in the trash by 7:05 A.M.

12 Neat people cut a clean swath through the organic as well as the inorganic world. People, animals, and things are all one to them. They are so insensitive. After they've finished with the pantry, the medicine cabinet, and the attic, they will throw out the red geranium (too many leaves), sell the dog (too many fleas), and send the children off to boarding school (too many scuffmarks on the hardwood floors).

Questions for Critical Thinking

1. When did you first become aware that this essay is written in a humorous vein?

2. What explanation does Suzanne Britt Jordan give for a sloppy person's behavior? Do you agree with her?

3. In paragraph 3, what examples does the writer list as projects the sloppy person plans to do? Do these plans seem admirable?

4. Does the author use the block method or the point-by-point method to contrast sloppy people with neat people?

5. In paragraph 11, the author states that "Neat people are no good to borrow from." Discuss the examples the author gives to support her statement. What makes them humorous? Suzanne Britt Jordan's ability to provide details that the reader recognizes as true about himself or herself is what makes her writing so appreciated.

6. Do you know anyone who has done the things listed in the concluding paragraph? Which type of person do you think the author is?

Writing in Response

1. Write an essay which takes the opposite viewpoint of Suzanne Britt Jordan. Defend the neat person and criticize the sloppy person.

2. Describe two people you know who have very different approaches to being neat and organized. Explain what it is like to be with each of them.

3. How would you describe the household in which you grew up? In what ways were your parents very organized? In what areas were they disorganized? What are the problems of growing up in a household that is extreme one way or the other?

4. Write an essay in which you give advice to a young couple setting up a household. How would you advise them in being neat and organized?

5. Suzanne Britt Jordan claims that sloppy people cannot part with anything. Write an essay in which you analyze your own attitude about possessions. What are the things you have a hard time parting with? What things do you especially like to collect and save?

Columbus and the Moon

TOM WOLFE

When events from history are placed next to current events, history often becomes more immediate and dramatic for us. This is what Tom Wolfe has done by bringing together the voyages of Christopher Columbus and the journeys to the moon that have been undertaken by modern astronauts. You may be surprised how many parallels there are between these fifteenth-century and twentieth-century events.

1   The National Aeronautics and Space Administration's moon landing 10 years ago today was a Government project, but then so was Columbus's voyage to America in 1492. The Government, in Columbus's case, was the Spanish Court of Ferdinand and Isabella. Spain was engaged in a sea race with Portugal in much the same way that the United States would be caught up in a space race with the Soviet Union four and a half centuries later.

2   The race in 1492 was to create the first shipping lane to Asia. The Portuguese expeditions had always sailed east, around the southern tip of Africa. Columbus decided to head due west, across open ocean, a scheme that was feasible only thanks to a recent invention—the magnetic ship's compass. Until then ships had stayed close to the great land masses even for the longest voyages. Likewise, it was only thanks to an invention of the 1940's and early 1950's, the high-speed electronic computer, that NASA would even consider propelling astronauts out of the Earth's orbit and toward the moon.

3   Both NASA and Columbus made not one but a series of voyages. NASA landed men on six different parts of the moon. Columbus made four voyages to different parts of what he remained convinced was the east coast of Asia. As a result both NASA and Columbus had to keep coming back to the Government with their hands out, pleading for refinancing. In each case the reply of the Government became, after a few years: "This is all very impressive, but what earthly good is it to anyone back home?"

4   Columbus was reduced to making the most desperate claims. When he first reached land in 1492 at San Salvador, off Cuba, he expected to find gold, or at least spices. The Arawak Indians were awed by the strangers and their ships, which they believed had descended from the sky, and they presented them with their most prized possessions, live parrots and balls of cotton. Columbus soon set them digging for gold, which didn't exist. So he brought back reports of fabulous riches in the form of manpower; which is to say, slaves. He was not speaking of the Arawaks, however. With the exception of criminals and prisoners of war, he was supposed to civilize all natives and convert them to Christianity. He was talking about the Carib Indians, who were cannibals and therefore qualified as criminals. The Caribs would fight down to the last unbroken bone rather than endure captivity, and few ever survived the voyages back to Spain. By the end of Columbus's second voyage, in 1496, the Government was becoming testy. A great deal of wealth was going into voyages to Asia, and very little was coming back. Columbus made his men swear to return to Spain saying that they had not only reached the Asian mainland, they had heard Japanese spoken.

5   Likewise by the early 1970's, it was clear that the moon was in economic terms pretty much what it looked like from Earth, a gray rock. NASA, in the quest for appropriations, was reduced to publicizing the "spinoffs" of the space program. These included Teflon-coated frying pans, a ballpoint pen that would write in a weightless environment, and a computerized biosensor system that would enable doctors to treat heart patients without making house calls. On the whole, not a giant step for mankind.

6   In 1493, after his first voyage, Columbus had ridden through Barcelona at the side of King Ferdinand in the position once occupied by Ferdinand's late son, Juan. By 15, the bad-mouthing

The NASA moon landing occurred in 1969.

feasible
possible

testy
irritated, impatient

ignominy
great personal humiliation

albeit
even though

lurid
sensational, gruesome

traumatized
wounded emotionally

of Columbus had reached the point where he was put in chains at the conclusion of his third voyage and returned to Spain in disgrace. NASA suffered no such ignominy, of course, but by July 20, 1974, the fifth anniversary of the landing of Apollo 11, things were grim enough. The public had become gloriously bored by space exploration. The fifth anniversary celebration consisted mainly of about 2 souls, mostly NASA people, sitting on folding chairs underneath a camp meeting canopy on the marble prairie outside the old Smithsonian Air Museum in Washington listening to speeches by Neil Armstrong, Michael Collins, and Buzz Aldrin and watching the caloric waves ripple.

7   Extraordinary rumors had begun to circulate about the astronauts. The most lurid said that trips to the moon, and even into earth orbit, had so traumatized the men, they had fallen victim to religious and spiritualist manias or plain madness. (Of the total 73 astronauts chosen, one, Aldrin, is known to have suffered from depression, rooted, as his own memoir makes clear, in matters that had nothing to do with space flight. Two teamed up in an evangelical organization, and one set up a foundation for

the scientific study of psychic phenomena—interests the three of them had developed long before they flew in space.) The NASA budget, meanwhile, had been reduced to the light-bill level.

8   Columbus died in 1509, nearly broke and stripped of most of his honors as Spain's Admiral of the Ocean, a title he preferred. It was only later that history began to look upon him not as an adventurer who had tried and failed to bring home gold—but as a man with a supernatural sense of destiny, whose true glory was his willingness to plunge into the unknown, including the remotest parts of the universe he could hope to reach.

9   NASA still lives, albeit in reduced circumstances, and whether or not history will treat NASA like the admiral is hard to say.

10   The idea that the exploration of the rest of the universe is its own reward is not very popular, and NASA is forced to keep talking about things such as bigger communications satellites that will enable live television transmission of European soccer games at a fraction of the current cost. Such notions as "building a bridge to the stars for mankind" do not light up the sky today—but may yet.

Questions for Critical Writing

1. This essay compares NASA's moon landing with Columbus's voyage to America. The first paragraph clearly sets up the comparison. What is the major point of comparison made in this first paragraph? Find the three expressions the author uses to signal the comparison throughout the paragraph.

2. What is the comparison made in the second paragraph? What word or expression is used to signal the comparison? Review the third paragraph. Again, determine what the comparison is and find the word that signals the comparison. Underline these words here and throughout the essay as you review the point-by-point comparisons.

3. Explain the pressures that were put on these explorers to make the voyages useful to the people back home.

4. Which point of comparison does the author say remains undetermined?

5. Discuss the concluding paragraph. Toward what central question has this essay been leading? Take a poll in your class to find out the attitude of your group toward this issue.

6. What did you learn about either Columbus or the NASA astronauts from reading the Wolfe essay that you did not know before?

Writing in Response

1. The fifteenth-century voyages of Columbus and the twentieth-century explorations of the astronauts might not at first seem to be comparable, but the author

shows us several points of comparison. Write a comparison of one of the following seemingly dissimilar sets of people or objects:

A ballet dancer and a football player

A senior citizen and a small child

A rock star and an opera singer

A successful executive with a homemaker

Underline the words and expressions you use as signals to make your comparisons. Review the list on page 000 before you begin.

2. Write an essay in which you agree or disagree with the argument that the exploration of space is worthwhile for its own sake, not because it may have any immediate application to our lives.

Requiem for the Champ.

JUNE JORDAN

requiem
a composition (musical or literary) for the dead

Many sports figures become heroes, but when one of these heroes falls from grace, a feeling of disillusionment inevitably follows. In the following essay, the African-American poet, essayist, and University of California professor June Jordan reflects on the life and career of one of these heroes, the boxer Mike Tyson. In the process of examining the tragedy of this fighter, who suffered his greatest defeat outside the ring, the writer makes some harsh observations, and even harsher judgments, on American society.

1   Mike Tyson comes from Brooklyn. And so do I. Where he grew up was about a twenty-minute bus ride from my house. I always thought his neighborhood looked like a war zone. It reminded me of Berlin—immediately after World War II. I had never seen Berlin except for black-and-white photos in *Life* magazine, but that was bad enough: Rubble. Barren. Blasted. Everywhere you turned your eyes recoiled from the jagged edges of an office building or a cathedral, shattered, or the tops of apartment houses torn off, and nothing alive even intimated, anywhere. I used to think, "This is what it means to fight and really win or really lose. War means you hurt somebody, or something, until there's nothing soft or sensible left."

2   For sure I never had a boyfriend who came out of Mike Tyson's territory. Yes, I enjoyed my share of tough guys and/or gang members who walked and talked and fought and loved in quintessential Brooklyn ways: cool, tough, and deadly serious. But there was a code as rigid and as romantic as anything that ever made the pages of traditional English literature. A guy would beat up another guy or, if appropriate, he'd kill him. But a guy talked different to a girl. A guy made other guys clean up their language around "his girl." A guy brought ribbons and candies and earrings and tulips to a girl. He took care of her. He walked her home. And if he got serious about that girl, and even if she was only twelve years old, then she became his "lady." And woe betide any other guy stupid enough to disrespect that particular young black female.

3   But none of the boys—none of the young men—none of the young Black male inhabitants of my universe and my heart ever came from Mike Tyson's streets or avenues. We didn't live someplace fancy or middle-class, but at least there were ten-cent gardens, front and back, and coin Laundromats, and grocery stores, and soda parlors, and barber shops, and Holy Roller churchfronts, and chicken shacks, and dry cleaners, and bars-and-grills, and a takeout Chinese restaurant, and all of that usable detail that does not survive a war. That kind of seasonal green turf and daily-life supporting pattern of establishments to meet your needs did not exist

quintessential
the most typical

gelid
very cold or icy

inside the gelid urban cemetery where Mike Tyson learned what he thought he needed to know.

4   I remember when the City of New York decided to construct a senior housing project there, in the childhood world of former heavyweight boxing champion Mike Tyson. I remember wondering, "Where in the hell will those old people have to go in order to find food? And how will they get there?"

5   I'm talking godforsaken. And much of living in Brooklyn was like that. But then it might rain or it might snow and, for example, I could look at the rain forcing forsythia into bloom or watch how snowflakes can tease bare tree limbs into temporary blossoms of snow dissolving into diadems of sunlight. And what did Mike Tyson ever see besides brick walls and garbage in the gutter and disintegrating concrete steps and boarded-up windows and broken car parts blocking the sidewalk and men, bitter, with their hands in their pockets, and women, bitter, with their heads down and their eyes almost closed?

diadems
crowns

6   In his neighborhood, where could you buy ribbons for a girl, or tulips?

7   Mike Tyson comes from Brooklyn. And so do I. In the big picture of America, I never had much going for me. And he had less. I only learned, last year, that I can stop whatever violence starts with me. I only learned, last year, that love is infinitely more interesting, and more exciting, and more powerful, than really winning or really losing a fight. I only learned, last year, that all war leads to death and that all love leads you away from death. I am more than twice Mike Tyson's age. And I'm not stupid. Or slow. But I'm Black. And I come from Brooklyn. And I grew up fighting. And I grew up and I got out of Brooklyn because I got pretty good at fighting. And winning. Or else, intimidating my would-be adversaries with my fists, my feet, and my mouth. And I never wanted to fight. I never wanted anybody to hit me. And I never wanted to hit anybody. But the bell would ring at the end of another dumb day in school and I'd head out with dread and a nervous sweat because I knew some jackass more or less my age and more or less my height would be waiting for me because she or he had nothing better to do than to wait for me and hope to kick my butt or tear up my books or break my pencils or pull hair out of my head.

8   This is the meaning of poverty: when you have nothing better to do than to hate somebody who, just exactly like yourself, has nothing better to do than to pick on you instead of trying to figure out how come there's nothing better to do. How come there's no gym/no swimming pool/no dirt track/no soccer field/no ice-skating rink/no bike/no bike path/no tennis courts/no language arts workshop/no computer science center/no band practice/no choir rehearsal/no music lessons/no basketball or baseball team? How come neither one of you has his or her own room in a house where you can hang out and dance and make out or get on the telephone or eat and drink up everything in the kitchen that can move? How come nobody on your block and nobody in your class has any of these things?

9   I'm Black. Mike Tyson is Black. And neither one of us was ever supposed to win anything more than a fight between the two of us. And if you check out the mass-media material on "us," and if you check out the emergency-room reports on "us," you might well believe we're losing the fight to be more than our enemies have decreed. Our enemies would deprive us of everything except each other: hungry and furious and drug-addicted and rejected and ever convinced we can never be beautiful or right or true or different from the beggarly monsters our enemies envision and insist upon, and how should we then stand, Black man and Black woman, face to face?

10   Way back when I was born, Richard Wright had just published *Native Son* and, thereby, introduced white America to the monstrous product of its racist hatred.

11   Poverty does not beautify. Poverty does not teach generosity or allow for sucker attributes of tenderness and restraint. In white America, hatred of Blackfolks has imposed horrible poverty upon us.

12   And so, back in the thirties, Richard Wright's *Native Son*, Bigger Thomas,

did what he thought he had to do: he hideously murdered a white woman and he viciously murdered his Black girlfriend in what he conceived as self-defense. He did not perceive any options to these psychopathic, horrifying deeds. I do not believe he, Bigger Thomas, had any other choices open to him. Not to him, he who was meant to die like the rat he, Bigger Thomas, cornered and smashed to death in his mother's beggarly clean space.

13 I never thought Bigger Thomas was okay. I never thought he should skate back into my, or anyone's community. But I did and I do think he is my brother. The choices available to us dehumanize. And any single one of us, Black in this white country, we may be defeated, we may become dehumanized, by the monstrous hatred arrayed against us and our needy dreams.

14 And so I write this requiem for Mike Tyson: international celebrity, millionaire, former heavyweight boxing champion of the world, a big-time winner, a big-time loser, an African-American male in his twenties, and, now, a convicted rapist.

15 Do I believe he is guilty of rape?

16 Yes I do.

17 And what would I propose as appropriate punishment?

18 Whatever will force him to fear the justice of exact retribution, and whatever will force him, for the rest of his damned life, to regret and to detest the fact that he defiled, he subjugated, and he wounded somebody helpless to his power.

19 And do I therefore rejoice in the jury's finding?

20 I do not.

21 Well, would I like to see Mike Tyson a free man again?

22 He was never free!

23 And I do not excuse or condone or forget or minimize or forgive the crime of his violation of the young Black woman he raped!

24 But did anybody ever tell Mike Tyson that you talk different to a girl? Where would he learn that? Would he learn that from U.S. Senator Ted Kennedy? Or from hotshot/scot-free movie director Roman Polanski? Or from rap recording star Ice Cube? Or from Ronald Reagan and the Grenada escapade? Or from George Bush in Panama? Or from George Bush and Colin Powell in the Persian Gulf? Or from the military hero flyboys who returned from bombing the shit out of civilian cities in Iraq and then said, laughing and proud, on international TV: "All I need, now, is a woman"? Or from the hundreds of thousands of American football fans? Or from the millions of Americans who would, if they could, pay surrealistic amounts of money just to witness, up close, somebody like Mike Tyson beat the brains out of somebody?

25 And what could which university teach Mike Tyson about the difference between violence and love? Is there any citadel of higher education in the country that does not pay its football coach at least three times as much as the chancellor and six times as much as its professors and ten times as much as its social and psychological counselors?

26 In this America where Mike Tyson and I live together and bitterly, bitterly, apart, I say he became what he felt. He felt the stigma of a priori hatred and intentional poverty. He was given the choice of violence or violence: the violence of defeat or the violence of victory. Who would pay him to rehabilitate inner-city housing or to refurbish a bridge? Who would pay him what to study the facts of our collective history? Who would pay him what to plant and nurture the trees of a forest? And who will write and who will play the songs that tell a guy like Mike Tyson how to talk to a girl?

27 What was America willing to love about Mike Tyson? Or any Black man? Or any man's man?

28 Tyson's neighborhood and my own have become the same no-win battleground. And he has fallen there. And I do not rejoice. I do not.

surrealistic
fantastic, unreal, dreamlike

citadel
a fortress or other place of control

a priori
existing from the start and based on belief, not fact

condone
to forgive or overlook

Questions for Critical Thinking

1. In paragraph 1, June Jordan compares the neighborhood of Mike Tyson's childhood with that of Berlin after World War II. What are the three words she wants us to remember? How does she make these three words stand out?

2. In paragraph 2, the author contrasts her own neighborhood in Brooklyn with Tyson's neighborhood. What are the differences?

3. What is June Jordan's definition of poverty? Do you believe her definition is correct?

4. In paragraph 8, June Jordan refers to people occupying their time by fighting with each other, "instead of trying to figure out how come there's nothing better to do." What is the result when people struggle against each other instead of struggling against their negative circumstances?

5. In paragraph 22, the writer states that Mike Tyson was never free. What does she mean?

6. What has June Jordan learned only during this last year?

7. Is this essay uplifting or depressing? What should be the social responsibility of a government toward its citizens who are struggling with poverty and lack of opportunity? What mistakes have government agencies made in the past and continue to make even now?

Writing in Response

1. Compare and contrast two neighborhoods with which you are familiar. How are they alike? How are they different? How does the environment play a role in how the people behave?

2. June Jordan points out the historical forces that have conspired against her people. Discuss these forces and the extent to which they continue to influence the direction of our society.

3. Write a paragraph in which you discuss the social conditions that lead to women being victimized by men.

4. Write a paragraph in which you propose how women could be better protected from what threatens them in our society today.

5. What causes two people who come from similar backgrounds to turn out very differently?

Ethmix!

BETSY ISRAEL

For most of our country's history, the many ethnic groups that make up our society have tended to remain separate from each other. In recent years, however, more and more people from different backgrounds have been marrying and forming new families. In the following essay, Betsy Israel discusses the kind of person who is the result of this modern trend, the person she calls "an ethmix."

dreidl

a spinning top, used in Hanukkah Games

1   Every year at holiday time there was that moment. After shuffling into the high school auditorium and taking our places on the risers below the orchestra, Mr. Callahan, the music teacher, would begin whipping his hands through the air, and we'd burst into *Joy to the World* or *Hark the Herald Angels Sing;* I, standing off to the side, would burst into a cold sweat. For after we'd finish these songs, Mr. C. would turn to me and to the two kids alongside and nod—our cue to start up. "I had a little dreidl, I made it out of clay. . . ." Being asked, at

age sixteen, to sing about a clay dreidl was, by itself, fairly humiliating. But it was, for me at least, also confusing.

2 I would be asked to sing the token Hanukkah song because my name was Israel: Clearly I was Jewish. But the truth was that we were only half Jewish, my father having been raised in a traditional Jewish family, my mother, the child of a Cuban immigrant and a Kansas farm boy, on another planet entirely. In our house we had not only menorahs, both electric and manual, but a Christmas tree and stockings and cookies shaped like angels and bells. Being asked, then, to sing *The Dreidl Song*—and told gently that I need not sing any songs referring to Christ (which is to say none of the others)—made me furious. I would walk home later, feeling embarrassed and angry—at my parents in some vague way, at myself for not being cooler, and also at the inevitable dumb girl in too-blue eye shadow and too-tight jeans who would fall in alongside me to ask earnestly, "Is it weird not to have Christmas?"

3 That was ten years ago. Back then, attending high school in a town divided strictly along ethnic and religious lines was tough if you didn't have the right answer to the "What are you?" question—and doubly worse if you looked so obviously out of it, nobody bothered to ask. In our town the right answers were always 1. Irish; 2. Italian; and/or 3. Catholic. Needless to say, the few times I was actually asked (I could, some people used to say, pass for Italian), I failed miserably. Today, of course, Jews marrying Gentiles—or Baptists marrying Buddhists, for that matter—is hardly cause for raised eyebrows. It's the odd high school, in fact, that doesn't have its share not only of half Jews and Catholic-Protestants but of black-whites and an ever-increasing number of Asian- or Hispanic-Americans. Coming from a family tossed several times through the ancestral blender is as common now as coming from a family known for its athletic ability or from one in which everyone has freckles.

4 Still, growing up between two worlds, whether the split is religious, ethnic, or cultural, is not quite as easy as growing up in a family that simply shares certain traits or talents. Whether we like it or not, our ethnic and religious backgrounds shape us profoundly. As children, our heritage is a key factor in helping us determine who we are in relation to the outside world—where we fit on the social spectrum and who else out there is "like" us. Not noticeably belonging to any one group is often upsetting, and these feelings of isolation, of not fitting in, easily carry over into adolescence—a time when everyone, even the fairest-haired among us, must struggle awfully hard just to seem seminormal. Sure, there were days when I felt almost normal, sometimes even lucky (I didn't, after all, have to spend my sunny Sundays in church). But there were as many times—usually just after some kid would pass my locker snickering, "Hey, Jew eat yet?"—when I'd feel a little like the cute neighborhood mutt we'd played with as kids: a half-breed, well liked but secretly pitied. At those moments I knew in my bones that growing up hybrid would always be, as we used to say, a truly mixed bag.

5 Feeling weird, it seems, is as common to ethmix kids as feeling bored in church is to others. Patti Rodriquez,* sixteen, of St. Louis grew up in a Cuban-Baptist-Catholic-family and considers herself something of an expert on the subject. "When we were kids, everybody went to Sunday school," she explains. "I felt funny for not having a church to go to. I was scared to tell the other kids I didn't go to church because they would think there was something wrong with me. And I never knew the Bible stories. I didn't know who Jason was or about Rachel. I would get really nervous when the teacher started talking about them. But I was too embarrassed to tell my parents how I felt. I thought it would hurt them."

6 Fifteen-year-old Karen Paulsen of Tallahassee, Florida, is half black, half white and is thus another authority on personal weirdness. "I never noticed color for a long time," she says. "I figured that's just how Mom and Dad are. But once, in fourth grade, my father,

menorahs
nine-branched candlesticks, used to celebrate Hanukkah

---

*All names of teens have been changed.

who's white, dropped me off at school, and this black kid laughed at me and said, 'Karen, look at your dad, he's *funny*.' And I started getting all inferior, thinking, 'What's wrong with me?'"

7   That was a question I asked a lot as I grew up, and it's a phrase that might well serve as an anthem of sorts for junior ethmixes. There are, after all, many things that you can look forward to outgrowing—having no breasts, for example, or having acne. But what can you do about a funny-sounding last name or eyes that don't look round and American? Not much, and so it's easy, in elementary or junior high school, for an ethmix girl to look at herself and feel doomed.

8   Dr. S. Peter Kim, M.D., an associate professor of psychiatry at New York University Medical Center and the director of NYU's Center for Trans-Cultural Developmental Studies, explains that at "about the time you turn ten the values of the outside world—of friends and teachers—come into play, and it can be hard to form a solid identity if your parents don't seem as American as they should, or as much like everyone else's. Children from bicultural families can have a really rough time adapting, especially since children that age have so little understanding of one another. That's when you get comments like 'You look funny,' which are usually just innocent and inquisitive but still very hurtful."

9   In adolescence, though, "We all suffer," Dr. Kim says. "Our bodies are changing rapidly, which leads to shattering questions about physical appearance: Will I be pretty enough? Will I get boyfriends? If you are the product of a bicultural environment, it can be even harder because you may look different from the kids around you. And the world outside the house becomes so very different from the one inside." Still, he adds, "These kids do adapt and often excel, especially if their parents help them to understand and appreciate their heritage."

10   And it was indeed true that by high school, the pressures, or at least the deep conviction that I was doomed to be forever weird, had faded. Other kids had abandoned their force-fed religions in rebellion. By the ninth grade, it was the strange kid in our school who *wanted* to

go to church. (Why go to mass when you could go to the mall or, better, the beach?) There were still moments of isolation—times like Saint Patrick's Day, when the high school would empty and I'd be left to attend an algebra class of three. But I was coming to feel less uncomfortable about it—no longer as angry as the child who'd once demanded to know, "Why can't we just be Catholic?" and instead just annoyed that others *assumed* I must have felt strange. That they felt sort of sorry for me.

11   Karen Paulsen says, "When I got to junior high, I started to wonder about the people who thought my color was weird. We lived in an integrated neighborhood then, and my parents seemed like any other parents; they fought and made dinner just like all the others. I mean, there were problems sometimes. I've always considered myself black—I never write 'other' in the space for race—but some blacks didn't, and still don't, accept me. I still get questions like 'What color are you?' I now have a friend who just snaps back, 'She's purple, can't you see?' And my mother supports me, too. Once a girl called me a halfbreed, and when I told my mother about it, she said, 'Forget it. She's a jerk. Blow it off.'" Adds Judy Holtz, a sixteen-year-old from Atlanta who grew up with a different kind of cultural split, a southern mother and a northern dad, "I used to feel weird around my southern relatives, like they were really backward or something. And my dad would be so abrupt with people, not like southerners, who always say 'Y'all come back' and stuff. He was always kind of rude. But I see now that there are two sides to it. Once when I was having a sorority tea, my dad came stomping through the den and didn't even say hello—something a southerner would never do—and kids just turned around to me and said, 'Judy, who's *that?*' I was totally embarrassed. But he is also a real bookworm. We used to get fifty-seven magazines here, and I think my mind was really formed by his being so strict this way, by the northern part of him."

12   Like Judy and Karen, I found the things that bothered or embarrassed me were, by my sophomore year or so,

becoming less upsetting and sometimes even sweet and funny—the way, for instance, my Jewish grandmother *still* tried to bribe us to attend Hebrew school (a losing proposition if there ever was one) or the way my mother's mother was turning spooky and spiritual, "seeking the answers" in Christian Science. Patti Rodriquez had always "wanted one of those grandmothers who baked cakes and knitted sweaters," but by high school, she, too, had found that it mattered less. "I had always preferred my mother's American relatives," she says, "because my Spanish relatives were always so emotional, and there was the language barrier. People used to laugh at things my grandmother said because they couldn't understand her. But as I got older, I started to feel a little bad that I hadn't been as close to my father's relatives. Now I feel proud that he came all the way here from Cuba to make a life with my mother and us. I used to think that the Cuban traditions, like 'the gifts from the wise men' at Christmas, were dumb. But now I'm glad we have them."

13 Part of this acceptance comes from looking around and discovering that younger family members have grown up relatively unaffected by the split. Judy Holtz says, "My little sister, who's seven, is much more southern than I am. I have more of my father in me, while she's more at home with the southern relatives." And Patti adds, "My Cuban grandparents didn't approve of my parents' marriage, and I think my brother and I picked up a lot of my mother's resentment against them. But it's all calm now, and my little sisters don't notice that anything's strange."

14 And accepting a slightly unorthodox cultural setup gets a *lot* easier when you see that it can work to your advantage—especially where boys are concerned. I mean, what was my mother going to say to us? She had, at age twenty, married a Jewish guy ten years her senior. So when one of my sisters began dating a long and increasingly strange string of boys all named Alan (one of them was a tattooed biker), my mother could only say, "Well, we'll see what happens." Patti says that her mother, like mine, "would

accept almost anybody." Says Karen, "I go out with boys who tend to share my views—who do not hate others and are accepting of all faiths and races. My mother supports those choices because they support her own view of the world."

15 It is this freedom to choose, born of a tolerance of others, that is perhaps the best part of growing up hybrid. My parents wouldn't flinch if I took up with a Hindu or an American Indian or a black man. And it is because of their basic beliefs that I would consider such choices in the first place. As Patti explains it, "I'm not so closed or one-wayed about things. It's made me a better person, more well rounded."

16 "Bicultural children are more flexible in their world views," says Dr. Kim. "And they are more tolerant in their relationships, more readily accepting. They have a much easier time standing in another person's shoes. And because they're less rigid, they're more mature psychologically, better able to perceive alternative ways of doing things."

17 This tolerance and freedom of choice extends beyond choosing boyfriends. Being exposed to more than one religion makes it easier—and often more meaningful—to choose one for yourself. Patti explains, "My parents gave me a choice—God is God, they said. So in eighth grade I started going to mass with friends, even though my family's only half Catholic. I liked it and wanted to go more, not because I wanted to fit in, but because I wanted to learn more about religion. A lot of people attend church for the wrong reasons. They go for the clothes or the social part. But I think you have to attend because you want to learn something about God."

18 For some of us, having a choice can mean choosing something unexpected, or coming up with a unique way to merge two very different worlds. Felicia Rafalkski, for instance, a fifteen-year-old New Yorker, recently joined a Unitarian church—a church without specific religious affiliation—at the suggestion of a friend. "I was half Roman Catholic and half Episcopalian," she explains, "but I never felt like I had any organized religion. When I would

go to a regular Catholic mass, I was really shocked by how strict it was. That's why I joined the Unitarians. You can worship any God you want. It's much more open." A thirteen-year-old boy in her church group adds, "I used to be weakly Jewish and Episcopalian, but I never had formal training. Then I became a Unitarian. Now whenever I go to a Jewish ceremony, it seems really weird—all the emphasis on the Torah. It seems totally strange to worship a book."

19   I don't know whether or not it's strange to worship a book. I still haven't reached any conclusions. But I do know that if I ever feel the need to, I will easily be able to slip in anywhere, making myself right at home. In the meantime, I can rest assured that my sisters and I have grown up to be special people,

more tolerant and, I think, more interesting than a lot of the kids we went to high school with. Once upon a time, the endless holidays in our house seemed strange—Hanukkah followed by Christmas; Easter, then a few weeks later, Passover. But I understand now that this was my parents' unique way of showing us how much diversity there was in the world—and how very much to celebrate. As the years have gone by, these holidays—even if noted only by card or by phone call—have become more than just a way of acknowledging our ethnic and religious roots. They have become the way my sisters and my parents and I remain a family, devoted to one another and bound together for life, precisely because there isn't anyone else who does things quite the way we do.

Questions for Critical Thinking

1. Adolescence is a time when many people have difficulty defining themselves and their place in society. When Betsy Israel uses the term "ethmix," she tries to define herself and analyze the issue in all its complexity. What is "ethmix" and how has its reality affected Betsy Israel's life? Give several specific examples from the essay.

2. Review the essay. Mark each paragraph with one of the following labels to classify the writer's examples: *personal experience, observation of those around her, report from outside authorities.*

3. In paragraph three, Betsy Israel remembers that when she was a child, the question "What are you?" was always answered by reference to nationality or religion or both. To what extent has this changed, or is the situation basically the same? In what other ways could people define themselves?

Writing in Response

1. Betsy Israel tells us that a "freedom to choose, born of a tolerance of others . . . is perhaps the best part of growing up hybrid." Write an essay in which you discuss other situations in which a person could be raised that would encourage the person to be tolerant of others. In your essay you might also want to point out situations you believe tend to actively discourage tolerance toward others.

2. Write an essay in which you compare the present social situation that Betsy Israel describes with the situation your parents encountered when they grew up. Based upon what you have heard during family discussions and what your parents have told you, how different is the world you live in, compared with the world your parents knew when they were young?

3. Write an essay in which you describe how you hope to raise your children so that they will be tolerant adults. What will you be able to tell them about your own childhood that will help them understand the need for greater tolerance? How can a parent be frank about the realities that exist in society without discouraging the child?

4. Write a description of the most flexible, unprejudiced person you have ever known. What do you believe was in this person's background that made him or her so free from prejudice?

Friends, Good Friends, and Such Good Friends

JUDITH VIORST

We tend to put different parts of our lives into separate categories. Our meals are divided into breakfast, lunch, and dinner; the day is divided into morning, afternoon, and evening. With a little creativity on our part, our teachers, classmates, coworkers, or friends could also be put into categories. In the following essay, the journalist and poet Judith Viorst places what she calls the "varieties of friendship" into different categories. As you read the essay, you might recognize at least some of the author's categories as the same basic groups you would use to classify your own friends.

1 Women are friends, I once would have said, when they totally love and support and trust each other, and bare to each other the secrets of their souls, and run—no questions asked—to help each other, and tell harsh truths to each other (no, you can't wear that dress unless you lose ten pounds first) when harsh truths must be told.

2 Women are friends, I once would have said, when they share the same affection for Ingmar Bergman, plus train rides, cats, warm rain, charades, Camus, and hate with equal ardor Newark and Brussels sprouts and Lawrence Welk and camping.

3 In other words, I once would have said that a friend is a friend all the way, but now I believe that's a narrow point of view. For the friendships I have and the friendships I see are conducted at many levels of intensity, serve many different functions, meet different needs and range from those as all-the-way as the friendship of the soul sisters mentioned above to that of the most nonchalant and casual playmates.

4 Consider these varieties of friendship:

5 1. Convenience friends. These are the women with whom, if our paths weren't crossing all the time, we'd have no particular reason to be friends: a next-door neighbor, a woman in our car pool, the mother of one of our children's closest friends or maybe some mommy with whom we serve juice and cookies each week at the Glenwood Co-op Nursery.

6 Convenience friends are convenient indeed. They'll lend us their cups and silverware for a party. They'll drive our kids to soccer when we're sick. They'll take us to pick up our car when we need a lift to the garage. They'll even take our cats when we go on vacation. As we will for them.

7 But we don't, with convenience friends, ever come too close or tell too much; we maintain our public face and emotional distance. "Which means," says Elaine, "that I'll talk about being overweight but not about being depressed. Which means I'll admit being mad but not blind with rage. Which means I might say that we're pinched this month but never that I'm worried sick over money."

8 But which doesn't mean that there isn't sufficient value to be found in these friendships of mutual aid, in convenience friends.

9 2. Special-interest friends. These friendships aren't intimate, and they needn't involve kids or silverware or cats. Their value lies in some interest jointly shared. And so we may have an office friend or a yoga friend or a tennis friend or a friend from the Women's Democratic Club.

10 "I've got one woman friend," says Joyce, "who likes, as I do, to take psychology courses. Which makes it nice for me—and nice for her. It's fun to go with someone you know and it's fun to discuss what you've learned, driving back from the classes." And for the most part, she says, that's all they discuss.

11 "I'd say that what we're doing is *doing* together, not being together," Suzanne says of her Tuesday-doubles friends. "It's mainly a tennis relationship, but we play together well. And I guess we all need to have a couple of playmates."

12 I agree.

13 *My* playmate is a shopping friend, a woman of marvelous taste, a woman who knows exactly *where* to buy *what*, and furthermore is a woman who always

Ingmar Bergman
Swedish director of modern psychological films

Camus
Albert Camus (1913–1960), French writer and philosopher

Lawrence Welk
popular American TV band leader

knows beyond a doubt what one ought to be buying. I don't have the time to keep up with what's new in eyeshadow, hemlines and shoes and whether the smock look is in or finished already. But since (oh, shame!) I care a lot about eyeshadow, hemlines and shoes, and since I don't *want* to wear smocks if the smock look is finished, I'm very glad to have a shopping friend.

14   3. Historical friends. We all have a friend who knew us when . . . maybe way back in Miss Meltzer's second grade, when our family lived in that three-room flat in Brooklyn, when our dad was out of work for seven months, when our brother Allie got in that fight where they had to call the police, when our sister married the endodontist from Yonkers and when, the morning after we lost our virginity, she was the first, the only, friend we told.

15   The years have gone by and we've gone separate ways and we've little in common now, but we're still an intimate part of each other's past. And so whenever we go to Detroit we always go to visit this friend of our girlhood. Who knows how we looked before our teeth were straightened. Who knows how we talked before our voice got un-Brooklyned. Who knows what we ate before we learned about artichokes. And who, by her presence, puts us in touch with an earlier part of ourself, a part of ourself it's important never to lose.

16   "What this friend means to me and what I mean to her," says Grace, "is having a sister without sibling rivalry. We know the texture of each other's lives. She remembers my grandmother's cabbage soup. I remember the way her uncle played the piano. There's simply no other friend who remembers those things."

17   4. Crossroads friends. Like historical friends, our crossroads friends are important for *what was*—for the friendship we shared at a crucial, now past, time of life. A time, perhaps, when we roomed in college together; or worked as eager young singles in the Big City together; or went together, as my friend Elizabeth and I did through pregnancy, birth and that scary first year of new motherhood.

18   Crossroads friends forge powerful links, links strong enough to endure with not much more contact than once-a-year letters at Christmas. And out of respect for those crossroads years, for those dramas and dreams we once shared, we will always be friends.

19   5. Cross-generational friends. Historical friends and crossroads friends seem to maintain a special kind of intimacy—dormant but always ready to be revived—and though we may rarely meet, whenever we do connect, it's personal and intense. Another kind of intimacy exists in the friendships that form across generations in what one woman calls her daughter-mother and her mother-daughter relationships.

20   Evelyn's friend is her mother's age—"but I share so much more than I ever could with my mother"—a woman she talks to of music, of books and of life. "What I get from her is the benefit of her experience. What she gets—and enjoys—from me is a youthful perspective. It's a pleasure for both of us."

21   I have in my own life a precious friend, a woman of 65 who has lived very hard, who is wise, who listens well; who has been where I am and can help me understand it; and who represents not only an ultimate ideal mother to me but also the person I'd like to be when I grow up.

22   In our daughter role we tend to do more than our share of self-revelation; in our mother role we tend to receive what's revealed. It's another kind of pleasure—playing wise mother to a questing younger person. It's another very lovely kind of friendship.

23   6. Part-of-a-couple friends. Some of the women we call our friends we never see alone—we see them as part of a couple at couples' parties. And though we share interests in many things and respect each other's views, we aren't moved to deepen the relationship. Whatever the reason, a lack of time or—and this is more likely—a lack of chemistry, our friendship remains in the context of a group. But the fact that our feeling on seeing each other is always, "I'm *so* glad she's here" and the fact that we spend half the evening talking together says that this too, in its own way, counts as a friendship.

---

dormant
quiet, as if asleep

endodontist
a dentist who specializes in specific diseases of the teeth

sibling
a person having one or more parents in common

questing
searching

24   (Other part-of-a-couple friends are the friends that came with the marriage, and some of these are friends we could live without. But sometimes, alas, she married our husband's best friend; and sometimes, alas, she *is* our husband's best friend. And so we find ourself dealing with her, somewhat against our will, in a spirit of what I'll call *reluctant* friendship.)

25   7. Men who are friends. I wanted to write just of women friends, but the women I've talked to won't let me—they say I must mention man-woman friendships too. For these friendships can be just as close and as dear as those that we form with women. Listen to Lucy's description of one such friendship:

26   "We've found we have things to talk about that are different from what he talks about with my husband and different from what I talk about with his wife. So sometimes we call on the phone or meet for lunch. There are similar intellectual interests—we always pass on to each other the books that we love—but there's also something tender and caring too."

27   In a couple of crises, Lucy says, "he offered himself, for talking and for helping. And when someone died in his family he wanted me there. The sexual, flirty part of our friendship is very small, but *some*—just enough to make it fun and different." She thinks—and I agree—that the sexual part, though small is always *some*, is always there when a man and a woman are friends.

28   It's only in the past few years that I've made friends with men, in the sense of a friendship that's *mine*, not just part of two couples. And achieving with them the ease and the trust I've found with women friends has value indeed. Under the dryer at home last week, putting on mascara and rouge, I comfortably sat and talked with a fellow named Peter. Peter, I finally decided, could handle the shock of me minus mascara under the dryer. Because we care for each other. Because we're friends.

29   8. There are medium friends, and pretty good friends, and very good friends indeed, and these friendships are defined by their level of intimacy. And what we'll reveal at each of these levels of intimacy is calibrated with care. We might tell a medium friend, for example, that yesterday we had a fight with our husband. And we might tell a pretty good friend that this fight with our husband made us so mad that we slept on the couch. And we might tell a very good friend that the reason we got so mad in that fight that we slept on the couch had something to do with that girl who works in his office. But it's only to our very best friends that we're willing to tell all, to tell what's going on with that girl in his office.

calibrated
adjusted

30   The best of friends, I still believe, totally love and support and trust each other, and to bare to each other the secrets of their souls, and run—no questions asked—to help each other, and tell harsh truths to each other when they must be told.

31   But we needn't agree about everything (only 12-year-old girl friends agree about *everything*) to tolerate each other's point of view. To accept without judgment. To give and to take without ever keeping score. And to *be* there, as I am for them and as they are for me, to comfort our sorrows, to celebrate our joys.

Questions for Critical Thinking

1. The author's introduction to this essay is contained in the first three paragraphs. What is her thesis in this introduction? What approach does she use in her introduction to arrive at her thesis? Do you think this is an effective way to begin an essay?

2. Which two paragraphs are nearly the same, word for word? Why do you think the author repeats an entire paragraph? Explain how this essay comes to an effective conclusion. What is the purpose of a conclusion?

3. When a scientific classification is made, each group in that classification must be *mutually exclusive*, that is, no one item can belong to more than one group.

Are Viorst's eight groups of friends mutually exclusive, or does the author's classification break down at some point? Can you think of any other group that you would add?

4. Brainstorm with your classmates to come up with a list of job situations in which workers might be asked to do a report involving classification. (For instance, a nurse categorizing the patients on the floor of the hospital or a salesperson categorizing the products available from the company's catalogue.)

Writing in Response

1. Judith Viorst is concerned mainly about female friendship. Write an essay that classifies the types of friends men are likely to have.

2. Compose an essay in which you choose a specific group of people to classify. You might choose *mothers, college students, brothers,* or *sports figures.*

3. How difficult is it to have friends of the opposite sex? Write an essay in which you classify the types of problems a person could encounter when that person's best friend is of the opposite sex.

4. Once a person has a family, how much time or energy is left for friendship? What type of friend tends to become less visible or important in a person's life, once a person is married and has his or her own family? To what extent does a family tend to replace a person's friends after marriage? Write an essay that classifies friendships after a person has married and has had children.

The Changing American Family

ALVIN AND HEIDI TOFFLER

No one denies that the American family has changed and will continue to evolve. The research and writing team of Alvin and Heidi Toffler have concluded that not all of these changes are necessarily bad. As they share the results of their research, they not only provide a broad historical review of some of the important changes the family has gone through, they also classify families according to types.

1   The American family is not dying. It is diversifying. This is the "secret" to understanding what is happening to ourselves, our children, and our society. Millions of people today are frightened about the future of the family. Dire predictions pour from the pulpit, the press, even from the White House. Emotional oratory about the need to "restore" the family is echoing through the nation.

dire
desperate, urgent

2   Unfortunately, our attempts to strengthen family life are doomed unless we first understand what is happening. And all the evidence suggests we don't.

fracturing
breaking up

3   Despite misconceptions, the American family system is not falling apart because of immoral television programs or permissive child-rearing or because of some sinister conspiracy. If that were

the problem, the solutions would be simpler.

4   To begin with, it is worth noticing that whatever is happening to family life is *not* just happening in the United States. Many of today's trends in divorce, remarriage, new family styles, and attitudes toward children are present in Britain, France, Sweden, Germany, Canada, even in the Soviet Union and Eastern Europe. Something is happening to families in all these countries at once.

5   What is happening is that the existing family system is fracturing—and taking on a new, more diversified form—because of powerful pressures arising from revolutionary changes in energy, technology, work, economics, and communications. If permissiveness and immorality play a role, they are far

less important than these other, larger pressures.

6 The whole world is changing rapidly, and it seems reasonable that you cannot have a revolution in all these fields without expecting a revolution in family life as well.

7 Human history has gone through successive phases—each characterized by a certain kind of family. In greatly simplified terms we can sketch these:

8 The First Wave family: Ten thousand years ago, the invention of agriculture launched the First Wave of change in history. As people shifted from hunting, fishing, and foraging, the typical peasant-style family spread: a large household, with grandparents and children, uncles and aunts and sometimes nonblood relatives, as well as neighbors, boarders or others, all living together and—most important—working together as a production team in the fields.

9 This kind of "extended" family was found all over the world, from Japan to Eastern Europe to France to the American colonies. It is still the dominant type of family in the nonindustrial, agricultural countries today.

10 The Second Wave family: Three hundred years ago, the Industrial Revolution exploded in England and triggered the Second Wave of change.

11 The old style family which worked so well as a production team in the fields did not fit well in the new evolving world of factories and offices. The elderly couldn't keep up with the clattering machines. Children were too undisciplined to be really efficient factory hands. And the industrial economy needed workers who could move from city to city as jobs opened up or closed. That was hard to do with a big family.

12 Gradually, under these pressures, families became smaller, more streamlined, with the husband going out to work in a factory or office, the wife staying home, and the kids marching off to school. Old folks were farmed out to their own apartments or nursing homes. Young people moved into their own apartments as soon as they could afford it. The family adapted to the new conditions and the so-called "nuclear" family became the most popular model.

13 This is the type of family that most of today's evangelists, politicians, and others have in mind when they say we must "protect" the family or "restore" it. They act as though the nuclear family were the only acceptable form of family life.

14 Yet today, as society is struck by a new shock-wave of technological, economic, ecological, and energy changes, the family system is adapting once more, just as it did three hundred years ago.

15 Because the economic and other conditions that made the nuclear family popular are changing, the nuclear family itself is less and less popular. America is no longer a nation of poorly educated blue-collar workers. Most of us work in service occupations or spend our time processing information. And today only some 7 percent of Americans still live in classical nuclear families. The nuclear family is simply no longer the norm—and it is not likely to become the norm again, no matter how much pulpit-pounding or breast-beating we do about it. In its place, a new family system is emerging.

16 The Third Wave family: This new system is harder to describe because it is not based on a single dominant family form but on a dazzling diversity of household structures.

17 For example, look at what is happening to single life. Between 1970 and 1978 alone, the number of people aged 14 to 34 who live alone nearly tripled in the United States. Today fully one-fifth of all households are live-alones. Some are alone out of necessity, others prefer it. Then there are the child-free couples. As James Ramey of the Center for Policy Research has pointed out, we are seeing a massive shift from "child-centered" to "adult-centered" homes. The number of couples who deliberately decide not to have children—whether for economic, psychological, or ecological reasons—has increased dramatically.

18 Next come the single-parent households. Divorce rates may be leveling out in this country, depending upon how they are measured, but broken nuclear households are so widespread that today as many as one out of seven children are

plummets
falls
wallowing
to surrender to an emotion

raised by a single parent. In big cities that may run as high as one in four.

19 In many countries at once, the single-parent household is becoming a key family form. Sweden gives one-parent households first crack at nursery and day-care facilities. Germany is building special blocks of apartments for them.

20 Then there is what we have called the "aggregate family." That's where two divorced people—each with kids—marry, and the kids from both sides come to know each other and form a kind of tribe. Often the kids get on better than the parents. It has been estimated that, before long, 25 percent of American kids may be part of such "aggregate families."

21 Trial marriages . . . single-sex households . . . communes . . . all can be found as people struggle to find alternatives to the nuclear model. Some of these will turn out to be workable alternatives; others will fall by the wayside.

22 We can also expect to see an increasing number of "electronic cottage" families—families in which one or both spouses work at home instead of commuting to the job. As the cost of gasoline skyrockets and the cost of computers and communication plummets, companies will increasingly supply their employees with simple work-at-home electronic equipment.

23 In such homes, we may well find husband and wife sharing the same work. Even children and old folks might pitch in, as they once did in the agricultural household. In our day, such "electronic cottage" families are as much an outgrowth of changes in energy, technology, and communications, as the nuclear family was a response to the factory system at the time of the Industrial Revolution.

24 In the new environment, nuclear households will no doubt continue to survive. For many people, they work. But this Second Wave family form will hardly dominate the future, as it did the recent past.

25 What we are seeing today, therefore, is not the death of the family, but the rapid emergence of a Third Wave family system based on many different types of family.

26 This historic shift to new, more varied and flexible family arrangements is rooted in and related to parallel changes now fast developing in other fields. In fact, we find the same push toward diversity at every level.

27 The energy system is diversifying, shifting from a near-total reliance on fossil fuels to new, alternative sources of energy. In the world of work, we see a similar trend: Older Second Wave industries engaged in mass production—turning out millions of identical items. Newer Third Wave industries, based on computers, numerical controls, and robots, custom-tailor their goods and turn them out in small runs. At the consumer level, we see an increasing variety of products.

28 The same shift toward diversity is even stronger in communications where the power of the great mass media is increasingly challenged by new "mini-media"—cable television, satellite-based networks, special-interest magazines. This shift toward diversity amounts to the demassification of the media.

29 In short, the whole structure of society is moving toward increased diversity. It is hardly surprising that the family system is in tune with this shift. The recent startling changes in American family structure are part of this larger move from a mass society to one that offers a far greater variety of life choice.

30 Any attempt to go backward to a simpler system dominated by the nuclear family—or by any one model—will fail, just as our attempts to save the economy by "reindustrializing" have failed. For in both cases we are looking backward rather than forward.

31 To help families adapt to the new Third Wave society, with its diversified energy, production, communications, and politics, we should encourage innovations that permit employees to adjust their work hours to personal needs. We should favor "flex-time," part-time work arrangements, job-sharing. We should eliminate housing tax, and credit regulations that discriminate against non-nuclear families. We need more imaginative day-care facilities.

32 An idea put forward by one businesswoman: a bank of word-processors and a

nursery located in a suburban shopping center, so that busy housewives or husbands can put in an hour or two of paid work whenever it is convenient for them, and actually have their kids right there with them.

33 In short, anything that makes it easier to combine working and self-help, job-work with housework, easier to enter and leave the labor force, could smooth the transition for millions of people who are now caught, as it were, between the old, Second Wave, family arrangements and the fast-emerging Third Wave family system.

34 Rather than wallowing in nostalgia and praising the "good old days"—which were never as good as they may seem in retrospect—we ought to be finding ways to make the new system more decent, responsible, morally satisfying, and humane. The first step is an understanding of the Third Wave.

Questions for Critical Thinking

1. The Tofflers argue that people should not be so upset about the changing American family. Find the paragraph where they begin to use classification as a method of developing their argument.

2. Explain each of the three distinct categories or "waves" described by the authors. Do you agree with this historical classification? Can you think of other ways to classify the family?

3. List the seven types of flexible families suggested in the third wave. Discuss what it is about the modern world that makes these "new" family groupings possible.

4. The Tofflers point out that only 7 percent of Americans still live in classic nuclear families. This fact frightens many people, even some who themselves are outside the nuclear family. What are some of the reasons behind these fears? Do these reasons make you less optimistic than the Tofflers are about the new family structures?

5. In paragraph 30, the writers point out that any "attempt to go backward to a simpler system dominated by the nuclear family . . . will fail" because that would mean looking backward instead of ahead. Do you agree or disagree, and why?

6. The Tofflers suggest we need to understand the *third wave* in order to make the new system "more decent, responsible, morally satisfying and humane." What are some of the methods they suggest? Do you think American society is moving toward greater understanding of the third wave family or not? Why?

Writing in Response

1. An often-repeated saying is, "The only thing you can be sure of in life is change." Most people have trouble adapting to change in their lives. Write an essay in which you classify the types of change that can happen to people during the course of their lives. You may want to include changes such as physical change, economic change, and social change. Be sure to provide good examples within each category.

2. Write an essay in which you classify the different kinds of families you have known. Use a different classification from the one used by the Tofflers. Devote at least one well-developed paragraph to each category.

3. The Tofflers suggest that employees need innovations that will permit them to adjust their working hours to their personal needs. Write an essay in which you classify the kinds of innovations that could be done by employers to make life better for families. What is the likelihood that your suggestions will actually be put into effect? Why or why not?

The Internet? Bah!

CLIFFORD STOLL

Electronics have already transformed our world, and new technology is being developed at an ever faster pace. Not everyone welcomes this technology, however, as the following essay indicates. Clifford Stoll's thoughts on the Internet may represent a minority point of view, but as you read his opinions on this popular means of communication, you might want to consider if there are parts of the writer's argument with which you are in agreement.

perplexed
puzzled

hacker
a person who illegally gains access to another's electronic system for money or information

virtual
existing in fact, although not named as such

pundits
people who give opinions

clamor
a loud outcry

cacophony
harsh, discordant sounds

myopic
blurry

1   After two decades online, I'm perplexed. It's not that I haven't had a gas of a good time on the Internet. I've met great people and even caught a hacker or two. But today I'm uneasy about this most trendy and oversold community. Visionaries see a future of telecommuting workers, interactive libraries and multimedia classrooms. They speak of electronic town meetings and virtual communities. Commerce and business will shift from offices and malls to networks and modems. And the freedom of digital networks will make government more democratic.

2   Baloney. Do our computer pundits lack all common sense? The truth is no online database will replace your daily newspaper, no CD-ROM can take the place of a competent teacher and no computer network will change the way government works.

3   Consider today's online world. The Usenet, a worldwide bulletin board, allows anyone to post messages across the nation. Your word gets out, leapfrogging editors and publishers. Every voice can be heard cheaply and instantly. The result? Every voice is heard. The cacophony more closely resembles citizens band radio, complete with handles, harassment and anonymous threats. When most everyone shouts, few listen. How about electronic publishing? Try reading a book on disc. At best, it's an unpleasant chore: the myopic glow of a clunky computer replaces the friendly pages of a book. And you can't tote that laptop to the beach. Yet Nicholas Negroponte, director of the MIT Media Lab, predicts that we'll soon buy books and newspapers straight over the Internet. Uh, sure.

4   What the Internet hucksters won't tell you is that the Internet is an ocean of unedited data, without any pretense of completeness. Lacking editors, reviewers or critics, the Internet has become a wasteland of unfiltered data. You don't know what to ignore and what's worth reading. Logged onto the World Wide Web, I hunt for the date of the Battle of Trafalgar. Hundreds of files show up, and it takes 15 minutes to unravel them—one's a biography written by an eighth grader, the second is a computer game that doesn't work and the third is an image of a London monument. None answers my question, and my search is periodically interrupted by messages like, "Too many connections, try again later."

5   Won't the Internet be useful in governing? Internet addicts clamor for government reports. But when Andy Spano ran for county executive in Westchester County, N.Y., he put every press release and position paper onto a bulletin board. In that affluent county, with plenty of computer companies, how many voters logged in? Fewer than 30. Not a good omen.

6   Then there are those pushing computers into schools. We're told that multimedia will make schoolwork easy and fun. Students will happily learn from animated characters while taught by expertly tailored software. Who needs teachers when you've got computer-aided education? Bah. These expensive toys are difficult to use in classrooms and require extensive teacher training. Sure, kids love videogames—but think of your own experience: can you recall even one educational filmstrip of decades past? I'll bet you remember the two or three great teachers who made a difference in your life.

7   Then there's cyberbusiness. We're promised instant catalog shopping—just

point and click for great deals. We'll order airline tickets over the network, make restaurant reservations and negotiate sales contracts. Stores will become obsolete. So how come my local mall does more business in an afternoon than the entire Internet handles in a month? Even if there were a trustworthy way to send money over the Internet—which there isn't—the network is missing a most essential ingredient of capitalism: salespeople.

8   What's missing from this electronic wonderland? Human contact. Discount the fawning techno-burble about virtual communities. Computers and networks isolate us from one another. A network chat line is a limp substitute for meeting friends over coffee. No interactive multimedia display comes close to the excitement of a live concert. And who'd prefer cybersex to the real thing? While the Internet beckons brightly, seductively flashing an icon of knowledge-as-power, this nonplace lures us to surrender our time on earth. A poor substitute it is, this virtual reality where frustration is legion and where—in the holy names of Education and Progress—important aspects of human interactions are relentlessly devalued.

icon
an image or symbol

fawning
seeking favor by flattery
relentlessly
without ceasing

Questions for Critical Thinking

1. How many paragraphs make up the introduction of this essay? Explain what the author does in his introduction. Is this an effective method for introducing a controversial issue?

2. Find the author's thesis and underline it in the text.

3. Find an example of the author's use of a quotation from an expert. Does he agree or disagree with the expert?

4. Students are taught not to include slang or informal language in their essays. Clifford Stoll, however, has used several slang words. How many of these words or expressions can you find? Why do you think the writer decided to use slang?

5. An effective argument considers the opponent's point of view. Review each paragraph in the essay and underline those sentences where Clifford Stoll presents the point of view of his opponents. What are Stoll's responses to each of his opponent's points? Do you think Stoll's point of view represents a majority or minority position?

6. Where does the writer use examples? Mark the paragraphs that contain examples. In each case, does he use a listing of examples or give an extended example?

7. What does the writer claim are the results of the continuing use of the Internet?

8. Based on what you know about the Internet and the information provided in this essay, do you feel persuaded that the Internet is a poor substitute for human interaction?

Writing in Response

1. The writer tells us that "computers and networks isolate us from one another." In an argument of your own, agree or disagree with this statement.

2. Stoll concludes that using the Internet devalues human interaction. Write an essay in which you argue that for some people the Internet makes possible a human interaction that would not otherwise be possible. (Brainstorm with your classmates to come up with a list of people who could benefit by having the use of the Internet in their homes.)

3. In paragraph 6, the writer argues against the use of computers in schools. Whether or not you have used computers as a learning tool, write an essay in which you agree or disagree that electronic methods of teaching have an important place in the classroom.

The Issue Isn't Sex, It's Violence

CARYL RIVERS

When Caryl Rivers wrote the following piece for the Boston Globe, *she was raising the issue of violence against women, an issue that is a continuing problem in our society. As you read the specific details the writer uses to convince us of her point of view, supply some illustrations from your own observations and reading, points that the writer could have used to support her argument.*

grisly
gruesome, ghastly

nifty
wonderful (here, used sarcastically)

torso
the trunk of the body

desecrating
violating something sacred

deliciously
delightfully

purveyors
suppliers

lepers
outcasts

proffers
offers for our acceptance

Mrs. Grundy
an imaginary person, used as a symbol of someone who is too prim and proper

garroting
strangling

sodomizing
sexually assaulting

Walter Cronkite
a popular television newscaster and commentator, now retired

1   After a grisly series of murders in California, possibly inspired by the lyrics of a rock song, we are hearing a familiar chorus: Don't blame rock and roll. Kids will be kids. They love to rebel, and the more shocking the stuff, the better they like it.

2   There's some truth in this, of course. I loved to watch Elvis shake his torso when I was a teen-ager, and it was even more fun when Ed Sullivan wouldn't let the cameras show him below the waist. I snickered at the forbidden "Rock with Me, Annie" lyrics by a black Rhythm and Blues group, which were deliciously naughty. But I am sorry, rock fans, that is not the same thing as hearing lyrics about how a man is going to force a woman to perform oral sex on him at gunpoint in a little number called "Eat Me Alive." It is not in the same league with a song about the delights of slipping into a woman's room while she is sleeping and murdering her, the theme of an AC/DC ballad that allegedly inspired the California slayer.

3   Make no mistake, it is not sex we are talking about here, but violence. Violence against women. Most rock songs are not violent—they are funky, sexy, rebellious, and sometimes witty. Please do not mistake me for a Mrs. Grundy. If Prince wants to leap about wearing only a purple jock strap, fine. Let Mick Jagger unzip his fly as he gyrates, if he wants to. But when either one of them starts garroting, beating, or sodomizing a woman in their number, that is another story.

4   I always find myself annoyed when "intellectual" men dismiss violence against women with a yawn, as if it were beneath their dignity to notice. I wonder if the reaction would be same if the violence were directed against someone other than women. How many people would yawn and say, "Oh, kids will be kids," if a rock group did a nifty little number called "Lynchin," in which stringing up and stomping on black people were set to music? Who would chuckle and say, "Oh, just a little adolescent rebellion" if a group of rockers went on MTV dressed as Nazis, desecrating synagogues and beating up Jews to the beat of twanging guitars?

5   I'll tell you what would happen. Prestigious dailies would thunder on editorial pages; senators would fall over each other to get denunciations into the Congressional Record. The president would appoint a commission to clean up the music business.

6   But violence against women is greeted by silence. It shouldn't be.

7   This does not mean censorship, or book (or record) burning. In a society that protects free expression, we understand a lot of stuff will float up out of the sewer. Usually, we recognize the ugly stuff that advocates violence against any group as the garbage it is, and we consider its purveyors as moral lepers. We hold our nose and tolerate it, but we speak out against the values it proffers.

8   But images of violence against women are not staying on the fringes of society. No longer are they found only in tattered, paper-covered books or in movie houses where winos snooze and the scent of urine fills the air. They are entering the mainstream at a rapid rate. This is happening at a time when the media, more and more, set the agenda for the public debate. It is a powerful legitimizing force—especially television. Many people regard what they see on TV as the truth; Walter Cronkite once topped a poll as the most trusted man in America.

9   Now, with the advent of rock videos and all-music channels, rock music has grabbed a big chunk of legitimacy. American teen-agers have instant access, in their living rooms, to the messages of rock, on the same vehicle that brought them Sesame Street. Who can blame them if they believe that the images they see are accurate reflections of adult reality, approved by adults? After all, Big Bird used to give them lessons on the same little box. Adults, by their silence, sanction the images. Do we really want our kids to think that rape and violence are what sexuality is all about?

10   This is not a trivial issue. Violence against women is a major social problem, one that's more than a cerebral issue to me. I teach at Boston University, and one of my most promising young journalism students was raped and murdered. Two others told me of being raped. Recently, one female student was assaulted and beaten so badly she had $5,000 worth of medical bills and permanent damage to her back and eyes.

11   It's nearly impossible, of course, to make a cause-and-effect link between lyrics and images and acts of violence. But images have a tremendous power to create an atmosphere in which violence against certain people is sanctioned. Nazi propagandists knew that full well when they portrayed Jews as ugly, greedy, and powerful.

12   The outcry over violence against women, particularly in a sexual context, is being legitimized in two ways: by the increasing movement of these images into the mainstream of the media in TV, films, magazines, albums, videos, and by the silence about it.

13   Violence, of course, is rampant in the media. But it is usually set in some kind of moral context. It's usually only the bad guys who commit violent acts against the innocent. When the good guys get violent, it's against those who deserve it. Dirty Harry blows away the scum, he doesn't walk up to a toddler and say, "Make my day." The A Team does not shoot up suburban shopping malls.

14   But in some rock songs, it's the "heroes" who commit the acts. The people we are programmed to identify with are the ones being violent, with women on the receiving end. In a society where rape and assaults on women are endemic, this is no small problem, with millions of young boys watching on their TV screens and listening on their Walkmans.

15   I think something needs to be done. I'd like to see people in the industry respond to the problem. I'd love to see some women rock stars speak out against violence against women. I would like to see disc jockeys refuse air play to records and videos that contain such violence. At the very least, I want to see the end of the silence. I want journalists and parents and critics and performing artists to keep this issue alive in the public forum. I don't want people who are concerned about this issue labeled as bluenoses and bookburners and ignored.

16   And I wish it wasn't always just women who were speaking out. Men have as large a stake in the quality of our civilization as women do in the long run. Violence is a contagion that infects at random. Let's hear something, please, from the men.

advent
coming

rampant
widespread, without limits or restraints

Dirty Harry
a cop who bends the rules to get justice in a series of five adventure movies in the 70s and 80s

The A-Team
an adventure show on television in the 80's starring Mr. T

sanction
approve

endemic
prevalent in or peculiar to a certain region or people

cerebral
intellectual (rather than emotional)

bluenosers
people with rigid moral ideas

contagion
a communicable disease

Questions for Critical Thinking

1. Sometimes an author of a persuasive essay chooses to provide anecdotes or examples before actually stating the thesis of the essay. Find the place in this essay where the author states her thesis. Can you restate her thesis in a single sentence of your own?

2. The author is worried that readers will confuse her topic with other closely related social issues. What are these other issues that could be confused with the specific topic of her essay?

3. The author claims that society would not stand for it if other groups were treated the way women are dealt with in the media. What groups does she

specifically name? Is she right? Are there other groups you could name? Why do you think this violence against women is allowed?

4. Although Caryl Rivers does not cite statistics or provide research from others in her essay, she does establish herself as an authority on the subject. What makes her an authority on her chosen subject?

5. What are the solutions she suggests for solving this problem? Are her suggestions realistic? What are the chances that this problem will be solved? What progress, if any, has taken place since she wrote this essay?

Writing in Response

1. Caryl Rivers makes a distinction between violence that occurs in a moral context and mindless MTV violence. Write an essay in which you point out examples of violence found in the media, and then argue why each example is an acceptable use of violence.

2. The author wrote this essay before computer technology brought us the Internet with its interactive capabilities. Write an essay in which you argue that a particular action must be taken to protect women and children from the dangers of this newest form of media communication.

3. Argue that the influence of modern music on teenagers is mostly good or mostly bad.

4. Sometime society ignores a problem, only to have it become more serious as time goes by. Follow Caryl Rivers' example and select a problem that our society has generally ignored. In your essay, explain the problem and then give several specific examples to illustrate the extent of the problem. Finally, suggest what should be done to change the situation.

5. Using four or five people you know as the sources for your examples, argue that television (or the computer, or the telephone) is an invention that is largely a positive force or a negative force in their lives.

Photo Credits

Literary Credits

INDEX